ECONOMICS

FIFTH EDITION TEACHERS' GUIDE

AQA

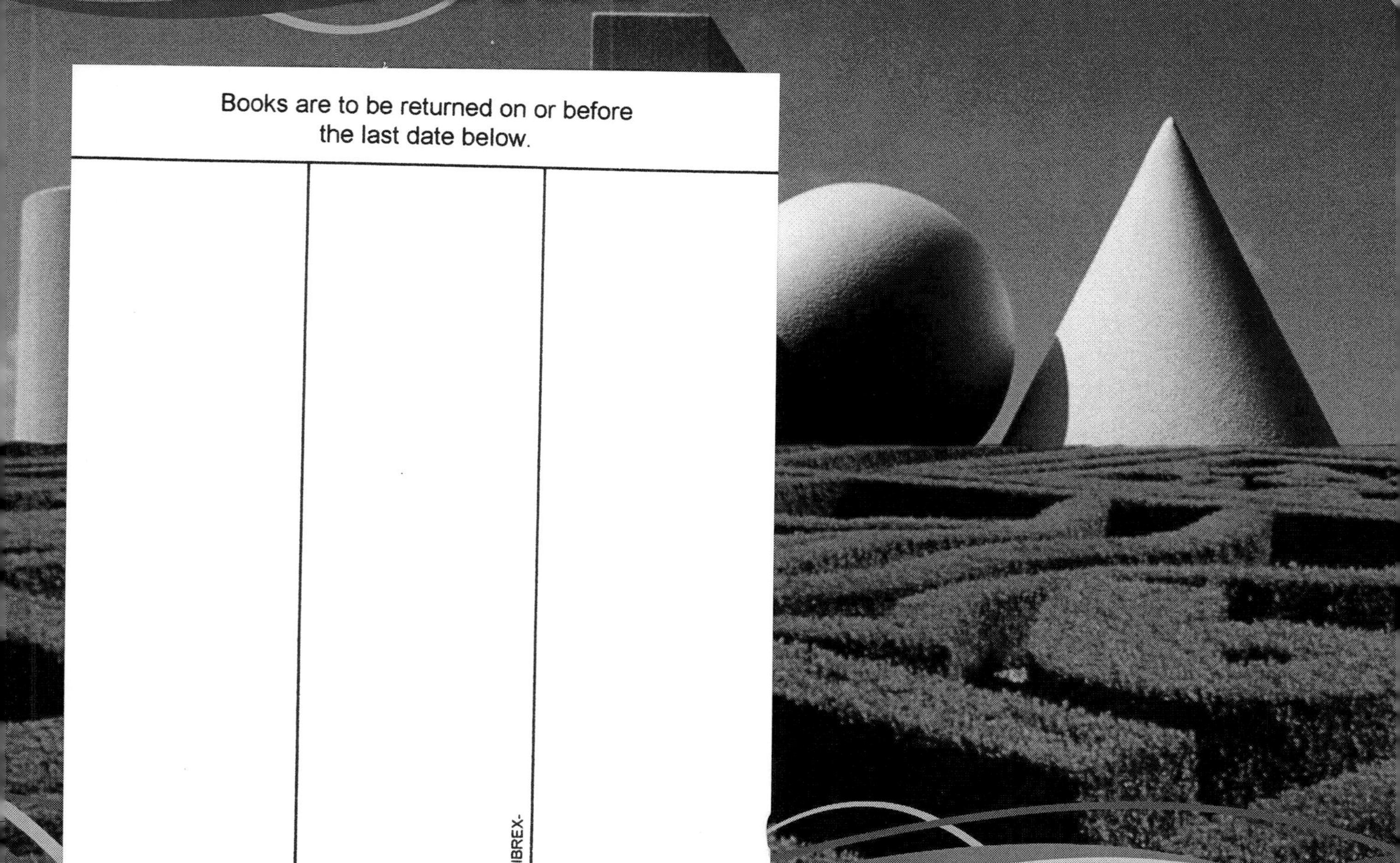

ALAIN ANDERTON

CP

298

Acknowledgements

Graphics by Kevin O'Brien
Cover design by Tim Button
Cover image provided by Shutterstock
Proof reading by Sue Oliver and Heather Doyle

British Library Cataloguing in Publication Data
A catalogue record of this book is available from the British Library

ISBN 978 1 4058 9239 1

Pearson Education
Edinburgh Gate
Harlow
Essex
CM20 2JE

First edition 1991 reprinted twice
Second edition 1996 reprinted twice
Third edition 2000 reprinted twice
Fourth edition 2006
Fifth edition 2008, Second impression 2008

Design page origination and production by Caroline Waring-Collins, Waring Collins Ltd, www.waringcollins.com
Printed by Ashford Colour Press Ltd., Gosport.

Contents

Preface

Economics (Fifth Edition) AQA Teachers' Guide contains suggested answers to questions and data questions in **Economics (Fifth Edition) AQA**. The information contained in the Teachers' Guide is designed to be photocopied within the purchaser's institution and copyright is waived.

Suggested answers

The Teachers' Guide provides suggested answers to questions in the students' book. In many cases there is a simple right or wrong answer to a question. In others, a variety of valid responses are possible. I have tried to indicate a number of possible arguments in the answers to these more open ended questions. However, other answers may be valid and this should be taken into account by teachers and lecturers when marking work or when giving them out as 'model answers' to students.

Specifications

Suggestions are provided on the relevant units in **Economics (Fifth Edition) AQA** which apply to particular areas of the AQA specification.

Thanks

I would like to thank Dave Gray for editing the book and Sue Oliver and Heather Doyle for proofreading. I would also like to thank my wife who has been an invaluable help to me in writing this book.

The author and Causeway Press would welcome any comments you have to make about the book, whether critical or otherwise. We hope that it will be a valuable resource for you and your institution.

Alain Anderton, 2008

The basic economic problem

Question 1

Nearly all resources are scarce and are called economic goods. A free good, in contrast, is one which is not scarce.

Congestion is an indication that road space is scarce. There are too many cars on the road to allow an individual motorist to proceed at a speed which he or she wants. Equally, car exhaust pollution leads to problems such as acid rain and global warming. Both of these environmental problems lead to resources having to be allocated to counteract their effects. Roads also have to be built using scarce resources. If fewer roads were built, more could be spent on, say, the public transport system. Hence, in these senses, roads are not a free good.

However, there are times of the day on particular roads when motorists are not adversely affected by the presence of cars. When driving a car at 6 o'clock in the morning, or going down a country lane, there is arguably no cost to other drivers. So, in this sense, roads are a 'free good'.

Most motorists implicitly assume that roads are free goods and fiercely defend their right to use roads at any time of the day without paying a toll. Hence, road tolls are deeply unpopular - the 'ultimate poll tax on wheels'. When discussing the issue, private motorists seem to put no value on time lost due to slower speeds or being stationary in a traffic jam. However, even if the time of private motorists is costless, that of commercial traffic such as lorries and taxis is not. Road congestion is therefore an economic issue involving economic goods rather than free goods.

Question 2

Minimum human needs of a teenager in the UK today could include material goods such as shelter, clothing and food and drink, and psychological and emotional needs such as love and self-esteem. The basic human needs of a teenager living in Bangladesh or sub-Saharan Africa might be little different. However, the exact form of material need may be different. For example, the Bangladeshi teenager may need to have a higher liquid intake in order to survive because of the hotter weather, whilst the person living in England may need a house designed for colder weather.

The ways in which the need is fulfilled will also differ. British teenagers may satisfy their need for entertainment by listening to CDs or MP3s. In contrast, the Bangladeshi teenager may be more concerned with basic needs such as collecting wood for burning for cooking.

Question 3

(a) Opportunity costs are the benefits lost from the next 'best' alternative when a choice is made. When a choice is made, people lose or miss out on the benefits from other courses of action. Therefore there is a cost associated with any choice. The opportunity cost to parents of spending £7 000 a year on fees and maintenance might be the benefits that could be gained from buying a digital television set, such as entertainment and relaxation. Alternatively, they could have invested the £7 000 and so the benefit lost might have been the interest or capital gain that could have been earned.

(b) If students borrowed £7 000 a year to pay for their fees and maintenance, there would come a point where they would have to pay the money back, some of it with interest. There is an opportunity cost to this. For example, the money might have been used instead to set up in business rather than finance three or more years at university. If the business were successful, the opportunity cost might be quite high. The student may also have used the money to travel. Typically, young people who travel also work whilst abroad. The whole experience of travel and work can build up experience which could be used to gain a better job in the future. The opportunity cost might be quite low, however, if the individual chose to spend the money on goods which yielded only short term benefits such as cars, holidays or drink.

Question 4

(a)(b)

Figure 1

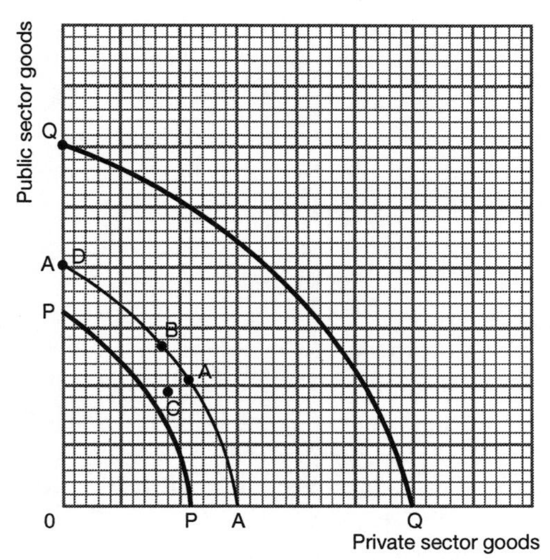

In Figure 1 here point C could be to the left or right of the production possibility frontier PP, but must not be to the right of the original frontier (AA). The production possibility frontier PP is drawn parallel to the original production possibility frontier in Figure 1, but does not have to be.

Data question

1. A production possibility frontier shows the different combinations of goods that an economy could produce if all resources were fully employed in the economy. It therefore shows the maximum amount of output that could be produced with the resources available.

For instance, in Figure 2 here, assume that the production possibility frontier for the economy is PQ. It could, therefore, produce no military services at all and devote all its scarce resources to producing OP of all other products. Alternatively, it could be at A, producing OS of all other products and OX of military services. Other possible combinations of products include those at point B and producing OQ of military services and no other products.

2. In most circumstances today, economies grow over time. Workforces become more productive because they are

Figure 2

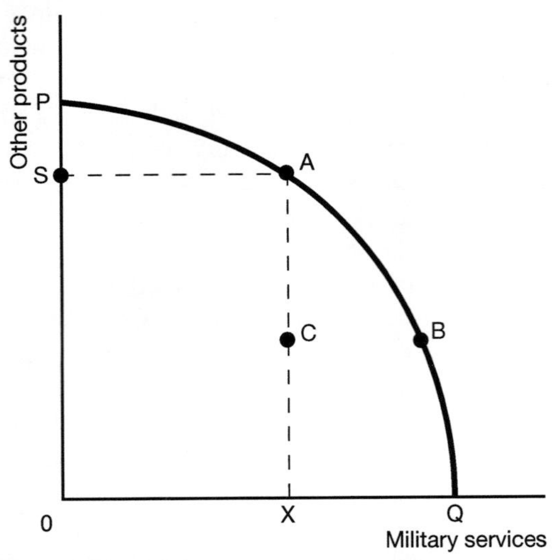

Figure 3

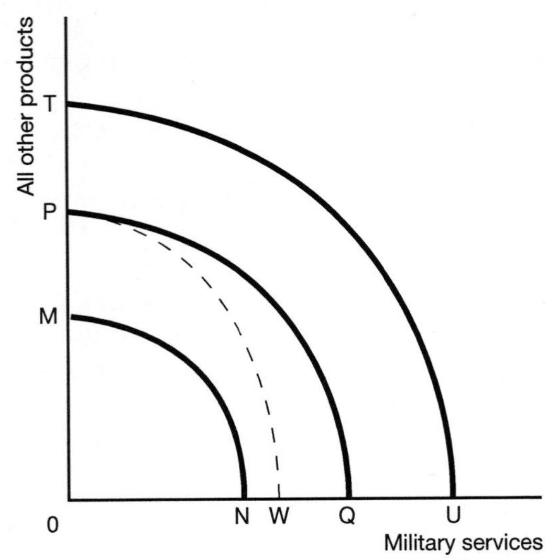

better educated. The amount of capital involved in production increases. Technological progress enhances the productivity of new capital compared to the capital it replaced. Economic growth is shown by a shift in the PPF outwards, to the right. In Figure 3 here, this is the shift from PQ to TU.

However, production possibility frontiers will shrink inwards if the amount and quality of resources are reduced. In Figure 3 this would be shown by a shift from PQ to, say, MN.

For example, in the Balkans, war from 1992 led to the destruction of a sizeable proportion of the capital stock of Bosnia-Herzegovina. This reduced the capability of the country to produce goods and services. Equally, in Kosovo, the country's infrastructure was severely damaged in the 1999 conflict leading to a shift inwards of the PPF. As for the aggressor, Serbia, its economy was damaged by the 1999 war. By 2006, its output was approximately three quarters of what it had been in 1989. This represents a significant inward shift of its production possibility frontier.

A second example of inward moving PPFs is given by the break-up of Eastern Europe. Many factories were closed down. Partly this was because there was no demand for their products. Partly it was because the factories were a danger to the local environment. Many workers, too, saw their skills written off. Used to working in a command economy, with obsolete equipment, they were ill-adapted to work in the new, more market-orientated economies that began to emerge. Countries that were slow to implement change were likely to have experienced falls in output, indicated by a move inwards of their PPFs. For example, in 2006, the national income of Georgia was only just over half what it had been in 1989. Russia's national income in 2006 was still 3.4 per cent below its 1989 value. In contrast, Eastern European countries which implemented reforms relatively quickly and efficiently saw their PPFs move outwards from their 1989 position. Hungary, for example, had a production possibility frontier in 2006 which was to the right of its 1989 position, with its national income 38.7 per cent higher.

Amongst developing countries, the Chinese economy has been the one which has most spectacularly transformed itself over the past thirty years. With growth rates averaging nearly 10 per cent a year, its PPF has been shifting outwards at a rate of 100 per cent approximately every 7 years.

3. A reduction in defence spending could have a complex mix of results. Initially, cuts in defence spending are likely to result in some unemployment in the economy. For instance, a cut in half of the defence budget would inevitably lead to a shrinkage in the numbers in the armed forces. These workers would not all immediately find new jobs. Hence, in Figure 2, there might be a movement from B on the PPF to C within the PPF. In the longer term, the economy should adjust and those workers could be absorbed into the non-defence labour force and the economy could return to A, on the PPF but with less defence services produced.

It could be argued that a cut of 50 per cent in the defence budget would lead to a shift inwards in the PPF, say from PQ to PW in Figure 3. Such a large cut would inevitably mean that a percentage of the country's capital stock, from army bases to industrial equipment to manufactured tanks and shells, would be rendered obsolete. These resources could not be transferred to civilian use and would therefore be lost forever. Cuts in military expenditure also harm the military capability of countries.

On the other hand, some of the resources that would have been used to produce defence services will now be devoted to investment in civilian industries. If there is an increase in overall investment expenditure in the economy as a result of resources being released from the defence industry, then in the longer term the PPF will shift outwards, from, say, PQ in Figure 3 to TU.

2 The function of an economy

Question 1

(a) A wide variety of goods and services is produced by households. For instance, many services are produced which are connected with eating. Shopping, storage of food, preparation of food, serving of food and washing up after a meal are examples. The household also provides accommodation services. Fixed capital, such as room space, furniture and appliances, yields services. So too does household labour when beds are made or rooms are cleaned. The household economy may also provide transport services. The person who drives the household car is effectively acting as a DIY chauffeur. When a parent collects a child from a disco or a party he or she is acting as a taxi driver. All forms of DIY activity create goods or services for the household economy. The household is also likely to provide services to the wider economy, mainly in the form of the hire of labour to an outside employer.

(b) Any production must be the result of the use of one or more of the factors of production. When cleaning a room, labour is combined with capital in the form of dusters, mops, brooms or vacuum cleaners, for instance. In many households, more and more capital is now being combined with labour to provide services. Nearly all households have cookers, washing machines and refrigerators, whilst increasingly they own freezers, microwave ovens and dishwashers. In the 1950s and 1960s there tended to be a division of labour based on male and female roles. The man provided services outside the home in return for a wage. He mowed the lawn, maintained the car and carried out DIY around the house. The woman brought up the children, did the cooking and cleaned the house. The children might have tidied their bedrooms, done some washing up and cleaned the car. This sexist division of roles has been breaking down in recent times. There are now far greater similarities in the work roles of men and women. People living on their own would, of course, provide all services themselves.

(c) Some services are usually provided for all family members. For instance, traditionally meals have been prepared for all family members to eat at the same time. The greater availability of convenience food, the use of microwaves and the variable nature of work and leisure activities means that this is less common today. Other services are provided for individuals. For instance, if you make your own bed or tidy your own room you are providing a service for yourself. Other services might be provided for groups of individuals. For instance, your mother might drive herself and your father to a restaurant.

(d) Many answers are possible here. But you may feel, for instance, that your father should do more household chores, or that your younger brother or sister should do more washing up. Equally, you may feel that your mother should provide a more frequent taxi service for your hectic social life rather than staying at home relaxing! Changes which are made to the organisation of the household economy should, however, either be aimed at improving its efficiency or producing a more equitable allocation of work and resources.

Question 2

(a) The buyers in the local Burscough market for grocery products are likely to be mainly individual households who live either in the town or within easy travelling distance of it, or workers who have jobs in the town. There may also be some purchases from local businesses but this is likely to be very small.

The sellers in the local market are the 2 independent grocers, the one convenience store and the one supermarket grocer. In addition, some supermarket chains may deliver to the area from online orders. There may also be a once or twice a week traditional market where sellers hire stalls.

(b) Meat and vegetables are complementary products. Shoppers who buy meat in the town are also likely to buy their vegetables locally. An increase in demand for meat, for example because more people have moved into the area, is likely to raise the demand for vegetables and vice versa. The supermarket in Burscough will sell both meat and vegetables under one roof, encouraging customers to buy them together.

Petrol will be needed by any buyer who used a car to go to the Burscough shops. Petrol would then be said to be in derived demand from vegetables. Equally, the shops in Burscough have to have their vegetables delivered to their premises. So deliveries require petrol. Again, petrol is in derived demand from vegetables.

Question 3

(a) The government might have been aiming to maximise the welfare of its citizens. By offering aid, it could mitigate the harmful impact of the closure on individual workers and on the local Birmingham community. Local businesses which had supplied parts to Rover would also receive aid because they would be reimbursed, at least in part, for deliveries made but not paid for in the run up to the point of receivership. These payments might make the difference between the survival of the supplier and it too going into receivership.
However, each year in the UK, thousands of businesses go into receivership and no help is given to them by the government. Therefore, it could be argued that the government was motivated more by political considerations than economic or welfare considerations. By giving aid upon the collapse of such a high profile company, the government could be said to be minimising the political fallout from what happened. This was particularly important because a general election was only a few weeks away. It could be argued that this was the British equivalent of 'pork barrel politics', spending money on a relatively small number of citizens in marginal constituencies in order to win their crucial support at election time.

(b) Trade unions exist to promote the interests of their members. Since trade union members were losing their jobs, their representatives, the trade unions, were anxious to maximise their future welfare. Ideally, workers' jobs would be maintained by finding another buyer for the company. This would also preserve the jobs of trade union members in supplier companies. If the firm were to cease to exist, trade unions argued that generous redundancy packages should be offered as well as training and the setting up of new firms which could reemploy those who had lost their jobs.

Data question

1. (a) A wide variety of economic resources - land, labour, capital and entrepreneurship - is used in the UK oil industry. For instance, the photographs show how labour is used to produce oil in the North Sea. Capital equipment in the form of oil rigs, refineries and petrol stations is used too. The crude oil pumped up from the sea bed is also an economic resource, an example of 'land'. Entrepreneurs also work in the industry, from the owners of companies working in the North Sea to independent petrol station owners.

(b) Specialisation is a system of organisation where economic units, such as oil companies, are not self-sufficient, but concentrate on producing certain goods and services and trading them with others. Specialisation occurs throughout the oil industry. An individual worker, for instance, would not be responsible for drilling for oil and refining it. Rather he or she is likely to specialise in one activity. Equally, capital equipment used on North Sea oil rigs cannot be used to put petrol into a car on a garage forecourt. It is specialised machinery used for a specific purpose. Plastic, which needs oil as a base product, is manufactured in different plants to oil refineries. Specialisation allows complex operations to be performed to get oil from the sea bed to the final customer. Without it, the North Sea would be unexploitable.

(c) Money is used to exchange goods and services in the oil industry. It buys in a wide variety of resources from individuals such as workers, firms such as catering companies, and government organisations. It pays for these resources by selling its products, shown in Table 3 of the student's book, from crude oil to petrol and diesel. Exchange inevitably involves a price at which goods are bought and sold. In a monetised economy, prices are set in terms of a currency. The international price of oil, for instance, is usually quoted in US dollars per barrel as in Figure 3 in the student's book. Prices can fluctuate as market conditions change. The price of oil, for instance, has fluctuated from below $10 a barrel in 1970 to over $60 per barrel in 2006.

(d) A market is any convenient set of arrangements by which buyers and sellers communicate to exchange goods and services. There is a large number of individual markets in which oil companies operate. For instance, they are in the contract catering market because many companies employ contract caterers to provide food on oil rigs. They operate within the international crude oil market, selling and buying oil. They also operate in the retail petrol market, selling petrol and other fuels to motorists.

2. (a) Betwen 2002 and 2006, the world price of oil more than doubled. As Figure 2, in the student's book shows, it rose from approximately $30 a barrel to nearly $70 a barrel. The objectives of oil companies with North Sea oil installations are likely to have been to maximise their profit. This is likely to have resulted in increased production. It will have become profitable at $70 a barrel to use techniques to extract oil from existing North Sea oil fields or from new fields that were not profitable at $30 a barrel.

(b) The UK government might have a variety of objectives. On the one hand, it may act to maximise the welfare of its citizens. This might involve maximising the tax revenues from the increase in price of North Sea oil. Or it might lead to tax and spending packages which maximised the output of North Sea oil in the long term. Or the government might see minimising the impact of higher oil prices as a priority. It could then reduce taxes on petrol as the market price rose. The government also might have other objectives, such as getting re-elected. Then they might pursue policies which would help MPs win marginal constituances. Using taxes and subsidies to encourage orders to be awarded to offshore equipment manufacturing in Scotland off the North Sea coast might be an example.

(c) UK motorists will almost all have the objective of minimising their fuel costs. Rising oil prices will lead to increases in the price of the petrol or diesel they are putting into their cars. Higher petrol prices might encourage them to shop around more in the short term. In the long term, assuming continued high oil prices, they will have greater incentives to buy more fuel efficient cars.

(d) Rising oil prices are likely to mean more work in the North Sea oil industry. Oil companies will be expanding their activities from what they would otherwise have been. Oil workers will seek to maximise their rewards from work. If their skills are in demand, they may be able to negotiate higher wages for themselves, or better conditions of work.

3 Economic data

Question 1

(a) There is a number of periods when the data show an upward movement in the original series and a downward movement in the revised series. These are the periods from May to June 1997, from August to September 1997 and from January to February 1998. In other periods both figures were rising at the same time, falling at the same time, the original figures were rising whilst the revised figures were static, or the original figures were falling whilst the revised figures rose.
(b) The three different measures of the annual average change in earnings provided different figures because the method of calculation of the average was different in each case. One difference between the three series was the weight given to changes in earnings by small businesses. The revised series gave greater weight to this than either the original series or the proposed new series.
(c) It is important that economic statistics are measured accurately. Inaccurate statistics will give a distorted picture of trends that are taking place and an unclear view about what is happening at a point in time. For example, the revised figures indicate that earnings appear to have been falling in 1997. The original and proposed new series figures show that they were rising.

This is important for two reasons. One is that economic theories are tested using real world data. If that real world data is inaccurate, then economists will not be able to build reliable models of the economy.

Second, decisions are often based on economic statistics. If the statistics are inaccurate then the outcomes of these decisions are likely to be undesired. For example, the revised series would have pointed to falling inflationary pressures between February 1997 and 1998. The government might then have reduced interest rates. But the proposed new series shows rising inflationary pressures over the period, which would indicate that interest rates should be rising.

Question 2

Table 1

	2003=100	£ billion at 2003 prices		
	Index of prices	Households' expenditure	Government expenditure	Fixed investment
2003	100.0	697	233	187
2004	102.4	716	245	197
2005	105.5	721	255	201
2006	108.4	733	265	217

Table 2

	2003=100	£ billion at 2006 prices		
	Index of prices	Households' expenditure	Government expenditure	Fixed investment
2003	100.0	756	253	203
2004	102.4	776	266	214
2005	105.5	782	276	218
2006	108.4	795	287	235

Question 3

(a) (b)

Table 3

	2003=100		
	Food and drink	Transport	Restaurants and hotels
2003	100.0	100.0	100.0
2004	103.6	104.4	106.0
2005	106.8	107.9	112.7
2006	112.2	111.3	116.6

Table 4

	2006=100		
	Food and drink	Transport	Restaurants and hotels
2003	89.1	89.9	85.8
2004	92.4	93.8	90.9
2005	95.2	97.0	96.6
2006	100.0	100.0	100.0

Question 4

(a) Both graphs in the student's book show the number of unemployed people calculated by the ILO (International Labour Organisation) measure. The number of unemployed is indicated in millions over a period of time. Figure 3 gives annual data and shows that over the whole period 1971 to 2007, the numbers unemployed rose from 1 million to 1.6 million. Within this period, there were four identifiable peaks in 1972, 1978, 1984 and 1993, reflecting the cyclical nature of unemployment. The highest level of unemployment was experienced in 1984 when unemployed reached 3.3 million. Figure 4 shows that unemployment rose slightly between 2004 and 2007 from 1.4 million to 1.7 million.
(b) Figure 3 gives the impression that there has been large rises and fall in unemployment, whereas Figure 4 would imply that unemployment has increased slightly. There is a number of reasons why this is so.

Figure 3 covers a much wider time period than Figure 4. There have indeed been large fluctuations in unemployment of the period 1971 to 2007, whilst 2004-2007, shown in Figure 4 was a period of slowly increasing unemployment. So the two graphs do not show the same data.

Second, the scales on the horizontal axes are different. Figure 4 is drawn with a larger horizontal scale than in Figure 3. This tends to give the impression that changes are less significant in Figure 4.

Third, the scale on the vertical axes ends at different points. In Figure 3, the scale starts at zero and end at 4.0 million, whereas in Figure 4 the scale starts at zero and ends at 2.0 million. Also, the actual height of the two graphs differs. Even if the scale were the same, the fact that Figure 4 is placed on the page higher than Figure 3 makes comparison more difficult.

Data question

Note: in Table 13, there was a mistake in the first impression of the 5th edition. This has been corrected in reprints. In the last column, under Revenue per screen at constant 2001 prices, the 1995 number should be 101.8 and not 237.0.

1. Certain trends can be identified from Tables 12 and 13. There was a 234.4 per cent increase in the number of cinema admissions over the period 1987 to 2006. The number of sites increased by 59.1 per cent and there was a 244.8 per cent increase in the number of screens. The much larger increase in the number of screens compared to sites reflects the growth of multi-screen cinemas over the period. Gross box office takings, revenue per admission and revenue per screen at current prices all rose over the period. At constant prices, stripping out inflation, the values of gross box office takings, and revenue per admission increased by 221.8 per cent and 37.8 per cent respectively over the period but revenue per screen fell by 5.9 per cent.

2. It is argued that index numbers make trends easier to identify from data. For example, it may be easier to see that the number of sites has increased by less as a proportion than the number of screens and admissions when index numbers are compared with a value of 100 rather than comparing figures such as 1 035 screens with 3 569 screens. It is also perhaps easier to see the extent of changes by examining index figures. For example, the large increase in gross box office takings at current prices over the period 1987 to 2006 is more easily identifiable by comparing an index of 615.6 with 100 than by comparing £762.1 million with £123.8 million. However, index numbers do not allow an evaluation of the importance of particular aspects of expenditure. So, for example, gross box takings may be broken down into age groups. Expenditure amongst those aged 16-21 may have increased by 20 per cent. If this group comprised 50 per cent of all film goers then the impact on total expenditure would be relatively great. It would not be possible to calculate these figures from index numbers. A further problem may be the choice of base year. The choice of a different base year leads to the calculation of different index numbers. For example, if 1995 were chosen as a base year rather than 1987, the index numbers for revenue per screen at constant 2001 prices would be 98.2 in 1987, 100 in 1995 and 92.4 in 2006 rather than 100 in 1987, 101.8 in 1995 and 94.1 in 2006. If a base year is chosen that is unrepresentative of the period studied, then the figures may be distorted and conclusions from the figures could be misleading.

3. (a) Over the period 1987-2006, the number of screens on offer to cinema viewers has increased by 244.8 per cent. At the same time the revenue per admission has risen by £3.02 at current prices and £1.19 at constant 2001 prices. This would tend to disprove the statement that 'revenues per admission and the number of screens cannot carry on rising'.

(b) The extent to which the statement is true in future may depend on a variety of factors. First, if cinema chains choose to push up revenues per admission (i.e. ticket prices), then the number of cinema goers will fall from what it would otherwise have been. The data show that rising ticket prices have been associated with a rising number of admissions between 1987 and 2006. However, the rising number of admissions has been due to a number of factors, including rising incomes, better facilities at cinemas, more screens, increases in film advertising, the arrival of videos and DVDs which encouraged consumers to see the film at the cinema first, and perhaps better films and changes in social attitudes to cinema. If ticket prices had not gone up at the same time, cinema admissions would have been even higher. So cinema chains have to choose between higher admissions and higher ticket prices. If they pushed the average price up to, say, £50 a ticket, few would want to go to the cinema. This would devastate the industry and lead to the closure of nearly all cinemas. So there is a limit to how much cinema chains can push up prices. The cinema chains will want to set the long term price at a level where they maximise their profits. To do this, they need to keep their cinemas relatively full and therefore to keep their ticket prices down to an affordable level.

As for the number of screens, they too cannot keep on rising. In 2006, there were 3 569 screens. If there were ten times this number, there would not be enough customers viewing to keep them profitable. The data show that increasing the number of screens has already resulted in a fall in the number of admissions per screen: between 1987 and 2006, the number of screens increased by 244.8 per cent whilst the number of admissions only went up 134.4 per cent. At some point, profit will begin to be hit and cinema chains will have to review their policy of opening more screens. There may be other limitations to opening screens. For instance, local authorities may refuse planning permission for new cinemas if they judge their local markets are saturated. Or there may be a technological revolution which hits the cinema market and its profitability, such as a growth in the use of broadband internet transmissions, digital television and pay-per-view television.

4 Positive and normative economics

Question 1

Positive statements are statements which can be supported or refuted by evidence. Normative statements are statements which are value judgements. In the passage, the first sentence is a positive statement. It is possible to find out whether or not London's business leaders are in fact hoping the government will fund the rail scheme for example by the use of survey methods. In the second sentence, 'Estimated to cost £16 ' is a positive statement, but what follows, 'is not cheap', is a normative statement, reflecting the opinion of the author.

There then follows a series of positive statements each of which can be supported or refuted: Crossrail will link Heathrow to the City; travellers have to change train to get to the City; in comparison with other major cities the services is poor and slow. The only possible normative element to this is the statement that the 'service is poor'. However, if this is defined as 'slow'.

The last paragraph contains two normative statements. 'The City of London is vital to the success of the UK economy' is a value judgement because there are no clear criteria laid out as to how success should be measured. 'The UK government should give this support' is also a value statement, giving the opinion of the author about government policy.

Data question

1. Positive statements are statements which are verifiable by proof. They are either true or false. A normative statement is one which contains a value judgment. It is not capable of being proved true or false. The question asks for at least six examples from the following.

Taking Bertie Ahern's letter sentence by sentence, we have:

- Positive statement - 'The defeat of the European Union's proposed constitution in the French and Dutch referendums has led to a renewed debate on the way forward for Europe.'
- Positive statement - 'As part of this debate, the Common Agricultural Policy has in recent months been the subject of much criticism, with repeated calls for further reform.'
- Positive statement - '2003 saw a radical reform of CAP, decoupling 'subsidies' from production.' Note though that describing the reform as 'radical' is normative.
- Positive statement - 'This reform is in its first year of implementation.'
- Normative statement - 'It would be both unfair and unwise to ask farmers to accept another radical reform now.'
- Normative statement - 'Farmers, like other business people, need a reasonable degree of stability in the policy environment in which they operate.'
- Normative statement - 'However, there is more at stake.'
- Normative statement - 'To try to overturn an agreement reached unanimously by the European Council as recently as October 2002 would be to send the wrong signal to Europe's people.'
- Normative statement - 'The public needs to see a Europe that stands by its agreements.'
- Positive statement - 'There are other issues too.'
- Positive statement - 'Reform would mean that European agricultural production would fall rapidly.'
- Positive statement - 'The food supply gap would be filled by imports from, for example, South America and Australia, which can produce at prices below European levels.'
- Normative statement - 'Europe's food supplies could, once again, become vulnerable.'
- Normative statement - 'Reform would also result in serious damage to the social and economic fabric of rural areas across Europe.'
- Positive statement - 'As for the scale of subsidies, the Organisation for Economic Co-operation and Development (OECD) has estimated that transfers to agriculture from both consumers and taxpayers amount to $103bn (£58bn) in the EU and $92bn (£52bn) in the USA, or 1.32 per cent of GDP for the EU and 0.92 per cent for the US.'
- Normative statement -'There is therefore broad comparability of support.' Note: it could be argued this is a positive statement. It depends whether 'comparability' is seen as positive or a value judgement.
- Normative statement - 'Calls for radical CAP reform are misplaced and outdated; they are based on a misunderstanding of the role of the CAP in European society and the world economy.'
- Normative statement - 'They are also based on a false premise about the relative cost of the CAP.'

Taking Tony Blair's statement sentence by sentence (Tony Blair was Prime Minister at the time of the statement):

- Positive statement - 'Our policy all along has been to get rid of subsidies for crops because we believe that this was a distorted way in which to support the rural economy.'
- Positive statement - 'Therefore what we have always argued for was a managed process of change in which you maintain sustainable livelihoods in the countryside but didn't do so at the expense of distorting world trade.'
- Positive statement - 'That was why we always argued for fundamental reform of CAP and we recognised that there had been some progress in that direction but we are arguing for more.' Note that these last two sentences are stating what the government has believed in the past. This can be verified or disproved and so they are positive statements. What they believed in the past (e.g. we believe there should be a managed process of change) was a value judgement and was therefore normative.
- Positive statement - 'We are still in a situation where some 80 per cent of the existing budget is directed towards the original 15 member states'
- Normative statement - 'and that does not allow the spending to be prioritised towards providing the infrastructure support that accession countries need.'
- Normative statement - 'Therefore we still have a distorted system.'
- Normative statement - 'There should be a policy of managed change which would include more efficient farming and viable, sustainable rural communities.'
- Normative statement - 'You cannot have a situation where we go into another decade with 40 per cent of the EU budget being spent on 5 per cent of the population.'

2. The Common Agricultural Policy is a policy which over the years has led to gross distortions within agricultural markets both within the EU and on a worldwide scale. It has been extremely costly to the vast majority of EU citizens and has bought benefits to a small minority. Further reform should be a high priority for the EU and yet agricultural interest groups seem to have a stranglehold on policy making at the highest levels.

The 2003 reform of CAP saw the decoupling of subsidies from production with regard to certain foods. The amount of money spent on farmers remained broadly the same, so EU taxpayers saw no benefit from the reform. If the CAP budget had been reduced, this would have freed up resources either to reduce taxes, or as Tony Blair pointed out, to use for other more important projects such as infrastructure support to accession countries. The scale of the transfers to the agricultural sector is enormous. As Bertie Ahern recognises, the OECD calculated these to £58 billion a year. For the EU 25, now with a population of 450 million, it means that CAP costs £129 per person per year. For a family of four, that means £516 a year. Tony Blair reminds us that 40 per cent of the current EU budget is spent on just 5 per cent of the population. This cannot represent good value for money for the ordinary citizen.

The benefits of CAP are not widely spread through the agricultural community as many believe. The existence of subsidies serves to drive up land prices. It is the owners of land who are the main beneficiaries. As the example of New Zealand, which eliminated farm subsidies in the 1980s, shows, farmers who rent their land would see their rents fall if CAP were abolished. They would be no worse off than before. Another statistic is that 80 per cent of CAP payments go to the 20 per cent of the richest farmers. Small farmers get relatively little of the CAP cash, and yet supporters of CAP make out that it is the small farmer in the isolated rural community who needs the most support.

CAP is also responsible for distorting world trade and keeping farmers poor in the Third World. If CAP were to be abolished and there was free trade in food commodities, the main beneficiaries on the world stage initially would be efficient farm producing countries such as the USA, Australia, New Zealand and Brazil. But poor African countries would benefit too. In the long term, eliminating farm subsidies would bring enormous trading benefits to the poorest countries in the world which could export food products to the rich countries of the world.

It should also be remembered that the 2003 'reform' only covered certain foodstuffs. Dairy products, for example, were not included and remain protected by the current inefficient quota system. The 'radical' reform that Bertie Ahern, the Irish Prime Minister, sees is a much watered down reform which countries like Ireland and France only agreed to after much political pressure.

The abolition of the Common Agricultural Policy is the only policy that makes any sense today. Imagine a situation where every industry claimed the right to be subsidised, or where every city, town and village claimed the right to have no change forced upon it. Imagine a situation where teachers or MPs were going on television and claiming that society owed their children and their grandchildren the right to inherit their jobs and their livelihoods. Bertie Ahern claims that 'calls for radical CAP reform are misplaced and outdated'. In a modern competitive world where consumers, workers and firms are expected to be flexible and where change is the norm, it is CAP that stands out as outdated.

5 The demand curve

Question 1

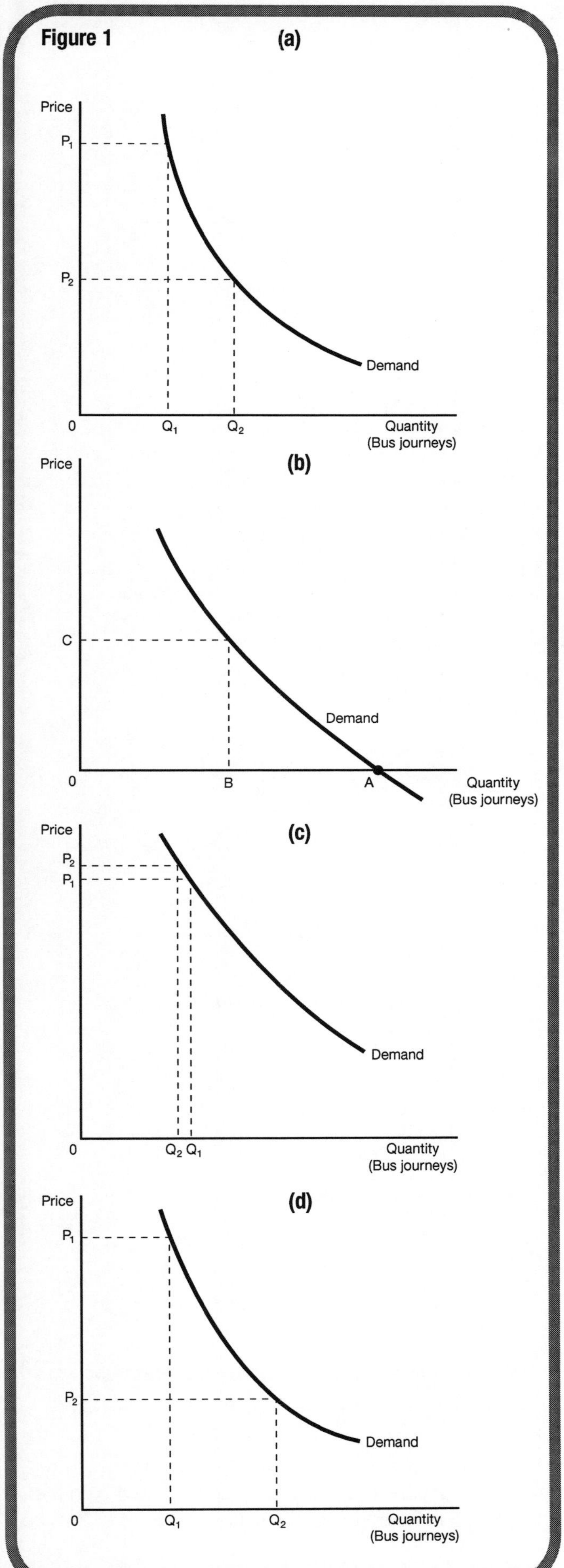

(a) Charging children half price rather than full price fares is likely to lead to an increase in the quantity demanded of bus journeys. For instance, at full price, P_1, in Figure 1(a), the number of children that will use a bus service is Q_1. If children are charged half price, P_2, then the quantity demanded rises to Q_2.

(b) Giving senior citizens free bus passes rather than charging them for each journey is likely to increase their quantity demanded of bus journeys. For instance, in Figure 1(b), if senior citizens had to pay an average fare of OC, they would demand OB bus journeys. By making journeys free and price per journey therefore fall to zero, quantity demanded increases to OA.

(c) If Stagecoach increased its price by 5 per cent, then the quantity demanded of bus journeys would be likely to fall. In Figure 1(c), an increase in price from P_1 to P_2 leads to a fall in quantity demanded from Q_1 to Q_2.

(d) Reduced fares after 9.30 will lead to an increase in the quantity demanded of journeys made. For instance, in Figure 1(d), the quantity demanded of journeys if the full price P_1 were charged would be Q_1. This can be compared to Q_2, the quantity demanded if the fare were 60 per cent cheaper.

Question 2

(a) and **(b)**

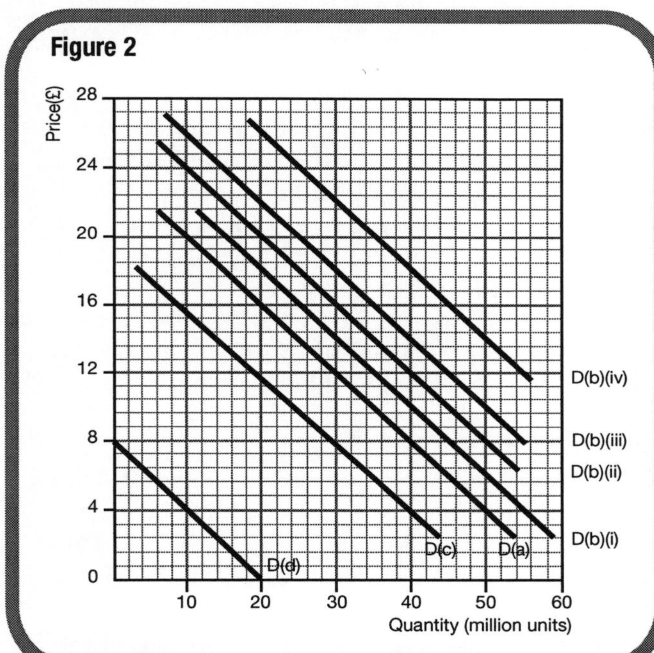

(c) Note: any demand curve drawn to the left of D(a) would be correct.

(d) Note: any demand curve which cuts the vertical axis at £8 would be correct.

Question 3

(a) Oil-fired central heating systems use oil as a fuel. If the price of oil goes up, so does the cost of running an oil-fired central heating system. Hence, if the cost of all other fuels remains the same, the demand for oil-fired central heating systems will fall. This is shown by a shift to the left in the demand curve for oil-fired central heating systems shown in Figure 3 from D_1 to D_2. In practice, the price of other fuels tends to rise when there are large oil price increases. So long as the rise in the price of oil is greater than the rise in the price of alternative fuels, the demand for oil-fired central

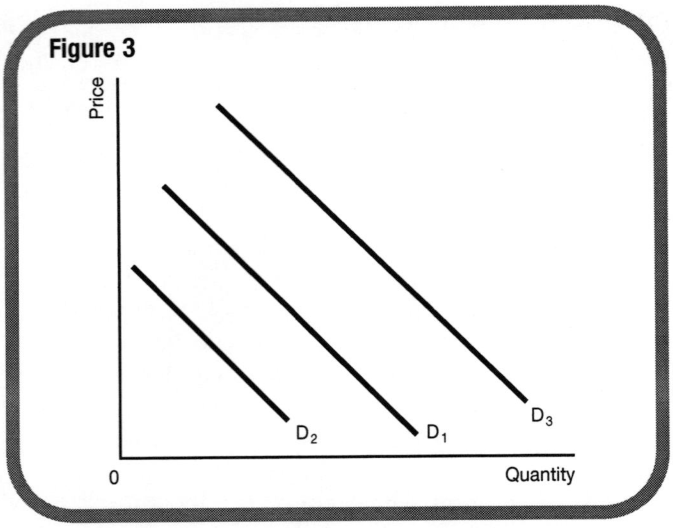

heating systems will tend to fall.

(b) The demand for luxury cars with low-mileage petrol consumption will fall if there is a substantial increase in the price of petrol. This is because the running costs of such cars will rise. The fall in demand is shown by a shift to the left in the demand curve, from D_1 to D_2 in Figure 3.

(c) The demand for rail travel is likely to rise. This is because the cost of motoring is likely to increase faster than any rise in rail fares due to higher fuel costs for rail operators. Motorists will therefore be tempted to use their cars less and travel by train. This rise in demand for rail travel would be shown by a shift to the right in the demand curve, from D_1 to D_3 in Figure 3.

(d) A rise in the price of oil is unlikely to have any direct effect on the demand for ice cream. The two goods are neither substitutes nor complements. Hence the demand curve for ice cream is likely to remain unchanged at D_1 in Figure 3. However, a sharp rise in the price of oil can have a significant impact on consumers' real incomes. Because consumers have to pay much higher oil prices, real incomes fall and this could have led to a small fall in the demand for ice cream, shown by a shift to the left in the demand curve, from D_1 to D_2 in Figure 3.

(e) A rise in the price of oil will add to costs for airlines because aeroplanes are fuelled by oil. They are likely to pass on these higher costs in higher ticket prices which in turn will reduce demand for airline travel. In Figure 4.3, this is shown by a shift to the left in the demand curve for air travel from D_1 to D_2. The shift to the left of the demand curve is, however, likely to be fairly small because the rise in airline ticket prices is likely to be small and many air travellers are unlikely to be deterred from buying a ticket by a small increase in prices.

Question 4

(a) An advertising campaign is likely to increase the demand for Activia at any given price. So, the Activia advertisement shown in the photograph should lead to an increase in sales for the product. This is shown diagrammatically by a shift to the right in the demand curve from D_1 to D_2 in Figure 4.

A fall in the population will reduce the number of consumers of yoghurt. This will lead to a fall in demand for Activia, all other things being equal. This would be shown by a shift to the left in the demand curve from D_1 to D_3 in Figure 4.

A rise in real incomes will mean that consumers will have more spending power available to buy Activia. Therefore, demand for Activia will rise, pushing the demand curve to the right from D_1 to D_2 in Figure 4.

A study which shows that yoghurt is good for health will lead to an increase in demand for Activia. This will push the demand curve for Activia to the right from D_1 to D_2 in Figure 4.

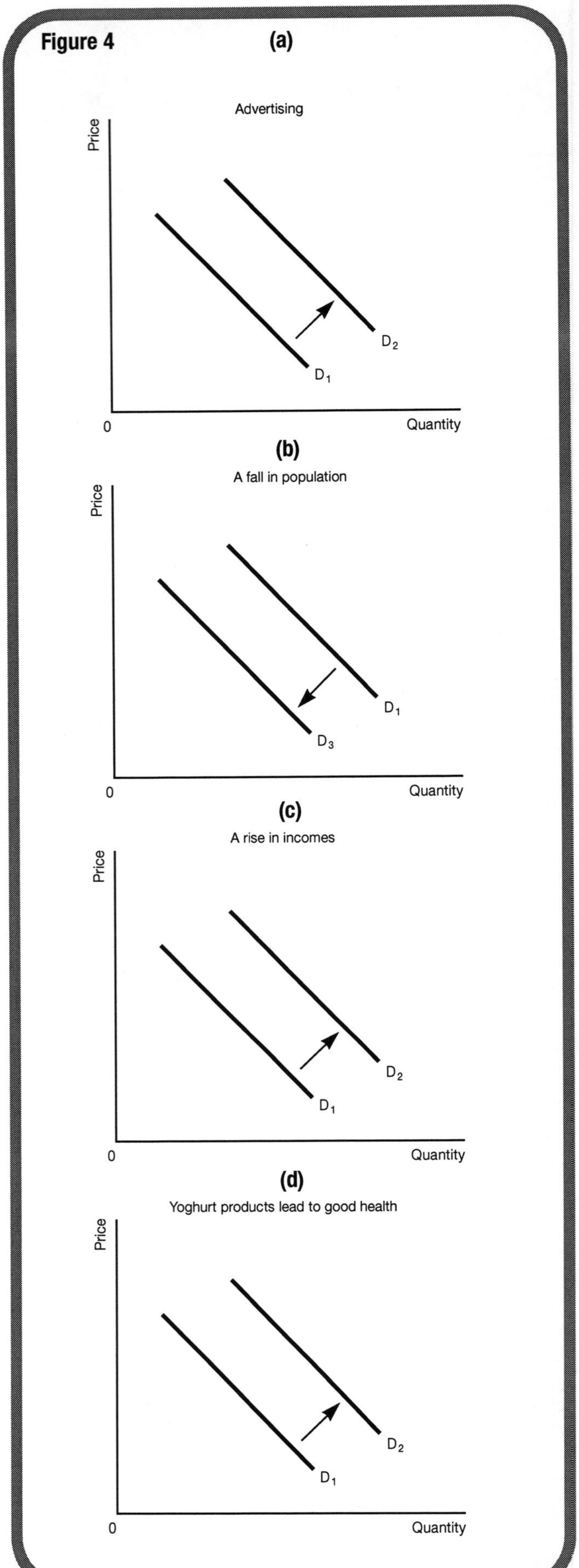

Question 5

(a) See Figure 5, demand curve A.
(b) (i) QD = 15 - 1/2 P
(ii) See Figure 4.5, demand curve B.
(c) (i) QD = 20 - 0.4P
(ii) See Figure 5, demand curve C.

Figure 5

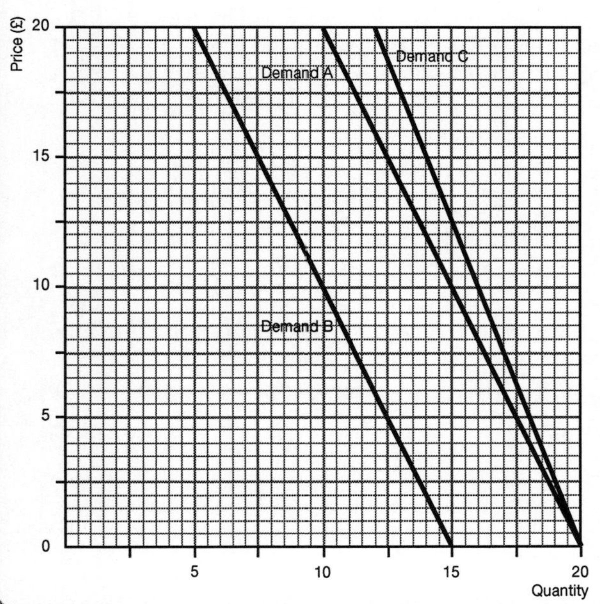

Table 1

Quantity (000 units)	Price (£)
1 500	100
1 330	200
1 160	300
990	400
820	500

(c) The market demand curve is drawn from the following data.

Table 2

Quantity (000 units)	Price (£)
2 000	100
1 850	200
1 660	300
1 490	400
1 320	500

Question 6

(a) and **(b)** The demand curves for answers (a) to (b) are shown in Figure 6.
The market demand curve for question (b) is drawn from the data in Table 1.

Figure 6

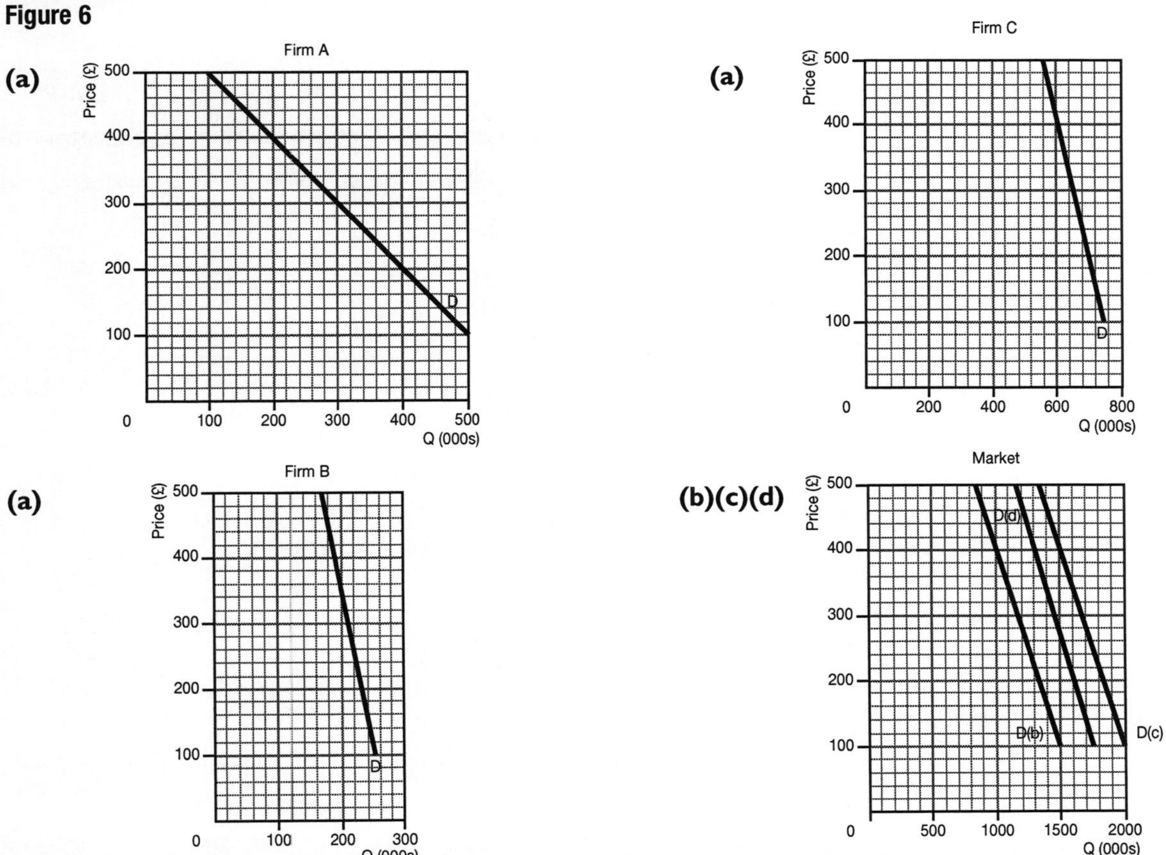

(d) The market demand curve is drawn from the following data.

Table 3

Quantity (000 units)	Price (£)
1 750	100
1 600	200
1 450	300
1 300	400
1 150	500

Question 7

(a) and **(b)**

Figure 7

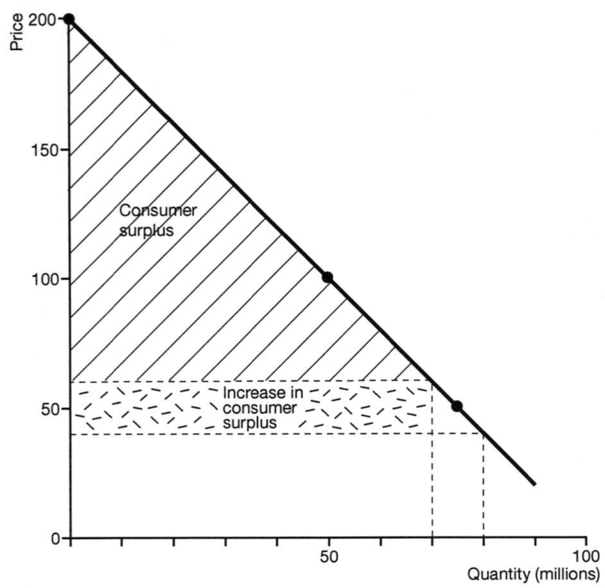

(c) The total consumer surplus at a price of £60 is shown by the shaded area in Figure 7. If the price of the product fell to £40 then there would be an extension in demand from 70 million units to 80 million units. As the price has fallen, then the price that the buyer is prepared to pay is relatively greater. Therefore the consumer surplus is greater by the dotted area shown in the figure.

Data question

1. The growth in numbers of children in independent has been greater than that for all schools over the period 1996 to 2006. Numbers in independent schools grew by 9 per cent between 1996 and 2003 and then remained roughly stable. In contrast, the number of children in all schools peaked in 2001 having grown over 3 per cent from 1996. But then numbers fell by approximately 2 per cent. Overall, therefore, over the period 1996 to 2006, independent school numbers grew by approximately 9 per cent but in all schools grew by only a little over 1 per cent.

2. (a) School fees have been rising over time. For example, in 2007, school fees rose by an average 5.9 per cent. This will lead to a contraction in demand for independent fee paying education. In Figure 8, a downward sloping demand curve is drawn. If prices rise from OA to OB, then quantity demanded will fall from OE to OF. If school fees were to fall, then there would be a movement down the demand curve showing an expansion of demand.

(b) A rise in school population numbers should lead to a rise in demand for independent school places. A rise in school population numbers shows that there are more children in the population needing to be educated. Therefore, at any given price (i.e. the level of school fees), there will be greater demand for places at independent schools. In Figure 9, the increase in demand is shown by a shift to the right in the demand curve from D_1 to D_2 for independent school places. At a school fee level of OA, demand for places increases from OB to OC. If overall school population numbers fall, the demand curve for independent school places will shift to the left showing a contraction in demand.

(c) A rise in spending on marketing and advertising for independent schools will lead to a rise in demand for independent school places. This will be a shown by a shift to the right in the demand curve from D_1 to D_2, shown in Figure 9. The data states that between 2001 and 2006, the average school's marketing budget rose from £33 966 to £59

Figure 8

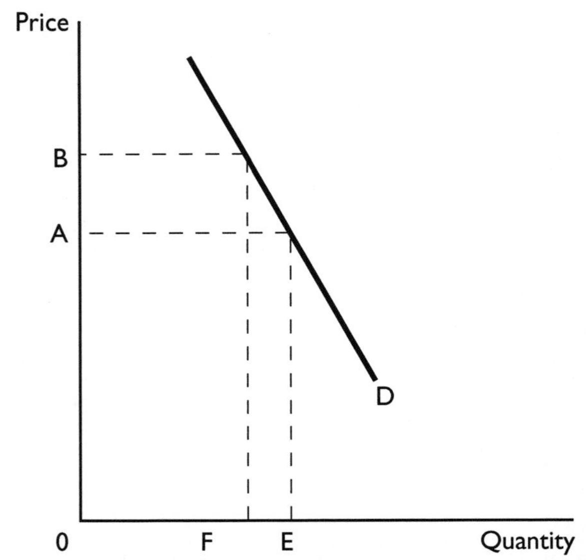

Figure 9

330. It is likely, therefore that this factor increased demand for independent education over this period. A fall in spending on marketing and advertising by independent schools will, in contrast, lead to a fall in demand for independent school places, shown by a shift to the left in the demand curve.

(d) A rise in the numbers of 'affluent, time-poor parents' should lead to an increase in demand for independent school places. A rise in the number of rich parents will shift the demand curve for independent school places from D_1 to D_2 in Figure 9 as more customers can now afford to send their children to independent schools. A rise in the number of 'time-poor' parents is equally likely to lead to an increase in demand for independent school places. With less time to spend on parenting, these affluent parents will be more prepared to spend money on their children's education, seeing schools as surrogate or substitute parents. A fall in the number of affluent, time-poor parents will have the opposite effect: demand for independent school places will fall.

(e) A rise in the amount of financial assistance means that more parents who could not otherwise afford to send their children to independent schools will now be able to do so. Therefore demand for independent school places will rise, shown by a shift to the right of the demand curve from D_1 to D_2. Conversely, a fall in financial assistance will lead to a fall in demand for independent school places. In the data, it states that the number of pupils receiving receiving financial help increased by 3.4 per cent in 2007.

3. Consumer surplus is the difference between the total amount paid by consumers for a product and what they would have been prepared to pay for it. What they would have been prepared to pay is shown by the demand curve. In Figure 10, if the demand curve for independent school education is D_1, then with school fees of OA, the quantity demanded of private school education is OH. Consumer surplus is ACJ, the difference between what parents actually paid, OAJH, and what they would have been prepared to pay which is OCJH.

The increase in average incomes of over 4 per cent a year will increase the demand for private school education, pushing the demand curve to the right to D_2. However, the question also states that fees have risen. So fees will now be higher than OA. Assume that higher fees leads to a movement up the demand curve D_2 to F with a fee level of OB. Note the quantity demanded of private education is now higher at OG but is not as high as it would have been if there had been an increase in income but no increase in fees.

With OG private education demanded, the amount of consumer surplus is BFE. Consumer surplus of BEF is higher than the previous level of consumer surplus, ACJ. This would suggest that the consumer surplus of parents buying private education has been rising in recent years.

However, there are circumstances where this would not be the case. Assume that price increases are so large that the quantity demanded falls below OH, the original level before the increase in incomes as shown in Figure 11. Despite substantial rises in incomes, less is being demanded.

Consumer surplus at a fee level of OL and a quantity of OK is LMN. This is less than that the previous consumer surplus level of ACJ.

In general, if the effect of the increase in fees more than outweighs the effect of increasing incomes, consumer surplus will fall. However, the data shows that number of pupils in private education rose over the period 1996 to 2006. Therefore the effect of increasing incomes has more than outweighed the effect of increasing fee levels. Consumer surplus is therefore likely to have risen rather than fallen over the past ten years.

Figure 10

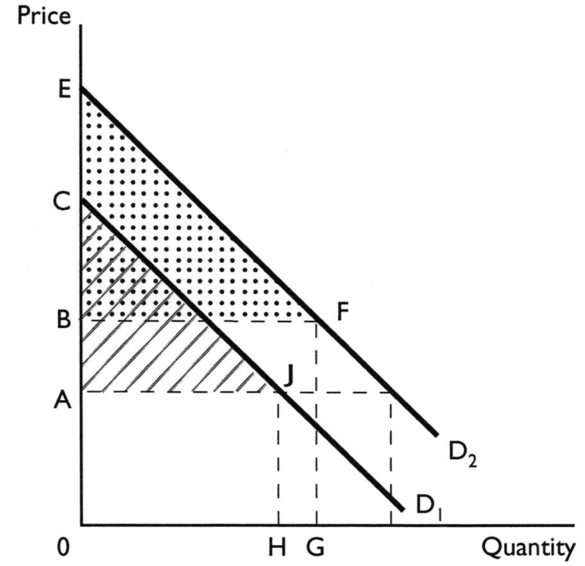

Figure 11

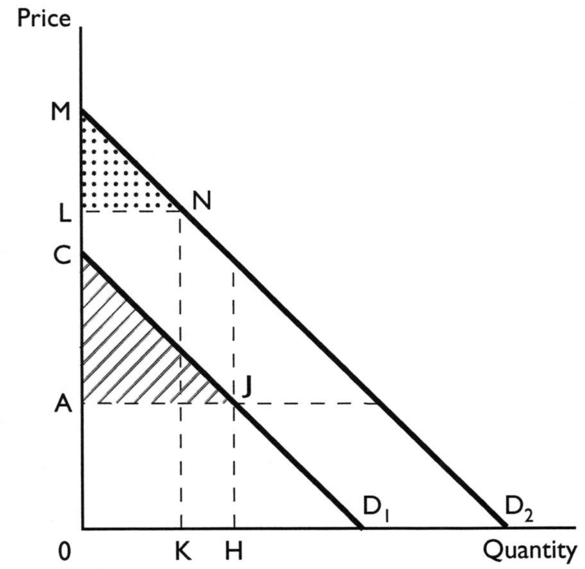

6 The supply curve

Question 1

(a) and **(b)** See Figure 1

Figure 1

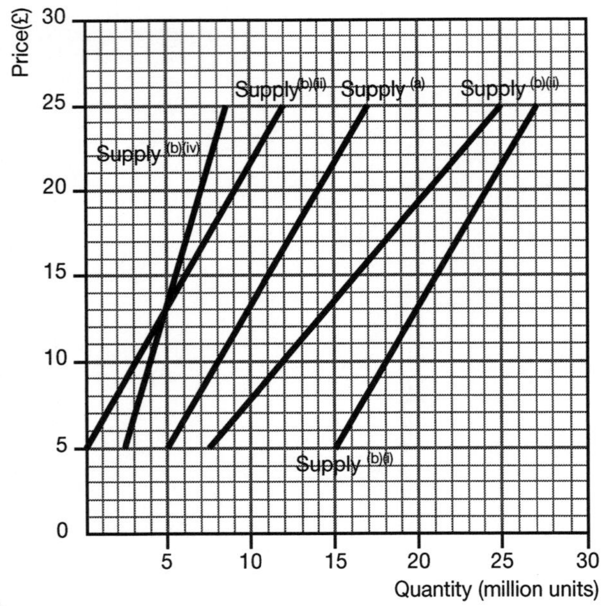

Question 2

(a) Earnings of workers, or wages, are a cost to firms. When wages rise, firms' costs rise too. This shifts the supply curve to the left, showing that firms want a higher price if they are to supply the same amount as before.

(b) (i) Firms' supply curves are likely to have shifted furthest to the left when wage increases were greatest. In 1976, for instance, average earnings rose by over 30 per cent. This is likely to have increased firms' costs substantially and led to a sharp shift to the left in their supply curves. 1981 and 1990 were other peak years for earnings when the supply curves of firms shifted further to the left than in surrounding years. Of these three peaks, 1976 was by far the highest.

(ii) The supply curve would have shifted least far to the left when changes in average earnings were at their lowest. In the period 1970 to 2007, there were a number of years when earnings growth was lowest compared to surrounding years. 1972, 1976, 1978, 1984 and 1996 all saw relatively low earnings inflation. Of these years, 1996 saw the lowest level of earnings inflation and hence in 1996 the supply curve for goods would have shifted least far to the left as a result of increases in costs.

Question 3

Advances in technology have vastly reduced the cost of calculators since 1970. The cost of the microchip used in a calculator has dropped at a startling rate. This has had the effect of pushing the supply curve right, as in Figure 2, from S 1970 to S 1975 to S Today.

Figure 2

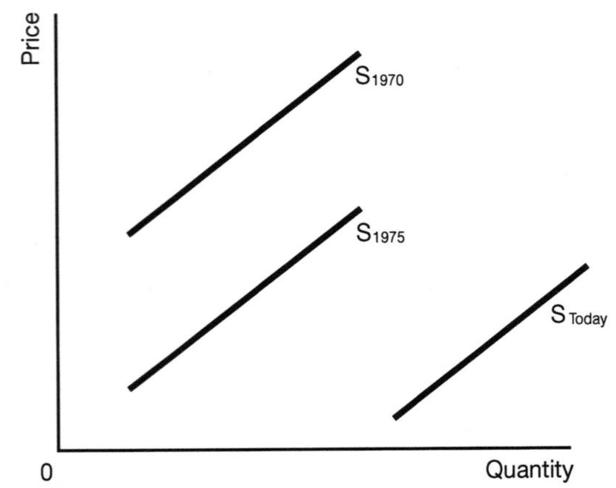

Question 4

Figure 3

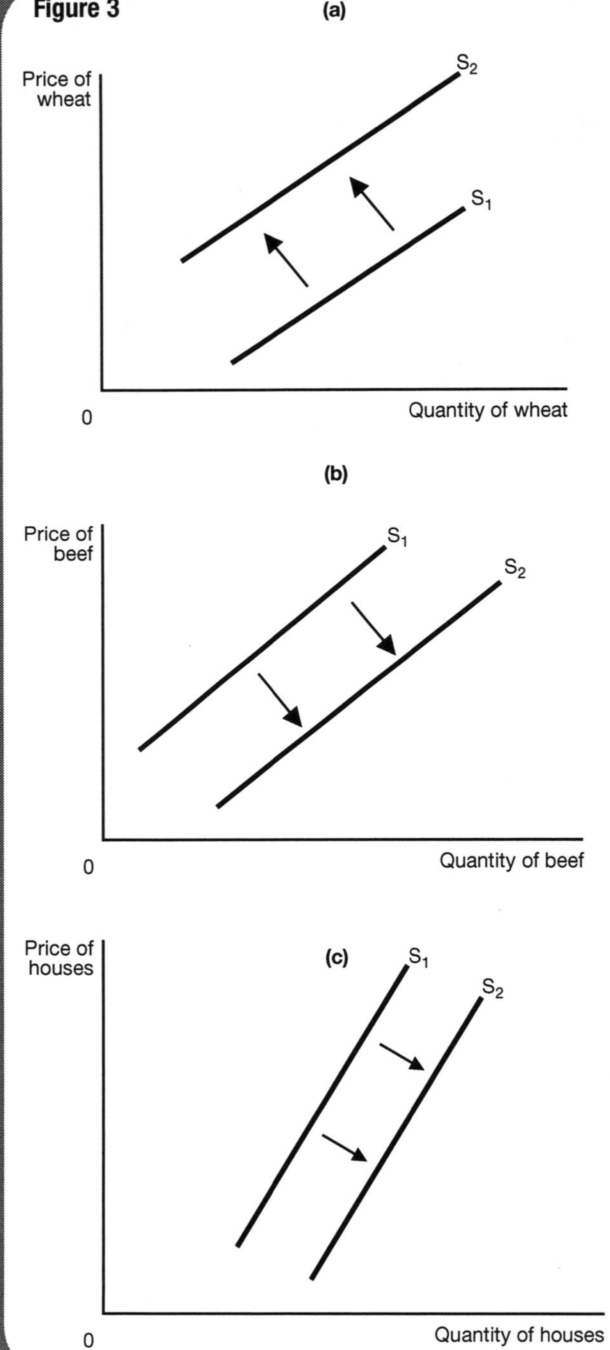

(a) A drought in Romania would reduce the supply of wheat in Romania and therefore the world. At any given price, less would be supplied. Therefore, the supply curve for wheat would shift to the left as in Figure 3.
(b) The new strains of grass represent an improvement in agricultural technology. Costs of production are likely to fall for beef because the new grasses allow ranchers to feed more cattle per hectare. Therefore there will be an increase in supply of beef. This is shown by a rightward shift in the supply curve in Figure 3. At any given level of quantity supplied, the price at which beef will be supplied will be lower because costs have fallen.
(c) Easing planning permission restrictions should make it easier to build more houses. The supply of houses will therefore increase. This is shown by a shift to the right in the supply curve for houses in Figure 3.

Question 5

(a) The market supply curve is drawn from the data in Table 1.

Table 1

Quantity (million units)	Price
12	1
20	2
28	3
36	4
44	5

Figure 4

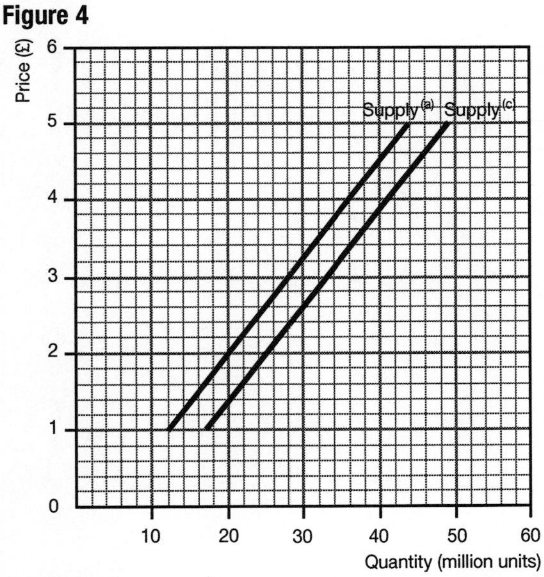

(b) (i) 12 million units.
(ii) 32 million units.
(c) See Figure 4, Supply(c).
(d) Greater productive efficiency means that firms are now able to produce the same amount at lower cost. So the introduction of new technology will increase supply and shift the supply curve of each firm to the right. This will therefore lead to a shift in the market supply curve to the right too, since the market supply curve is derived by adding up the individual supply curves of firms.

Data question

1. The price of coffee over the period 1987 to 2007 fluctuated between US$0.40 and US$2.00. Prices were broadly falling between 1989 and 1993 and again between 1995 and 2002, although the latter period included a large spike in prices in 1998. Prices broadly rose between 1993 and 1995 and then again from 2002 to 2007. Overall, the price was roughly the same at the end of the period in 2007 as at the beginning in 1986 at just over US$1 per lb.
2. (a) Severe frosts in coffee growing regions will reduce coffee yields. At any given price, less will be supplied to the market as a result. Hence, there will be a shift to the left in the supply curve of coffee, shown in Figure 5 from S_1 to S_2. For example, the frosts in Brazil in the mid-1990s led to large increases in the price of coffee.

Figure 5

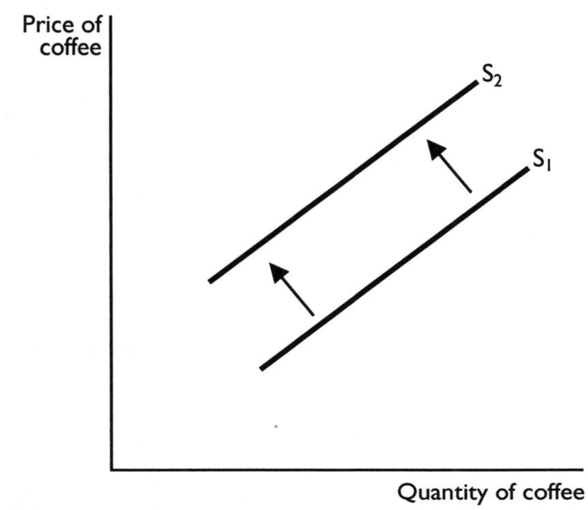

(b) Changes in costs for coffee growers will lead to either an increase or a decrease in supply of coffee. If costs fall, coffee growers will be prepared to supply the same amount of coffee at a lower price. This will shift the supply curve to the right in Figure 6 from S_1 to S_3. Conversely, if costs rise, the supply curve will shift to the left from S_1 to S_2. For example, between 2005 and 2007, production did not increase despite higher prices. This was because costs of production, such as oil prices had increased considerably. Rising costs reduced the profit incentive to increase production.

Figure 6

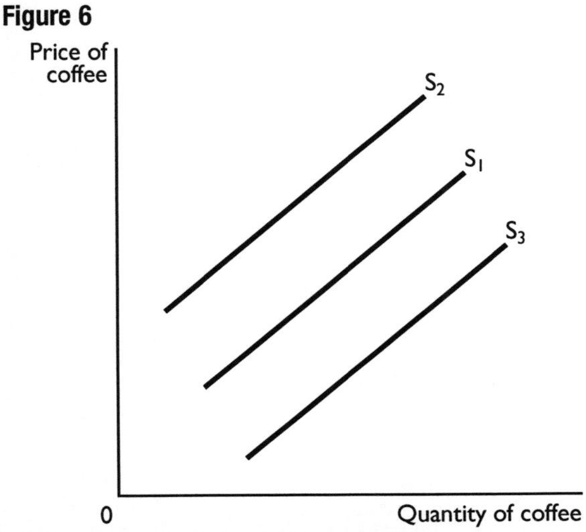

(c) A change in the price of coffee will lead either to a movement up or down the supply curve of coffee. If prices rise, coffee growers will supply more coffee to the market. In Figure 7, there would be a movement up the supply curve from, say, A to B. If prices fall, coffee growers will supply less coffee to the market. In Figure 7, this would be shown by a movement down the curve from, say, A to C. For example, in the second half of the 1990s, relatively high prices led to increased production. Vietnam, at this time, moved from being an insignificant producer of coffee to being a major world producer.

Figure 7

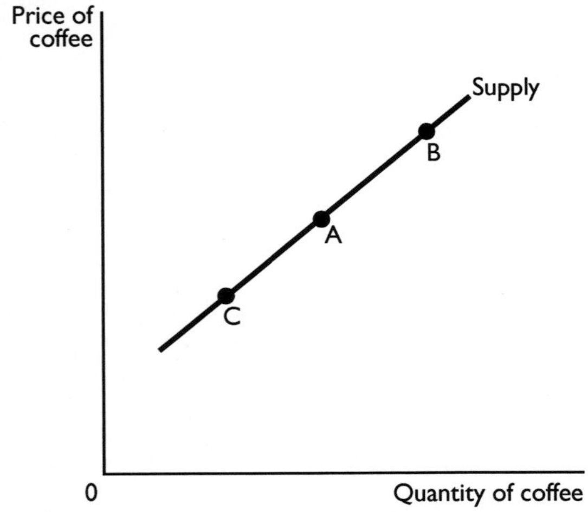

(d) Dumping of coffee stocks onto world markets will lead to an increase in the supply of coffee at any given price. This will shift the supply curve from S_1 to S_2 in Figure 8. For example, the failure of the coffee cartel at the end of the 1980s and the subsequent sell off of coffee stocks from the cartel led to a major fall in price.

Figure 8

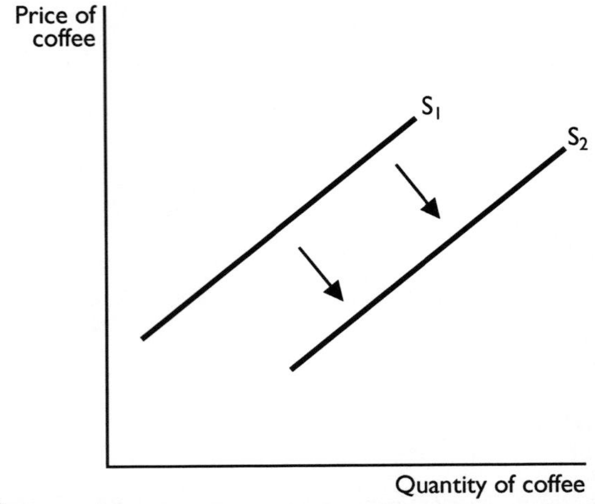

3. Severe frosts in Vietnam would not benefit Vietnamese producers. They would see their output fall as their crops were damaged. On the other hand, a fall in world supply resulting from lower Vietnamese production would lead to higher world prices for coffee. Therefore, other producers, such as those in Brazil, would benefit. They would be able to sell their crops at a higher price than would otherwise have been the case. Given that Vietnam is the world's second largest coffee producer, the fall in Vietnamese supply due to frost could have a significant impact on world supplies. The larger the fall in Vietnamese production, the greater the loss to Vietnamese producers but the greater the gain to coffee producers elsewhere in the world.

7 Price determination

Question 1

(a)

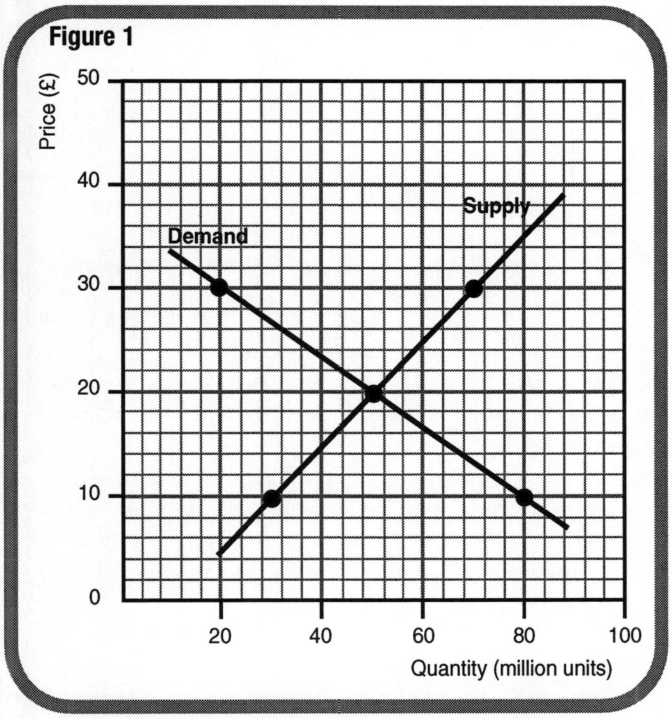

(b) The equilibrium price is £20 (i.e. where demand equals supply).

(c) (i) Excess demand (i.e. where demand is greater than supply) exists at a price of £10.

(ii) Excess supply (i.e. where supply is greater than demand) exists at a price of £30.

(d) (i) At £10 there will be a shortage in the market because 80 million units are demanded but only 30 million supplied.

(ii) At £40 there will be a glut on the market because 90 million units will be supplied but demand is zero.

(iii) At £22 there will be a glut on the market because 44 million units will be demanded whilst 54 million units will be supplied.

(iv) At £18 there will be a shortage because 56 million units will be demanded whilst 46 million will be supplied.

(v) At £20 there will be neither a glut or a surplus because demand equals supply and the market is in equilibrium.

Question 2

(a) New production facilities, which came on stream in the late 1970s, led to an increase in the supply of nickel. This shifted the supply curve to the right, from S_1 to S_2 in Figure 2 The result would have been a fall in price from OF to OE all other things being equal.

(b) The world recession in the early 1980s led to a fall in the demand for nickel. This was because the demand for products in which nickel is used, such as stainless steel, fell. A sharp drop in the price of nickel resulted. In Figure 3 the fall in demand from D_1 to D_2 leads to a fall in price from OF to OE.

(c) When the industry closed capacity in the early 1980s it reduced the supply of nickel to the market. This, in Figure 4, led to a shift in the supply curve to the left and a rise in the price of nickel to OF from what it might otherwise have been at OE.

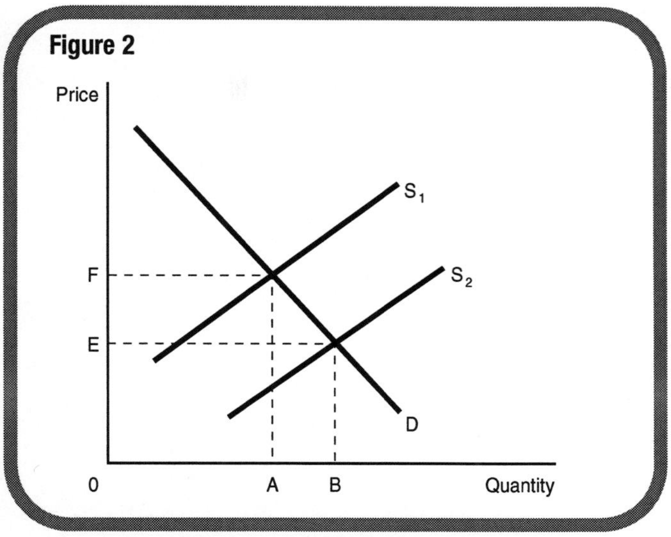

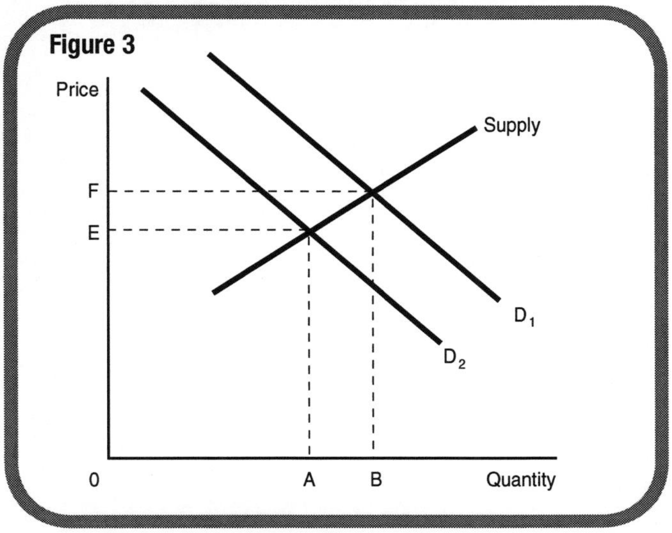

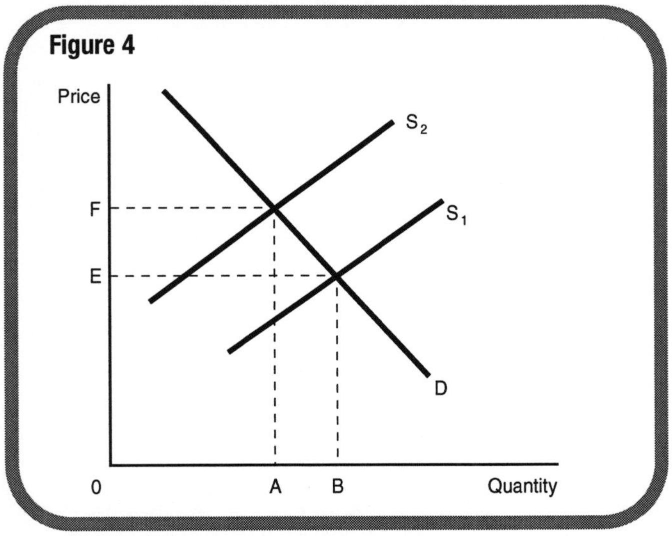

(d) The increase in demand from Japanese stainless steel producers led to a sharp increase in the price of nickel from $1.87 a lb to over $9 per lb. This is shown in Figure 5 by a shift to the right in the demand curve with a rise in equilibrium price from OE to OF.

(e) The invasion of Kuwait by Iraq in 1990 led to a rise in the price of nickel. This was because the demand for nickel rose as buyers feared an increase in demand for the metal in armaments and a possible fall in supply if some nickel producing countries decided to withdraw sales from the world markets. This is shown in Figure 6 with the demand curve shifting to the right. Speculators may also have withheld supplies that they would otherwise have sold in the hope that

Figure 5

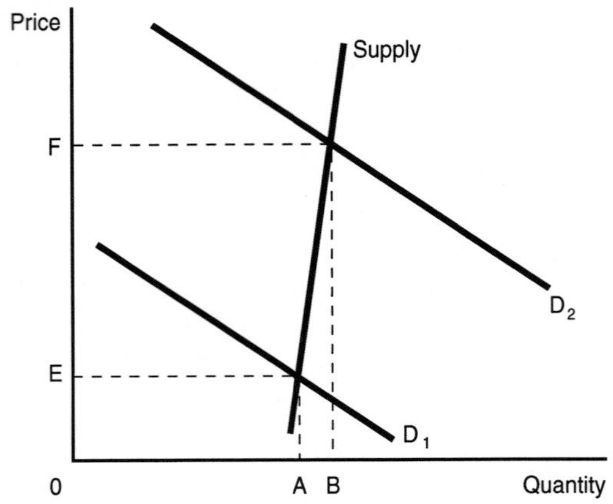

Figure 6

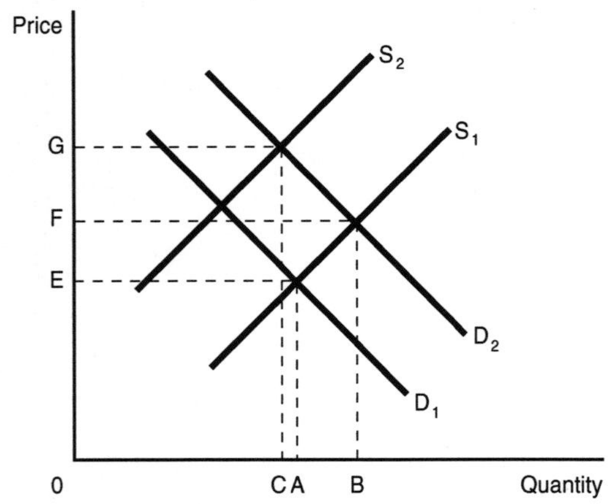

Figure 7

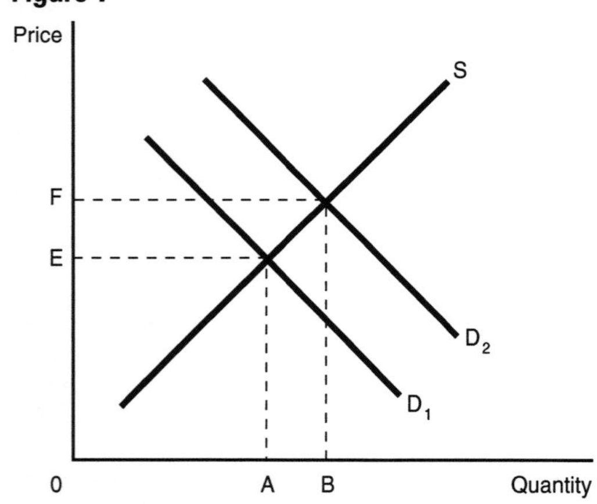

they could sell later at a higher price, decreasing the supply of nickel to the market. This is shown by the shift to the left in the supply curve in Figure 6.

(f) Economic growth in 1994 will have led to an increase in demand for nickel as the demand for goods in which nickel is a raw material rose. This is shown by a shift to the right in the demand curve in Figure 7. The price rose from OE to OF as a result.

(g) The 1998 Asian crisis led to a sharp fall in demand for all goods and services in the countries affected. This caused a consequent fall in demand for nickel, in derived demand from other goods and services. This is shown in Figure 8. The fall in demand is shown by a shift to the left in the demand curve.

Figure 8

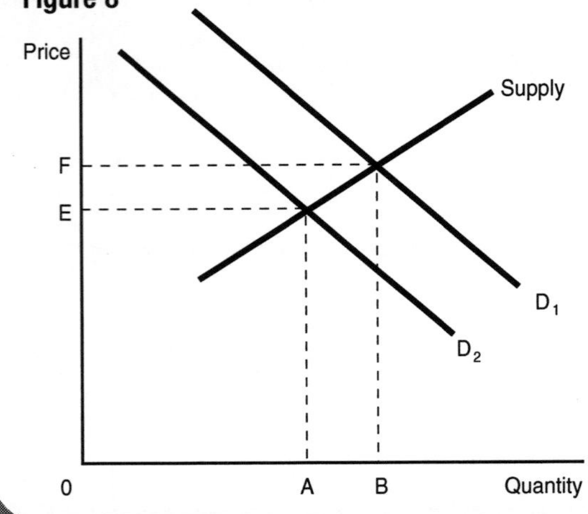

This leads to a fall in price, from OF to OE and in the quantity bought and sold in equilibrium from OB to OA.

(h) China, with the world's largest population, experienced fast economic growth between 2003 and 2007. Economic growth is likely to lead to an increase in demand for raw materials to feed extra production. This increase in demand then led to an increase in the price of nickel to levels not seen since the late 1980s. The increase in demand can be seen in Figure 5 with the demand curve shifting to the right from D_1 to D_2 and price increasing from OE to OF.

Question 3

(a) In the run up to Christmas 2006, retailers had large amounts of unsold stock. They had ordered too much stock from their suppliers and were unable to sell it at full price. This is shown in Figure 9. The supply curve is assumed to be vertical because retailers have bought the stock already. In this short period of time, there is a fixed amount of stock in the supply chain. Full price being charged was OF. At this price, OB was supplied but OA was demanded. There was therefore excess supply of AB. Retailers could have chosen to reduce their prices before Christmas to eliminate the excess supply by holding pre-Christmas sales, but the data state they chose not to do so.

Figure 9

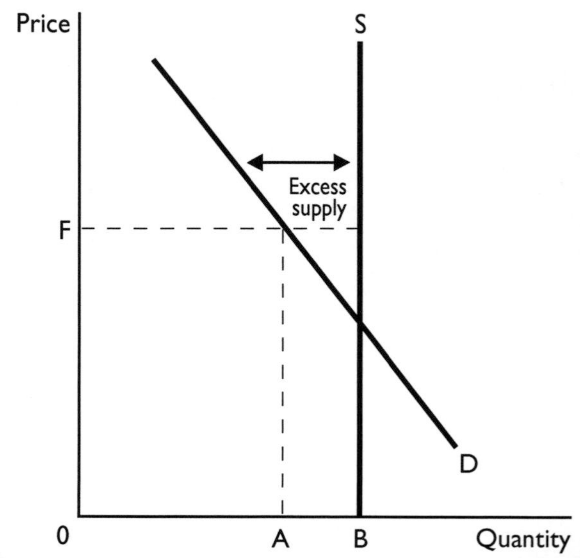

(b) To restore equilibrium to the market, producers lowered their prices by holding a sale. They were then able to 'off-load' their unwanted stocks at reduced prices. In Figure 10, equilibrium between demand and supply was restored by a fall in price to OE where demand equals supply.

Figure 10

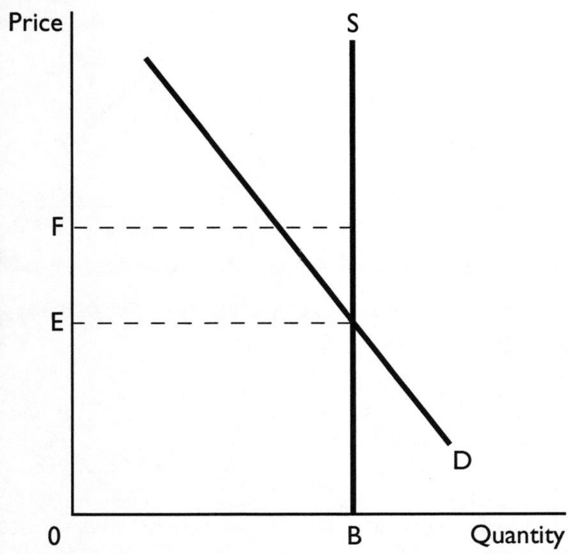

Data question

1. (a) Demand is shown by consumption in Figure 8 of the students' book. So, in 2001, world demand was approximately 14 950 000 (14.95 million) tonnes.

(b) Supply is shown by production in Figure 9 of the students' book. So, in 2001, world supply was approximately 15,600,000 (15.6 million) tonnes. Note that this can only be an estimate since world supply would also include the net amount of copper taken out of stock. If more copper were taken out of stocks than were put in, then world supply would have been higher than 15.6 million tonnes.

2. Prices in a free market are determined by the forces of demand and supply. In 2002, demand roughly equalled supply. But between 2003 and 2006, demand as measured by consumption was greater than supply as measured by production. As a result, the price of copper rose four-fold over the period from approximately US$1,500 per tonne to a maximum of US$7 500 per tonne.

3. The price of copper is likely to remain high in 2007 and 2008, if not increase. On the demand side, demand remains strong. Figure 10 of the students' book shows that demand from China, a major source of increased demand for world copper due to high investment in construction, was growing strongly, having weakened in 2005 and 2006. On the supply side, expansion of production is likely to be weak. Severe inflation in the copper mining industry has meant that much of the increase in the price of copper has not flowed through to higher profits. Instead, it has been paid out to factors of production such as labour. So the profit incentive to bring new mining projects on stream has not been as strong as the data in Figure 8 of the students' book showing the increase in copper prices might suggest. Even so, 'marginally profitable mining projects are now 'more feasible'. Even then, however, it can take years if not decades to bring new projects to the production stage. So the impact of increased investment is likely to be felt in the medium to long term rather than the short term.

The other factor affecting prices is the level of stocks. If stock levels are high, stocks can be drawn down, reducing price pressures in the market. However, the data states that stocks of copper were 'low' in 2007. Hence, any increase in demand for copper is likely to result in higher prices in 2007-2008.

The most likely scenario for 2007-08 can be illustrated using a demand and supply diagram. Increasing demand for copper is shown by the shift in the demand curve from D_1 to D_2 in Figure 11 here. With producers unable to increase the supply of copper by very much (i.e. the supply of copper is price inelastic) because of a lack of physical copper mines and equipment, most of the increase in demand results in higher prices of AB although there is some increased output of EF.

Figure 11

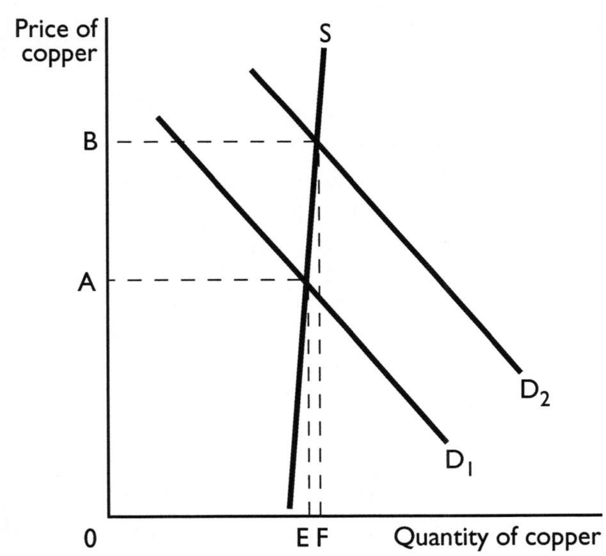

8 Interrelationships between markets

Question 1

(a) (i) Electricity and gas may be substitutes because one can be used instead of the other. For instance, electricity can be used to power central heating systems rather than gas. On the other hand, they can also be complements. For instance, gas fired central heating systems require electricity to power the pump or fan mechanism which takes hot water or air round the system.
(ii) Tea and milk are complements in the UK because tea is generally drunk with milk. On the other hand, tea can be a substitute for milk in that a consumer may have a cup of tea rather than a drink of milk.
(iii) Bus and train journeys can be substitutes. For instance, a person may travel from London to Glasgow by train or by bus. On the other hand, they can also be complements. For instance, a journey to work may involve both a train and a bus journey.
(iv) Chocolate bars and crisps can be substitutes. A consumer may buy either a chocolate bar or a packet of crisps as a snack. On the other hand, they could be complements if, for instance, a chocolate bar and a packet of crisps are included in a lunch box.
(b) (i) In terms of the amount consumed, electricity and gas are far more likely to be substitutes than complements. The amount of electricity needed to run a gas fired heating system, for instance, is minimal in comparison with the gas burned to generate the heat.

In the UK, tea and milk are far more likely to be complements than substitutes. Milk on its own is far less popular a beverage than tea with milk.

Bus journeys and train journeys are more likely to be substitutes, mile for mile. When they are complements, the bus journeys made are likely to be relatively short.

Chocolate bars and crisps are more likely to be substitutes than complements. In only a small percentage of instances when a chocolate bar or a packet of crisps were eaten on their own would the other snack also be eaten.
(ii) Assume that gas and electricity are substitutes. A rise in the price of gas will lead to a rise in the price of electricity. In Figure 1, a fall in the supply of gas leads to a rise in its price from OE to OF. This results in a fall in quantity demanded from OB to OA as consumers switch to electricity which is now relatively cheaper. This increase in the demand for electricity is shown by a shift to the right in the curve for electricity. Whilst GH more is consumed, the equilibrium price rises from OJ to OK.

Assume that tea and milk are complements. A rise in the price of milk will lead to a fall in the price of tea. In Figure 2, a fall in the supply of milk leads to a rise in price of milk from OE to OF. The rise in the price of milk discourages people from drinking beverages such as tea with milk. Hence the demand for tea falls, shown by a shift to the left in the demand curve for tea. GH less tea is demanded whilst the price drops from OK to OJ.

Assume the bus journeys and train journeys are substitutes. A rise in the price of train journeys will, all other things being equal, lead to a rise in the price of bus journeys. In Figure 1, a fall in the supply of train journeys leads to a rise in its price from OE to OF. This results in a fall in quantity

Figure 1

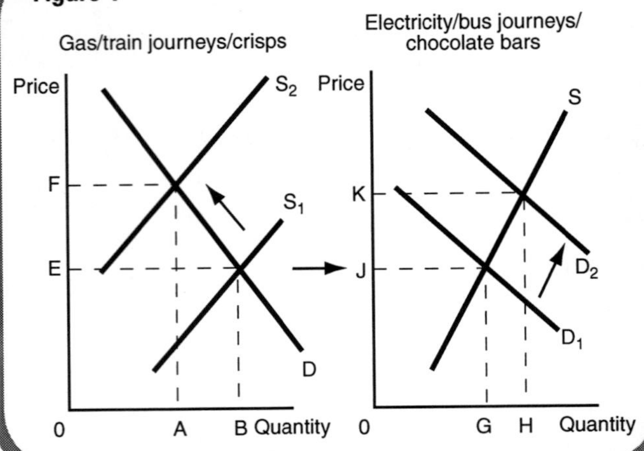

Figure 2

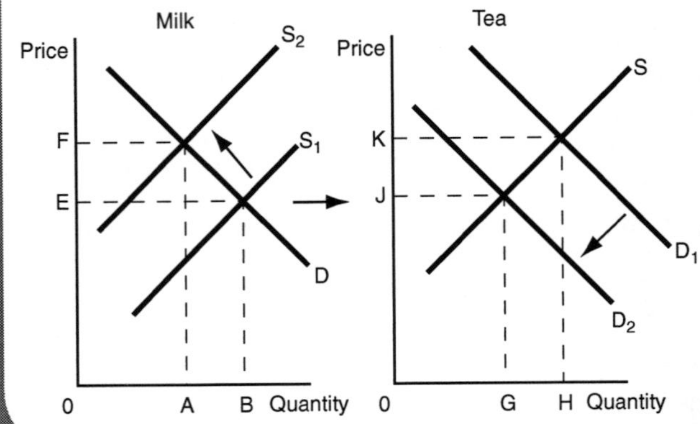

demanded from OB to OA as consumers switch to buses which are now relatively cheaper. This increase in the demand for buses is shown by a shift to the right in the curve for buses. Whilst GH more is consumed, the equilibrium price rises from OJ to OK.
Assume the crisps and chocolate bars are substitutes. A rise in the price of crisps will, all other things being equal, lead to a rise in the price of chocolate bars. In Figure 1, a fall in the supply of crisps leads to a rise in its price from OE to OF. This results in a fall in quantity demanded from OB to OA as consumers switch to chocolate bars which are now relatively cheaper. This increase in the demand for chocolate bars is shown by a shift to the right in the curve for chocolate bars. Whilst GH more is consumed, the equilibrium price rises from OJ to OK.

Question 2

(a) Derived demand is when the demand for one good is the result of or derived from the demand for another good. So milk is in derived demand from porridge because, in order to eat porridge, most consumers make porridge by combining it with milk.
(b) The data suggests that there has been an increase in demand for porridge because of the latest fashion in diet: the Glycemic or GI diet. In Figure 3 (a), the increase in demand for porridge is shown by a shift to the right of the demand curve from D_1 to D_2. Equilibrium quantity demanded therefore increases from OA to OB. As a result, there is an increase in demand for milk because milk is in derived demand from porridge. In Figure 3 (b), this is shown by a shift to the right in the demand curve for milk from D_1 to D_2, with equilibrium

Figure 3

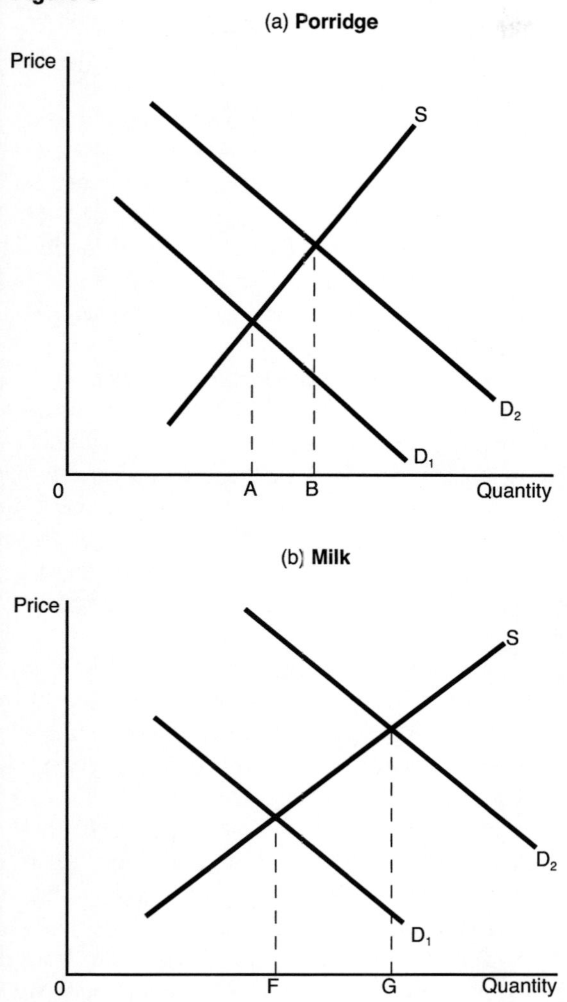

quantity demanded increasing from OF to OG.

(c) There are several reasons why the price of milk might not go up. One is that the increase in demand might be so small that it has no effect on the price. In the year to April 2005, demand increased by 35 million litres compared to the 4.45 billion litres sold in 2004, a 0.8 per cent increase. 0.8 percent might not be sufficiently large to trigger a price rise.

A second reason is that the supply of milk might be highly responsive to changes in price. Farmers might be prepared to supply more milk at roughly the same price as before. In Figure 4, the supply curve is flat (i.e. perfectly elastic, see unit 9) and so the increase in demand, shown by the shift in the demand curve from D_1 to D_2, has no impact on equilibrium price, P, despite sales increasing from OA to OB. There are a variety of reasons why supply might be highly responsive to changes in price. One is if most of the costs facing farmers are fixed and it is relatively costless to supply small amounts more of milk to the market.

Figure 4

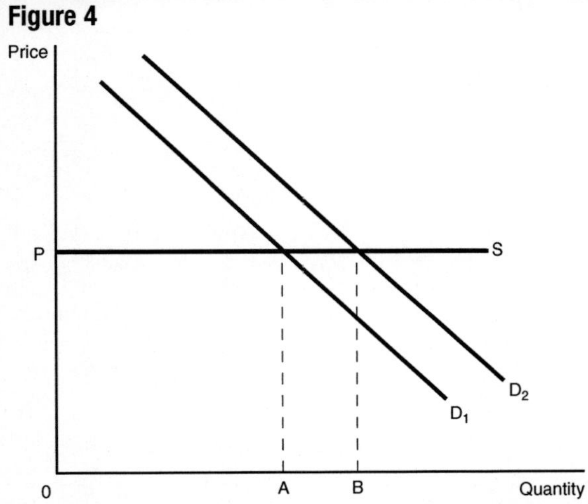

A third reason might be that the major buyers of wholesale milk, the supermarkets, have such large market power that they can tell farmers to supply them with more milk at no increase in price. The extent of the power of the major supermarkets over farmers has been debated fiercely in recent years with farmers complaining that supermarkets can virtually dictate prices to farmers.

Question 3

Joint supply is when two or more goods are produced together, so that a change in supply of one good will necessarily change the supply of the other goods with which it is in joint supply. If the demand for withdrawals from fee paying cash machines increases, then companies operating such machines will increase the number of machines available. Companies are also profiting by selling advertisements on these machines. An increase in demand for cash withdrawals will increase the number of advertisements which could be sold. Economic theory would suggest that the price of advertisements will therefore fall. In Figure 5 (a), the increase in demand for withdrawals from cash machines increases supply from OA to OB. As a result, more advertisements are supplied, in Figure 5 (b), pushing the price of advertising space down from OF to OG.

Figure 5

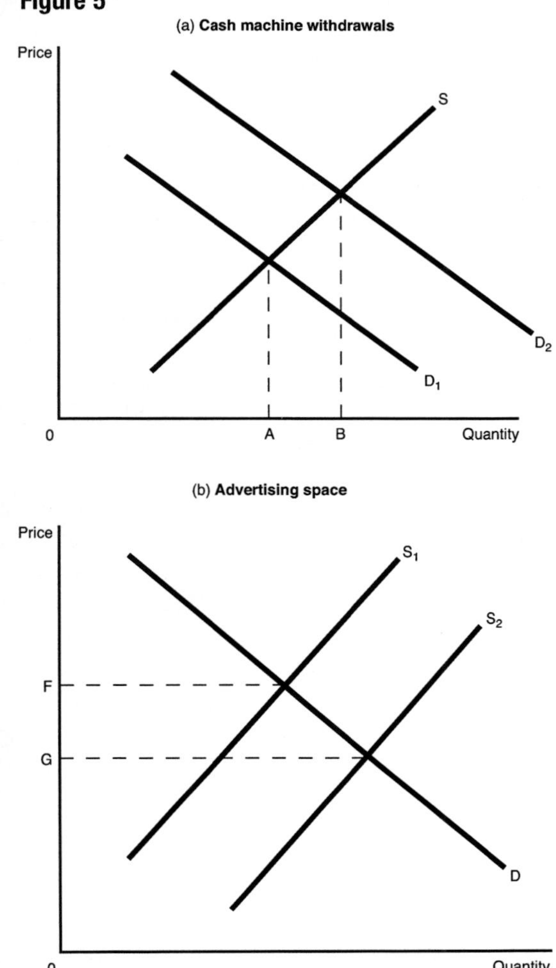

It could be argued, however, that cash machine owners will be able to push up the price they charge to advertisers. A large company, like a drinks multinational, might not be interested in buying advertising space with a cash machine company which only owns 30 cash machines because the advertising opportunities are too limited. But it might be interested in buying space if a single cash machine company operates 1 000 machines. Demand for advertising space would therefore increase, pushing up its price.

Data question

1. (a) Land is a derived demand because it is demanded as a result of the demand for other goods and services. For instance, farmers demand land because consumers buy food in the shops. Homeowners demand land because they want somewhere to live.

(b) Land is in composite demand because it can be demanded for two distinct uses. For instance, a field could be used either for farming or for building an estate of houses. An urban site could be used for residential housing or industrial buildings.

(c) Land is sometimes in joint supply because it can produce two or more goods. For instance, a forest area could be used both to produce timber and for recreation by walkers. A field of wheat will give both wheat and hay.

(d) Land is in joint demand with buildings because both are demanded at the same time. A building must be located on a plot of land. Therefore, someone buying or renting a building must also buy or rent the plot of land on which it is located.

2. (a) A growing population puts pressure on land use. The increase in population, forecast to reach 64.7 million in England by 2021, means greater demand for housing, schools, shops, leisure facilities and places of work. This greater demand increases the demand for land since land is in derived demand from these other goods and services. A growing population will therefore move the demand curve for land to the right.

(b) A shifting population means that some areas of the country are far more affected by a growth in the population than others with a consequent effect on demand. For instance, areas in Figure 7 in the Sstudent's book which have been suffering from falls in population could well have seen falls in land prices, all other things being equal. Areas which have experienced the fastest population growth, such as the South West, should, all other things being equal, have experienced the fastest rises in prices.

(c) Increasing affluence will increase demand for land. With more money, individuals want to buy more goods and services. Advances in technology mean that goods can often be produced in less factory space than before and hence the pressure on land from manufacturing is not particularly great. However, services can be very land hungry. For instance, a new motorway, which provides travel services, creates a demand for land from the government. A new McDonald's or cinema complex will take up land. Thus, increasing affluence can lead to increases in demand for land particularly near urban centres. However, as the example of France shows, increasing affluence can also lead to rural depopulation. If enough people are attracted from isolated rural areas to the towns in a short space of time, demand for land in isolated rural areas can fall.

3. There are many, particularly in the construction industry, who believe that loosening green belt regulations would bring benefits. They argue that green belt regulations have driven up the price of land. For instance, according to a 1994 study commissioned by the Department of the Environment, housing land in Reigate in Surrey was 3.6 times the price it would have been if there were no green belt policies in the area. For Beverley in Yorkshire, the figure was 2.2 times. With such high land prices, the price of housing is artificially increased, making it much more difficult for those on relatively low incomes to afford decent housing and forcing those on higher incomes to live in smaller houses than they would otherwise have done.

As far as industrial property is concerned, higher land prices increase the costs of UK firms, which have to be passed on to UK consumers. Higher land prices also make the UK less internationally competitive viz a viz those countries with much lower land prices. A loosening of green belt regulations for housing might lower land prices in urban areas and make land more affordable for industry. Thus industry would benefit even if green belt regulations were not loosened for industrial development.

The farming community is also probably a net loser from green belt regulations. Without green belt regulations, farming land could be sold to builders, pushing up the price of agricultural land particularly near urban centres. Farming land would thus be more marketable to its owners.

There are many, however, who strongly support green belt regulations. Nimbys are likely to gain disproportionately from their existence. In most cases, having a new housing estate, factory or bypass built at the bottom of your garden will lead to a loss in value of your property and worsen your quality of life. Most Nimbys would not protest if a housing estate were to be built ten miles away from their homes, but would protest vigorously if it were built immediately next to them. Nimbys do not need blanket green belt regulations to safeguard them in a particular location. All they need is a regulation which says that building will not be permitted in their area. However, the easiest and safest way in Britain's current political climate to ensure that such a local regulation exists is to defend the overall green belt regulations in place since the Second World War.

Ecologists point out that green belt policies have been a successful way of preserving the environment. They would argue that new housing in rural areas leads to environmental degradation. Loss of wildlife and plant life is too high a cost to bear for the sake of putting up a few houses or industrial units. There are also groups such as ramblers and blood sports enthusiasts who argue that the countryside provides considerable benefits in the form of recreational use. The benefits to be gained from being able to walk in the countryside, or hunt foxes far outweighs any benefits from encroaching urbanisation.

One major problem of coming to any conclusion is that it is difficult to place a value on each cost and benefit. Another is that there would be many losers as well as gainers from a loosening of green belt regulations. How to reconcile these losses and gains is a highly contested issue.

9 Price elasticity of demand

Question 1

Price elasticity of demand is the percentage change in quantity demanded divided by the percentage change in price. Hence: **(a)** 2; **(b)** 3; **(c)** 1/2 or 0.5; **(d)** 1/9 or 0.11; **(e)** 5/7 or 0.71; **(f)** 8/11 or 0.73.

Question 2

The formula for price elasticity of demand is:

$$\frac{\Delta Q}{Q} \times \frac{P}{\Delta P} \quad \text{or} \quad \frac{\Delta Q}{Q} \div \frac{\Delta P}{P}$$

Hence:
(a) 1/2 or 0.5; **(b)** 2; **(c)** 1/3 or 0.33; **(d)** 2; **(e)** 0; **(f)** 0.27.

Question 3

(a) A 10 per cent increase in the price of petrol is unlikely to have any immediate significant effect on quantity demanded of petrol. The short term elasticity of demand for petrol is highly inelastic because it has very few good short term substitutes. Car owners, for instance, will not change their cars to more fuel efficient models overnight because the price of petrol has gone up 5p a litre. In the longer term, however, the elasticity of demand is much higher because consumers can change the equipment they use. Following the 1973-4 quadrupling of the price of oil, for instance, sales of oil fired central heating systems slumped in the UK as consumers switched to gas fired central heating systems.
(b) Fresh tomatoes are likely to have a higher short term elasticity of demand than petrol. Tomatoes have a number of good substitutes. If the price of tomatoes is too high, consumers will buy, for instance, tinned tomatoes or eat hot meals instead of salads containing tomatoes. However, it is not possible to say whether demand is elastic or inelastic without further evidence.
(c) A 10 per cent increase in the price of holidays offered by a tour operator, with no similar increase in price offered by other tour operators, is likely to lead to a significant fall in demand for these holidays. Many package tours are bought on price and therefore demand is likely to be elastic. On the other hand, if the tour operator is offering holidays in a niche market, or it has a very strong brand image, then demand could be inelastic. If it operates in a niche market there is likely to be little competition and consumers will therefore have no alternative but to pay the higher price for the holiday. If the tour operator has a strong brand image, consumers will be less price sensitive than would otherwise have been the case.
(d) Ford cars have a certain brand image and therefore demand for Ford cars in the short term is likely to be relatively inelastic. This would especially be true if consumers thought that rises in the price of Ford cars would be followed later in the pricing season by rises in the prices of other makes of cars. In the longer term demand for Ford cars is likely to be more elastic than in the short term if the 10 per cent increase in price differential proves permanent. Despite branding, Ford is unlikely to be able to prevent consumers switching to other makes of cars whose prices have not gone up and therefore are now relatively better value.
(e) Mars Bar as a brand is very strong in the UK. It is widely recognised and is one of the market leaders in the chocolate bar market. Consumers have strong preferences in this market and will not buy many competing bars to Mars Bars on taste grounds. This would suggest that demand for Mars Bars is inelastic, with a 10 per cent price rise having little effect on the quantity purchased.

However, this is unlikely to be the case. If demand for Mars Bars was price inelastic at their present price, it would pay Mars to increase the price because the total revenue (the number sold times the price) would then increase. For instance, if a 10 per cent rise in price resulted in a fall in quantity demanded of 6 per cent, spending on Mars Bars would increase by approximately 4 per cent. Moreover, Mars would save on costs because it could then produce 6 per cent fewer Mars Bars, further increasing profits for the company.

The fact that Mars Corporation (a US company) is not increasing its prices today suggests that it believes that demand is elastic. A 10 per cent rise in price would lead to a fall of more than 10 per cent in quantity demanded as consumers switched to other now cheaper brands.
(f) As with Mars Bars, GQ magazine might at first seem to have an inelastic demand. It has a strong brand image and is widely read by young males. However, again as with Mars Bars, it could be argued that it would be in the interests of GQ to increase prices today if demand was indeed in elastic. It could raise revenue whilst saving on costs because of lower print runs. The argument is more complicated than with Mars Bars because GQ also generates income from advertising. The lower the circulation, the lower the amount that the magazine can charge per advert and the less attractive the magazine as an advertising medium. Even so, it is unlikely that a few per cent reduction in circulation would substantially lower advertising rates or the number of adverts being placed. So, as with Mars Bars, the owners of GQ probably believe that demand is elastic.

Question 4

(a) Demand is elastic on a straight line demand curve at all points on the upper half of the line. Therefore:
(i) demand is elastic between £4.50 and £9.00;
(ii) demand is inelastic between £0 and £4.50.
(b) (i) £0; **(ii)** £9; **(iii)** £4.50.

Data question

1. In the data, it mentions price rises for Hovis bread of 10 per cent, a pint of milk of 10 per cent and Italian pasta of 20 per cent. The formula for price elasticity of demand is

$$\frac{\text{\% change in quantity demanded}}{\text{\% change in price.}}$$

The effect on demand can therefore be calculated by multiplying the percentage change in price by the price elasticity of demand. For individual products, these are therefore likely to be:

- for Hovis bread, with a price rise of 10 per cent a price elasticity of demand of -0.4, a fall in quantity demanded of 4 per cent;
- for pints of milk, with a price rise of 10 per cent and a price elasticity of demand of - 0.36, a fall in quantity demanded of 3.6 per cent.
- for Italian pasta, with a price rise of 20 per cent and a price

elasticity of demand of -0.94, a fall in quantity demanded of 9.4 per cent.

2. Price elasticity of demand measures the responsiveness of changes in quantity demanded to changes in price. When demand is price inelastic, it means that a percentage change in price will result in a smaller percentage change in quantity demanded. For example, if bread has a price elasticity of demand of -0.40, shown in Table 5 of the students' book, then a 10 per cent rise in price of bread will result in a lower percentage fall in quantity demanded of bread: in this case of 4 per cent.

Milk and bread have such low price elasticities of demand because they have few good substitutes. They form part of the staple diet of households in the UK. Large changes in price, therefore, are unlikely to see much change in the decision to purchase these items.

Some economists would also argue that bread and milk are necessities rather than luxuries. Necessities, they argue, have a low price elasticity of demand. However, in this case, bread and milk are arguably necessities because they have few good substitutes. If they had more good substitutes, their price elasticity of demand would be likely to be higher.

Some economists would also argue that bread and milk have low price elasticities of demand because households spend a relatively small proportion of their total income on these items. However, this is unlikely to be a good explanation given the intense price competition, particularly with bread, before the rises in price in 2007. Households would presumably have been indifferent to price cuts in bread when these were occurring. Hence, it is difficult to see why supermarkets would have bothered to lower bread prices.

3. The estimated average price elasticity of demand for cereal and cereal products other than bread is -0.94 according to calculations made by Defra economists from the 2000 National Food survey. There are a number of reasons why the price elasticity of demand for pasta is almost certainly different from this.

One is that the -0.94 is an average for all non-bread cereal products. Pasta is only one of many such products. Whether the price elasticity of demand for pasta is higher or lower than 0.94 is likely to depend on the degree to which other products have good substitutes. If pasta has fewer good substitutes than other products in the group, then the demand for pasta is likely to be more inelastic. Support for this would come from the fact that pasta is a fairly narrowly defined product compared to 'all cereal and cereal products other than bread'. In general, the more narrowly defined the product range, the fewer the substitutes it will have and therefore the lower will be its price elasticity of demand.

Another reason why the price elasticity of demand for pasta is unlikely to be exactly 0.94 is that the calculation is based on survey evidence from the National Food Survey. However, statistically reliable is the National Food Survey, it is unlikely to be 100 per cent accurate. Small variations in accuracy are likely to affect the calculation for the price elasticity of demand for pasta.

Another issue is that different formulas can be used to calculate price elasticity of demand. Exactly which formula is used will produce a different number for the price elasticity of demand of pasta.

10 Elasticities

Question 1

The formula for income elasticity of demand is:

$$\frac{\Delta Q}{Q} \times \frac{Y}{\Delta Y} \quad \text{or} \quad \frac{\Delta Q}{Q} \div \frac{\Delta Y}{Y}$$

Hence:
(a) 20/100 x 10/4 = +0.5
(b) 5/15 x 6/1 = +2
(c) -10/50 x 25/10 = -0.5
(d) 3/12 x 100/25 = +1
(e) 50/200 x 10/1 = +2.5
(f) 5/25 x 20/-2 = -2

Question 2

(a) Gas and electricity are substitutes for each other. Therefore if the price of electricity rises, there is likely to be an increase in the demand for gas, all other things being equal. Hence the cross elasticity of gas for electricity is likely to be positive.
(b) Tennis shorts and tennis rackets are complements. Hence if the price of tennis rackets increases, fewer people are likely to play tennis and hence fewer people will buy tennis shorts. The cross elasticity of demand of tennis shorts for tennis rackets is therefore likely to be negative.
(c) Luxury cars and petrol are complements. A substantial increase in the price of petrol, as occurred for instance in 1974, is likely to lead to a fall in demand for luxury cars as consumers buy more fuel-efficient vehicles. Therefore the cross elasticity of demand of luxury cars for petrol is negative.
(d) The demand for paper and the demand for socks are largely unconnected. A rise in the price of socks is unlikely to have any impact on the demand for paper. Hence the cross elasticity of demand for paper for socks is likely to be zero.
(e) It is not immediately obvious what is the cross elasticity of demand of compact disks (CDs) for MP3 downloads. On the one hand, it could be argued that the demand for CDs and MP3 downloads is linked to ownership of players. A buyer who wants something to play in the car or on their hi fi system at home may always buy CDs for that purpose. On the other hand, they may always buy MP3 downloads to play whilst on the move, walking or on a train or bus. The relative price of one format to the other will not persuade consumers to switch from one to the other. In this case, the cross elasticity of demand would be around zero.

Alternatively, it could be argued that MP3 downloads are a substitute for a CD. If the price of MP3 downloads fell by, say 20 per cent, but the price of CDs were maintained, then some consumers may switch from buying CDs to MP3 downloads. Alternatively, if the current price differential between CDs and MP3 downloads were narrowed by a fall in the price of CDs, then it could be that consumers would buy more CDs and fewer MP3 downloads. In this case, the cross elasticity of demand would be positive.
(f) Sainsbury's own brand baked beans are substitutes for Tesco's own brand baked beans. So it might seem reasonable to argue that their cross elasticity is positive; a rise in price in Tesco beans will lead to consumers switching to Sainsbury's beans. However, the cross elasticity is likely to be very low because few people shop around on a single item between supermarkets. A 10 per cent rise in Tesco beans is unlikely to lead to a rush of shoppers doing their weekly shop at Tesco and then going to Sainsbury's to pick up their beans.
(g) Virgin Cola and Coca Cola are substitutes. Where they are sold together in the same store, a rise in price of Coca Cola could have a significant impact on sales of Virgin Cola as consumers switch brands on price. Experience of the launch of Sainsbury's Classic Cola and Virgin Cola showed that cheaper brands can secure some share of the market despite the very heavy branding of Coca Cola. However, soft drinks are also sold in small retail outlets and in the pub and restaurant trade. Often, only one or possibly two brands will be stocked, usually Coca Cola and/or Pepsi Cola. A change in price of Coca Cola will then have no impact on demand for Virgin Cola because consumers are not being given the opportunity to buy Virgin Cola at the point of sale. So the overall cross elasticity of demand is positive, but how positive depends upon what proportion of sales of cola drinks are being made by outlets which stock both Coca Cola and Virgin Cola.

Question 3

The formula for price elasticity of supply is:

$$\frac{\Delta Q}{Q} \times \frac{P}{\Delta P}$$

Hence:
(a) 3/0 x 4/2 = infinity;
(b) 3/3 x 6/2 = 3;
(c) 3/6 x 8/2 = 2;
(d) 3/7.5 x 9/2 = 18/10 or 1.8;
(e) 3/4.5 x 7/2 = 21/3 or 2.33.

Question 4

(a) All the foods in Table 3 in the student's book are price inelastic in demand and one, prepared fish, even has an elasticity of 0. The lowest price elasticity foods tend to be those with few good substitutes. For instance, liquid milk, fresh potatoes and bread could be considered as staples or necessities of the British household diet, which people are prepared to carry on buying even if the price rises. Some of the goods with higher elasticity demand, in contrast, have good substitutes and could be seen as luxuries in the British diet. A rise in the price of frozen peas, for instance, could lead to consumers shifting to other types of frozen vegetable. Price increases in 'other fruit and fruit products' could lead to consumers buying different types of fruit such as bananas.

Another possible explanation of higher price elasticities is that they are relatively expensive items in the household budget. Carcass meat, fresh fish, other cereal and cereal products, frozen convenience cereal foods, meat products and processed fruit and fruit products are expensive per kilo bought. Because they might therefore form a larger part of the household budget than, say, potatoes or milk, they are more price sensitive than these cheaper staples.
(b) (i) Household expenditure is equal to the number of items bought (quantity) times the average price of each item. Price rises of goods which have a very low price elasticity will lead to little change in the quantity demanded of these goods. Therefore expenditure on them will rise significantly when there is a rise in their price, pushing up total household expenditure. The four foods which have the lowest price elasticity of demand are prepared fish (0.00), fresh potatoes

(-0.12), liquid wholemilk and skimmed milk (-0.17) and processed and shell fish (-0.17).

(ii) Household expenditure on an item will rise so long as demand is price inelastic. However, the closer price elasticity comes to the value of -1.0, the less expenditure will rise when price rises. The four foods which have the highest price elasticity of demand are other cereal and cereal products (-0.94), other fruit and fruit products (-0.81), fresh fish (-0.8) and sugar and preserves (-0.79). So when prices rise for these products, there will be the least increase in household expenditure of all the foods shown in the table.

Data question

Note: in the first impression of the 5th edition there was a misprint in Table 8. This has been corrected in reprints. Spending on men's outer garments for the tenth decile should be £10.70, not £1.70.

1. (a) Table 8 of the student's book shows how expenditure on clothing and footwear and on transport varies with income. Data for three decile groups are given, the lowest decile by income, the fifth decile and the highest decile by income for 2005-06. The Table also shows how total household expenditure changes with income.

Total household expenditure increases 6.5 times between the lowest and highest decile from £153.60 per week to £989.70 per week. In contrast, expenditure on clothing and footwear increases 6.5 times, from £8.00 to £52.00 per week. Expenditure on transport increases even more, from £13.20 to £161.90 per week, a 12 fold increase. So expenditure on both clothing and footwear and transport increases by more than the average as income increases; and expenditure on transport increases more than clothing and footwear.

(b) Table 7 of the student's book shows how expenditure on clothing and footwear and transport has increased over time, between 1980 and 2005-06. Expenditure on clothing and footwear has increased by less than the average increase in total household spending, falling from 8.1 per cent of total expenditure in 1980 to 5.1 per cent in 2005-06. Expenditure on transport too has increased by less than the average, falling from 14.6 per cent of total household expenditure in 1980 to 13.9 per cent in 2005-06.

2. Clothing and footwear is likely to have a lower, not a higher, income elasticity of demand than transport. Income elasticity is defined as the responsiveness of quantity demanded to a change in income and is measured by dividing the percentage change in quantity demanded by the percentage change in price.

Considering both changes in income levels at a point in time, shown in Figures 3 and 4 and in Table 8 in the student's book, and changes in spending over time shown in in Table 7, the increases in spending on clothing and footwear are less proportionately than increases in spending on transport as income rises. For example, in Figures 3 and 4, the lowest 5 deciles by income spent approximately 5 per cent or less of their total expenditure on clothing and footwear. The top five deciles spent a little more but the range for all deciles was only from 4.6 per cent of income to 5.5 per cent. In contrast, the bottom decile by income spent 8.5 per cent of their income on transport but this rose to over 16 per cent for the top decile. So the proportion spent on clothing and footwear rose far less as income rose than for transport. Similarly, in Table 7, real household disposable income increased 100 per cent between 1980 and 2005-06. Expenditure on clothing and footwear rose over that period but fell as a proportion of total expenditure. So too did expenditure on transport but the fall as a proportion of total spending was very small and much smaller than that for clothing and footwear.

3. The components of spending in Table 8 Level which are likely to have the highest income elasticities are those where spending increases proportionately the most as income increases. Table 1 here shows the percentage increase in spending for the tenth decile compared to the first decile in descending order for the two types of expenditure. So for clothing and footwear, 'dry cleaners, laundry and dyeing' and 'men's outer garments' are likely to have the highest income elasticity of demand. For transport, it is rail and tube fares and purchase of vehicles.

Table 1 Weekly household expenditure, £, on clothing and footwear and transport by gross income decile group 2005-06; percentage change in spending between bottom and top decile groups

	First decile £	Tenth decile £	% change, first decile to tenth decile
Dry cleaners, laundry and dyeing	0.10	1.10	1,000
Men's outer garments	1.10	10.70	872.7
Men's under garments	0.10	0.80	700.0
Women's outer garments	3.20	21.50	571.9
Accessories	0.30	20	566.7
Girls' outer garments (5-15)	0.30	1.60	433.3
Footwear	1.70	90	429.4
Childrens' under garments (under 16)	0.10	0.50	400.0
Women's under garments	0.50	2.20	340.0
Boys' outer garments (5-15)	0.40	1.30	225.0
Infants' outer garments (under 5)	0.30	1.0	233.3
Haberdashery and clothing hire	0.0	0.60	na
Total clothing and footwear	8.0	52.0	550.0
Rail and tube fares	0.40	8.20	1,950.0
Purchase of vehicles	4.10	71.80	1,651.2
Other motoring costs	1.90	23.80	1,152.6
Petrol, diesel and other motor oils	3.70	38.20	932.4
Other travel and transport	1.70	14.80	770.6
Combined fares	0.50	3.60	620.0
Bus and coach fares	0.90	1.70	88.9
Total transport	13.20	161.90	1,126.5
Total household expenditure on all goods and services	153.60	989.70	544.3

4. Table 8 of the student's book would suggest that bus and coach travel have a very low income elasticity of demand. An exact value for income elasticity of demand cannot be calculated from the table because the income figures given are ranges rather than individual numbers. However, if we assumed that average total household income of the bottom decile were £130 and for the top decile was £1 500, income elasticity of demand for bus and coach travel would be the percentage change in quantity demanded for travel (which we assume can be measured by the percentage change in expenditure), which is 89% (100% x [£1.70 - £0.90)] ÷ £0.90), divided by the percentage change in income, which is 1 054% (100% x [£1500 - £130]÷ £130). This estimated value for income elasticity of demand is therefore 0.084.

An alternative calculation would be to compare income elasticity between the first decile and fifth decile by income, and the fifth decile and the top decile. Assuming the same income figures as above, and an average income figure of £400 for the fifth decile, the percentage change in quantity demanded is 55.6 per cent for the first to fifth decile and 21.4 per cent for the fifth decline to tenth decile. The percentage change in incomes are 208 per cent and 275 per cent respectively. So the income elasticities of demand for the first to fifth decile is 0.27 and for the fifth to tenth decile is 0.078.

Whichever calculation is used, the income elasticity of demand for bus and coach fares is almost zero. This means that as income rises, there is hardly any increase in demand for bus and coach journeys. However, the evidence in Table 8 does not show that income elasticity of demand for bus and coach fares is negative. Bus and coach journey's are not an inferior good according to this evidence. Bus and coach transport has a future in the UK but the evidence would suggest that demand for bus and coach transport is unlikely to increase as incomes rise over time, all other things being equal.

In practice, all other things will not be equal. In recent years demand for bus and coach transport has risen, arguably due to investment by bus and coach companies in more and better vehicles and more services being offered. On the other hand, average fares have been rising in comparison with the cost of motoring which would depress demand. The income of consumers is therefore only one of many factors which will determine the success of the bus and coach industry in the future.

11 Normal, inferior and Giffen goods

Question 1

As income increases, households increase their consumption of normal goods, but reduce their consumption of inferior goods. Therefore chicken, bananas, and pickles and sauces were normal goods, whilst sugar and bread were inferior goods. Butter was an inferior good between 1985 and 1995, but it is difficult to say from the evidence for 1995-2005/6 whether it was normal or inferior over this period.

Question 2

Normal goods are goods where a rise in price leads to a fall in quantity demanded because of the substitution effect and the income effect. Hence jeans and compact discs are both normal goods according to the data.

Inferior goods are goods where a rise in price leads to a rise in quantity demanded because of the income effect and a fall because of the substitution effect. However, the substitution effect is greater than the income effect and so a rise in price leads to an overall fall in quantity demanded. Hence bacon and baked beans are inferior goods in the data.

A Giffen good is one where a rise in price leads to a rise in quantity demanded because of the income effect and a fall because of the substitution effect. However, the income effect is so great that it outweighs the substitution effect and so a rise in price leads to an overall increase in quantity demanded. Hence bus rides are Giffen goods in the data.

Question 3

The data might suggest that increased share prices lead to higher demand for shares and vice versa. For example, both in October 1987 and early 2000, share price falls were associated with falls in the number of shares being bought. The bursting of the dotcom bubble in 2000 which led to a sharp fall in share prices saw transactions fall from 2.6 million in March 2000 to 1.1 million in December 2002.

It can be argued that this supports the theory that for some goods, the demand curve for shares is upward sloping. The higher the price of shares, the greater will be the quantity demanded. However, a more plausible explanation is to suggest that the demand curve for shares shifted to the left and right when there is a change in expectations. When share prices are high and there is a 'bull' market, investors tend to believe that share prices will rise further. This causes them to demand more shares, shifting the demand curve for shares to the right. When share prices are falling in a 'bear' market, investors expect shares to fall in price in the future. This reduces demand for shares, shifting the demand curve to the left.

Data question

1. The number of trips taken by British residents has been increasing over time. As Figure 4 in the student's book shows, the number of trips taken in the UK has increased from 105 million in 1989 to 145 million in 2006. The number of overseas trips has increased from 25 to 60 million. It should be noted that these figures include business trips as well as holidays.

The main holiday destination abroad for British tourists, as Figure 5 in the student's book shows, is Spain with 27.3 per cent of the market in 2005. The second most important destination was France, with 16.6 per cent of the market in 2005. The other most popular destinations are Greece, Turkey, Italy, Portugal, the Irish Republic and the USA. Of these, Turkey and the USA have seen considerable increases in their share of the market since 1971, although all destinations have seen an increase in numbers given the large increase in the numbers of tourists going abroad.

Table 5 in the student's book shows the number of visits to the most popular tourist attractions in the UK. Museums and galleries saw a significant rise in the number of admissions between 1981 and 2006, although the Natural History Museum went against this trend. Both theme parks, Blackpool Pleasure Beach and the Pleasure Beach at Great Yarmouth, have seen visitor numbers fall. Wildlife parks and zoos have seen their admissions remain broadly stable. Of the three historic houses and monuments given, Stonehenge has seen visitor numbers increase by 80 per cent and Edinburgh Castle by 50 per cent whilst the Tower of London has seen broadly static visitor numbers.

In terms of social class, Table 6 in the student's book shows that the higher the social class, the more likely it is that a holiday will be taken each year and that this holiday will be abroad. For social groups D and E, 57 per cent took no holiday, whilst only 20 per cent went on holiday abroad. For social groups A and B, the comparable figures were 18 per cent and 59 per cent.

Within the UK, the most popular holiday destinations in 2005 were Devon and Cornwall, the North West and Scotland.

2. A normal good is one where as income increases so too does the the demand for the good. Between 1989 and 2006, real household disposable income per head increased by nearly 50 per cent. Therefore, if tourism is a normal good, the number of holidays taken should have increased. Both Figures 4 and 5 show that this has been the case.

3. Figure 4 shows that holidays taken abroad are a normal good since numbers have increased as income has increased. All the foreign tourist destinations given in Figure 5 in the student's book have seen the numbers of British tourists increase between 1971/1981 and 2005 even though some have seen a substantial fall in their market share. However, trips taken in Great Britain by UK residents in Figure 4 declined between 2001 and 2004 despite rising disposable income per head. Trips taken in the UK therefore could be argued to have been an inferior good over this period. This conclusion should be treated with some caution. Figure 4 includes business trips as well as holidays and so it might have been UK business trips which have been in decline. Equally, there may have been other factors at work in causing the decline such as large rises in costs of trips taken in the UK or large falls in the cost of holidays taken abroad.

Table 5 would suggest that some tourist attractions might be inferior goods. In particular, the two theme parks in Blackpool and Yarmouth have seen declining visitor numbers at a time of rising incomes.

4. (a) One problem facing Great Yarmouth is the weather. British holiday makers have been increasingly going abroad for their holidays to secure hotter and more reliable weather. Another problem is location. Great Yarmouth is far away from large centres of population and has to rely on holiday makers who are taking longer holidays in the area. A third problem is the quality of other attractions in the local area. Foreign tourism in the UK, for instance, is centred on London because of the large number of sites to be seen. UK tourists going to Florida are attracted both by the sun and by attractions such as Disneyworld. Great Yarmouth does not have a sufficiently large number of high quality tourist attractions to make it a growing centre for holiday activities.

(b) Great Yarmouth faces the challenge of attracting more visitors as real income grows over the next ten to twenty years to reverse the decline it has seen. It can do little about the weather or its location. However, it can attempt to maximise its strengths. First, it needs to ensure that existing holiday accommodation and attractions are competitive with other UK holiday destinations. Price and quality are the key elements here. Second, it needs to develop new attractions in Great Yarmouth and the surrounding area. Great Yarmouth needs to become a centre for tourists who wish both to come to the town but also to use it as a base for touring the surrounding countryside. Third, the town needs to fight for better transport links, both road and rail. Better transport links will encourage more day trippers.

12 Indirect taxes and subsidies

Question 1

(a) 101.1p.
An increase in the price of petrol from 28.6p to 32.3p before tax would have no effect on excise duty. The price including excise duty would go up 3.7p from 82.3p to 86.0p (32.3p + 53.7p). With VAT at 17.5 per cent, the cost of VAT would now be 15.1p rounded to the nearest 0.1p (86.0p x 17.5%). The cost at the petrol pump would then be 101.1p (86.0p + 15.1p).
(b) 102.0p.
If the government increased excise duty from 53.7p to 58.2p, the cost after excise duty but before VAT would increase to 86.8p (28.6p + 58.2p). With VAT at 17.5 per cent, the cost of VAT would be 15.2p (86.8 x 17.5%) rounded to the nearest 0.1p. The cost at the petrol pump would now be 102.0p (86.8p + 15.2p).
(c) 94.7p.
If VAT were reduced to 15 per cent, the cost at the petrol pump would fall to 94.7p (82.3p + [82.3 x 15%]) rounded to the nearest 0.1p.
(d) 26.6p.
The petrol cost before tax is 28.6p per litre. If the government subsidised the cost before tax by 2p, the price would fall to 26.6p per litre.

Question 2

(a)

Figure 1

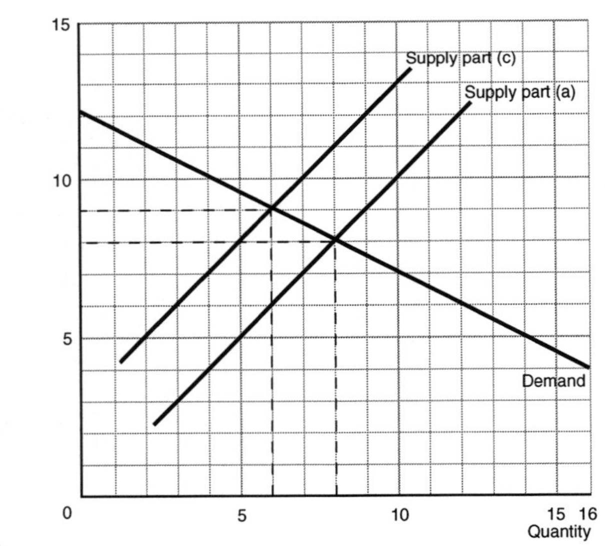

(b) The equilibrium quantity demanded and supplied is 8 units where demand equals supply.
(c) See Figure 1.
(d) 6 units.
(e) £9.
(f)(i) £1.
The incidence of tax per unit on the consumer is the difference between the original equilibrium price of £8 and the new equilibrium price of £9 following the introduction of the tax. So it is £1.
(ii) £2.
The incidence of tax per unit on the producer is the difference between the tax per unit of £3 and the incidence of tax on the consumer, shown above to be £1. So it is £2.
(g)(i) £3.
This is simply the information already given in the question.
(ii) £18.
Total government revenue is the the tax per unit, £3, times the quantity sold when the tax is applied, 6 units. So the total government revenue is £18.
(h) £28.
Producers before the tax was imposed received the equilibrium price, £8, times the equilibrium quantity sold, 8 units, making total revenue of £64. After the tax is imposed, producers only receive £6 per unit (which can either be read off the graph or is the new equilibrium price of £9 minus the tax of £3), and sell only 6 units. So total revenue is £36. So revenue will change by £64 - £36 or £28.

Question 3

(a) If hard cheese were to become subject to VAT at 17.5 per cent, the supply price would rise by 17.5 per cent at any given level of output. In Figure 2, this is shown by a shift of the supply curve to the left from S_1 to S_2. At a quantity supplied of OA, the supply price would rise from OF to OG. Alternatively, at a price of OF, supply would fall from OA to OB following the imposition of VAT.

Figure 2

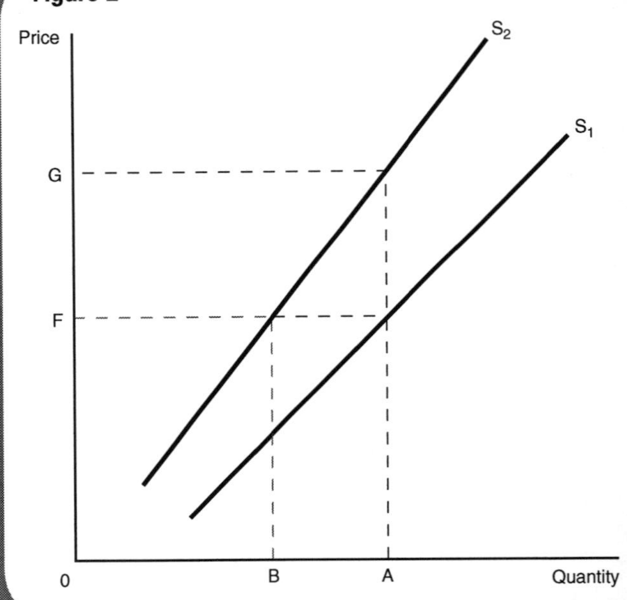

(b) The price of hard cheese is most unlikely to rise by 17.5 per cent following the imposition of VAT. This is because part of the tax increase will be absorbed by producers. In Figure 11.3, the original equilibrium price is OA. With the imposition of VAT, the supply curve for cheese shifts from S_1 to S_2 leading to a new equilibrium price of OB. However, OB is less than OA plus 17.5 per cent. The tax of 17.5 per cent is the distance BC. So the increase in price of AB paid by consumers is less than 17.5 per cent. The part of the tax not paid by consumers, AC, is absorbed by producers who now receive a lower price for their product.
(c) The imposition of VAT on hard cheese might lead consumers to buy less hard cheese and turn to healthier products. This could include orange juice, and so the demand

Figure 3

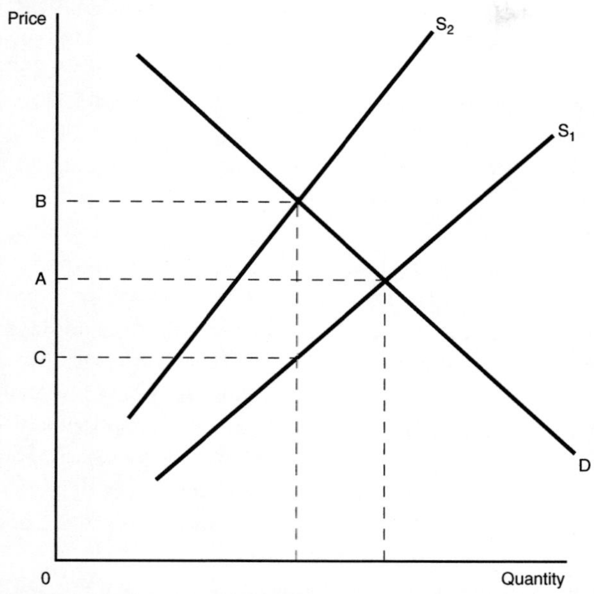

for orange juice could increase. If this were to happen, hard cheese and orange juice would be substitutes.

(d) If the demand for fatty foods were price elastic, it would mean that a 17.5 per cent imposition of VAT would lead to a more than 17.5 per cent drop in demand. The higher the elasticity, the larger the drop in demand. For example, if fatty foods had an elasticity of 1.1, a 17.5 per cent tax would lead to a fall in demand of 19.25 per cent. If elasticity were 2.0, the imposition of a 17.5 per cent tax would lead to a 35 per cent drop in demand.

This can be shown on a demand and supply diagram. In Figure 4 (a), the 17.5 per cent rise in price of EF, resulting from the shift in the supply curve from S_1 to S_2, leads to a much larger percentage fall in quantity demanded from OA to OB. This can be contrasted with Figure 4 (b) when demand is inelastic. The fall in demand resulting from the imposition of tax is much less than in Figure 4 (a).

Question 4

(a) and **(b)** One of the characteristics of a 'good' indirect tax designed to raise revenue for the government is that it does not discourage consumption of the product. Not only does this not alter the patterns of consumer preferences, but it also raises the maximum amount of revenue for the government for every pound spent on a commodity. In terms of price elasticity of demand, this means that indirect taxes should be levied on goods which have as low an elasticity as possible. Imposition of VAT on fuel and light and food (with price elasticities of 0.47 and 0.52 respectively) would raise significantly more tax per pound spent than the imposition of VAT on services (with a price elasticity of 1.02).

Data question

1. There is a number of reasons why the government might want to raise the level of Vehicle Excise Duty on the purchase of SUVs. One relates to the environment. SUV's tend to have very poor fuel consumption. Therefore they contribute more per mile both to global warming through the emission of greenhouse gases and to atmospheric pollution in cities such as London.

However, it could also be argued that the government might want to increase tax revenues by imposed taxes on SUVs. With a highly price inelastic demand for these vehicles, tax revenues are likely to be high.

2. The demand for SUVs is likely to be less elastic than for ordinary cars. This is because SUVs are a niche market within the larger car market and buyers of SUVs are less price sensitive than the ordinary motorist. They have already shown this by buying an above average cost vehicle and being prepared to pay the above average cost of running it. So the imposition of a purchase tax of, say, £2 000 or £5 000 on SUVs is unlikely to have that much impact on quantity demanded.

In Figure 5, demand for SUVs is shown to be inelastic. The imposition of a flat tax of CB has little effect on demand, pushing it down from OE to OF. Note that because demand is inelastic, manufacturers will be able to pass on most of the tax to motorists. Prices increase from OA to OB leaving manufacturers to pay just CA of the tax per vehicle.

The more elastic the demand curve for SUVs, the greater will be the fall in quantity demanded following the imposition of a tax.

3. A 'significant reduction' in purchases could be interpreted in a number of ways, but the economic analysis remains the same

Figure 4

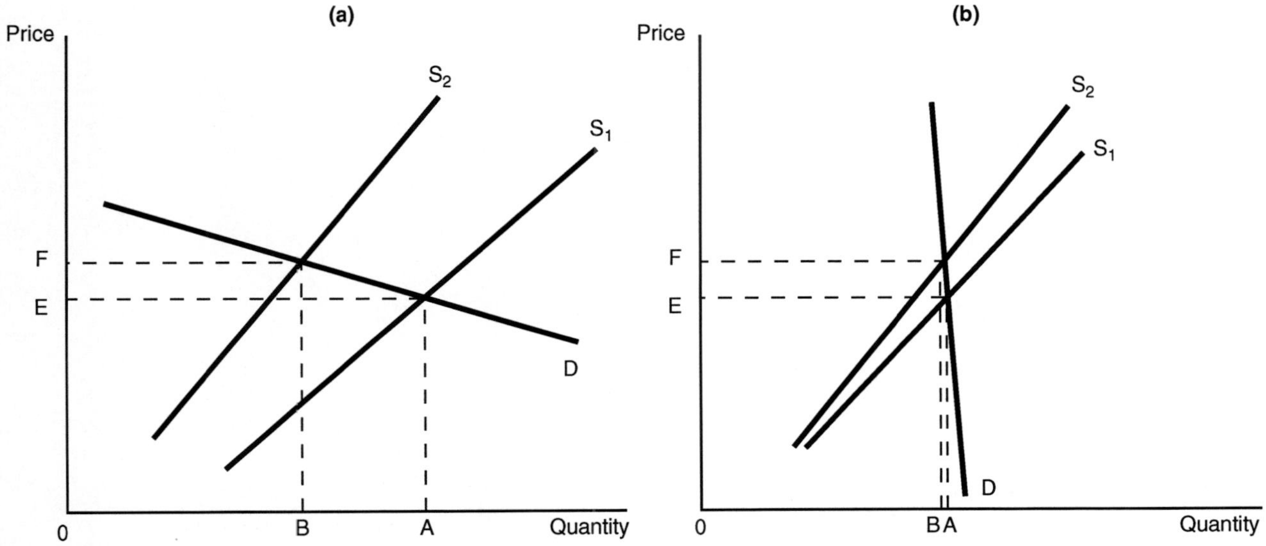

Figure 5

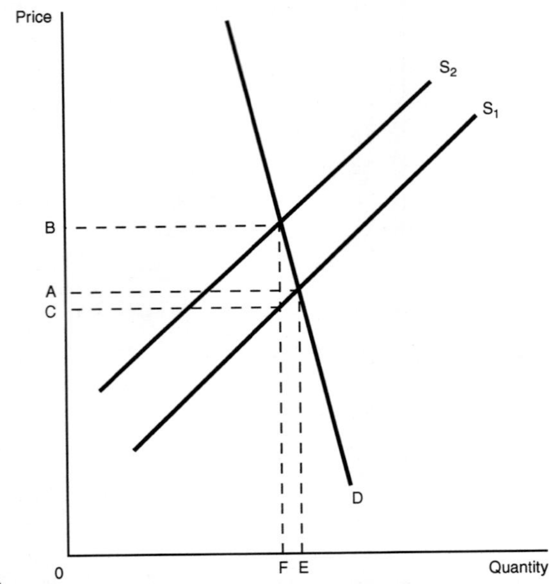

whether it is, say, a 20 per cent reduction or a 50 per cent reduction.

Assume that a significant reduction is 25 per cent. Price elasticity of demand measures the responsiveness of changes in quantity demanded to changes in price and is calculated by dividing the percentage change in quantity demanded by the percentage change in price. If the price elasticity of demand for SUVs is 0.8, then the price of new SUVs would have to rise by 31.25 per cent to cut demand by 25 per cent. Table 3 in the student's book shows the price ranges of selected SUVs in 2007. Assume that the average new SUV costs £20 000. Then a 31.25 per cent tax would mean imposed a tax of £6 250 per vehicle. If the government wanted to achieve a 50 per cent fall in demand, the tax would have to be £12 500 per vehicle. At the bottom end of the SUV market, this would be more than the 2005 price of these vehicles.

Since Vehicle Excise Duty is a specific tax, if it were raised by the same amount on all SUVs, it would then favour more expensive SUVs because it would represent a lower proportion of the existing price. So demand for Land Rover Discovery vehicles would be likely to be less affected than demand for Suzuki Grand Vitaras. However, it could be that more expensive SUVs have poorer fuel consumption and cause more pollution than cheaper SUVs. A tax would then have the perverse incentive of driving down sales of less damaging vehicles whilst leaving more sales of more expensive vehicles relatively less affected.

The lower the price elasticity of demand, the greater will need to be the increase in tax to cause the same fall in demand. If price elasticity of demand were 0.4 and average price were £20 000, the tax would need to be £12 500 per vehicle to achieve a 25 per cent fall in demand. For a 50 per cent fall, it would need to be £25 000 per vehicle.

Such large increases in tax would be difficult to justify politically. 'Chelsea tractors' are therefore likely to continue to be popular with the motoring public.

13 Markets and resource allocation

Question 1

In a free market, there are many buyers and sellers. Firms, which produce goods and services, compete amongst themselves to sell their products. In the photograph, for instance, there are many brands of biscuits on sale produced by a number of different biscuit manufacturers. Each biscuit manufacturer has to produce a number of different types of biscuit because of different tastes amongst consumers. If one manufacturer only produced, say, ginger nut biscuits, then it would take only a small share of the market because other manufacturers would be producing many other types of biscuits preferred by consumers. Firms also have to minimise costs and prices. If two firms produce identical products, but one is much cheaper than the other, then consumers will tend to buy the cheaper product. Firms which produce the products consumers want to buy are rewarded by high sales and profits. Firms which fail to satisfy consumers are likely to sell low volumes and may make such low profits or losses as to force it out of the market.

It could be argued that firms can impose their wishes on consumers through marketing methods such as advertising. Whilst marketing can influence spending patterns, no amount of marketing will persuade customers to make repeat purchases of products they do not wish to buy. In the biscuit market, where consumers make frequent repeat purchases, their knowledge of the products they buy is high and therefore they are able to make rational decisions between competing products.

Question 2

(a) Prices act as signals in a free market. In the market for flat screen televisions, the fall in price of flat screen televisions signals to consumers that they are more affordable and hence more consumers will buy them. To producers, it is a signal that market supply has increased and that they have to take action. Either they have to cut their costs to remain profitable or they have to cut their production to a point where they move back into profitability.

(b) Prices act as incentives. When prices fall, consumers have an incentive to increase their purchases of flat screen televisions. Firms have to make choices. Lower prices could mean that they are unable to manufacture flat screen televisions at the price they are receiving. This provides them with an incentive to leave the market. Or, as is the case with Pioneer, low prices provide them with an incentive to cut costs, for example by closing factories or sacking staff. By cutting their most inefficient production facilities, Pioneer will be able to cut average costs of production and, it hopes, to return to profitability. This change in resource allocation has been a direct consequence of the fall in prices.

Question 3

Profits act as signals for resource allocation by firms. If profits are high, firms will invest to expand output in the hope of making even higher profits. In the case of Samsung, it is attempting to erode the market share of Apple's iPod since the iPod is enormously profitable. In one quarter alone, the first quarter of 2005, Apple quadrupled its profits compared to the year previously because of iPod sales. Profit is providing Samsung with the incentive to invest in and market new products. High Apple profits are providing Samsung with the signal that it too could earn high profits in the market. Profit also rations resources. If Samsung fails in its attempt to make significant inroads into the market, it will have to withdraw because profits will not be high enough or it might make losses. The article suggests that Samsung is unlikely to win its battle with the iPod because consumers are looking for a 'cool', easy to use product. Samsung's product is complex, even if it provides more functions than an iPod. Equally, it did not at the time of launch of Samsung's products, have that 'cool' image which has made the iPod such a success.

Data question

1. Figure 3 in the student's book shows that commodity prices fluctuated in a 20 per cent band range between January 2006 and September 2006. From October 2006, corn and palm oil prices then rose substantially. By the end of February 2007, corn prices were double what they had been at the start of January 2006, whilst palm oil prices were 40 per cent higher. Wheat remained with the 20 per cent band, ending up approximately 18 per cent higher at the end of the period. Crude oil in contrast ended the period at approximately the same level as at the start of the period.

2. The rationing function of prices allocated scarce resources between competing uses. So higher prices for crops such as yellow corn which can be used to produce ethanol are diverting resources from food crops such as soyabeans and industrial crops such as cotton to yellow corn production. For example, US farmers planned to plant 11 per cent less acres of soyabeans in 2007 and fewer acres for cotton and using the land to grow yellow corn.

The signalling function of prices is to give information to buyers and sellers about whether to purchase or produce goods. Higher prices for biofuels is raising their price relative to other commodities such as wheat, soyabeans and cotton.

The incentive function of prices acts to change how buyers and sellers behave in the market. Higher prices for crops used to make biofuels act as an incentive for farmers to grow more of these crops. Lower relative prices for non-biofuel crops acts as a disincentive for farmers to grow these crops. Equally, higher prices for biofuels acts as a disincentive for buyers of biofuels to make purchases. In the data, for example, it states that the Spanish engineering company Abengoa is threatening to halve production at its largest bioethanol plant because of the high price of its raw material, wheat.

3. The 2020 EU 10 per cent biofuels target was designed to be ecologically friendly. Substituting renewable crop resources for a non-renewable resource, crude oil, would help conserve a finite resource and ensure that future generations will have more to consume themselves.

Unfortunately, the move to biofuels has come at a time of rising world demand for food from emerging Third World countries such as China. With rapidly rising incomes, their populations are increasing their demand for food products. The result is that world food prices have been rising. Rising prices act to ration food. Rich western consumers will hardly alter their spending patterns but the poorest in the world on very limited budgets will be forced to eat less.

Some economists are predicting that the move into biofuels will cause starvation in some countries amongst very poor households. Other economists argue that the rise in food prices will be relatively short lived. The rise in the prices of food crops will lead to an increase in supply as farmers bring land into use which at the moment is fallow or in some alternative use. Higher prices will also encourage more intensive methods of cultivation, for example, making it profitable to use more fertilisers. However, unless supply is perfectly elastic in the long term, increased demand for food products will cause some permanent increase in price. This must put at risk the most vulnerable low income households in the world from the threat of starvation and malnutrition.

14 Production, specialisation and exchange

Question 1

(a) Specialisation involves economic units concentrating on particular activities. In the photograph, a garment manufacturing factory is shown. Materials such as cloth, thread and buttons are combined to produce a completed garment. Specialised machinery, such as sewing machines are used. Workers have particular skills which they employ to make garments.

Specialisation requires that goods and services be traded. For example, workers trade their time at work for food and other products. The garment manufacturer trades its finished products for money which it then uses to buy cloth, pay the wages of workers and give a profit to the owners of the firm.

(b) (i) Firms are likely to benefit in a number of ways from specialisation. Workers making garments become highly skilled by constantly carrying out the same activity. Repetition of tasks speeds up the rate of work and reduces errors. Workers are able to use specialised machinery such as sewing machines. The layout of the factory should help reduce the amount of time spent making each garment. Greater efficiency enables firms to compete in the marketplace. The more efficient a firm, the more likely it is to win orders and make a profit.

(ii) Specialisation can give rise to disadvantages for firms. Workers may become bored carrying out the same job, which can affect their motivation, attendance and concentration. If there is a breakdown in a piece of specialised machinery, such as a sewing machine, it can bring work to a halt for an employee. If, say, there is an electricity disruption, work in the whole factory could halt. A small group of workers may equally have the power to bring all production to a halt if they strike in pursuit of their demands. It may not be possible to transfer workers with specialised skills from one job to another if work needs to be done in a different area. Specialisation may therefore add to costs of production unless work is organised relatively efficiently and there are relatively few interruptions to the working system.

Data question

1. (a) Specialisation is a system of organisation where economic units, such as firms, are not self-sufficient but concentrate on producing certain goods and services and trading them with other economic units. For example, JVC is a firm which specialises in manufacturing electronic goods. It buys in factors of production and turns them into finished products which it then sells to other firms and consumers.

(b) The division of labour is specialisation by workers. For example, workers at JVC specialise in doing a particular job. Through specialisation, they are able to build up knowledge and expertise in performing a range of specific tasks. By co-operating with other workers, they are able to be far more productive as a group than if every worker attempted to perform every task.

(c) Exchange occurs when goods and services are swapped for other products or for money. At JVC, for example, workers exchange their time working for the company for money. They can then exchange that money for other goods and services such as food and heating. JVC exchanges the products it sells for money. It can then use that money in exchange for factors of production such as raw materials, labour and capital.

2. JVC can only exist because money acts as an efficient medium of exchange. Take a society where money did not exist but where everything was bartered. Any business like JVC would have to spend large amounts of its time in the process of bartering. It would have to find acceptable goods to exchange for the labour of its workers from the sale of its products. This is likely to be difficult if not impossible given the number of workers that JVC employs and their different needs. An efficient medium of exchange such as money is therefore needed. This allows JVC to buy factors of production using the same medium of exchange that it uses to sell its products.

Without an efficient medium of exchange, it is very difficult if not impossible, for large firms like JVC making complex products to exist. Using barter, for example, JVC is most unlikely to be able to assemble the complex mix of factors of production that it uses in its production processes.

15 Economic efficiency and market failure

Question 1

(a) Firm A is less technically efficient than its competitor. It produces the same amount of outputs but uses more inputs. When producing 60 units of output, it uses 2 more units of labour than its competitor.
(b) Firm B is less productively efficient than its competitor. This is because it employs the same number of factors of production as its competitor to produce the same output, but its total costs are higher.
(c) (i) Combinations (1) and (3) are technically efficient.
(ii) Combinations (1) and (2) are productively efficient.

Question 2

(a) Privatisation in the UK had the effect of increasing productive efficiency. This is because, following privatisation, costs fell. For instance, staff were cut in all industries whilst firms switched to cheaper suppliers where possible. This is shown in Figure 1. Before privatisation, the economy may have been working at the point A within the production possibility frontier. After privatisation, as costs of production fell, the economy was able to produce more goods and services. The economy therefore moved to the right of A to a point such as B. The point B is on the production possibility frontier, implying that all resources are now allocated efficiently. Consumption at B allows consumers both to consume more output from the privatised utilities and more output of all other goods and services.
(b) Privatisation also led to a change in allocative efficiency. Figure 2 shows point A, the point of production before privatisation. After privatisation, the electricity companies demanded less coal. There was therefore a movement along the curve from A to B, showing that at the new point of consumption, less coal was demanded and more of all other goods were produced. It could be argued that the economy was not on the production possibility frontier to start with because there was productive inefficiency. The economy might then have moved from a point within the boundary to the right of B, such as point C, to B following privatisation.

Figure 1

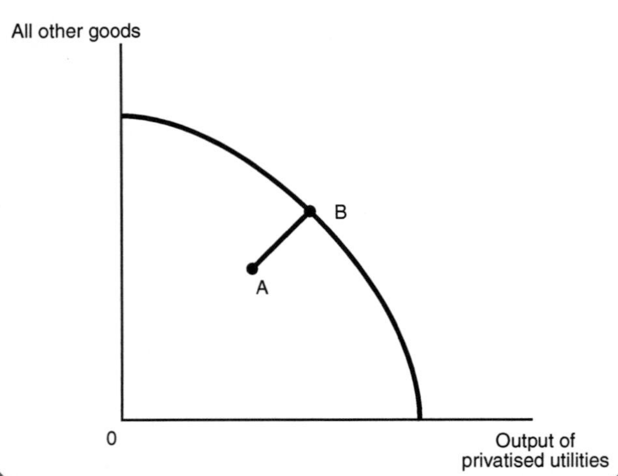

Figure 2

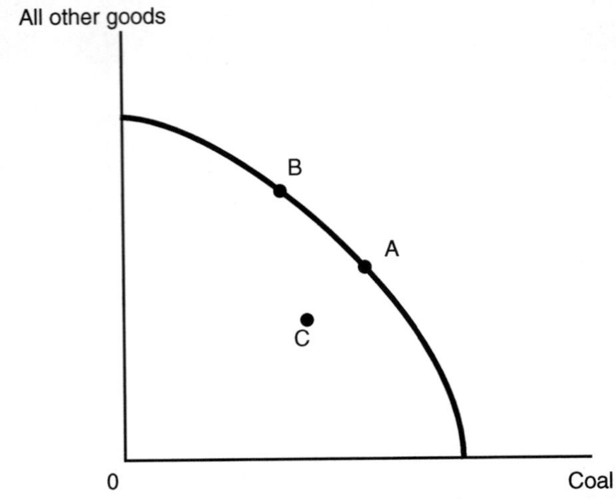

Question 3

(a) The merger is likely to give rise to financial economies of scale because the new building society would be able to 'borrow at a cheaper rate'. Increased size would reduce the risk that the Nationwide would default on its loans. Hence, lenders will be prepared to make loans at a lower rate of interest.

Technical economies will be gained because the same amount of business will be generated with the use of less capital. The Nationwide is proposing to close 180 branches as well as The Portman's mortgage and administration centre in Wolverhampton. Hence, a larger scale of production enables existing resources to be utilised more fully.

Marketing economies of scale will be gained. The new society will have 'lower marketing costs' such as 'saving on costs such as advertising'. The larger building society could spend the same amount on advertising. However, because it is a larger building society, every £1 spent on advertising is likely to result in a greater number of products sold or amount deposited or borrowed. Average marketing costs will therefore fall.
(b) Productive efficiency is likely to increase because of increased economies of scale as a result of the merger. In

Figure 3

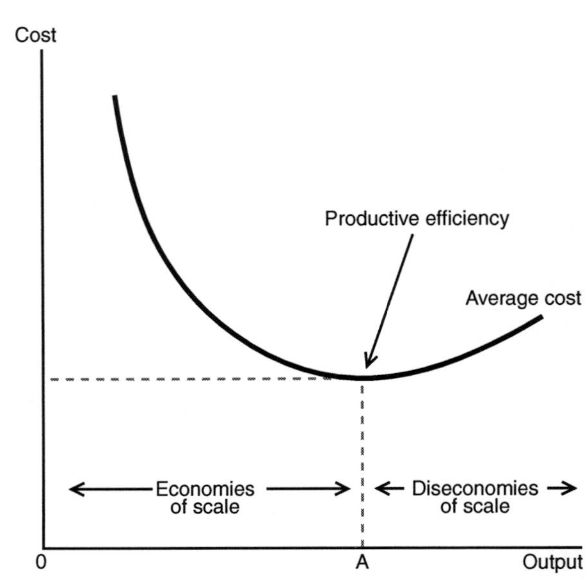

Figure 3, increased size is likely to result in a movement down the average cost curve towards the point where output is OA. The data suggests that the Nationwide, despite already being the UK's largest building society before the merger, was not operating at the lowest point of its average cost curve. If it had been, then there could be no economies of scale to be gained by merging with The Portman. There is no indication from the data that even after the merger the Nationwide was operating at the lowest point of its average cost curve. Further takeovers or mergers could therefore increase the building society's productive efficiency even further.

Data question

1.

Tesco Competition in the market place usually leads to efficiency. It drives down costs because higher priced producers lose sales to lower priced producers. This leads to productive efficiency. It also leads to allocative efficiency because the most successful firms are the ones which provide the goods and services that consumers wish to buy. With the example of Tesco, both Harry Tuffins and The Association of Convenience Stores believe that the actions of the supermarket giant amount to unfair competition. Tesco in Ludlow was clearly attempting to reduce the impact of the opening of a new Harry Tuffins store in the town. Harry Tuffins would provide greater competition for Tesco and take customers away from its local store. The fear would be that Harry Tuffins would eventually close down, reducing competition in Ludlow. However, it could be argued that Tesco's actions increased efficiency for consumers in Ludlow. If Tesco responded to Harry Tuffins' arrival by permanently lowering average prices in its store, and Harry Tuffins survived in the long term, then consumers would benefit.

Yixing In Yixing, there is economic inefficiency. Factories which are creating pollution are not paying to clean up the externalities they have created. Their costs of production are lower but this has only occurred because local residents have paid part of the price through damage to their health and their environment.

Coalmining communities Efficiency in former coalmining communities is impaired because of factor immobility. Workers have not left these communities in sufficient numbers to eliminate unemployment. Equally, capital has not moved into these communities to create the workplaces which would create jobs. With factor immobility, there is a potential loss of production in the economy. Output is lower than would otherwise be the case. Hence there is allocative inefficiency. Also, high unemployment has led to a wide range of heightened inequalities. In former coalmining communities, average incomes and educational attainment are lower whilst illness is higher.

Older workers Retirement and old age is a serious issue today. The data suggests that some workers are failing to save for their retirement. This could be the result of market failure because of information failures. Individuals often find it difficult to make correct decisions about how to allocate their resources between the present and the future. The present, with pressure to spend on everything from houses to alcohol, is relatively well known. Life in 20 or 30 years times is less certain. So there is an inbuilt tendency for individuals to overspend today at the expense of income in retirement.

There is another aspect to market failure in this situation. Low incomes in retirement lead to poverty and inequality.

Burkina Faso In Burkina Faso, income per head in 2007 was just $516. The poverty that results leads in itself to market failure. Markets have led to unacceptable levels of poverty.

16 Public and merit goods

Question 1

A public good is one that possesses two characteristics. First, consumption of the good by one individual does not reduce the amount available for consumption by another individual. Second, once produced, no individual can be excluded from benefiting. In the case of lamp posts, the lighting given to one person does not diminish in any way the ability to give lighting to other people. Furthermore, once provided, it is impossible to exclude people in the area from benefiting, whether or not they have contributed to the upkeep of the lighting.

Question 2

A merit good is one which would be underprovided if left to the free market system. Education is extremely expensive. The cost of a state primary school place for a year, for instance, averages £1 500. Independent secondary day school fees usually start at around £7 000 per year. Most parents cannot afford private schooling for their children and many could not afford cheaper state education if they had to pay the full cost at the point of consumption. Therefore, many parents would choose not to send their children to school at all, or force them to leave early, or opt for cheaper schools if they were given a completely free choice. In the photograph in the student's book, child labour is a direct response by parents to the cost of sending children to school and to the wage benefits that can arise if the child is sent out to work.

Education gives rise to significant externalities. For instance, education is a prerequisite for working life in a modern economy like that of the UK. Those with the lowest educational qualifications form a disproportionate number of workers who have low productivity, earn low pay, may be exploited, as in the case of child labour, or are unemployed. In a Welfare State, these individuals have to be supported through the benefit system. They tend to contribute less tax than more educated individuals, increasing the tax burden on everyone. Low levels of education are also associated with many who commit crime and are in prison.

Question 3

Dental care is arguably a merit good. Without government intervention, too little dental care will be bought in a free market. Those who do not receive regular dental care are more likely to develop serious problems which might need attention under the NHS and therefore be a cost to the taxpayer. Dental ill health can also affect time off work. In the case of children who cannot be responsible for their own dental care, lack of dental care may lead to physical and psychological problems as adults.

For the taxpayer, the most expensive of the three options is the first. Direct free provision by the state for all is most likely to provide the highest take up on the part of citizens for dental care. However, it could be argued that there would be overprovision in that citizens will consume more than the social benefit created. For instance, if the NHS provided free treatment to straighten children's teeth, this could be seen as unnecessary treatment.

Subsidising treatment is a cheaper alternative for the taxpayer. However, by passing some of the cost onto consumers, it could be that too few will come forward for treatment. This would particularly be the case if parents of children, senior citizens or those on low incomes were forced to make a contribution to their dental care or that of their dependants. This could lead to a less than optimal consumption of dental care.

Compulsory insurance would cost the taxpayer nothing but the cost of enforcement of the policy. However, it is likely that there would be widespread evasion, particularly by those on low incomes. This would lead to a less than optimal consumption of dental care. Insurance is likely to widen inequalities compared to both the other options. High income earners under the present subsidy system tend to use private dentistry anyway. With insurance, those with low incomes would be forced to take out insurance, leaving them less income available to spend on all other goods. Insurance systems also tend to be highly expensive to administer, creating bureaucracy as patients or dentists claim back money from insurance companies, whilst patients are also paying small sums in insurance premiums.

Data question

1. A public good is one which possesses two characteristics. The first is non-rivalry: consumption by one economic agent does not reduce the amount available for consumption by another economic agent. Second is non-excludability: once provided, all economic agents benefit or suffer whether they wish or not. Television broadcasting can be an example of a public good if television signals are sent out unscrambled. It is non-rival in that my reception of the television signal does not reduce the ability of my neighbour to receive the signal. It is non-excludable in that once sent out, everyone can choose whether or not to tune in to the television broadcast. The broadcaster cannot choose who is to receive the signal and who is not.

2. (a) Cable television and Sky satellite television is different to public broadcasting in the UK. Their systems prevent anyone who has not subscribed to their service from receiving their broadcasts. So it is excludable. However, it is non-rival. Once broadcast, my consumption of the programme does not affect the ability of another viewer to see the programme. Sky satellite television is also not totally excludable. If I do not pay for a subscription, I can still see a big football match on Sky by going to a local pub or going round to a friend's house where there is a subscription to Sky. Therefore it could be argued that some broadcasting is a quasi-public good, which is defined as a good which is non-rival but does not possess perfectly the characteristics of being non-excludable.

(b) A merit good is a good which, for whatever reason, is seen to be underprovided by the market mechanism. For example, education for children would be underprovided if left solely to market forces because many parents would not have sufficient income to pay for their children to go to school. Yet having children receive a proper schooling is vital to the success of the whole economy over time. Hence, society requires that children go to school.

In the case of television, it could be argued that some television is a merit good. If left to free market forces, as it mainly is in the USA, it is clear that the quality of most television output would be poor. In the USA, there is plenty of choice of channels, but there is very little that is of any quality. In contrast, the BBC is often regarded as the 'world's best broadcaster'. Some would argue that the quality of broadcasting doesn't matter. If millions of people are prepared to sit through poor quality broadcasting, then that is their choice. They have the power to turn off their television set. Others would argue that television is a vital part of the culture of a nation. It has a 'vital role in informing and challenging viewers'. Certainly, evidence from other countries is clear that markets lead to a very different provision of programming from the BBC. So, if the BBC is seen as providing higher quality television, then it could be argued that there is market failure. In that case, quality broadcasting could be seen as a merit good.

3. Liquidating the BBC and giving its channels to commercial broadcasters is likely to lead to market failure. Commercial broadcasters are financed in two ways: either through advertising, or through subscriptions or some combination of both. When financed through advertising, commercial broadcasters want maximum ratings for the lowest cost programming. The evidence from other countries is that this leads to low quality programming. When financed through subscriptions, the results are mixed. However, even the best subscription channels are not as well regarded for the overall quality of mix of programmes as the BBC.

The data also discuss the issue of national sporting events. The result of Sky buying up the rights to Premier League football in the early 1990s was that football which could be seen for free on BBC or ITV could now only be seen by those who bought a Sky subscription. Commercial companies like Sky would like to buy the exclusive rights for all major national sporting events but cannot do so because this was made illegal in 1996. This shows some of the dangers of leaving broadcasting to free market forces. National events become mere opportunities for commercial broadcasters to earn profit without any regard to the national interest.

Overall, in terms of value for money, quality and choice, it is difficult not to conclude that liquidating the BBC would lead to market failure.

17 Externalities

Question 1

(a) The left hand photograph shows an example of topiary - cutting a hedge or tree to a particular shape, in this case to show an elephant. Passers by are likely to find this attractive but will not pay for the pleasure they receive. So the social benefit is likely to be higher than the private benefit. Therefore it is an example of a positive externality.

The middle photograph shows examples of litter on a beach. The spilled litter is an example of a negative externality where the social cost is greater than the private cost. This is because those who have created the litter have not paid for its disposal but the litter is an eyesore for those passing by. The litter might also pose a threat to wildlife.

The right hand photograph shows a tree being cut down in a forest. Felling the tree might lead to soil erosion and increased global warming because the tree might otherwise have been capturing carbon dioxide. The company felling the tree is unlikely to pay either of these costs. So the social cost of felling trees is likely to be higher than the private cost paid by the timber company.

Question 2

(a) Fly-tipping creates an externality because the social cost of fly-tipping is greater than private cost. The private cost to the business or individual getting rid of the waste is loading the waste into a car or truck and driving it somewhere to be dumped. To society, the cost is this private cost plus the cost of clearing up the waste and disposing of it safely. The data suggests the externality created by fly-tipping is costing society £100-£150 million a year. This is likely to be an underestimate because not all waste which is fly-tipped is cleared by local councils.

(b) Fly-tippers weigh up the private costs and benefits to them of dumping waste. If the likelihood of detection is low, and if caught the fine is also low, there is little incentive for them to dispose of waste legally. For example, a fly-tipper might dispose of waste which it would otherwise cost £2 000 to dispose of legally. If the maximum fine if caught is only £500, then the maximum 'profit' the fly-tipper can make if there is a 100 per cent certainty of being caught will be £1 500. But if the probability of being caught is only 1 in 100, then the likely fine is only £5 (£500 x 1 ÷ 100). The less likely the detection, the greater the average 'profit' the fly-tipper can make.

(c) Matching fines to environmental damage is a much better way of dealing with problems such as fly-tipping than fixed fines. In an ideal situation, the fine for fly-tipping should be equal to the cost of clean up and disposal plus a further fine adjusted for the likelihood of getting caught.

In the example of fly-posting, the likelihood of getting caught is very high because only the clubs and concert promoters putting on an event have any interest in getting posters up advertising those events. So it is relatively easy to find the guilty party. The fine should then be set equal to the cost of removing the posters, as will be the case under the Clean Neighbourhoods and Environment Act.

If there is a one in ten probability of an environmental offender being caught, then the fine should reflect this to deter all potential environmental offenders. For example, in the case of roadside tipping of waste, the chance of detection is small. So the fine is probably going to need to be several times the cost of clean up to deter potential environmental offenders.

Question 3

(a) A negative externality is created when social cost is greater than private cost. In the case of cans and bottles, if they are used only once and then thrown away, their disposal creates an externality unless it is included in the individual cost of the purchase to either the producer or consumer. A further externality exists if manufacturers of cans and bottles do not pay the full social cost of production. For example, they might use electricity which has been generated and has created greenhouse gases. But the cost of this environmental damage has not been included in the price of the electricity.

(b) The German scheme is an example of extended property rights. This is because the price of buying a product supplied in a recyclable can or bottle has been increased between 25 and 50 cent. This sum is then refunded if the can or bottle is returned for reuse. The 25-50 cents can be seen to represent the environmental cost of disposing of the can or bottle if used once. Property rights have thus been extended over the cans and bottles, raising their price and thus providing an incentive for consumers to return them for recycling.

(c) The scheme will reduce externalities because it provides an incentive for consumers to return used cans and bottles. The environmental cost of recycling is still positive in that, for example, greenhouse gases are emitted when cans and bottles are returned by truck to a recycling plant. However, this environmental cost is lower than if the cans and bottles were disposed of after one use and then new bottles and cans had to be manufactured.

Question 4

(a) A negative externality occurs when social costs are greater than private costs. Cigarette smoking causes negative externalities primarily because of the health problems it creates. Cigarette smokers have a reduced life expectancy and a greater change of getting illnesses which reduce their quality of life and can force them to stop working. Non-smokers can be affected too because of passive smoking. The data states that a leaked report estimated that second-hand smoke increases 'the risk of heart disease by an estimated 25 per cent'. The exact value of the negative externality is the difference between the price paid by consumers for cigarettes, including tax, and the full cost to society of smoking, including cost of production of cigarettes, the cost to the employers of days off work from smokers and the cost to the health service of treating smoking-related illnesses in patients.

(b) Governments have used both bans on advertising and taxes to reduce cigarette smoking. The tobacco industry has long argued that bans on advertising have no impact on the quantity bought of cigarettes. They argue therefore that the demand curve for cigarettes will not shift to the left when a ban is imposed. In practice, this is most unlikely. Since the cigarette industry argue that advertising is effective in making consumers shift from brand to brand, it is most likely that an advertising ban would also lead to a fall in demand. In Figure 1, the demand curve shifts from D_1 to D_2 following a ban. As a consequence, the equilibrium quantity bought and sold falls from OA to OB.

Increased taxes on cigarettes will also lead to a fall in the equilibrium bought and sold. In Figure 2, the increase in tax is shown by the shift to the left of the supply curve from S^1 to S^2. As a consequence, there is a movement back along the demand curve reducing quantity demanded from OA to OB. Note that the demand for cigarettes is shown to be price inelastic. As a result of a price rise, there is a less than proportionate fall in quantity demanded. The more inelastic is demand, the less effect a rise in taxes will have on the quantity demanded of cigarettes.

It is not possible to say which would be the most effective of the two methods in reducing cigarette smoking. There is no data given about the effects of a ban. The data does give some indication about the price elasticity of demand for cigarettes in Germany. A rise in prices from €3.00 to €3.80, a 27 per cent increase, has led to a fall in quantity demanded of 13 per cent. This would suggest that the price elasticity of demand for cigarettes is approximately 0.5. However, the data suggests that the effects of the price rise have not been fully felt and that there will be further reductions in demand which would increase the value of price elasticity of demand. It is also the case that price elasticity will differ depending on what price is currently being charged for cigarettes, and that the demand curve may differ between countries.

Figure 1

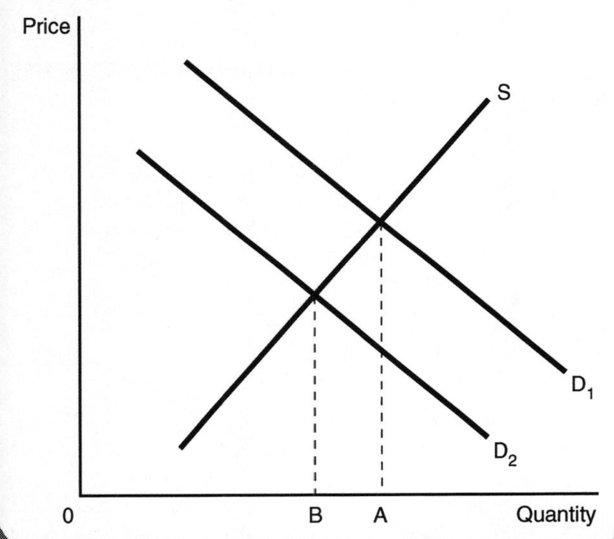

Figure 2

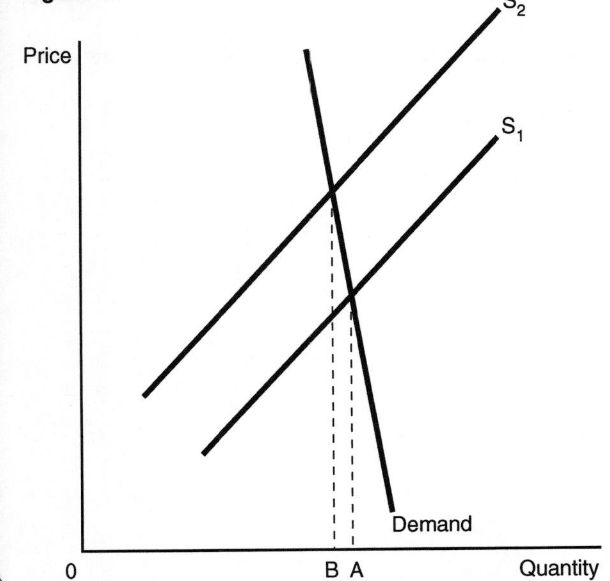

Question 5

(a) An emission permit is a permit to pollute which can be bought and sold. Under a system of emission permits, an organisation such as a national government or the EU would issue permits to individual firms. These firms would then not be able to exceed the limits on pollution specified in the permit. However, if they polluted less, they could sell this part of the permit to another firm which found that it was exceeding its pollution limits.

(b) Emission permits cut pollution levels at least cost. To understand why, consider two firms making the same product, one in the USA and one in Poland. Each receives identical emission permits. However, both are currently producing 10 per cent more emissions than they have emission permits. It will cost the Polish firm £10 million to reduce its pollution levels to the required limit, but it will cost the US firm only £2 million. To bring emissions down by 20 per cent would cost the Polish firm £20 million and the US firm £5 million. If both cut their emission levels by 10 per cent under a simple regulatory regime, it will cost £12 million (£10 million plus £2 million).

However, if the Polish firm bought permits from the US firm, it could carry on polluting at its present level if the US firm cuts its pollution levels by 20 per cent at a cost of £5 million. Society gains from this second solution because only £5 million worth of resources are used to cut pollution instead of £12 million. The Polish firm would gain if it could buy the extra permits at a cost of less than £10 million (£20 million - £10 million), whilst the US firm would gain if it could sell the 10 per cent pollution permit at more than £3 million (£5 million - £2 million). Hence tradable permits are a more efficient way of reducing pollution than simple regulation.

(c) It could strongly be argued that UK producers are being put under an unfair competitive disadvantage because of UK policy on emissions. Unlike other countries which have signed up to the Kyoto Protocol, the UK has unilaterally increased its emission cuts from the 12.5 per cent agreed at Kyoto to 20 per cent. Much of the burden of the emission cuts is being imposed on heavy industry including power generation. This means that raw material costs, particularly electricity, will be higher in the UK that they would otherwise have been had the target been kept at 12.5 per cent. Since other Kyoto countries have limited themselves to 12.5 per cent cuts, any firm with locations in the UK is likely to suffer.

However, not all UK firms will suffer. For many UK firms, particularly in service industries, inputs which are likely to be affected by the 20 per cent target are only a very small part of their costs. Therefore, the erosion of competitiveness with overseas firms is likely to be minimal. Another reason why many UK firms will not suffer is because they are not in the tradable sector of the economy. Only some goods and services can be traded with foreign countries. Even amongst those industries most affected, there are examples where transport costs are very high and which would limit the impact of price increases. Mass market glass manufacturer, for example, has high transport costs for the finished product. Hence, it is likely to remain competitive close to its customers even if costs increase.

Data question

1 (a) The private cost of generating electricity from nuclear power stations are those costs which are borne by the producer. This would be the cost of building the nuclear power stations, running them and then decommissioning them. In Figure 13 in the student's book, the overall cost of generating nuclear power is estimated to be between £31 and £45 per megawatt.

(b) The social cost of nuclear energy is the private cost plus any externalities created. Externalities are costs which are borne by society but not by the producer. For example, if a UK nuclear plant went into meltdown, as at Chernobyl in Russia in 1986, most of the cost would be born by others than the owner of the nuclear generating plant. The nuclear generator could well go out of business as a result of the huge costs that it would face following a meltdown. Society would then pick up the costs. Equally, as suggested in the data, if radioactive material fell into the hands of terrorists, then there could be a major incident whose costs would not be borne by the producers of nuclear energy.

The data also point out that some nuclear waste will still be dangerous in 1,000 years' time. It is most unlikely that the cost of dealing with this waste will be borne by today's producers. It will be future generations who will pay the bill for dealing with the waste. This then represents an externality.

2. Carbon emissions from coal and gas fired electricity power stations represent an externality to society. They contribute to global warming, which over the next 100 years will result in wide ranging costs across the world. But the power generators are not paying towards those costs. Hence, the government imposes environmental taxes on electricity generators in the form of the carbon levy. Environmental groups argue that this carbon levy is set at too low a level because the social costs of electricity generation are too high compared with the social benefits even with the tax.

This can be shown in Figure 3. If left to free market forces, output of the power generators would be at OA where marginal private cost equalled marginal private benefit. However, the marginal social cost curve shows that negative externalities occur at this level of output. Only if output were to be OC would marginal social cost equal marginal social benefit. According to environmentalists, current taxes do reduce output to OB, nearer the socially optimal level of OC than OB, but still not at the socially optimal level. The marginal tax needs to be EK, not FH as at present.

3. The proposal from the environmental group to cut the number of miles travelled by 20 per cent would cause a major change in transport arrangements. At present, travellers place a high private benefit on both road and air travel. They are prepared to spend a significant part of their income on travel. Trebling the price of petrol and freezing the number of air flights into and out of the UK would place severe restrictions on travel leading in Figure 3 to a movement up the demand or marginal social benefit curve for travel. Given that the demand for road travel is arguably fairly inelastic, the loss of consumer surplus from a cut in road travel could be substantial. So the main disadvantage to this proposal would be a large cut in private benefits. There would be a fall in social costs. For example, there would be fewer accidents and less noise pollution. This would be an advantage of this proposal.

The alternative proposal is to build nuclear power stations which would reduce the UK's emissions of CO_2 gases. The advantage of this solution would be that the estimated private cost would be little different from generating energy from more polluting coal and gas fired power stations. However, environmental groups argue that the costs are far higher than those suggested by government. They point to the large cost of decommissioning plants. They also argue the risks involved with nuclear power are so great that this must rule nuclear power out as a solution.

If environmental groups are correct in saying that the potential externalities of nuclear power are unquantifiably large, then limiting travel is the best solution. On the other hand, if government estimates of the social costs are correct, then restricting travel would lead to a major loss of welfare compared to building nuclear power stations. Building new nuclear power stations would then be the best solution.

Figure 3

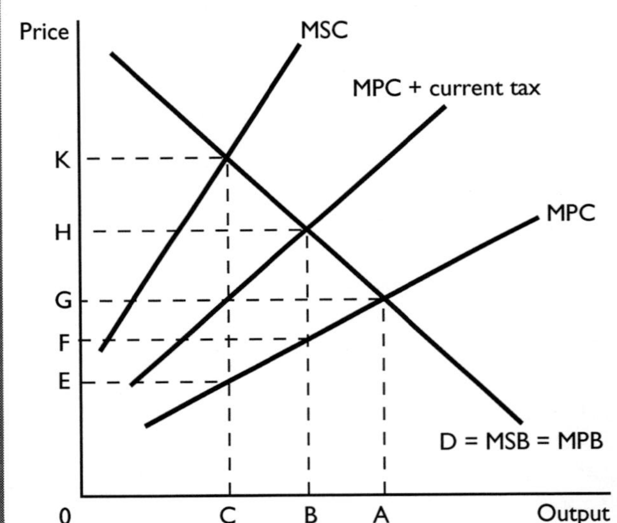

18 Competition

Question 1

(a) The market structure of the dry cleaning market has a number of features. One is that there are a large number of firms in the industry. In 2004, there were an estimated 4 500 outlets and the largest firm, Johnson Service Group, had 638 outlets. An estimated 64 per cent of the market is supplied by small independent firms. So there are probably well in excess of 2 000 firms in the industry.

There is freedom of entry to and exit from the industry. Barriers to entry are relatively low. For example, it is relatively cheap to set up a dry cleaning firm and the technology of dry cleaning is readily available. The fact that there are so many firms in the industry also suggests that there are relatively few economies of scale to be had, again reducing the barriers to entry.

Dry cleaning services tend to be homogeneous. It is difficult for any single business to develop such a strong brand that it would keep customers loyal to its service rather than that of a rival.

There is perfect knowledge in the industry because the technology of dry cleaning is available to any entrant.

(b) The market structure of the dry cleaning industry would suggest that it is highly competitive, if not perfectly competitive for the reasons described in (a). There are two factors which might suggest the industry is not perfectly competitive. One is the existence of Johnson Service Group with its 638 outlets and its brand name of 'Sketchley's'. It probably has some weak control over the market in areas where it operates. The other is the growth of supermarket groups in the industry. This is shown by the increase in the number of out of town outlets in Figure 1 in the student's book. As yet, supermarket groups only have a small share of the market but the lower prices they charge and their ability to afford new licences and the latest equipment might be affecting the ability of other firms in the industry to gain business.

(c) Supermarket groups have a tendency to dominate sectors in which they operate. It could be that in future they will come to achieve a high market share in the dry cleaning industry as customers bring their suits in to be dry cleaned along with buying the groceries. Given that 4-5 supermarket chains dominate the UK grocery market, dry cleaning could become an imperfectly competitive industry. Competition as defined by competition among the many would decline.

The supermarket groups might argue that they have such a small share of the existing market that it is unlikely they will come to dominate the market in the future. Equally, they might argue that convenience is often more important to customers in this market than price. Being able to take clothes to a local dry cleaner a few minutes away from home might be more important than saving £5 by taking it to a supermarket miles away from home.

Overall, the entry of supermarket groups has undoubtedly made the market more competitive in the short term. Consumers have greater choice of where to take their dry cleaning. However, if the supermarket share of the market grows significantly over the next few years, competition is likely to be reduced as local dry cleaners are forced out of business.

Question 2

(a) Abnormal profit is profit over and above normal profit, the profit needed to keep resources in use in an industry. The sandwich market in the UK is a growing market and if a few firms dominated the market, they might be able to use their market power to charge prices high enough for them to earn abnormal profit. However, the sandwich market is highly fragmented. According to the data, there are 5 000 independently owned sandwich shops. There are chains, the most important of which are Pret A Manger and Subway, but there are only 700 chain outlets, a fraction of the 5 000 outlets of independently owned shops. Because of the large number of firms in the industry, it is would be difficult for any single firm to earn abnormal profit. If a firm charged high prices, it would lose customers to outlets charging lower prices. Hence, abnormal profits would be competed away.

The fact that the market is growing does not affect the competitive pressures on the market. A growing market will encourage new independent firms to enter the industry, providing fresh competition for incumbent firms and so limiting their ability to raise prices and earn abnormal profits.

Question 3

(a) Three types of efficiency can be distinguished. Productive efficiency occurs when there is production at lowest cost. Allocative efficiency occurs when resources are used to produce the goods and services that consumers wish to buy. Dynamic efficiency occurs when resources are allocated efficiently over time.

Increased competition in the European rail freight market is likely to lead to greater productive efficiency. Existing nationalised rail companies have little incentive to reduce their costs. The data say that a lack of competition has led to 'disorganisation and inefficiency'. The companies coming into the market, such as Rail4Chem, will gain market share by charging lower prices. They are able to do this because their operations will be more productively efficient than those provided by nationalised industries.

Increased competition is also likely to lead to less allocative inefficiency. In the data, Matthias Raith, managing director of Rail4Chem, is quoted as saying that 'traditional railways have long overcharged certain customers'. Ewout Sandker, policy manager for the European Shippers' Council is also quoted as saying that 'Users saw an immediate change in the traditional railway company's behaviour, its service orientation' when the Dutch rail company lost contracts to a new entrant. Prices which are too high and poor service are examples of allocative inefficiency.

Increased competition is likely to lead to increased dynamic efficiency. Future prices are likely to be lower and service better. One example of this is that in France, SNCF is investing E500 million in new locomotives to speed up journey times and increase reliability. This is a direct response to the competitive threat posed by new entrants.

Data question

1. A number of trends are described in the data, two of which are asked for by the question.

One of these is for chains of high-street outdoor retailers either to shrink in size or close down altogether. For example, Blacks Leisure Group was due to close more than 40 of its

Milletts stores in 2007 because of poor profitability.

Another trend is for mass market retailers to increase their share of the market. Stores like Halfords, Woolworths and Argos have been increasing their sales of cheaper equipment used by customers who only go walking or climbing occasionally.

A third trend is for Internet sales to increase. The Internet has allowed relatively small shops to gain extra customers.

A fourth trend is for specialist retailers to adopt new shop formats with 'bigger outlets and in-store attractions such as rock climbing walls and wet areas to test goods'. By becoming destinations in their own right, like garden centres, these specialist stores hope to attract more customers.

2. The UK outdoor equipment retailing industry is a competitive industry. There are a large number of different firms in the industry, none of which has significant market share. Most of the market is made up of small independent retail shops. There are also specialist chains such as Milletts. Finally there are general retailers such as Argos or Woolworths which also sell outdoor equipment.

Barriers to entry to the industry are relatively low. It is relatively cheap to set up as an independent. Equally, the cost for a general retailer, such as a major supermarket chain, to sell a range of goods within its existing stores would be relatively low.

There is weak product branding amongst retailers. For example, some customers will show brand loyalty to specialists such as Cotswolds Outdoor or Graham Tiso. However, most customers will shop around for convenience or price.

Knowledge within the industry is arguably perfect. Retailers have access to the same knowledge and there are no trade secrets.

3. Increased competition in the industry has arguably led to increased efficiency. Productive efficiency has increased because large general retailers like Halfords and Woolworths have entered the market. They have reduced costs and prices. As a result, less efficient retailers such as Milletts have been forced to contract or even leave the market. On the other hand, there is no indication that costs and prices have fallen amongst specialist outdoor equipment retailers which sell up-market specialist equipment to serious enthusiasts.

Efficiency, resulting from competition, has also increased because consumers have more choice. They are able to cast their spending votes on cheap products or on expensive products. Because profits are low, shown by the fact that some firms are leaving the industry or scaling down their operations, consumers are not exploited by monopoly firms.

It could also be argued that there is dynamic efficiency in the market. The face of the market is changing over time to respond to consumer needs. Some firms are leaving the industry and others are entering it to take advantage of new consumer tastes. Existing firms, like Cotswolds Outdoor, are changing their product offering.

Overall, increased competition is leading to both greater static and dynamic efficiency in the market for outdoor equipment.

19 Monopoly and efficiency

Question 1

(a) A monopoly, in theory, is a firm which is the sole supplier in its market. Intel is not the sole supplier of microchips for personal computers (PCs), but it does have 80 per cent of the market. This makes it an effective monopolist, able to maintain high profits through creating barriers to entry to the market.
(b) Intel has maintained its monopoly powers over its market by creating barriers to entry. A key barrier to entry has been Intel's research and development programme which has given it a technological advantage over competitors. It has protected this through patents on its products. It has also stayed ahead of the competition through frequent product launches.

Rivals, however, such as AMD (Advance Micro Devices) would argue that Intel's market dominance has been achieved through unfair competitive practices. In a law suit, it alleges that Intel has bribed customers to stock Intel powered devices at the expense of rivals such as AMD. For example, Intel agreed to pay Dixons, the UK high street retailer, if it kept AMD powered machines to below 10 per cent of its sales. Equally, it agreed to pay Toshiba 'market development funds' of $25-$30million 'on the understanding that Toshiba will not use any AMD microprocessors in its PCs'.

Question 2

(a) A local monopoly is one where a firm in a local area has no effective competition. For example, if in a rural area, there is only one supermarket outlet within a thirty mile radius, that supermarket is likely to have a local monopoly because customers will not be willing to travel much greater distances to go to another supermarket.
(b) Supermarkets are likely to vary their prices according to how much local competition there is in the market. Where local competition is intense, supermarkets are likely to charge low prices in order to attract customers to their stores. When there is effectively no local competition, supermarkets can charge higher prices knowing that customers have no choice but to shop with them. This policy allows the supermarkets to maximise their profits.
(c) Tesco, like any firm, has to decide on what price will maximise its profits. Raising average prices is likely to increase the profit per unit sold. However, higher prices are likely to lead to some customers going elsewhere to buy their groceries. Higher prices are therefore likely to lead to less sales volume. Maximum profit is achieved when profits would fall because of lost sales volume if prices were raised. Tesco would argue that it charges very low prices to customers. This only makes sense in terms of profit because low prices attracts customers to its stores, whereas higher prices would lead to fewer customers and lower overall profit. The data suggests that Tesco takes account of the willingness of customers to pay by charging different prices in different stores according to the amount of local competition. This way it is able to maximise the amount of producer surplus it can earn by minimising the level of consumer surplus its customers gain by shopping at Tesco.

Question 3

(a) Since the beginning of the twentieth century, land based telecommunications have enjoyed a monopoly in their market. However, from the 1980s onwards, a new technology, mobile phones, began to challenge the dominance of land based telecommunications.

Mobile phones potentially have the power to destroy land based markets. In practice, the two are likely to co-exist, with cost and convenience being the deciding factors for consumers using them.
(b) Customers have benefited in two ways from the breakdown of the monopoly on land line telephone companies. First, they have been given choice about which technology to use. Mobile telephones have some convenience and technological advantages over land line telecommunications and vice versa. Second, customers have benefited from falling prices. Land line operators had been mainly state monopolists. The new mobile phone companies have tended to be private sector companies in competition with these monopolies. The land line operators have been forced to reduce their prices or face further erosion of their markets. This process of competition has been aided by the privatisation of many of these state monopolies and the introduction of competition into the land line market.

Question 4

(a) Royal Mail until the 1 January 2006 had a monopoly on the collection and delivery of mail to business and residential customers. Even after this date, Royal Mail is likely to have retained an effective monopoly on these services if the example of New Zealand and Sweden is replicated. Monopolists, to maximise profits, restrict output and charge higher prices than if the market were competitive. Hence, consumers are exploited and pay higher prices than they would otherwise if they had a choice of providers. Having a regulator in the form of Postcomm means that Royal Mail is limited in its ability to exploit its customers. Hence, customers of Royal Mail gain from being protected by Postcomm.
(b) Introducing competition means that customers will have a choice about which company to use for postal services. This should help reduce prices and improve services. Royal Mail is likely to react to competition by attempting to prevent its customers from using the service provided by rival companies. It may therefore compete more aggressively on price and attempt to improve its own customer service levels.

Data question

1. A patent gives the owner a legal right to exclusive use of an invention or technology for a number of years. Patents therefore confer monopoly powers on their owners because they are the sole suppliers of that invention or technology. For example, Tate&Lyle holds a patent on the artificial sweetener, sucralose, which prevents rivals from copying it.
2. Firms take out patents to protect their property rights. They have usually invested money in research to develop a technique or process. They expect to gain a commercial return from this investment. This commercial return would be considerably smaller if competitors could gain immediate access to its use. By taking out patents, they can prevent competitors from gaining access to the technology. In the case of sucralose, Tate&Lyle has been a huge success for the

company. 20 per cent of its profits now come from sales of sucralose and it 'can't keep up with demand' according to the data. It holds patents on the product until 2020 which should allow it to maintain high profits on the product. However, other firms, particularly Chinese firms, are attempting to produce a similar product without violating the patents that Tate&Lyle has taken out. High profits encourage other firms to engage in research and development themselves to put their own patented products on the market.

3. Market efficiency can be defined in terms of dynamic efficiency and two types of static efficiency, productive efficiency and allocative efficiency. Patents encourage dynamic efficiency because the existence of patents prevent firms from copying profitable new products put onto the market by rival firms. This then encourages them to engage in research and development to develop their own new products. Hence, in markets when product innovation is important, patents ensure that firms have a strong incentive to bring new products to the market. In the case of artificial sweeteners, Tate&Lyle's monopoly on the production of highly profitable sucralose provides a strong incentive for rival firms to develop better artificial sweeteners. One response, from rival Nutrasweet has been to develop Neotame, a sweetener which doesn't taste as good as sucralose but is very cheap to produce and buy.

However, patents may not lead to static efficiency. The existence of high profits on successful patented products limits competition. Firms with patents are under less pressure then to ensure productive efficiency, production at lowest average cost. Equally, there will not be allocative efficiency. Firms with successful patents charge high prices to customers by restricting output. Prices would be lower and output higher if the market were competitive. When Tate&Lyle's patent on sucralose expires in 2020, it will be forced to reduce its prices because of competition in the same way that Nutrasweet was forced to reduce its prices on aspartame. In that case, when the patent expired at the end of the 1990s, the price collapsed from $100 per lb to $9 per lb, slashing profits from 75 per cent of sales value to 15 per cent of sales value.

It can be argued therefore that patents lead to both market efficiency and market failure. In the long term, patents lead to dynamic efficiency, but in the short term to static inefficiency.

20 Market stabilisation

Question 1

(a) Overall, the stock of privately rented properties more than halved between 1961 and 1991 from 5.0 million to 2.2 million.
(b) (i) The introduction of registered rents in the 1960s placed a cap on the rent of properties. This was a maximum price landlords could charge. Because this was below the equilibrium market rent, it meant the quantity supplied of rented properties fell. In Figure 1, the equilibrium rent initially is OA. A maximum rent of OB is then applied. This led to a movement back along the supply curve with only OG being supplied.

Figure 1

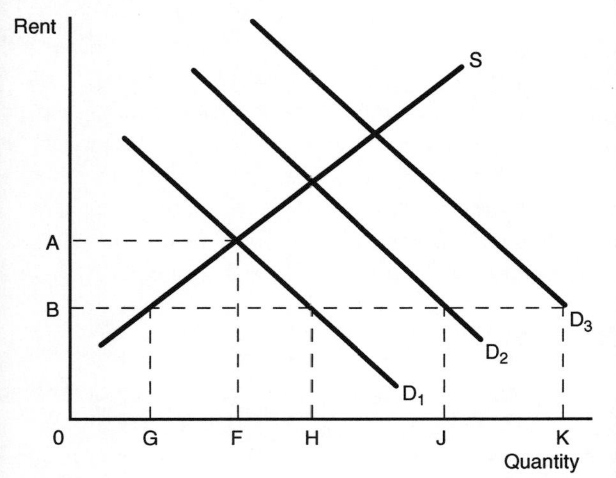

(ii) Meanwhile, excess demand for private rented property rose. In Figure 1, at the equilibrium rent of OA, OF is demanded and supplied. But with rents at OB, OG is supplied but OH is demanded. There is therefore excess demand of GH. Excess demand between 1961 and 1991 increased over time. The movement down the supply curve took decades to achieve because tenants had the right not to be evicted. Landlords could not reclaim their property unless tenants left voluntarily. However, demand was increasing, shown by the shift in the demand curve to the right, because incomes were increasing over time. At a rent of OB, demand increased over time from OH to OJ to OK. Excess demand therefore grew.
(c) The introduction of assured tenancies allowed landlords to charge market rents and gave them the right to reclaim their rented property from tenants if they wished to do so. This led to a rise in the quantity supplied of privately rented housing but also a fall in quantity demanded. In Figure 2, rents under previous legislation were capped at OA. This maximum rent led to OF being supplied, OG being demanded and excess demand of FG. Assured tenancies allowed landlords to raise rents to the market clearing price of OB. Quantity supplied therefore increased to OH whilst quantity demanded fell also to OH. As a result, OH was now the equilibrium quantity of rented housing.

Question 2

(a)(i) 'EU cereal stocks now at their highest for a decade' mainly because of a bumper harvest from the ten new member states of the EU. Across the EU, production of cereals were up 25 per cent in 2004 compared to 2003. However, in Hungary the increase was 89 per cent whilst in the Czech Republic the increase was 54 per cent. The EU sets a minimum price for cereals. If supply is so great that the free market price threatens to go below this minimum intervention price, the EU buys up the excess supply from the market, putting it into stock. Hence, bumper harvests tend to lead to increases in stock. In 2004, the EU had committed itself to buying up 13.5 million tons of cereal for intervention.

This can be shown in Figure 3. Due to a bumper harvest, the supply curve for cereals shifts from S_1 to S_2. As a result, the new equilibrium market price is OA. But this is below the intervention price of OB. So the EU has to buy up FG to raise the price back to OB. FG represents the increase in EU stocks of cereals.
(ii) One way of reducing EU stocks is to sell cereal that would otherwise have been sold into stock onto world markets. However, the world market price for cereals is below the intervention price in the EU. Therefore, the only way the EU can achieve this is to offer subsidies to EU farmers who sell their cereal outside of the EU. This subsidy has to be large

Figure 2

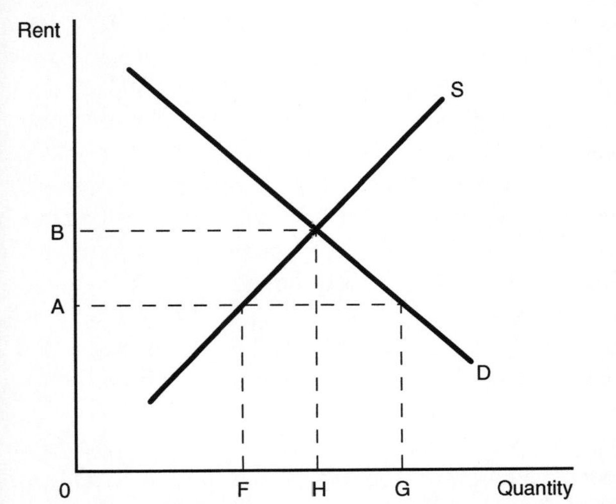

Figure 3

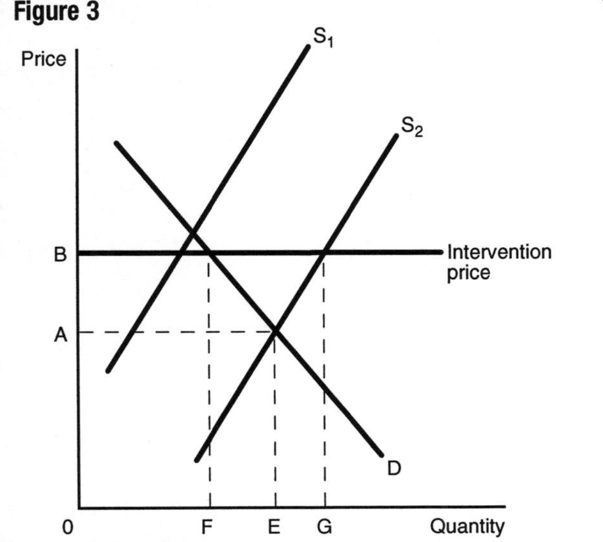

Figure 4

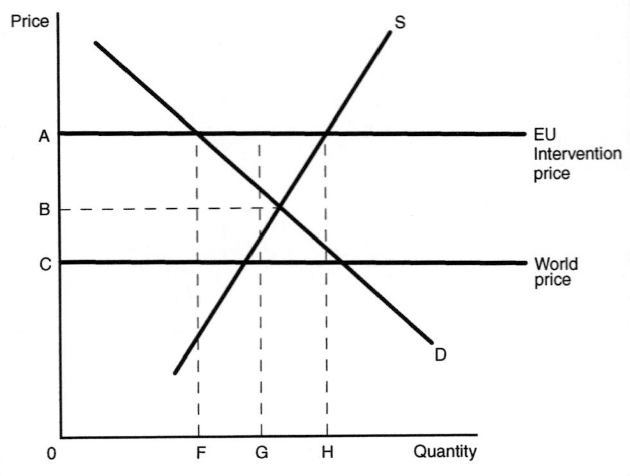

Figure 5

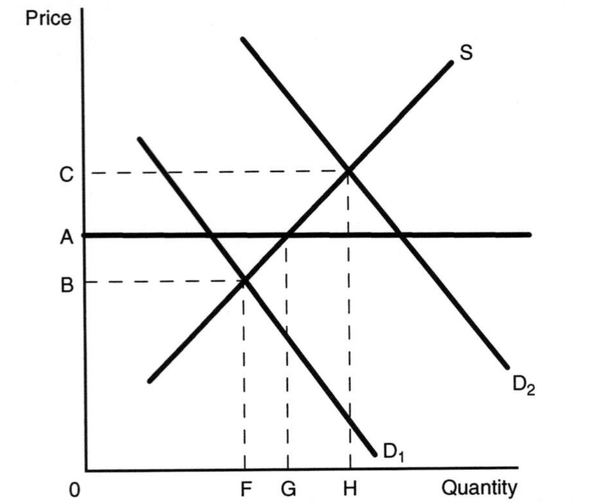

enough to reduce the price of cereals to world prices.

This can be shown in Figure 4. The world free market price for cereals is OC. The free market price in the EU is higher at OB but this is below the intervention price of OA. Instead of buying up stock to increase the price to OA, the EU offers a subsidy of AC per unit. This reduces the price of cereals to OC per unit. This is the difference between the price the farmers would have received if they had sold their stock into intervention and the the world market price of cereals. The EU will limit the amount of cereal sold under export subsidies. In Figure 4 it is assumed that the EU is willing to sell FG for export with subsidies. Given that excess supply at the intervention price is FH, this leaves GH of the excess supply of FH to be bought into stock.

(b) EU grain farmers, particularly those in Eastern Europe where supply increased the most, benefited because they were able to sell all their grain at the EU intervention price. If they had not been able to do so, they would otherwise have received a much lower price. EU taxpayers, in contrast, were significant losers. They had to pay the bill for all the grain that was bought up for stock or sold below cost onto world markets.

Question 3

(a) The International Tin Council (ITC) operated a buffer stock scheme. When price threatened to go below a minimum price, the ITC would step into the market and buy up tin so increasing demand. When price was above the minimum price, the ITC could choose to sell tin from its stockpile. This can be shown in Figure 5. The intervention price is OA. When demand is D_1, the equilibrium free market price is below the intervention price and so the ITC had to buy up FG of tin on world markets to return the price to OB. If demand is D_2, the equilibrium price is OC. At this price, the ITC can sell GH of tin from its stockpile leading to a fall in price to the intervention price of OA.

(b) The ITC's performance in the 1970s and 1980s was mixed. According to the data, and as shown in Figure 7 in the student's book, the ITC did not have sufficiently large quantities of tin in stockpiles to prevent a sharp rise in the price of tin particularly in the second half of the 1970s. In the first half of the 1980s, it had difficulty finding the finance to buy up tin as tin prices fell due to a recession in world markets. In late 1985, the ITC ran out of funds and it was disbanded.

(c) In the late 1970s and early 1980s, the price of tin was high because of a commodity price bubble. Demand for tin was high and suppliers were not able to match the increase in demand with an increase in supply. Hence the price of tin rose. By the 1990s, the ITC had been disbanded and free market forces were determining the price of tin. Demand was subdued in relation to supply and hence prices were much lower than in the bubble period of the late 1970s and early 1980s.

Data question

1. A buffer stock scheme is a scheme whereby an organisation buys and sells in the open market so as to maintain a minimum price in the market for a product. The International Natural Rubber Organisation (INRO) was an example of such a scheme. It was committed to supporting the market price of rubber. When prices were falling, it might step into the market and start buying rubber. Increasing demand raised the price from what it would otherwise have been. If prices reached a high level, INRO could sell rubber from its stocks. This would give it funds to use when it wanted to buy rubber and would also help stabilise prices.

2. INRO had built up stocks of rubber by 1999 because it had recently been a net buyer of rubber in the markets. Figure 8 in the student's book shows that in four of the six years between 1992 and 1997 production had exceeded consumption. This put downward pressure on rubber prices which INRO had attempted to stem by buying in the market.

3. Rubber prices began increasing from a low of 45 Singapore cents per kilogram at the end of 2001 and by 2006 had peaked at 270 Singapore cents, an increase of 500 per cent. In August 2002, the world's three largest producers of rubber, Malaysia, Indonesia and Thailand, set up IRCo to 'co-ordinate production and exports of the three countries'. However, it is unlikely that IRCo had much if any influence over the price of rubber in the early 2000s. A commodity price boom sent the price of rubber soaring. To stabilise the price, IRCo would have had to increase supply to the market, for example by selling from a stockpile. However, IRCo had no such stockpile and it would not have been in the interests of the three producing countries to have artificially depressed the price in the circumstances. As Figure 11 in the student's book shows, world production increased from 6.7 million tonnes in 2000 to 9.7 million tonnes in 2006 an increase of 45 per cent. However, in

2006 production exceeded demand and this may account for the falls in rubber prices in that year. But the data does not give any indication that IRCo was responsible for the increase in production or for stabilising prices round an intervention price. Therefore, it is probably the case that IRCo had little or no influence on the price increases in rubber shown from 2001.

21 Government failure

Question 1

(a) Markets fail, according to the data, because producers are able to sell goods which are not fit for human consumption. Consumers do not necessarily have the knowledge about the products they buy which would enable them to make rational choices. So consumers, even in Victorian times, would not have wanted to buy diluted sulphuric acid when they thought they were buying vinegar. However, the data are also implying that consumers may be willing to buy goods, such as pork or eggs, where they pay only the private cost and not the full social cost. Markets are unlikely to take into account the value of cruelty to animals in the production of food. Hence, externalities are created.

(b) There is little disagreement that governments should intervene to make sure that firms sell products which are safe and which conform to the description given to them. However, it could be argued that government regulation is too tight. It prevents individuals, for instance, from setting up food preparation businesses in their own homes without conforming to government regulation. Excessive government regulation, which discourages new businesses, creates costs, such as higher unemployment or loss of wealth generation.

In the case of animal welfare, many food producers, including farmers, do not agree that practices such as battery hen production are cruel to animals. They therefore deny that such farming practices create externalities. If this were the case, then tighter government regulation to improve the living conditions of animals on farms is an unnecessary expense and simply leads to consumers having to pay too high a price for their food. Resources are misallocated because, instead of being able to spend more on clothes or holidays, consumers are being forced to pay for unnecessary changes in farming practice. Animal welfare groups would disagree and would probably argue that there are still considerable externalities present in the production of food. At its most extreme, this argument would suggest that any system which kills animals for food creates an externality in that humans have no right to kill any animal to eat.

Question 2

(a)(i) Table 1 in the student's book shows that the party's policies have led to a redistribution of income from the poor to the rich. The bottom 60 per cent of individuals now take a lower proportion of total income than before. The bottom 20 per cent have been worst affected, seeing their share of total income drop by 40 per cent. The top fifth of income earners, in contrast, have seen their share of disposable income rise from 35 per cent to 43 per cent. Greater inequality in society, all other things being equal, is often seen as contributing to a lowering of welfare. If nothing else, it indicates greater horizontal and vertical inequity.

(ii) The main argument used to justify a widening of inequality is that it contributes to the welfare of even the lowest strata of society because their absolute levels of income are higher than they would have been. For instance, assume that the rate of growth in the economy is 9 per cent over the period because of increased incentives instead of 2 per cent previously. At 9 per cent rather than 2 per cent, national income will be double what it would otherwise have been at the end of the 10 year period. The bottom 20 per cent are therefore better off getting 6 per cent of this doubled national income rather than 10 per cent of what it would otherwise have been.

So, to justify the conclusion that welfare has increased or diminished due to greater inequality of income, we need to know about growth rates of income in the economy and how inequality has affected these growth rates.

(b) The party can win elections because it can draw on the support of the top 40 per cent of the electorate by income. These voters will vote for the right wing party either because it has or will make them better off, or it will make them no worse off. The data suggest that the top 20 per cent of income earners will contribute 18 per cent (90 per cent of 20 per cent) of the national vote immediately. If the next 20 per cent contribute, say 14 per cent, the party already has 32 per cent of the vote. It only needs another 8 per cent from the bottom 60 per cent of the electorate to secure a majority with 40 per cent of the vote.

Data question

1.(a) There is arguably market failure in the market for traditional fuels because their social cost exceeds their private costs. Burning fossil fuels leads to emissions of greenhouse gases. This causes global warming which could lead to significant increases in world temperatures over the next 100 years. In turn, this will give rise to large costs to society because of the economic and social dislocation that will occur. In Figure 1, the marginal private cost of burning fossil fuel is shown by the MPC line. Equilibrium consumption is OB. But the marginal social cost is higher, shown by the MSC line. The socially optimal level of consumption is OA. Therefore AB shows too much is produced and consumed. There is a welfare loss to society shown by the triangle GJK.

Bio-fuels can help solve this problem because they can be carbon neutral. Growing bio-fuel crops reduces carbon in the atmosphere whilst burning ethanol increases carbon. The two cancel each other out. This helps reduce the market fuel from all types of fuel.

(b) Government failure occurs when government intervention leads to a net welfare loss compared to the free market solution. Bio-fuels create government failure because they are not produced in an efficient way. The United States should import its ethanol from Brazil where the sugar cane industry can efficiently convert sugar cane into bio-fuel. Instead, it imposes high taxes on ethanol imported from this efficient source and gives its farmers subsidies to grow bio-fuel crops. The US tax and subsidy regime distorts the working of the free market. Government failure also occurs because it leads unintentionally to widening inequalities. The US ethanol programme has led to large rises in world food prices. Those who suffer the most are the poor in the Third World who do not grow their own crops. With a fixed income, they cannot afford to buy as much food as before. The result is greater levels of malnutrition.

2. Public choice theory is theory about how and why public spending and taxation decisions are made. In the United States, individual groups can have an undue influence on political decision making. This is traditionally known as 'pork-barrel politics'. The farming lobby is one such group and it exercises its power in two main ways. First, large farming industries spend large amounts of money lobbying different branches of the US government. By acting together, they can

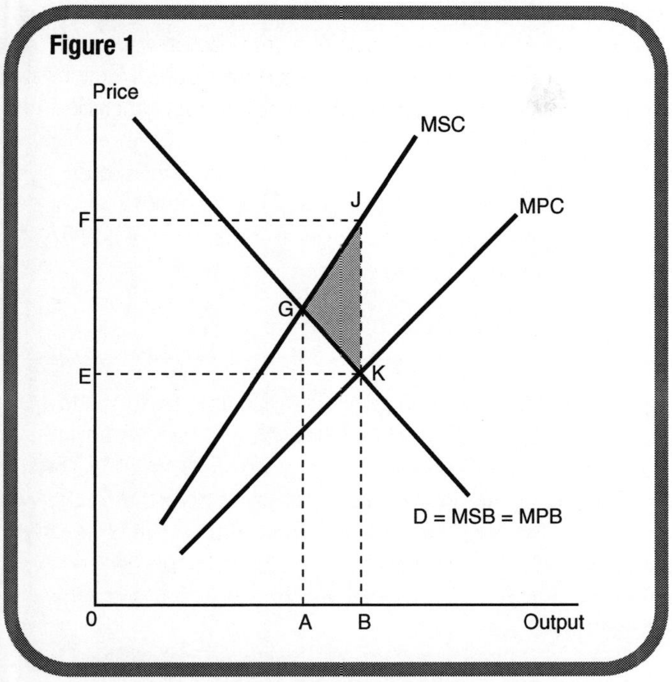

exercise undue influence. Second, farming voters are key voters in the race to choose a president. The voters of Iowa, a predominantly rural state, can derail a bid for the presidency because they vote early in the round of primary elections. Therefore no presidential candidate is willing to come out with an anti-farming message.

22 National economic performance

Question 1

Note: in Table 1 there was a mistake in the first impression of the 5th edfition. This has been corrected in reprints. Average economic growth for France in 2000-2007 was 2.0 per cent and not 2.7 per cent as stated. The answer below assumes that France's economic growth was 2.0 per cent.

(a) The country with the highest average economic growth in these years was:
(i) Japan; **(ii)** Mexico; **(iii)** Mexico and the United States; **(iv)** Mexico; **(v)** Mexico.
(b) Measuring national economic performance is complex because a number of different variables need to be taken into account. However, if economic growth is the key measure of long term national economic performance, then Mexico has enjoyed a better economic performance over the period 1961-2007. In Table 1 in the student's book, in four of the five the periods shown, Mexico's average annual growth rate was higher than that of Germany, whilst in the other period it was the same. Mexico's average annual growth rate over the whole period 1961-2006 was 4.1 per cent whilst that of Germany's was 2.6 per cent.
(c) Of the seven countries shown in Table 1 in the student's book, the United Kingdom had the lowest average annual rate of economic growth in the periods 1961-1973 and 1974-79. In the 1980s and the 1990s, its economic performance was a little better but still below the average of the seven countries shown. However, in comparison with European countries its performance was better. Between 1980 and 1989, the UK's economic growth averaged 2.4 per cent per annum compared to 2.2 per cent for Germany, Italy and France combined. In the 1990s, UK annual average growth of 2.1 per cent was approximately the same as the average growth rate of Germany, Italy and France. However, between 2000 and 2007, UK average annual growth was 2.7 per cent compared to an average 1.7 per cent for the three European countries. Over the whole period 1961-2007, the UK's average annual rate of economic growth was 2.4 per cent compared to 3.0 per cent for France, 3.0 per cent for Italy and 2.6 per cent for Germany. This would be consistent with saying that UK GDP was higher than these other European countries in 1961, fell below them in the mid 1990s and today is roughly comparable.
However, economic growth is only one aspect of 'economic performance' and is not the same as growth in living standards. More data is needed if we were to conclude that living standards were the same in 2007 in the UK, France, Germany and Italy. Equally, more data would be needed to conclude that the UK's national economic performance was worse relative to other European countries in the 1960s and 1970s but better from the mid 1990s onwards. Table 1 below summarises the average annual growth rates for 1961-2007 for the seven countries in the question.

Table 1 Average annual growth rate, %, 1961-2007

	%
United States	2.9
Japan	4.6
Germany	2.6
France	3.0
Italy	3.0
Mexico	4.1
United Kingdom	2.4

Question 2

(a) The data give two indicators of economic performance. For the first, the unemployment rate, the UK has performed much better than the eurozone between 1995 to 2007. The unemployment rate in the UK was always below that in the eurozone. Moreover, the unemployment rate in the UK nearly halved from 8.5 per cent to 5.2 per cent over the period whilst the eurozone unemployment rate only fell from 11.5 per cent to .9 per cent..
The second indicator given is economic growth. Annual economic growth was higher in the UK in most years between 1995 and 2007. Average growth in the UK over the period was 2.8 per cent compared to 2.2 per cent for the eurozone.
However, it should be remembered that unemployment and economic growth are only two measures of economic performance. Without other data, such as inflation rates or balance of payments data, it is not possible to say conclusively that the UK's economic performance was better than that of the eurozone.
(b) Economic growth and unemployment tend to be linked. When economic growth is high, unemployment tends to fall as extra workers are needed to produce more output. When economic growth is low, unemployment tends to rise because the rate of growth in labour productivity is higher than the rate of growth of output. The UK's higher rate of economic growth compared to the eurozone therefore partly explains why the UK's unemployment rate fell more than the eurozone's unemployment rate between 1995 and 2006. Equally, though, there may have been other factors at work, such as changes in productivity.

Question 3

(a) The performance of the UK economy can be measured in a number of different ways. Four such measures would be economic growth, unemployment, inflation and the current account on the balance of payments.
In the short term, the 2005 bombings would reduce the number of foreign tourists coming to the UK. The World Travel and Tourism Council (WTTC) predicted that there would be 600 000 fewer tourists in 2005. This would reduce predicted spending in the UK by £927 million, according to the WTTC, and therefore reduce economic growth. According to the data, £927 million is 2 per cent of tourist spending, and tourist spending accounts for 4 per cent of GDP. Therefore, there would be a negative impact on GDP of 0.08 per cent.
Unemployment in the UK would rise because tourism directly or indirectly creates 2.8 million jobs according to the data. If 0.08 per cent of jobs were lost, this would represent a total loss of 2 240 jobs.
The current balance position of the UK's balance of payments would deteriorate. If it is assumed that all of £927 million loss of spending would have come from foreigners spending their own currency to buy pounds, the current account position

would deteriorate by £927 million. This would be smaller if some of the £927 million were goods and services bought from foreign suppliers by UK firms in the tourist industry. Tea towels with scenes from London printed on them might be sold in tourist shops in London but be manufactured in India. If they sold for £2.50 in a London shop and cost 25p to import, then the current account would deteriorate by £2.25.

The impact on inflation is likely to be minimal. If anything, however, inflationary pressures are likely to be reduced. A fall in spending will lead to a fall in demand and so a fall in the rate of increase of prices.

(b) The long term might be defined as 'after 2007'. After this point, the WTTC predicted that tourism would return to normal. Hence, there are unlikely to be any significant long term effects on economic performance of the 2005 bombings. The WTTC points out that this assumes that UK authorities take appropriate action to reassure tourists and that no serious terrorist incident reoccurs. However, short term decisions might have a long term impact. For example, a hotel company might decide in 2006 not to build a hotel in London. This would then have a small but long term effect on hotel capacity in London in the long term. Equally, a foreign travel company might reduce the number of English tours it offers its customers in the short term, but fail to put these back in its brochures in the long term despite the fact that there might be demand for them. Such long term effects are difficult to predict and identify.

Question 4

(a) Four economic objectives mentioned in the 2007 Budget speech were

- inflation;
- growth;
- employment;
- environmental objectives.

(b) The Chancellor in his budget speech states that economic growth was 'sustained' and built on the 'foundation of the longest period of economic stability and sustained growth in our country's history'. He also stated that the 'British economy is today growing faster than all the other G7 countries'.

In terms of inflation, he stated that 'our forecast and the consensus of independent forecasts agree that looking ahead to 2008 and 2009 inflation will be on target'. He also mentions 'continued low inflation'.

However, on the environment, he talked about 'setting a framework for environmental action' and 'securing support for a strengthened European carbon trade scheme on the road to a global scheme'. This would suggest that there was plenty of initiatives towards creating policies which might affect environmental change but that existing schemes were not delivering the required impact to achieve the current and future objectives set by the government. Unless new policies were introduced, the government would fail to meet its targets.

Data question

Note: in Figure 8 there was a mistake in the first impression of the 5th edition. This has been corrected in reprints. The labels for the line have been reversed. Ireland had lower unemployment than the Czech Republic at the end of the period.

1. The performance of an economy can be measured in a number of different ways. Four such measures would be economic growth, unemployment, inflation and the current account on the balance of payments.

The economic performance of the Irish economy was arguably better than that of the Czech economy over the period 1994 to 2006. Economic growth was the same or higher in every year apart from 2005. On average, inflation was lower in the first half of the period, although it was higher in the second half of the period. Unemployment in Ireland was on a downward trend to 2001 whilst in the Czech Republic it rose. Admittedly, the unemployment rate was over three times as high at the start of the period in Ireland than in the Czech Republic, but by the end the unemployment rate in Ireland was nearly half what it was in the Czech Republic. Both countries saw an overall deterioration in their current account position, but Ireland had a better current account position than the Czech Republic throughout almost all the period.

2. One problem for Ireland identified in the data is a possible future lack of competitiveness. Lower wages in other EU countries, particularly in Eastern Europe, and worldwide such as in China, might encourage firms based in Ireland to close down their operations and move elsewhere. In the Czech Republic, a possible problem for the future is the continuing restructuring of its industry to be able to compete in the EU.

If firms relocated from Ireland to lower wage countries such as the Czech Republic and China, economic growth in Ireland would begin to slow. Unemployment would be likely to rise because of lower output whilst the current account position on the balance of payments could deteriorate if lower output meant less exports. But lower wages is not the only factor in determining the location of industry. Factors such as the skills and education of the workforce, transport costs, nearness to markets and infrastructure can also be important. In the data, it states that Ireland has invested heavily in education, building up the human capital of its workforce in recent times. Particularly where a highly skilled workforce is needed, Ireland may have a competitive advantage over, say, the Czech Republic. Key to Ireland's future success will be its ability to orientate its economy towards industries in which it has a comparative advantage.

For the Czech Republic, its future growth remains dependent too upon a continued restructuring of its economy towards industries in which it has a comparative advantage. With high unemployment, there is a danger that both the government and trade unions will attempt to preserve jobs in industries which are uncompetitive. The government may also be reluctant to give tax breaks and grants to foreign companies in the belief that this is too costly to the Czech tax payer. However, such policies are likely to increase the country's problems. The Czech Republic needs to be outward looking, attracting investment from foreign firms to create industries of the future rather than preserve industries of the past. Ireland's success has crucially been built upon foreign investment. The Czech Republic could learn from Ireland's success if it is to avoid a disappointing future economic performance.

23 The economic cycle

Data question

1. The economic cycle is the regular fluctuation in the level of economic activity around the productive potential of the economy. Figure 1 in the student's book illustrates the four phases of the cycle.

In the recovery phase, the economy is growing out of a recession. Unemployment might be falling as consumer spending, investment and GDP rises. Inflationary pressures might be relatively small as the economy approaches its long run trend level of output. The very start of the period shown in the data could be argued to be part of this stage of the cycle.

Equally, it could be argued that in 1987 the economy was already in boom, the top of the cycle when GDP is high, inflationary pressures are building up and spending is growing fast. However, in a boom, the economy is often growing at an unsustainable rate. In 1988 and 1989, GDP was still growing fast but inflationary pressures were apparent from the middle of 1988.

After a boom, the economy goes into a downturn. The downturn is apparent in the data in 1989 and 1990. Spending and GDP growth slows and, after a time lag, unemployment begins to rise. Inflation too might still be rising at the start of the downturn but eventually will begin to fall as it did in 1991.

Downturns are followed by recessions or depressions. There is no accepted definition of a recession but the UK government defines it as occurring when GDP falls in two successive quarters. The economy was arguably in recession between 1990 and 1992. Unemployment began to rise as consumer spending and investment fell. Inflation falls rapidly.

Recession is followed by recovery again. The data shows that the economy went into recovery from late 1992 with GDP beginning to rise again. At the start of the recovery phase, unemployment is still likely to be rising because unemployment is a lagged indicator in the cycle.

2. A demand side shock is a shock which affects aggregate demand. In the Lawson boom, the shock was caused by the government raising interest rates sharply and then holding them at a high level for several years. High interest rates lowered demand for consumer and investment goods. This then fed through to slowing growth of GDP and eventually pushed the economy into a recession.

24 The circular flow of income

Question 1

(a)

Figure 1

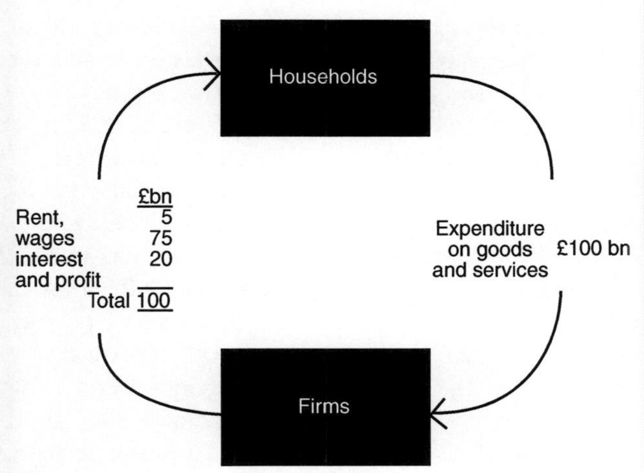

(b) On the income side, total income would equal £125 billion, made up of £100 billion in wages, £5 billion in rent and £20 billion in interest and profit. Expenditure on goods and services would now equal £125 billion.

Question 2

(a) Gross domestic product at market prices is the key measure of national income today. It is a measure of national income which includes the value of indirect taxes but does not include the value of net investment income from abroad.

Gross value added at basic prices is gross domestic product at market prices minus the value of indirect taxes plus the value of any subsidies. It does not include the value of net investment income from abroad.

Gross national income at market prices is gross domestic product at market prices plus the value of net investment income from abroad.

Net national income at market prices, is gross national income at market prices minus the value of depreciation of the nation's capital stock.

(b) The data support the view that changes in GDP at market prices broadly reflect changes in other measures of national income. In Figure 3 in the student's book, the four lines showing four different measures of national income broadly move in parallel over the period 1980 to 2006. There are some minor divergences, such as at the end of this period. However, these are relatively insignificant.

Question 3

(a) Governments need to collect two sets of statistics in order to calculate GNP per capita. First they need to collect GNP statistics. GNP could be measured using the output method, the income method or the expenditure method. Second, governments need to collect population statistics, for instance by conducting a census or updating census material through registers of births and deaths. A country like the USA with a GNP many times that of the UK has a broadly similar GNP per capita because its population is also much larger.

(b) (i) and **(ii)** Economists are particularly interested in using statistics to test hypotheses and build economic models of the economy. An economist might postulate that high investment leads to high per capita incomes. One way of testing this is to correlate the two sets of statistics for different economies. In Figure 3 in the student's book, for instance, can the difference in GNP per capita between the UK and the USA be accounted for by past investment performance?

Both economists and government are interested in making policy recommendations based upon economic evidence. For instance, if it were decided to transfer resources from rich to poorer nations, which countries should gain and lose from this transfer? GNP per capita figures would be crucial in making any recommendations. Economists and governments are also interested in making judgments about economic welfare. GNP per capita figures are an important measure of living standards and economic welfare in society. The GNP per capita figures in Figure 3 of the student's book show, for example, that the average Norwegian has a much higher income than the average citizen of Malawi or Madagascar.

Question 4

(a) There is an incentive for workers to work in the hidden economy because workers can then avoid paying taxes on their income. In the UK, there are two taxes on income gained through employment. One is income tax and the other is National Insurance contributions. In the formal economy, these are deducted from workers' wages through the PAYE system by employers. In contrast, the self employed have to fill in a tax return each year declaring their income. The temptation for self employed workers is then not to declare all of their earnings to the tax authorities and so save themselves tax.

(b) Workers such as painters and decorators are far more likely to be self employed than teachers or civil servants. They therefore have much greater opportunities to evade tax. A gardener, for example, may receive much of her income in cash from clients and it is therefore difficult for the Inland Revenue to trace how much income she is earning. A teacher, in contrast, will be paid a salary by an employer. The teacher may do some work, such as private tuition, in the hidden economy. However, unlike the gardener, this will be only a fraction of the teacher's income.

(c) A more flexible workforce is likely to increase the size of the black economy. Part time, casual and self employed workers all have far greater opportunities to defraud the Inland Revenue than full time employees. Casual workers, for instance, may be paid cash in hand with the employer avoiding paying employers' National Insurance contributions and maybe other taxes on the contract like VAT. The self employed, as explained above, have greater opportunities for working in the hidden economy than employees.

Question 5

(a)(i)(ii)

Table 1

Year	Nominal GDP per head of the population, £	Real GDP per head of population at 2006 prices
1948	246	6 150
1958	447	7 210
1968	788	9 381
1978	2 991	11 869
1988	8 272	15 319
1998	14 798	18 002
2006	21 452	21 452

The value of nominal GDP per head is calculated by dividing nominal GDP by the population. It should be remembered in Table 2 in the student's book that the former is in billions whereas the latter is in millions.

The value of real GDP per head at 2006 prices can be found be taking the nominal GDP per head already calculated, and multiplying it by the ratio of prices in 2006 to prices in the other year. For instance, the 1948 value of real GDP per head is £246 (nominal GDP per head) × 100 ÷ 4.0 (the ratio of the price level in 2006 to 1948).

(b) The data show that real GDP per head has increased 3.5 times in the 58 year period 1948-2006. This increase reflects the enormous growth in material well being for most of the UK population over that period. Goods which were considered completely beyond the reach of most people are now commonplace luxuries. At the same time, it must be remembered that GDP per head, whilst taking into account changes in prices and changes in population, does not tell the economist about other factors which affect living standards. For instance, the quality of many goods has increased over time. A car today is far more reliable than a car made over 40 years ago, but this cannot be deduced from GDP figures. On the negative side, it can be argued that pollution has considerably increased over the past 50 years leading to negative externalities which are not measured by GDP. The data tell us nothing about how income was distributed. Some people may have become worse off over the period despite substantial rises in average incomes. The data also say nothing about the proportion of income devoted to defence and investment, both of which reduce resources available for consumption.

Data question

Living standards

Life is not fair. If you are born today in Ethiopia in East Africa, you will almost certainly be very poor in comparison with others in the rest of the world. If you were born in the USA, you stand a reasonable chance of enjoying one of the highest standards of living in the world.

There are many ways in which the standard of living of an individual in a country can be measured. Economists tend to use GNP per capita. GNP, or Gross National Product, is a measure of the income generated by the whole economy. Dividing it by the number in the population gives a measure of average income per person. In Tanzania, this is $730 per year measured at purchasing power parity rates. In the USA, it is over 50 times larger at $41 950. In between these two extremes, there is a wide range of incomes. A poorly developed country like the Czech Republic has a per capita income of $20 140. For a richer European country like the UK it is $32 690. For a middle income Third World country like Colombia, it is $7 420.

National income statistics provide a broad measure of living standards. It is very difficult, for instance, for a country with a low GNP per capital to provide good health care or education for its citizens. Hence, a poor country like Tanzania is characterised by low life expectancy, high levels of malnutrition and high levels of adult illiteracy. Taking three Third World countries with different incomes, there is a correlation for Tanzania (GNP per head $730), Indonesia (GNP per head $3 720) and Colombia (GNP per head $7 420) between GNP per capita and adult illiteracy rates, and GNP per capita and under 5 mortality rates. All three countries have poorer health and education indicators than a poor First World country like the Czech Republic. However, once countries have reached the levels of income achieved by New Zealand, the UK or the USA, for instance, good health provision and education are determined more by spending priorities and national policies than by differences in GNP.

National income is also well correlated with other measures of the standard of living. For instance, citizens of Third World countries like Tanzania or Indonesia are unlikely to have the Internet in their homes whilst a significant minority do not have access to safe water or sanitation. The number of fixed line and mobile phone subscribers per 1000 of the population is also correlated to national income.

However, national income as a measure of living standards does have its limitations. On the environmental front, poor countries consume far fewer resources than a country like the USA. For example, electric power consumption in the United States per head of the population is 233 times that of Tanzania. Much of this electricity production will have come from burning coal, a non-renewable resource. Rich countries could be argued to be enjoying a high standard of living now but at the expense of future generations.

It is also true that the poorest citizens of many First World countries like the United States are far poorer than the richest citizens of even the poorest Third World countries like Tanzania. The gap between rich and poor varies from country to country. The standard of living of the average citizen of a country can be very different to the richest and the poorest.

Defence spending can impact on living standards. There is no correlation between the percentage of GDP spent on defence and national income per head. Pakistan, a poor country, spends 3.3 per cent of its GNP on defence, whilst New Zealand, a rich country, only spends 1.0 per cent. The heavier the defence spending, the less is available for consumption and investment. Hence, the lower the level of defence spending, the higher the standard of living, all other things being equal.

National income per capita, then, is a good rough and ready measure of differences in living standards between countries. However, countries with broadly similar GDPs per capita can vary considerably in terms of living standards depending upon a range of factors such as the distribution of spending and income and the resources devoted to the environment.

25 Consumption and saving

Question 1

(a) Table 1 in the student's book shows that consumption and disposable income have broadly increased over time. What is more, there is a strong correlation between increases in consumption and increases in income, such that consumption for most of the period has only been a little less than income.

(b) (i)

Table 3

	APC	MPC
1966	0.96	0.74
1976	0.95	-1.08
1986	0.97	1.45
1996	0.93	1.49
2006	0.99	1.86

(ii) For a household, saving is the difference between disposable income and consumption. In each of the years, consumption was less than disposable income. Hence, households added to their stock of savings by saving a proportion of their disposable income. The proportion saved was highest in 1996 when the APC was at its lowest.

Question 2

One way in which the housing market can affect consumption levels is through the wealth effect. If house prices rise, homeowners become wealthier. They are then likely to spend part of that increased wealth on goods and services.

A second way is through housing turnover. When homeowners move house, they tend to buy consumer durables such as carpets and curtains and new furniture for their new house. A rise in housing turnover then increases such spending whilst a fall decreases consumer spending.

A third way is through equity release or mortgage equity withdrawal. When buying a new house, a homeowner may borrow more than they need to finance the purchase. This extra money is then spent. Equally, homeowners many remortgage their property, increasing their debt but the money borrowed is then spent.

Question 3

(a) The expenditure data shown in Figure 2 in the student's book shows that real spending on housing, water, electricity, gas and other fuels rose a little between 1988 and 1990 before falling in 1991 and 1992. Then it broadly increased over the period 1988 to 2007. Spending on food and non-alcoholic beverages was broadly flat between 1988 and 1992 but has since been slowly rising. In contrast, spending on durable goods fell in the late 1980s and early 1990s and then rose to 2007. Spending on durable goods has seen the fastest increase over the whole period more than doubling from £10 billion to £26 billion at 2003 prices. In contrast, expenditure on housing, water, electricity, gas and other fuels only increased from £28 billion to £33 billion and expenditure on food and non-alcoholic beverages increases from £13 billion to £17.5 billion.

Interest rates rose sharply from 7.5 to 15 per cent over the period 1989-90, before falling to nearly 5 per cent in 1994. Over the rest of the period 1995 to 2007, interest rates have broadly remained the same but have fluctuated within the range 3.75 per cent to 7.75 per cent.

(b) Increased interest rates should lead to a downward movement in spending. This is because the cost of borrowing to finance consumption increases. It also increases mortgage repayments, which leaves less money to spend on other goods and services. Finally, increased interest rates may have an effect on household wealth because they tend to dampen activity in the housing market and stock prices fall. With reduced wealth, consumers will spend less.

The data indicate that durable goods do seem to have been affected by interest rates. The fall in spending on consumer durables from their peak in 1989 coincided with very large increases in interest rates. Large cuts in interest rates in 1991 and 1992 then helped to increase spending on durables from 1992. However, the small changes in interest rates from 1994 do not seem to have had much effect on the growth of spending on consumer durables.

Interest rates seem to have little impact on consumption of food and non-alcoholic beverages. This is what would be expected since these items are unlikely to be bought on credit. They are also considered necessities by households and therefore are less likely to be affected by falls in income after mortgage payments or by changes in wealth.

Equally spending on housing, water, electricity, gas and other fuels appears to be little affected by changes in interest rates. This might seem surprising given that the cost of most mortgages changes as interest rates change. However, the housing component of final expenditure does not include mortgage payments. Instead, the value of expenditure on owner occupied housing is the imputed rent on that housing. This does not change very much with interest rates. Expenditure on housing also includes rents paid by tenants to landlords.

It can therefore be seen that interest rates can play an important role in affecting some items of consumption expenditure but not others. Interest rates are therefore only a weak determinant of consumption expenditure.

Question 4

Figure 2 in the student's book shows that there will be a small fall in the population aged 0-19 between 2003 and 2026. The population aged 20 to 59, who will form most of the working population, will also see a small fall. However, the numbers of retired people will increase throughout the period.

These demographic changes are likely to have significant effects on consumption and saving. People aged 20 to 44 tend to save very little, and often accumulate substantial debts, such as when houses are purchased. Falling numbers of people in this age bracket are therefore likely to reduce consumption in the economy.

Equally, 45-59 year olds are the economy's major savers. The numbers in the age bracket are predicted to remain roughly constant and so savings should be maintained.

Those over 60 tend to draw on their savings to finance consumption. Growing numbers of senior citizens should therefore increase consumption.

The question facing policy makers is how the increased consumption from those aged 60 and over will be paid for when there will be little if any extra saving in the economy from those aged 20 to 59.

Data question

THE DETERMINANTS OF SAVING

Trends in saving since 1975

The level of saving in the economy, the difference between households' disposable income and their final expenditure, has grown over time as incomes have risen. This growth has not been even, however, and this is reflected in a changing average propensity to save. Over the whole period 1975 to 2006, the broad trend in the APS has been downwards. It started the period in 1975 at approximately 0.09 and ended the period in 2006 at 0.042. However, there have been considerable fluctuations in the APS with two peaks being experienced in 1980 and 1992 at 0.12 and 0.11 respectively.

Factors affecting saving

There is a number of factors which affect saving. One important determinant is the level of income. The higher the level of personal disposable income, the higher the level of saving. Higher interest rates encourage saving because they provide a higher rate of return. Rising inflation tends to increase saving because households see the real value of their wealth being eroded by inflation and hence increase their savings to compensate for this. Unemployment tends to increase savings because households become more reluctant to spend money, particularly on consumer durables. They also save to safeguard against a drop in income resulting from unemployment. The composition of households may affect saving too. 40-60 year olds tend to be the largest savers in the economy because they have often paid off most of their mortgage and their commitments to their children disappear whilst their incomes are at their highest. The larger the proportion of these households in the economy, the higher will be the average propensity to save.

Case study 1975-2006

The 1970s and early 1980s were difficult economic times. As Figure 4 in the student's book shows, real household disposable income stagnated in the mid 1970s and early 1980s. Inflation was at record levels. When inflation is high, savings are likely to be high too partly because households need to rebuild the real value of their stock of savings. But stagnant income and inflation also produces uncertainty. When times are uncertain, consumers put off buying consumer durables on credit and choose to save instead. The same scenario of rising inflation combined with a recession in the late 1980s and early 1990s helped increase the APS at the time.

House prices too had an effect on saving. The difficult times of the second half of the 1970s, early 1980s and late 1980s into the early 1990s coincided with falling or stagnant house prices. This dented consumer confidence and also meant that a major component of consumer wealth was either declining or not increasing. A low APC tended to coincide with periods when house prices were rising. For example, the fall in the APS from the mid-1990s occurred as house prices took off.

Levels of interest rates are correlated with savings. The mid 1970s, the early 1980s and the late 1980s were all periods of high interest rates and high levels of saving. High interest rates encourage households to save. But equally they tend to be associated with high levels of inflation. Both can provide a causal link between savings and interest rates.

26 Investment

Question 1

The photograph shows the interior of a branch of a bank in the area where customers carry out their bank transactions.

(a) There are statement machines, cash dispensers and rapid deposit machines or paying in machines, which are at the back of the area on the photograph. On the right are reception windows where customers can also make deposits and payments. Bank employees at these desks operate computer terminals to handle the transactions of customers. There is display information which might contains details of mortgages, accounts, loans and interest rates. The building in which the bank is situated is also an example of physical capital. These areas also often have interview rooms attached, which is an example of past investment.

(b) The people in the photograph are examples of human capital. The customers shown standing in the queue, for instance, will have received education at a school, college or university and will have been further trained by their employer.

(c) The customers of the bank are likely at the moment or at other times to deposit money with the bank. This is an example of saving.

(d) All the physical capital shown is depreciating minute by minute. In ten years' time, almost all the capital shown in the photograph will have been replaced, whilst the building itself will need continuous maintenance.

Question 2

(a) High interest rates are likely to lead to lower investment. In Figure 1, interest rates of r1 will lead to investment of OA. If, however, interest rates were lower at r_2, then investment would be higher at OB. The high rates of interest in the UK therefore put UK firms at a disadvantage compared to overseas competitors because they have to pay more for funds to finance investment. This discourages UK firms from borrowing and therefore investing.

Figure 1

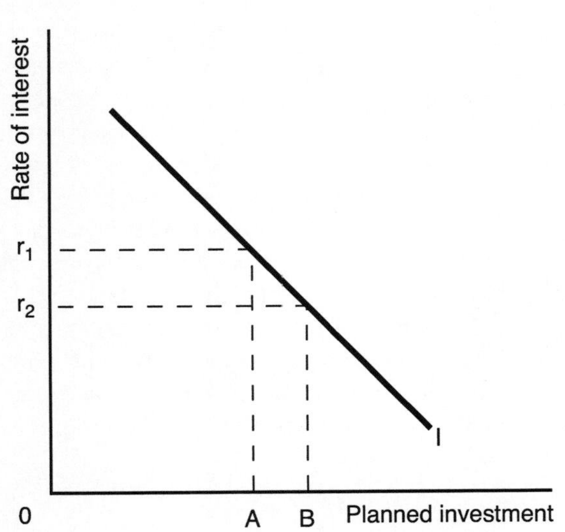

(b) If Britain were to join the euro, interest rates in the UK would come into line with interest rates in the rest of the eurozone. This is because interest rates are set by the European Central Bank in the eurozone and not by the individual central banks of each country. If UK rates have tended to be above those in the rest of Europe, joining the euro would lead to a fall in UK interest rates. This would encourage investment in the UK as can be seen from Figure 1.

Question 3

(a) A rise in the real prices of commercial property means that the cost of one type of capital good has risen. This means that the expected rate of return on investment projects will tend to decline. For instance, if a company was considering expanding into new premises, a rise in property price might force it to shelve its plans because the rate of return would be too low. Hence, the investment schedule will shift from I_1 to I_2 in Figure 2.

Figure 2

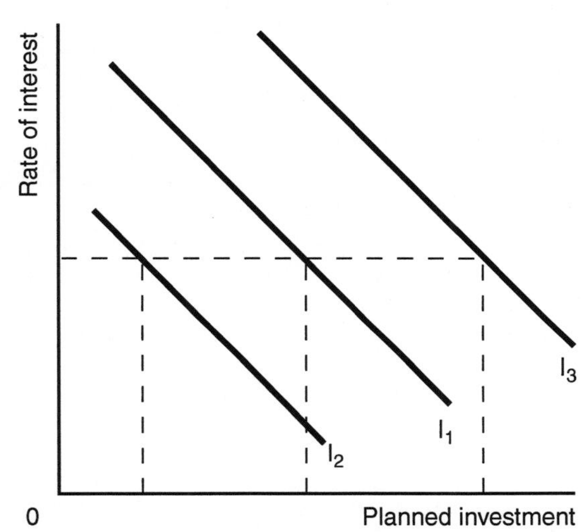

(b) A government subsidy to industry for the introduction of micro computers will increase the rate of return on investment projects involving micro computers. Hence, investment will rise, shown by a shift in the investment schedule from I_1 to I_1 in Figure 2.

(c) A booming economy is likely to increase the rate of return on investment. Firms will sell more goods than expected, which will tend to increase their profitability. Moreover, a booming economy raises business expectations about the future, making firms more likely to invest. Hence, the investment schedule will shift to the right, from I_1 to I_1 in Figure 2

(d) A fall in the price of computers and computer aided tools reduces the price of capital. Hence, the rate of return on investment projects requiring computer capital will rise. The investment schedule will then shift to the right, from I_1 to I_3 in Figure 2.

(e) A crash on the New York Stock Exchange will damage consumer and business confidence. Firms will now feel more pessimistic about the future and there will be a reduction in the expected rate of return on investment projects. The investment schedule will shift to the left in Figure 2 from I_1 to I_2.

Question 4

(a) Calculations of figures in brackets are rounded to two significant figures. Other calculations may give slightly different answers.

Year 1 I = 2 x (£105m - £100m) = £10m
Year 2 I = 2 x (£110.25m - £105m) = £10.5m
Year 3 I = 2 x (£115.76m - £110.25m) = £11.02m
Year 4 I = 2 x (£121.55m - £115.76m) = £11.58m
Year 5 I = 2 x (£127.63m - £121.55m) = £12.16m

(b) (i)

Year 1 I = 2 x (£110m - £100m) = £20m
Year 2 I = 2 x (£121m - £110m) = £22m
Year 3 I = 2 x (£133.10m - £121m) = £24.2m
Year 4 I = 2 x (£146.41m - £133.10m) = £26.62m
Year 5 I = 2 x (£161.05m - £146.41m) = £29.28m

(ii)

Year 1 I = 2 x (£102.5m - £100m) = £5m
Year 2 I = 2 x (£105.06m - £102.5m) = £5.13m
Year 3 I = 2 x (£107.69m - £105.06m) = £5.26m
Year 4 I = 2 x (£110.38m - £107.69m) = £5.38m
Year 5 I = 2 x (£113.14m - £110.39m) = £5.50m

Data question

Note: in the first impression of the 5th edition there is a misprint. This has been corrected in reprints. Question 1 and 2(b) should refer to 2007 not 2004.

1. Figure 4 in the student's book shows that investment in British manufacturing industry has been cyclical. with three peaks in 1990, 1998 and 2006-07. The trend in investment in real terms, however, has been flat with investment at the end of the period shown in 2007 being no higher than it was at the start of the period in 1987.

In the Lawson boom of 1987-88, when GDP rose particularly fast, so too did investment. When the economy began to slow down in 1989 and 1990, investment carried on booming, reaching peaks of around £4.5 billion per quarter. However, investment began to fall in mid-1990 and carried on falling till the end of 1993 when it reached a low of £3.3 billion per quarter. During this time, the economy went into a deep recession. Recovery began in late 1993 and investment followed, peaking in 1998 at £5.1 billion per quarter. Between 1998 and 2003, investment fell back reaching a low of £3.4 billion per quarter in 2004 before slightly recovering again.

2. One factor which affects investment is the rate of interest. If rates of interest are very high, the opportunity cost of investment - putting money into bonds and bank deposit accounts - is very high. Moreover, investment projects which are financed from borrowed funds carrying these high rates of interest have to be much more profitable than if interest rates are low. The very high interest rates, shown by base rates in Figure 5 in the student's book, of the late 1980s certainly must have discouraged investment and led to the sharp fall in investment between 1990 and 1993. Equally, the fall in interest rates from 1990 to 1993 will have eventually encouraged firms to invest. Relatively low interest rates in the period between 1993 and 1998 will have helped sustain the boom in investment in that period although they fail to explain why investment fell significantly from 1998.

Much of British manufacturing investment is financed from the retained profits of companies. It would therefore seem plausible to argue that when company profits are high, investment will tend to be high. When company profits are low, firms will have less to retain and will therefore cut back on their investment. The data give some support to this hypothesis. There was a sharp increase in company profits from 1991 to 1997 after which company profits fell. This mirrored what happened to investment with investment increasing between 1993 and 1998 before falling back.

As has already been described in (1.), investment fluctuates with the trade cycle. When the economy is doing well, investment tends to rise. When the economy goes into recession, investment tends to fall. The accelerator theory suggests that investment and past changes in income are linked through capital-output ratios, the amount of capital needed to produce a given level of output. If income is rising particularly fast as in the Lawson boom of the late 1980s and there is a positive output gap, investment will need to be high in order to produce the higher level of output. In a recession, with a negative output gap, investment will be low because there is less need for capital and hence the fall in investment spending in the recession of 1990-92. When the economy began to pick up from 1993, the need for investment spending re-emerged and hence investment rose. However, the fall in manufacturing investment cannot be explained particularly well by output gap figures after 1998.

Perhaps of more significance is the relationship between the output of manufacturing industry and manufacturing investment. Between 1987 and 1998, manufacturing output and manufacturing investment were positively correlated. Rises in manufacturing output coincided with rises in investment and vice versa. Between 1998 and 2007, manufacturing output broadly stagnated and this coincided first with a fall in manufacturing investment to 2004. If output is stagnant, the need for new investment will be less initially because new investment is not needed to provide extra output. By 2004, however, manufacturing investment began to pick up again possibly because of the slight upturn in manufacturing output at the time and possibly because the need for replacement investment was greater.

The data give no evidence about other possible causes of investment such as the cost of capital goods, technological change, expectations and government policy.

3. Investment is determined by a number of different factors. As already explained, profitability, interest rates and changes in income can all help explain investment in the late 1980s and 1990s.

However, many of the determinants of investment are interlinked through the trade cycle. Recessions are characterised by, and can be caused by, high interest rates. So in a recession firms are likely to invest less because interest rates are high and because the rate of return on investment as measured by profits tends to fall. Similarly, recovery tends to be marked by improved investment opportunities. So the timing of the trade cycle is probably the most important macro-economic factor which firms should take into account when making investment decisions. On the other hand, firms need to recognise that their orders and their business may flourish despite a recession. Equally they may find trading conditions difficult despite a boom. So making investment decisions remains a difficult process and is likely to be influenced by many factors.

27 Government spending, exports and imports

Question 1

(a) One reason for the increase in government spending is that the government wishes to provide more goods and services. In the data, it states that the Labour government has increased spending on health and education. Another reason is to boost demand in the economy. This creates jobs and reduces unemployment.

(b) An increase in the budget deficit could occur for a number of reasons. In the case of the Labour government from 2001-2007, it occurred because government spending rose faster than taxation. But equally government spending could rise when taxes fall. Or government spending and taxes could both fall but government spending falls less fast than taxes.

Government spending and taxes are injections to and withdrawals from the circular flow of income. So if, for example, government spending, an injection, rises by £20 billion into the circular flow and taxation, a withdrawal, rises by £15 billion, then there is a net injection of £5 billion. Income will therefore rise by at least £5 billion. There could be a larger increase if there is a net multiplier effect.

Data question

1. One reason why DEK is a successful exporter is that it is price competitive. Use of automation keeps down the cost of labour in the overall cost. As a result, its UK plant in Weymouth has only slightly higher costs than its Chinese plant despite paying much higher wages. Another reason is that it has cutting edge technology which allows it to produce a large number of variants of machines. Products can be adapted to the customer's needs. Not only does technology allow it to be a specialist producer but also order times are very short. So a customer ordering a machine can receive it two weeks later.

2. UK exporters can be successful against a much lower labour cost producer like China in future if it maintains its technological lead. Technology may allow it to remain price competitive because the technology allows labour to be a small part of the total cost. Or technology can allow it to supply products to customers which they can't buy from any Chinese manufacturer.

However, Chinese manufacturers are renowned for gaining technology from Western companies operating in China. They will secure the best of today's technology over time. Therefore, unless UK exporters like DEK retain their technological lead, they will find themselves overtaken by the Chinese. To remain successful exporters, companies like DEK must continue to invest in developing new technologies and staying ahead of their rivals.

28 Aggregate demand

Question 1

Economic theory suggests that the aggregate demand (AD) curve is downward sloping. As the price level rises, all other things being equal, aggregate demand in the economy will fall. This is the phenomenon illustrated in each of the three examples in the text. In all three cases, the rise in inflation was accompanied by historically high levels of interest rates. This reduced both consumption and investment which in turn reduced GDP.

Question 2

(a) The increase in real investment expenditure between 2000 and 2005 will have led to an increase in aggregate expenditure and therefore aggregate output. The aggregate demand (AD) curve will have shifted to the right, from AD_1 to AD_2 in Figure 1.

(b) The large rise in interest rates between May 1987 and October 1989 will have led to a fall both in consumption and investment spending. This will have led to a fall in aggregate demand, shown by a shift to the left in the AD curve from AD_1 to AD_3 in Figure 1.

(c) The large cuts in taxes in the Lawson Budget of 1987 will have led to an increase in consumption expenditure as households' disposable incomes rose. This in turn will have led to an increase in aggregate expenditure and therefore output. The AD curve will then have shifted to the right, from AD_1 to AD_2 in Figure 1.

(d) The 50 per cent fall in London stock market prices between December 1999 and January 2003 led to a substantial fall in wealth for a minority of individuals and businesses. This will have led to a fall in consumption, shifting the aggregate demand curve to the left from AD_1 to AD_3 in Figure 33.1.

Figure 1

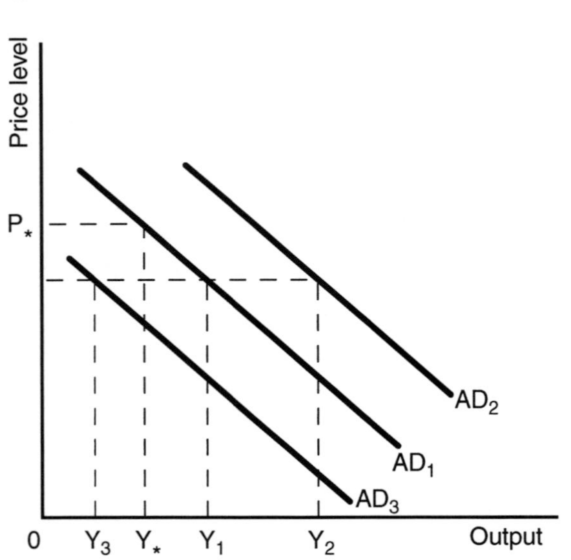

(e) The fall in the savings ratio between 1992 and 2004 will have been mirrored by a rise in the consumption ratio. Aggregate demand and output will have risen. Hence the AD curve will have shifted to the right, from AD_1 to AD_2 In Figure 1.

(f) The increase in planned public expenditure by the Labour government between 2000 and 2007 on education and healthcare will have led to a rise in aggregate expenditure and therefore aggregate output. The AD curve will therefore have shifted to the right, from AD_1 to AD_2 in Figure 1.

(g) The more than 25 per cent rise in the sterling exchange rate between 1996 and 2000 will have led to an fall in exports and a rise in imports. This is because the UK became less competitive compared to its international trading partners as a result of the appreciation of the currency. Lower exports and higher imports will have reduced aggregate demand. Hence the AD curve will have shifted to the left, from AD_1 to AD_3 in Figure 1.

Question 3

The proposed £150 million investment in the development scheme at Bo'ness would have a multiplier effect throughout the local and national economies. This is because the new spending by ING Real East, a property development company, would create further spending in the economy. For instance, the money spent on a new marina, harbour front apartments and townhouses, a hotel and waterside shops, restaurants, cafes and bars would initially go to construction companies. They would pay their workers and their suppliers for goods and services rendered. They would also pay their shareholders or owners a share of any profits made on the Ford contracts. This money would then be spent, further creating income, and further moving round the circular flow of income. Although much of the initial benefit might be concentrated in the local economy, the spending would flow out to the whole economy eventually.

Data question

1. Aggregate demand is the total of all demand or expenditure in the economy at any given price. So it is the total of consumption, investment, government spending and the difference between exports and imports.

2. A measure of aggregate demand is GDP at market prices, shown in Figure 6 in the student's book. GDP rose continuously throughout the period 2000-2007 because growth in GDP was positive. Growth fluctuated over the period between a high of 4.3 per cent in the first two quarters of 2000 and lows of 1.6 per cent in the first quarter of 2001 and the second quarter of 2005.

The components of aggregate demand, shown in Figure 6 in the student's book, performed differently during this period. Consumer spending grew in the range 1 per cent to 6 per cent per quarter. There were sharp changes in investment spending, growing at between - 2 per cent and + 10 per cent a quarter. There were also sharp fluctuations in levels of government spending ranging from 1 per cent to 5.5 per cent per quarter. Import and export growth slowed after 2000, rose sharply in 2005-06 before falling sharply in 2006-2007. Throughout much of the period 2000-2007 import growth was greater than export growth.

3. Figures 8 to 12 in the student's book show factors which might have affected the level of aggregate demand. Figure 8 shows short term interest rates. The relatively high interest rates in 2000 will have had a negative influence on both consumption and investment spending. The fall in interest rates to 2003 will then have stimulated consumption and investment whilst the subsequent rise from 2003 will have reduced spending. Bank base rate is positively correlated with growth in GDP at market prices. When growth in GDP was high, so too were interest rates and vice versa. This is the opposite of what might be expected given that high interest rates should dampen spending. However, the Bank of England which controls bank base rate was deliberately attempting to reduce high growth in GDP and boost low growth as part of its inflation policy. Without such intervention, the range of growth of consumer expenditure and investment might have been much larger.

Inflation, shown in Figure 9, was relatively low throughout the period. It is therefore unlikely to have had much impact on any component of aggregate demand.

The exchange rate, shown in Figure 10, should have had some effect on exports and imports. The exchange rate index of the pound averaged 100.4 over the period 2000-2007, for most of the time fluctuating within a fairly narrow range. There was a temporary sharp fall in the value in 2003 and a rise in the value of the pound in 2006-2007. Falls in the value of the pound should have boosted exports and led to fewer imports and vice versa. However, it is difficult to see any trend in actual export and import values shown in Figure 6 in the student's book. This suggests that other factors apart from the exchange rate were more important in determining these variables.

Unemployment, shown in Figure 11, fell between 2000 and 2004 before rising again in 2005-2007. Unemployment reduces consumer confidence and the rise in unemployment between 2001 and 2002 might have been one factor in explaining the fall in the rate of growth of consumer expenditure in those years. However, the change in unemployment was relatively small over the whole period and therefore it probably had little effect on overall aggregate demand.

Figure 12 shows changes in average house prices. Of the components of aggregate demand, consumption is the most affected by changes in house prices. If they rise particularly fast, households become wealthier and therefore they tend to spend more money. Housing booms also encourage people to move houses more often and each house move generates extra consumption expenditure in itself. 2000-2007 saw a sustained increase in house prices, with a peak of 25 per cent occurring in the last quarter of 2002. These increases in house prices will have been one of the factors holding up the growth in consumer spending over the period.

4. The UK experienced a mild downturn between 2001 and 2002 with quarterly growth in GDP falling from a high of 4.3 per cent in 2000 to a low of 1.6 per cent in 2002. If this was mainly due to the downturn in the world economy, this would be reflected in lower exports. Figure 6 in the student's book indeed shows that there was a substantial fall in growth of exports in 2001. In the last quarter of 2001 and the first quarter of 2002, exports actually fell. However, it is the difference between exports and imports which contributes towards aggregate demand. Growth in imports too fell at this time although not by as much as exports. Therefore, the trade balance, X - M, must have had some deflationary impact on aggregate demand.

Exports minus imports is a relatively small component of aggregate demand. It is difficult to see, however, from the data what else could have caused the weakening of GDP growth. Growth in consumer expenditure in 2001 was actually increasing whilst GDP growth was falling. Then when GDP growth picked up again in 2002, growth in consumer spending began to fall. The overall trend in government spending in these two years was upward. Investment fell in 2001, perhaps due to a loss of confidence because of the international slowdown, but recovered sharply in 2002.

Overall, the downturn in the world economy was probably the major factor in determining slower economic growth in 2001-2002.

29 Aggregate supply

Question 1

(a) Assuming that the prices of all factor inputs were fixed, a rise in real GDP in 1988 will have led to an increase in short run aggregate supply. In Figure 1, this is is shown by a movement along the SRAS curve. With real national output increasing from OA to OB, the price level will have increased from OE to OF.

(b) Assuming that the prices of all factor inputs were fixed, a fall in real GDP in 1991 will have led to a fall in short run aggregate supply. In Figure 2, this is is shown by a movement along the SRAS curve. With real national output falling from OA to OB, the price level will have fallen from OE to OF.

Question 2

(a) If real national output in the 2nd quarter of 1992 was the same as in the fourth quarter of 1988, but average prices had increased 27 per cent, there will have been a movement up the vertical long run aggregate supply curve. Real national output has not changed but the price level has increased. This is shown in Figure 3. Real national output remains the same at OA but the price level has increased from OB to OC.

(b) In 2004-2005, the price of crude oil approximately doubled. This is likely to have led to an increase in the price level but the long run aggregate supply curve will not have shifted. In Figure 3, the price level has increased from OB to OC, but output is unchanged at OA. An alternative answer would be to argue that the rise in crude oil prices led to some capital equipment, such as oil fired boilers, being scrapped earlier than would have been the case. This will have reduced the productive potential of the economy, shifting the LRAS curve back and to the left.

(c) A rise in money earnings between 2000 and 2004 will not in itself have led to a growth in productive potential in the economy. So the LRAS curve will not shift. However, there will be a movement up the the LRAS curve because higher wages is likely to have fed through to higher prices. So in

Figure 1

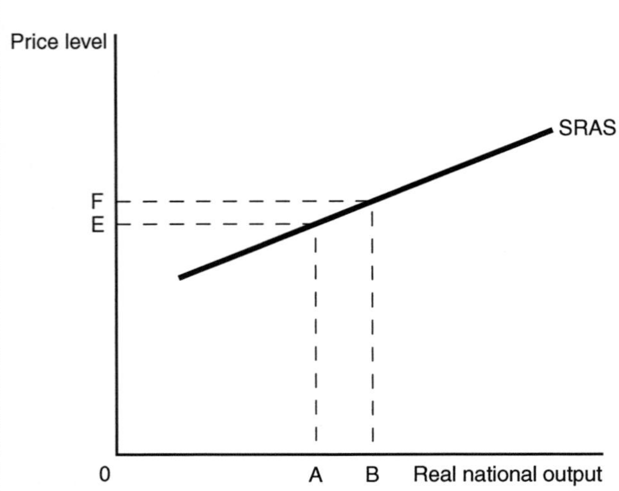

Figure 2

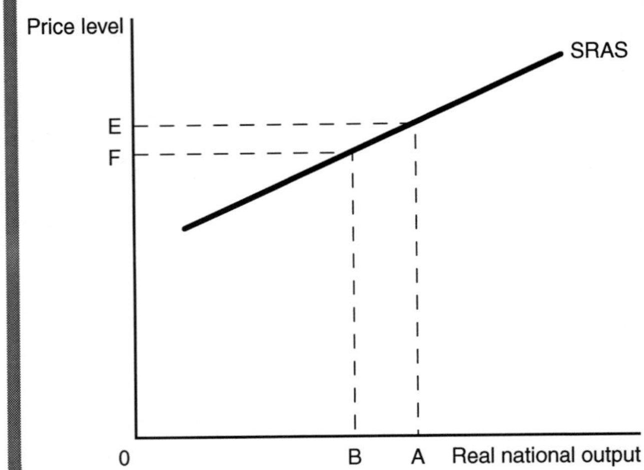

Figure 3

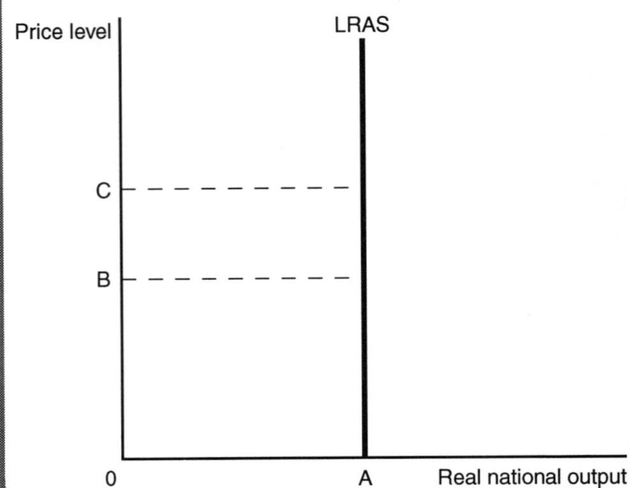

Figure 4

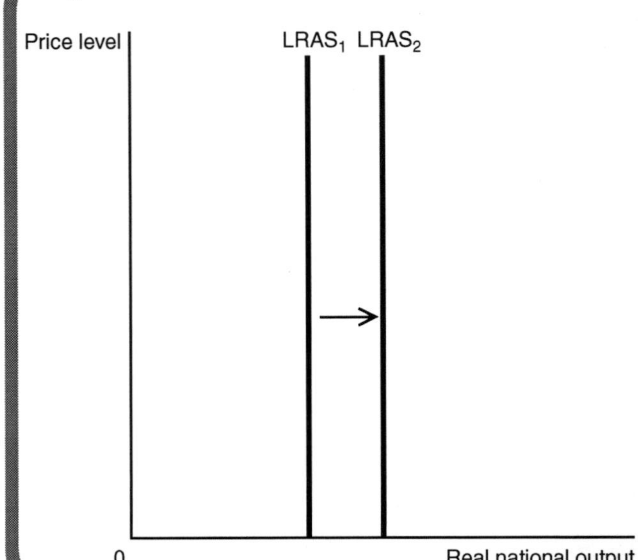

Figure 3, the price level will increase from OB to OC.

Question 3

(a) The economy was operating on its long run aggregate supply curve when the output gap was zero. Hence, the years when the output gap was zero for at least quarter were 1973, 1974, 1975, 1976, 1977, 1978, 1979, 1986, 1991, 1997, 1999, 2001, 2004, 2005 and 2007.

(b) Over time, the LRAS curve for the UK economy is shifting outwards at around its long term trend rate of growth of 2.25 per cent. Deviations from this trend rate of growth are shown by positive and negative output gaps. However, the existence of an output gap does not mean that the productive potential of the economy is not increasing. It simply means that actual output is different from potential output. Therefore the LRAS curve will have been shifting to the right between the years when actual output and potential output were equal. This is shown in Figure 4.

(c) In these years, damage was done to factor inputs. For example, factories and buildings were closed and demolished even though they had potential for further use. Workers became long term unemployed and suffered from deskilling. This could have resulted in a fall in long run aggregate supply in those years, shifting the LRAS to the left as shown in Figure 5.

Figure 5

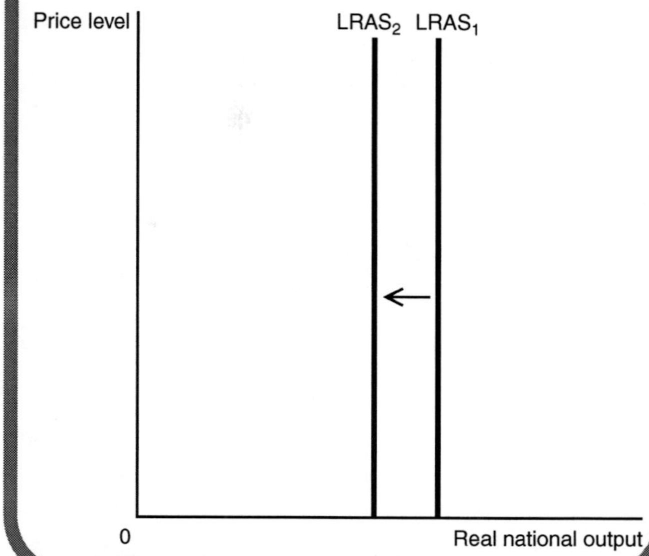

Question 4

(a) (i) The National Minimum Wage (NMW) might prevent the labour market from clearing. This is because the NMW might be set at too high a level for the demand for labour to equal its supply. In Figure 6, the equilibrium wage is OA. But the NMW is above this minimum wage at OB. Hence, unemployment of GH arises.

(ii) The National Minimum Wage sets a floor to wages. It could therefore be argued that this sets a floor to prices since wage costs are arguably the most important factor in determining prices in the economy. If there is unemployment, wages cannot fall below the NMW and so prices cannot fall further to clear the market. Hence, the long run aggregate supply curve is not vertical but is the shape shown in Figure 7. The effect of the minimum wage is shown by the horizontal part of the curve.

(b) The data would suggest that the NMW is set at too low a level to have much impact on the labour market. The data states that 'despite NMW increases running ahead of both inflation and average earnings over the past three years, there has been no negative employment effect.' This would suggest that the LRAS curve is in fact vertical. Not everyone agrees with this. The British Retail Consortium argued that the increase in the NMW in October 2006 would lead to 35 000 job losses, an indication that the labour market would not clear at the higher NMW. However, the British Retail Consortium have a vested interest in arguing for lower pay since lower pay could increase their profits. Until there is firm evidence that the NMW is causing unemployment, their views should be treated with caution.

Figure 6

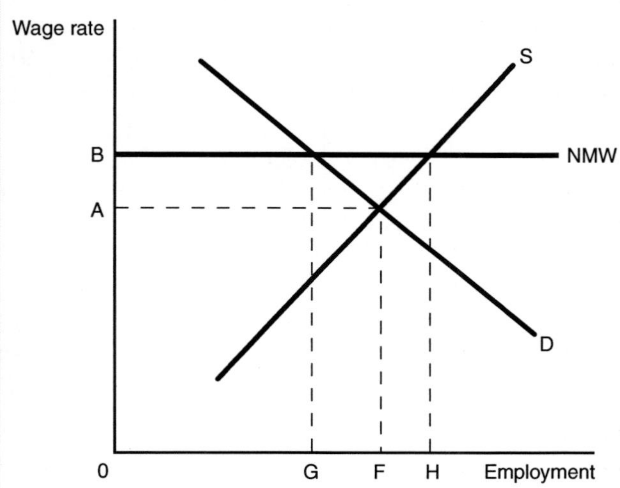

Data question

(a) The short run aggregate supply curve will have shifted sharply upwards over the period. Prices doubled between 1974 and 1979, whilst GDP rose by less than 10 per cent. The rise in the short run aggregate supply curve was caused by a

Figure 7

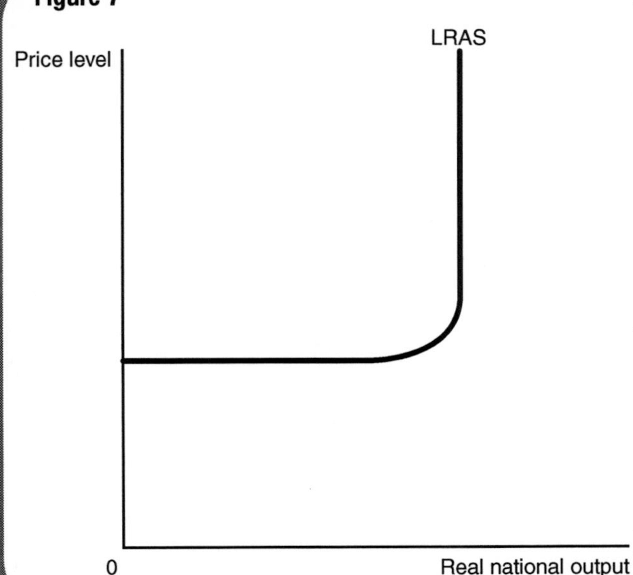

number of factors. Import prices increased by three quarters with the oil price rise being the single most important increase within this total. Wages more than doubled, outstripping inflation. Indirect taxation is also likely to have increased, although there are no figures given for this in the data. These changes can be shown in Figure .8. The short run aggregate supply curve will have been continually shifting upwards, from $SRAS_1$ to $SRAS_2$ to $SRAS_3$.

(b) Long run aggregate supply is likely to have expanded, but at a rate below the trend rate. Long run aggregate supply is determined by the quantity and quality of factors of production available. Gross physical investment slightly fell over the period as a percentage of GDP, but given rising GDP levels, actual investment levels in money terms was broadly constant. Hence, there is likely to have been some growth in capital stock, even allowing for higher than average rates of depreciation due to changing production methods in the wake of the 1973-74 oil crisis. Nevertheless, investment as a percentage of GDP fell over the period as growth in investment failed to keep pace with growth in the overall economy. This is perhaps one factor in explaining why growth in GDP itself was below trend over the period.

The rise in unemployment from half a million to one and a half million is likely to have reduced the growth in human capital from what it would otherwise have been. Improved education and training will have increased human capital over the period. However, unemployment destroys human capital. Some workers, particularly older workers, leave the workforce prematurely because they are unable to get another job, taking with them their skills and experience. Other workers become partially deskilled in periods between jobs.

This can be shown in Figure 9. The long run aggregate supply curve under more normal economic circumstances would have shifted from $LRAS_1$ to $LRAS_2$. However, the difficult economic times meant that the shift in the LRAS curve was less than would otherwise have been the case and so it only shifted from $LRAS_1$ to $LRAS_3$.

Figure 8

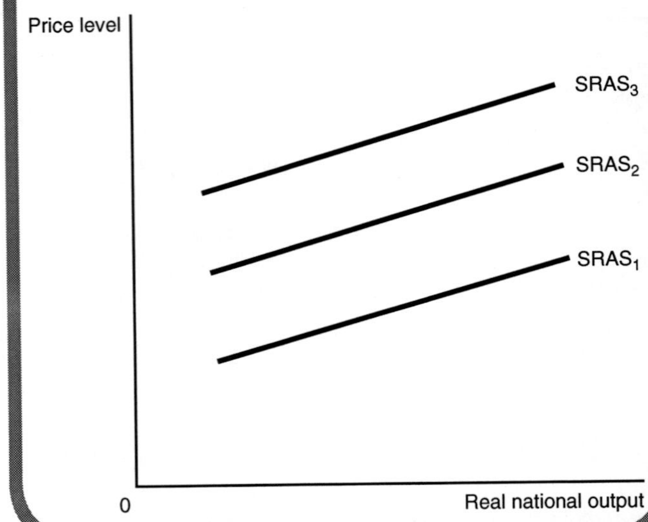

Figure 9

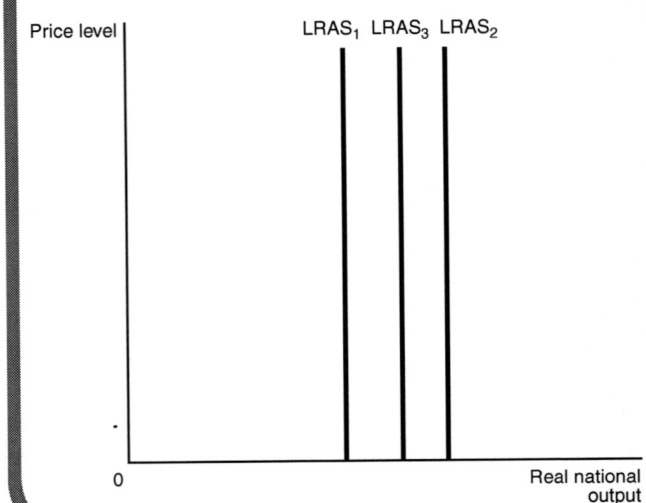

30 Equilibrium output

Question 1

(a) According to classical economists, the long run aggregate supply curve is vertical. An increase in demand, therefore, will only lead to an increase in prices.

Assuming that the economy is at full employment (i.e. unemployment is at its natural rate), a resolution of the strike in favour of the strikers will first increase short run aggregate supply (SRAS), shifting the SRAS curve upwards, and second increase aggregate demand (AD), shifting the AD curve to the right. The SRAS curve will shift upwards because it is drawn on the assumption that wage rates are constant, whereas here wage rates are increasing. The AD curve will shift to the right because the workers will now spend more. (We are assuming here that the government does not pay for the increasing wages by cutting expenditure elsewhere or by raising taxes.) The shifts of these two curves lead to a movement up the long run aggregate supply curve. Prices would increase, but the level of output and employment in the economy would remain the same.

If the economy were at less than full employment, both the Keynesian and classical economists would agree that a rise in workers' pay, all other thing being equal, would tend to increase both output and prices because the increase in aggregate demand would help move the economy nearer to its full employment level.

(b) If the action was unsuccessful then there would be no effect on either wage rates or aggregate demand. Hence neither the AD curve or the AS curve would shift. Prices and equilibrium output would therefore be unaffected.

Question 2

(a) Increasing taxes is likely to lead to a reduction in the level of aggregate demand in the economy. In Figure 1 the 1981 rise in taxes is shown by a shift to the left of the aggregate demand curve from AD_1 to AD_2. If the economy were at full employment in 1981, the economy would have started at point A. It would then have moved to point B down the short run aggregate supply curve. Unemployment would have risen.

Figure 1

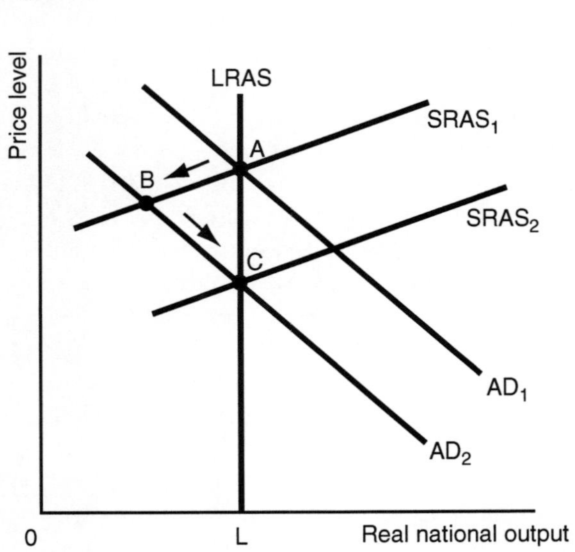

Figure 2

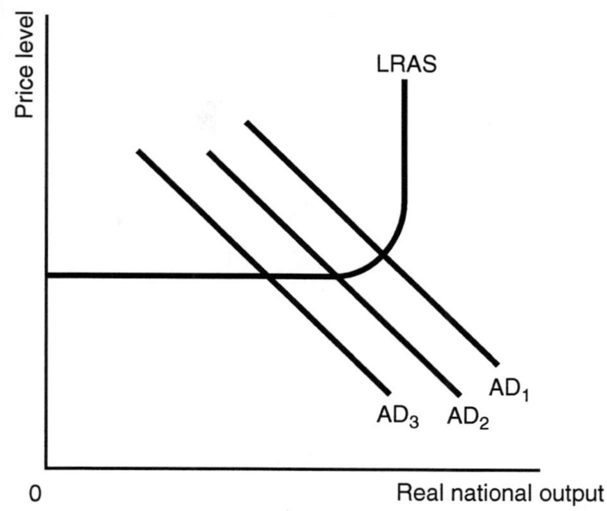

However, in the long run the economy would return to its previous level of unemployment at C (the natural rate), but prices would be lower. In reality the cut in taxes did not result in a fall in the AD curve. Because there were strong inflationary pressures in the economy, the AD curve shifted upwards, but the cut in taxes meant that the AD curve did not shift upwards as much as it would otherwise have done, and hence inflation was lower than it would otherwise have been.

If the economy had not been at full employment the analysis is little different. The rise in taxes would have led to a fall in aggregate demand. Output would have fallen and unemployment would have risen in the short term, but in the long run the economy would have returned to full employment output at a lower rate of inflation.

(b) Keynesian economists disagreed strongly with Geoffrey Howe's policy in 1981 of raising taxes. Faced with the worst recession since the 1930s, they argued that the rise in taxes would lead to even greater unemployment, with little or no effect on the inflation rate. In Figure 2 the long run aggregate supply curve is drawn at first horizontal and then rises till it reaches the full employment level of output, where it becomes vertical. If the level of aggregate demand in 1981 prior to the Budget was AD_1 then a rise in taxes would have pushed the AD curve left to, say, AD_2. There would have been a substantial increase in unemployment as output fell, whilst the effect on prices would have been negligible. If the March 1981 AD curve had been AD_2, the rise in taxes, which pushed the AD curve to the left to AD_3, would have had no effect on prices because the economy was already operating at mass unemployment levels. The correct policy prescription, according to Keynesian economists, was to lower taxes in order to stimulate aggregate demand.

Question 3

(a) Classical or supply side economists would argue that these measures would lead to an increase in aggregate supply. On the one hand, the government is cutting its budget deficit by cutting spending. This will release resources to be employed by the more productive private sector of the economy. On the other hand, it is stimulating employment in the economy by a

Figure 3

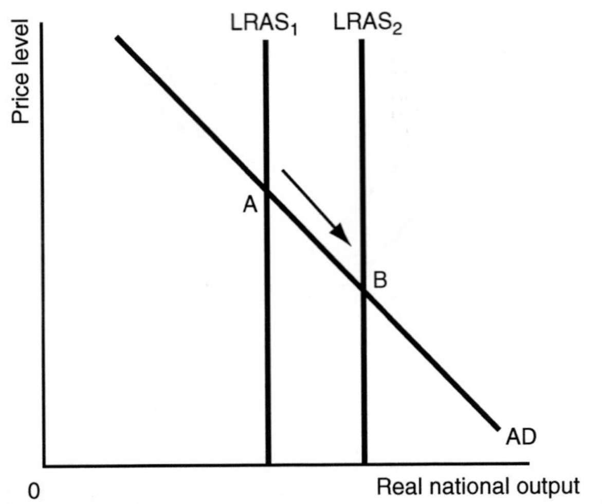

Figure 4

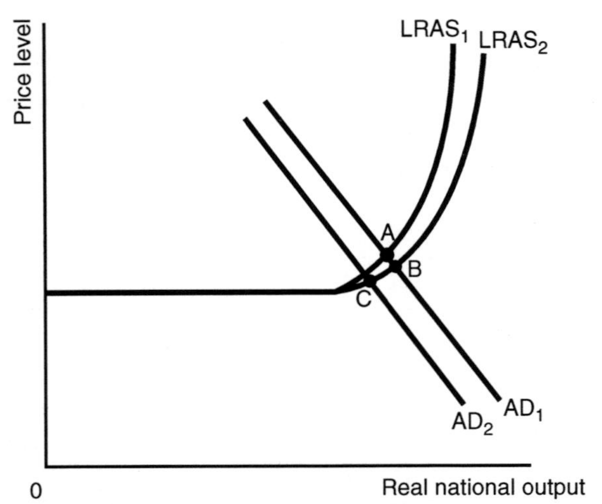

Figure 5

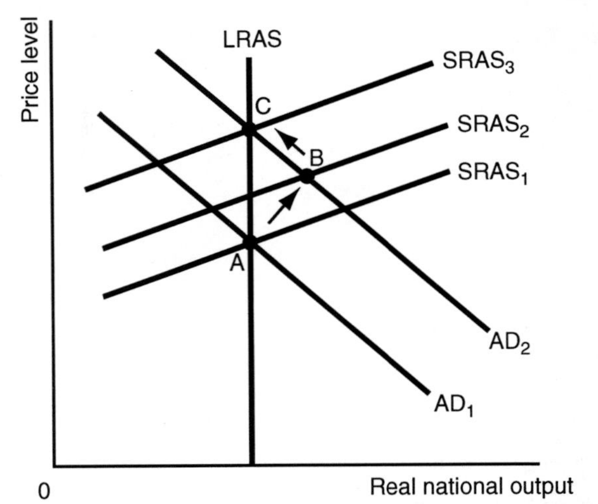

Figure 6

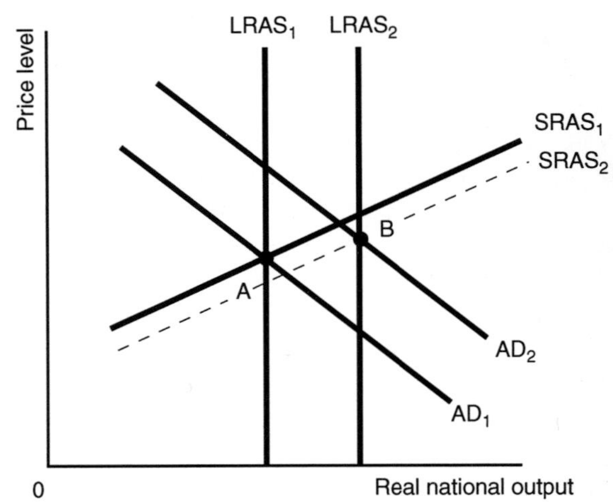

range of measures from cutting employment taxes to helping the low paid gain access to housing. The rise in aggregate supply is shown by a shift in the vertical long run aggregate supply curve in Figure 3 from $LRAS_1$ to $LRAS_2$.

(b) Keynesian economists would be more sceptical of the beneficial effects of the measures. On the one hand, they would question the extent to which measures such as cutting employment taxes will raise employment and thus long run aggregate supply in the economy. On the other hand, they would point out that the overall impact of the budget is deflationary. In Figure 4, the employment measures shift the LRAS curve slightly to the right from $LRAS_1$ to $LRAS_2$. If aggregate demand remained the same the economy would move from A to B. However, the overall deflationary impact of the budget leads to a fall in aggregate demand from AD_1 to AD_2. As a consequence, the economy moves to C on the new LRAS curve. However, output is lower at C than at A and hence there is likely to be more and not less unemployment than originally.

Question 4

(a) (i) A 10 per cent rise in earnings in the economy will lead to an increase in aggregate demand as workers spend their extra wages. In Figure 5, the aggregate demand curve will shift to the right from AD_1 to AD_2.

(ii) At the same time, wage rates have increased and therefore the short run aggregate supply curve will also have risen from $SRAS_1$ to $SRAS_2$.

(iii) In the long term, the economy must return to a point on its long run aggregate supply curve. There is likely to be continued wage inflation in the economy pushing the SRAS curve upwards towards a long run equilibrium position of C. In the long run, prices will have risen but output will remain unchanged.

(b) (i) An increase in real spending by government on education and training, all other things being equal, will increase aggregate demand in the economy, shown by a shift to the right in the aggregate demand in Figure 6.

(ii) The short run aggregate supply curve should remain unchanged initially since there are no short term upward cost pressures implied by extra spending on education and training. In the long term, however, the SRAS curve is likely to shift downwards because the productivity of labour will have increased, lowering the effective wage cost of producing a unit of output.

(iii) The increase in spending is likely to increase long run aggregate supply because the amount of human capital available for production is likely to be higher. In Figure 6 this is shown by the shift to the right in the LRAS curve. In the long term, the economy therefore moves from A to B. Output will increase. The effect on the price level will depend on the extent of the shift in the AD curve compared to the LRAS curve.

(c) (i) An increase in the average long term real rate of interest from 3 per cent to 5 per cent is likely to reduce aggregate demand because both consumption and investment will be affected negatively.

(ii) The short run aggregate supply curve is likely to shift upwards because costs to industry of borrowing money will increase.

(iii) The rate at which long run aggregate supply shifts to the right is likely to fall because less investment will reduce its growth rate. The overall impact on long run output is likely to be a reduction in its growth rate. The effect on the price level will depend on the relationship between the shift to the right in the AD curve and the shift to the left of the LRAS curve.

Data question

1. (a) A variety of demand side factors helped keep growth in demand subdued in 2005. One factor was higher interest rates which will have helped dampen both consumption and investment. Another was higher petrol prices and higher gas and electricity bills. Because these products tend to be necessities for most households, consumers were forced to cut back on other expenditure to pay for the higher bills. This reduced consumer confidence and willingness to take out loans. Subdued growth in the housing market meant that growth in household wealth was lower than in 2004, again helping to subdue growth in consumer spending. Unemployment was up slightly which will have helped dampen growth in consumer spending too.

(b) The main short run supply side factor affecting the economy in 2005 was the doubling in oil prices. This led to a fall in short run aggregate supply as its effects were felt throughout the economy from transport, to heating, to other fuel prices. The short run aggregate supply curve therefore shifted to the left.

2. The rise in real national output was low and below trend in 2005 because of subdued increases in aggregate demand combined with a fall in short run aggregate supply because of oil price rises. In Figure 7, if aggregate demand had grown at its trend rate, the aggregate demand curve would have shifted from AD_1 to AD_3. However, subdued growth meant that the aggregate demand curve only shifted to AD_2. On the supply side, short run aggregate supply fell, shifting the curve from $SRAS_1$ to $SRAS_2$. The result is that short run equilibrium real national output increased from OA to OB. However, had aggregate demand increased at its trend rate and had there been no oil price shock, real national output would have been at OC.

3. A recession in the USA would affect countries world wide as demand for imports into the USA fell. This would affect the UK directly through lower UK exports to the USA. But it would also affect it indirectly as other countries suffered lower national income because of lower exports to the USA. They would then import less from the UK. Exports are a component of aggregate demand. So a recession in the USA would lead to a fall in aggregate demand in the UK. This is shown in Figure 8 where the aggregate demand curve shifts to the left from AD_1 to AD_2. As a result, in the short run, there is a fall in real national income from OA to OB, but also a fall in the price level because of reduced demand-side pressures on prices from OH to OG. In the long run, if the long run aggregate supply curve was LRAS in Figure 8, there would be a movement down the AD_2 curve and equilibrium output would return to OA, but at the lower price level of OF.

4. It could be argued that it is relatively unimportant in the long term if there are large deviances from the long term trend rate of growth of the economy. By definition, the economy will return to its long run equilibrium position over time. The only cost will be short term costs, such as to those who are made unemployed in a recession, or those who suffer because inflation is higher than average in a boom.

Other economists would argue that these short run costs are significant and lead to a large loss of welfare in the economy over time. Moreover, it can be argued that a 'boom and bust' economy tends to have a lower long run trend rate of growth than one where the output gap is kept close to zero over time. In recessions, both physical and human capital can be destroyed. Factories and places of work can close down forever whilst the long term unemployed lose valuable work skills. Large booms and busts also produce uncertainty, with businesses unsure whether to invest or not. If investment is lower in a boom and bust economy, then long run average growth rates will also be lower.

Figure 7

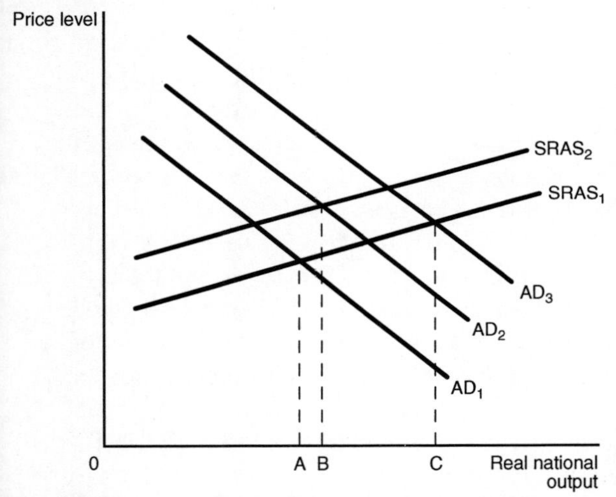

Figure 8

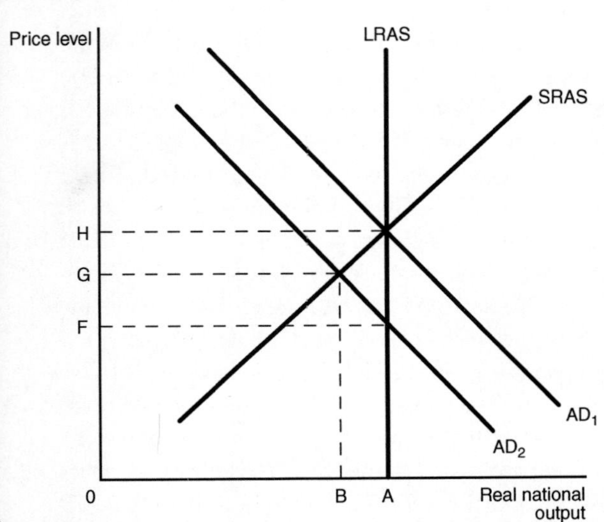

31 Economic growth

Question 1

(a) As Figure 5 in the student's book shows Spain has a higher rate of unemployment than either the Euro area of the United States. In 2006, for example, Spain's unemployment rate stood at 8.5 per cent compared to 7.9 per cent for the Euro area and 6 per cent for the United States. Throughout the period 1991-2006, Spain's unemployment rate was higher than the Euro area of the United States.

The data suggest that Spain has failed to bring its unemployment rate down to European levels because of its inability to address its 'poor productivity record'. Economic growth has not been high enough to take up the slack in the labour market. The data puts some of this down to the existence of 'garbage jobs', jobs which are short term, offer little security and give few benefits. These jobs discourage workers with permanent contracts to move jobs and to be entrepreneurial.

(b) Economic growth in Spain could have been higher in the 1990s and 2000s. One factor limiting growth has been a failure to give sufficient training to the workforce. The widespread use of temporary contracts, covering 35 per cent of the workforce compared to an EU average of 12 per cent, has meant that employers have been reluctant to spend money on training when employees are likely to move on quickly. Less training means less investment in human capital and this affects growth in labour productivity and ultimately economic growth itself.

A second factor has been a discouragement of the entrepreneurial spirit in Spain. The widespread use of temporary contracts has encouraged workers to put their energies into securing a job with a permanent contract rather than consider setting up in business themselves. Equally, those with full time contracts have been discouraged from becoming entrepreneurs because if their business failed, there might be considerable difficulty in getting a permanent job back again. Less entrepreneurial activity affects economic growth because fewer new businesses are being set up.

A third factor limiting growth has been the discouragement of labour mobility and labour flexibility. With 35 per cent of all jobs classified as temporary, getting and retaining a permanent job has become a major goal for Spanish workers. With so many temporary jobs, there is a much smaller pool of permanent jobs for those already with permanent jobs to apply to if they want a change of job. So permanent workers tend to stay longer in their existing jobs than would otherwise be the case. This prevents the market from getting the right worker into the right job and leads to lower productivity than would otherwise be the case. Lower productivity means lower economic growth.

Question 2

(a) Economic theory would suggest that the higher the level of investment, the higher the rate of economic growth in the economy. Investment increases the capital stock of an economy and hence helps to shift the production possibility frontier of the economy outwards. The greater the capital stock, the greater the productive potential of the economy.

(b) The data in Figure 6 in the student's book would suggest that there is a reasonable level of correlation between investment and economic growth. Countries such as Ireland, New Zealand and Australia with high levels of increase in fixed capital formation also have high economic growth rates over the period 1993-2006. Countries such as Japan, Germany and Italy with low or even negative annual increases in fixed capital formation had relatively low levels of economic growth.

Clearly, other factors apart from gross investment are determining the rate of economic growth since the correlation is not perfect. For example, Finland over the period grew almost as fast as countries such as New Zealand, Australia and Turkey with annual average increases in fixed capital formation of almost twice its level.

The data could be used to support two hypotheses. One is that increases in investment cause increases in GDP. However, the data could also support the theory that changes in GDP cause changes in investment. It is not possible from the data to say which of these causal relationships is correct.

Data question

1. (a) Economic growth is the increase in the productive potential of the economy. It is commonly measured by the increase in GDP on an annual basis. In the short term, this can be an unreliable measure because GDP growth can represent economic recovery - the movement of the economy from less than full employment to full employment. Over long periods of time, however, average annual GDP growth rates are a good measure of growth in potential because the booms and slumps of the business cycle are evened out.

(b) Ireland has seen higher economic growth than either the UK or the average for the Euro area over the period 1991 to 2006. At its height, between 1995 and 2000, Ireland was growing at an average rate of 10 per cent per annum compared to 2 or 3 per cent for the UK and the Euro area. Such high economic growth was unsustainable in the long term for Ireland. However, even in 2006, at the end of the period, Ireland's growth rate was over 5 per cent compared to 3 per cent for the UK and the Euro area.

2. Some economists argue that high levels of capital investment can give an economy a much better chance of having high levels of economic growth. Capital investment increases the productive potential of the economy and so raises its ability to produce goods and services. Countries with high levels of investment as a proportion of their GDP should therefore grow faster, all other things being equal, than countries which invest less of the GDP. Figure 10 in the student's book shows that Ireland has increased its level of investment at a faster rate than both the UK and the Euro area over the period 1991 to 2006. Therefore it could be argued that investment has been key to Ireland's success in growing its level of GDP over the period.

However, the data shown in Figure 10 in the student's book doesn't actually show the levels of capital investment in the UK, the Euro area and Ireland. Instead, it shows the annual percentage change in investment excluding housing. Throughout the period 1991-2006, Ireland tends to have the highest percentage change of the three countries or areas. But it could be be that investment in Ireland started off from a very low base and that even by 2006, Ireland was investing a smaller proportion of its GDP than both the UK and the Euro area. So the data should be be treated with caution in discussing this issue.

Figure 1 in the student's book shows that Ireland has had above average increases in labour productivity growth in the business sector over the period. Labour productivity is important for economic growth because if output per worker increases over time, so it is likely that GDP will also increase. Labour productivity is determined by factors such as education and training of the workforce. The data states that education has been a key factor in 'Ireland's economic success'. So too has been 'flexible working practices' which enable workers to move around the economy to maximise their earnings but also to maximise their output for employers. Equally, high labour productivity is often linked with high levels of physical capital. The ability of Ireland to attract multinational companies, for example through low business taxes, has led to an increase in investment. Such investment has also had a spin off in terms of knowledge in the economy. Workers who have been employed by multinational companies have then been able to set up their own businesses, often competing with their former employers. Higher labour productivity has also come from an exodus from low productivity agricultural jobs to higher productivity manufacturing and service sector jobs.

Figure 9 in the student's book shows how unemployment has fallen in Ireland at a much faster rate than in the UK and the Euro area. In 1991, unemployment stood at a very high 15 per cent. By 2006, it was just over 4 per cent. Not merely has unemployment fallen, but the Irish economy has seen in recent years a steady inflow of workers from abroad. Putting all the workers into jobs has led to higher levels of GDP than would otherwise have been the case. So part of Ireland's success story has been been about increasing the utilisation of labour, a scarce resource.

There are other factors too which could be argued have helped Ireland. Entrepreneurial activity, such as seen in Galway, has boosted growth. So too has wage moderation which has helped the macroeconomic management of the economy. Low income taxes may have boosted incentives to work.

So Ireland's success in maintaining higher economic growth than the UK or the Euro area over the period can be attributed to a variety of factors, including increased capital investment. Increased capital investment has not been the sole cause of economic growth but it has probably played an important part. In the long run, however, economic history suggests that Ireland cannot grow at a faster rate than its economic partners once it has achieved a comparable level of national income per head. High levels of capital investment, as shown by the example of Japan in the 1990s, does not guarantee high economic growth.

32 Unemployment

Question 1

(a) (i) Unemployment increased in quarters when inflows to the pool of unemployment exceeded the outflows. Hence, unemployment rose from 2005 Q3 to 2006 Q3.
(ii) Unemployment decreased in quarters outflows to the pool of unemployment exceeded the inflows. Hence unemployment fell from 2006 Q4 to 2007 Q2.
(b) Unemployment was lower in 2005 Q3 than in 2007 Q2 because the inflows were less than the outflows overall during the whole period. Inflows were a cumulative 4 961 700 whilst outflows were 4 964 400. Hence unemployment was 2 700 lower in 2005 Q3 compared to 2007 Q2.

Question 2

(a) Katie Morris is likely to be seasonally unemployed. She works in a seasonal industry, the holiday industry. She works during the season but out of season, she finds herself out of work despite wanting to work.
(b) John Penny is likely to be frictionally unemployed. He lost his job only two weeks ago and is currently seeking employment. For him to be suffering from either structural or cyclical unemployment, the period of unemployment would have to be much greater.
(c) Manus O'Brien is likely to be suffering from structural unemployment. He is seeking work but has not had a job for 12 years. This would suggest that jobs are not available for him to take.
(d) Clare Livingstone is likely to be cyclically unemployed. If the housing market is depressed, this suggests that the economy is in a recession. She has been out of work for 6 months so it is unlikely she would still be classified as frictionally unemployed.
(e) Gavin is most likely to be classified as structurally unemployed. He is unable to get a job at the same level as before. However, he might be cyclically unemployed. Recessions can last for 2 years or more.

Question 3

(a) A range of problems is identified in the data including poor psychological health and greater risk of marriage break-up. The unemployed found it harder to find employment than those in jobs because they were less likely to mix with those in work and partly because of this had less access to information about jobs.
(b) The problems of the unemployed impose high costs on the rest of society. For instance, marital breakdown creates one parent families which often have to be supported by the state and whose members can be psychologically damaged themselves by the break up of the family. Psychological stress will often be accompanied by treatment on the NHS, pushing up costs to the taxpayer.

Data question

1. The ILO measure of unemployment is based on a survey of employment called the Labour Force Survey. 60 000 households with over 100 000 adults are surveyed. To be classified as unemployed, an individual has to be without a paid job, be available to start a job within a fortnight and has either looked for work at some time in the previous four weeks or been waiting to start a job already obtained. The claimant count measures the number of people claiming benefit for being unemployed.
2. Cyclical unemployment occurs when the economy is in recession. There is too little aggregate demand to employ all workers who wish to work at the going wage rate. However,

Figure 1

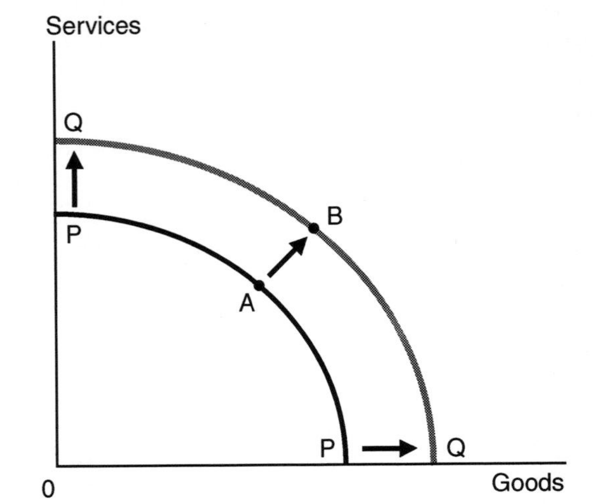

Figure 2

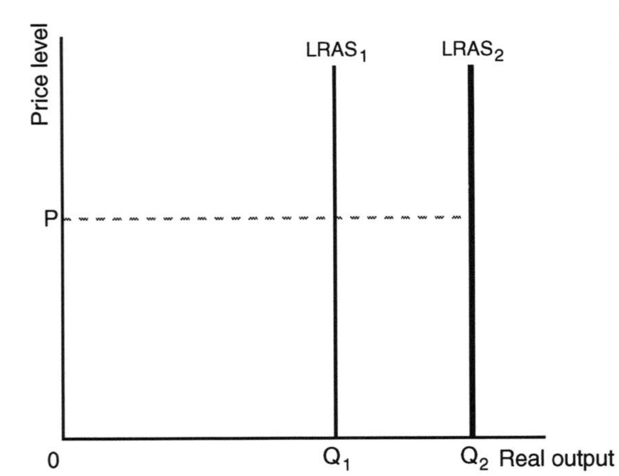

Figure 3

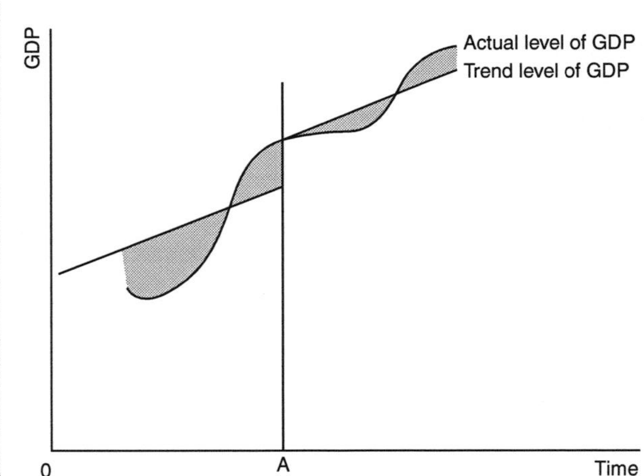

in 1979 and 2007, the data states that it could be argued that the economy was in boom. Therefore, unemployment in those years was mainly structural. This is when the pattern of demand and production changes over time and workers are left unemployed. For example, in 1979, manufacturing industry was shrinking, leaving high levels of unemployment across regions which had been dependent upon manufacturing for employment. In 2007, structural unemployment was much more localised, with pockets of high unemployment scattered across all regions of the UK.

3. In 2007, the economy was in boom. It could be argued that it was operating on its production possibility frontier at the point A in Figure 1. Alternatively, it could be argued that it was operating at the level of output shown by its long run supply curve $LRAS_1$ in Figure 2. However, there was still large amounts of structural unemployment. The official level of unemployment was 1.7 million. Much of the unemployment was located in small geographical pockets round the country where unemployment rates were particularly high. In addition, there was also considerable hidden unemployment. For example, 2.4 million people in 2007 were receiving incapacity benefit. Some of those were capable of holding down a job. If these individuals who were structurally unemployed could return to work, GDP could be even higher. In Figure 1, a reduction in structural unemployment would be shown by a shift to the right of the production possibility frontier from PP to QQ increasing output to, say, B. In Figure 2, it would be shown by a shift to the right in the long run aggregate supply curve from $LRAS_1$ to $LRAS_2$. It could also be shown in Figure 3 by a shift upwards in the long run trend rate of growth of the economy at the point in time A.

33 Inflation

Question 1

(a) Prices in Russia at the start of the period were increasing considerably. Already in 1991, prices had doubled, but in 1992 inflation, the rate of increase in prices, was approximately 2500 per cent. Inflation then fell, but only dipped below 100 per cent in 1996. In 1997, inflation was minimal, but increased to an estimated 50 per cent in 1999, before falling back again. Since 2000, inflation has been relatively low at less than 10 per cent.
(b) Hyperinflation is a very high rate of inflation. Russia clearly experienced hyperinflation in the early 1990s with inflation rates reaching approximately 2 500 per cent. However, since the mid-1990s, inflation has been relatively subdued.

Question 2

(a) One factor is the increase in pay settlements. An increase in wages leads to higher costs for firms and hence rising cost-push inflation when firms pass on those higher costs to customers in the form of higher prices. Another factor is the increase in profit margins by firms. Increasing profit margins means firms charge higher prices.
(b) One factor causing demand-pull inflation is 'strong consumer demand'. Consumption is the most important part of aggregate demand. So an increase in consumer spending will increase aggregate demand leading to demand-pull inflation.
(c) One factor is rising labour productivity. Labour productivity is defined as output per worker. With rising labour productivity, more can be produced with the same quantity of resources. If labour productivity rises by 3 per cent, this can offset the impact of a 3 per cent rise in wages. Hence, demand can increase without there necessarily being demand-pull inflationary pressures. Another factor is the likelihood of a rise in interest rates by the Bank of England. A rise in interest rates will act to dampen both consumer and investment spending. With lower aggregate demand than would otherwise have been the case, demand-pull inflationary pressures will ease.

Question 5

(a) The pensioner on a fixed income lost 2.8 per cent of her purchasing power in 2005 and 3.2 per cent in 2006.
(b) The saver saw a real loss of 0.8 per cent on her savings in 2005 and a real loss of 0.7 per cent in 2006.
(c) It is not possible to say whether the taxpayer was worse off in 2006 than in 2005 because there are no figures to compare the fiscal year year 2005/6 with 2004/5. However, in April 2006, the increase in tax allowance was 2.9 per cent, roughly the rate of inflation for 2005. Hence the income taxpayer will have been neither better off nor worse off in real terms.
(d) It is not possible to say whether the mother was worse off in 2006 than in 2005 because there are no figures to compare the financial year year 2005/6 with 2004/5. However, in April 2006, the increase in child benefit was 2.6 per cent, roughly the rate of inflation for 2005. Hence the mother will have been neither better off or worse off in real terms.

Data question

1. The period 1997-2006 was a period of strong growth for the economy ranging from a high of 3.8 per cent in 2000 to a low of 1.8 per cent in 2005. GDP saw little deviation from its trend level. In 2000, there was a positive output gap of 0.8 per cent of GDP, whilst the largest negative output gap was in 2005 at 0.5 per cent of GDP.

Strong growth led to falling unemployment. The rate of unemployment fell on the ILO measure from 7.2 per cent in 1997 to 4.7 per cent in 2005 although it then picked up a little in 2006 to 5.4 per cent. Inflation remained low throughout the period ranging on the CPI measure from a high of 2.1 per cent in 2006 to a low of 0.8 per cent in 2000.

2. The demand-pull theory of inflation states that inflation is caused by excess demand in the economy - too much money chasing too few goods. Conversely, a reduction in demand in the economy leads to falling inflation rates.

There is little evidence from the period 1997-2006 to support a demand-pull hypothesis. Changes in inflation are not particularly well correlated with changes in aggregate demand as measured by levels of economic growth or the size of the output gap. However, it should be remembered that the Bank of England was using interest rates to manipulate the level of the aggregate demand in order to stabilise inflation at a CPI range rate of 2 per cent plus or minus 1 per cent. The apparent lack of correlation could therefore be seen as evidence that the Bank of England has been highly successful in operating this policy.

The cost-push theory of inflation states that inflation is caused by rising costs in the economy. The main cost is wages. However, import costs and changes in profits are important too. An exogenous shock is assumed to give a significant increase in costs. Firms pass those costs on to consumers in the form of higher prices. Workers then demand higher wage increases to compensate for falls in their real wages, whilst firms increase prices to maintain profit margins. Higher domestic prices make the economy less internationally competitive and could lead to a fall in the value of the currency, leading to higher import prices. Hence, there is a continual interchange between higher prices and higher costs and back again.

Throughout the period 1997 to 2006, there was strong growth in average earnings from a minimum of 3.4 per cent in 2003 to a high of 5.2 per cent in 1998. Growth in profits was strong too with only two years, 2000 and 2001 recording a fall in profits. With regard to imports, in most years, import prices fell partly due to increasing globalisation and the ability of the UK to buy increasing amounts of low cost imports from countries such as China and India. 2005-06 saw significant increases in import prices which are likely to have added inflationary pressures to the economy. However, overall, it is difficult to see any correlation from the statistics between changes in costs and changes in inflation. Again, it could be argued this has been due to Bank of England policy. It has responded to any substantial increase in cost-push pressures by raising interest rates, thus limiting their impact on inflation. Equally, it could be argued that the significant levels of net inward migration, peaking at 223 000 in 2004, and positive increases in labour productivity (output per worker) have helped reduce cost-push inflationary pressures. Inward migration has helped reduce pressure on wages to increase whilst increased labour productivity has allowed firms to offset at least part of their higher wage bills through increased production per worker.

Inflation throughout the period 1997 to 2006 has remained subdued. There have been both demand-pull pressures on the economy and cost-push pressures. However, inflation has remained relatively low. It could be argued that neither demand-pull or cost-push pressures have been large enough to lead to large changes in the rate of inflation. This period would therefore have been a period of low inflationary pressure. Equally, it could be argued that the Bank of England, through its operation of monetary policy, has been very successful at keeping inflationary pressures to a minimum.

34 The balance of payments

Question 1

(a) (i) Exports of manufactured goods (£20 bn); sale of coal to foreign countries (£2 bn).
(ii) Imports of food (£10 bn); purchase of oil from abroad (£8 bn).
(iii) Earnings from foreign tourists (£5 bn); earnings from nationals overseas which are repatriated (£7 bn); payments by foreigners to domestic financial institutions for services rendered (£1 bn).
(iv) Interest, profits and dividends paid to foreigners (£4 bn).
(b) (i) Balance of trade = visible exports minus visible imports = £22 bn - £18 bn = £4 bn.
(ii) Balance on invisible trade = invisible exports minus invisible imports = £13 bn - £4 bn = £9 bn.
(iii) The current balance = the balance of trade + the invisible balance = £4 bn + £9 bn = £13 bn.
(c) (i) If it cost the country £3 bn to export products in its own ships, then there would be no effect on the balance of payments, assuming all the £3 bn came from domestic costs.
(ii) If, on the other hand, it was using foreign shipping companies, the £3 bn would then become an invisible import. So whilst the balance of trade would be unaffected, the balance on invisible trade would be £3 bn worse at £6 bn whilst the current balance too would be £3 bn down at £10 bn.

Question 2

(a) The Czech Republic was a success story in the 1990s and 2000s. It achieved high rates of growth of up to 6 per cent per annum as Figure 1 in the student's book shows, with an average rate of growth of 3.4 per cent, one and a half times that of the euro area.
(b) The current deficit shown in Figure 1 may not pose a problem for the Czech Republic. The country will have been importing financial capital to finance its economic development. If the country continues to grow at the rate it did in the 1990s and the early 2000s, it should have no problem repaying loans in the future.

However, if the current balance deficit has been mainly made up of imports of consumers goods and services, the foreign debt built up will prove to be an increasing burden to the Czech Republic. Equally, if Czech growth rates were to collapse, then it could find that it might no longer afford to keep up with repayments on loans. This would inevitably lead to a contraction in the domestic economy as resources were diverted from consumption and investment to paying off foreign debt.

Question 3

(a) The USA has experienced a current account deficit for nearly all of the period shown in the data. By 2007, the deficit was estimated to have reached 6 per cent of GDP. In contrast, Japan has experienced a current account surplus throughout the period, typically of between 1.5 and 5 per cent of GDP.
(b) Running a persistent surplus has enabled Japan to build up a large stock of wealth abroad. It has lent money to other economies and invested in them. For instance, Japanese car manufacturers have built car plants around the world. The benefit is that Japan is then able to earn interest and profits on its overseas investments. It is like a household earning interest on a large sum of money saved in a bank account. For Japan, this large foreign 'nest egg' may prove vital in the next forty years. The country has a rapidly ageing population and it may find it difficult to provide the pensions to support its retired population. Its foreign assets could then be seen as a pension fund, to be drawn down as time goes on to finance its pensioners.

The costs of running large surpluses are two fold. First, Japan could be consuming at much higher levels today if it were not exporting so much and importing so little. An average current account surplus of 2.5 per cent of GDP shown in Figure 2 in the student's book is 2.5 per cent not available for domestic consumption. Second, the Japanese surplus has caused considerable trade friction with the USA, which has accused it of destroying jobs in America and trading unfairly. The USA and other countries may be tempted to use trade restrictions against Japan in retaliation.

Data question

1. The visible trade balance remained in deficit throughout the period 1987 to 2006. It deteriorated sharply during the period 1987 to 1989 and again from 1997 to 2006. During the period 1992-98 the deficit fluctuated at just below 2 per cent of GDP before deteriorating to 6.4 per cent of GDP by 2006.

Net investment income deteriorated slightly between 1987 and 1991 before broadly increasing over the rest of the period to 2006. This increase was recorded despite a fall in the UK's net wealth overseas.
2. The current account is made up of trade in goods, trade in services, investment income and current transfers. The data show balances for two of these four components. In the late 1980s, and then from 1998-2006, the sharp deterioration in the visible trade balance will have had an adverse effect on the current account position. However, these falls will have been partially offset by the rise in net investment income over the period.
3. The deterioration in the trade gap in 2006 to 6.4 per cent of GDP was a worrying trend. Although UK trade in services and investment income remained in positive balance, trade in goods still remains a significant component of exports and imports for the UK. Further falls in the balance of trade are likely to lead to further deterioration in the overall current account position. At 3.7 per cent of GDP, the current account deficit on the balance of payments was arguably unsustainable in 2006. If it continued at that level, foreigners might no longer be willing to lend UK borrowers money or invest in the UK. A balance of payments 'crisis' or 'credit crunch' would then arise with the most likely outcome being a sharp fall in the value of the pound and a major recession in the UK economy.

On the other hand, the deficit on trade in goods might improve in the future. Equally, there might be offsetting rises in the balance of trade in services or in net investment income. There must be a question mark, though, with these scenarios. First, the UK exports approximately twice as many goods as services by value. For every 1 per cent fall in exports of goods, there must be a 2 per cent rise in exports of services to compensate. Second, since 1995, the UK has seen a deficit on the value of net international assets. The UK government, firms and citizens owe more to foreigners than they owe to the UK. So far, because of higher returns on UK assets overseas, net investment income has been positive. But if the

UK continues to be a net borrower overseas because of substantial current account deficits, net investment income could well turn from being positive to negative. This would then almost certainly lead to a crisis.

If the 2006 deficits were a one-off event with an improvement in later years, then it is unlikely to have been been of much significance. If it is part of a broader trend for the balance of trade in goods to deteriorate over time, at some point in the future there is likely to be a foreign exchange crisis with investors overseas unwilling to lend or invest more in the UK. This could be a dangerous and damaging scenario for the UK economy.

35 Fiscal policy

Question 1

(a) (i) The PSNCR is the Public Sector Net Cash Requirement. It is the amount of cash that government has to borrow if its revenues are less than its spending. Government is central government, local government and state owned industries and other bodies. If government revenues exceed government spending, the government has a negative PSNCR and is able to repay part of its debt.
(ii) For the government to have a budget surplus, its revenues must be greater than its spending and so the PSNCR will be negative. This occurred in 1988, 1989, 1990, 1991, 1999, 2000 and 2001. Note that the budget surplus in 1988 and budget deficits in 1987, 1998 and 2002 were very small and therefore are difficult to read off the graph in Figure 1 in the student's book.
(b) The National Debt is the total of accumulated past debts minus any repayments. If the government is running a budget deficit, a positive PSNCR, it is adding to the Debt. Hence in any year where the PSNCR is positive, the National Debt will rise. On the other hand, if there is a budget surplus and so the PSNCR is negative, the government is able to repay debt and the National Debt will fall. For instance, between 1972 and the late 1980s, and most of the 1990s, and since 2002, when there was a budget deficit, the National Debt rose. In the late 1980s, and late 1990s when there was a budget surplus, the National Debt fell.
(c) To pay off the National Debt, the public sector would have to run consistent budget surpluses. The larger the average annual negative PSNCR, the quicker the National Debt would be repaid.

Question 2

(a) A rise in income tax rates is likely to reduce aggregate demand. With less spending power, workers will cut their consumption and hence cut aggregate demand.
(b) A cut in council tax rates is likely to increase aggregate demand. The cut in taxes will increase households' spending power and thus lead to an increase in consumption.
(c) A cut in spending on education is likely to reduce aggregate demand. The cut in spending could filter through to the whole economy in a number of different ways. For instance, if fewer teachers are employed, then there will be a loss of spending from those who would otherwise have had jobs. If the cut falls on new building, contractors will receive fewer orders and some of their workers may be laid off.
(d) The rise in VAT rates will tend to reduce aggregate demand because the volume of goods that consumers can afford to buy with a given income will fall. The increased spending on the NHS, on the other hand, will lead to an increase in aggregate demand. The overall impact on aggregate demand of the two measures will depend upon the relative effect on aggregate demand of one compared to the other.

Question 3

(a) If investment, government spending or any other autonomous variable changes, then there is likely to be an even greater effect on aggregate demand. The relationship between these two figures is known as the multiplier. For instance, if firms increase their investment spending, this creates orders for other firms. These firms use the money to pay wages to workers, dividends to shareholders and create orders for other firms. Workers spend the wages creating more orders for firms. And so on. The result is that the initial increase in investment has led to an even greater final increase in income and aggregate demand.
(b) In 1975 and 1976, the Labour government cut the budget deficit by raising taxes and reducing public expenditure. This is likely to have reduced national income from what it would have been, and indeed by more than the government cuts because of the multiplier effect. For instance, the fall in the budget deficit of over £1 000 million in 1976 is likely to have reduced national income by more than £1 000 million.
(c) The more relaxed fiscal stance in 1978 is likely to have raised inflationary pressures but increased output. In Figure 1, the rise in the budget deficit pushes the aggregate demand curve from AD_1 to AD_2. The economy moves up the short run aggregate supply curve from A to B. The price level rises but so does output. The assumption is that, even at B, the economy is at less than full employment and the long run aggregate supply curve, not shown on the diagram, is to the right of B.

Figure 1

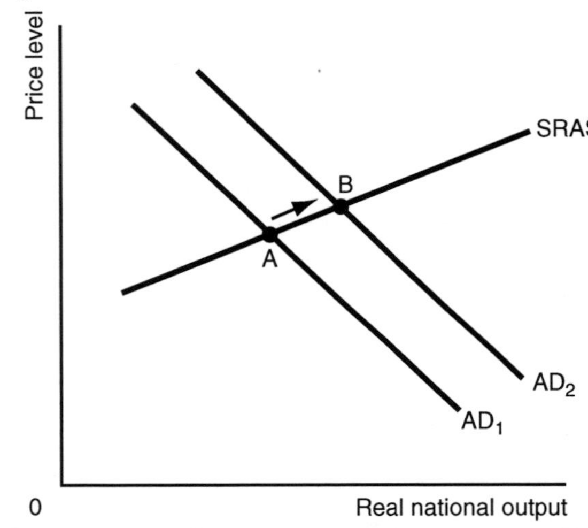

Question 4

(a) The large rises in public spending between 2003 and 2007 not matched by increases in taxes will have led to a rise in the budget deficit given that the PSNCR was positive in 2003. This in turn will have led to an increase in aggregate demand. In Figure 2, the aggregate demand curve shifts from AD_1 to AD_2. In the short term, this increases real output from Q_1 to Q_2, which will be recorded as economic growth (although strictly speaking the long run aggregate supply curve would have to shift for this to be genuine growth). Unemployment is likely to fall since more is being produced. Inflation will rise. In Figure 2, the price level rises from P_1 to P_2 as a result of the increase in aggregate demand. The current balance is likely to deteriorate because higher spending will lead to increased demand for imports. There might also be a negative effect on exports if UK firms divert goods from the export market to a booming domestic market.
(b) The virtual freezing of government spending in the early 1980s at a time when tax revenues were rising will have led to

Figure 2

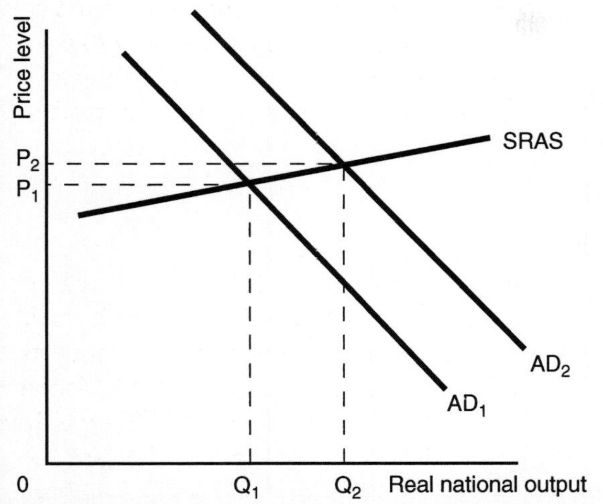

Figure 3

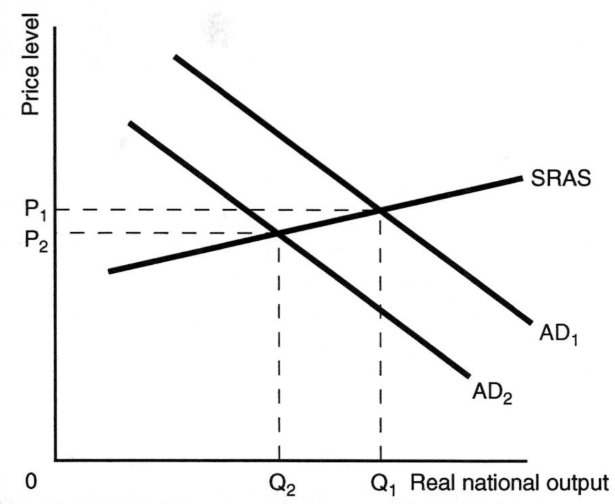

a fall in government borrowing (or a rise in the government budget surplus). The freezing of government spending will have had no effect on aggregate demand, although presumably if it hadn't been frozen, aggregate demand would have increased as government spending increased. However, the increases in taxes will have reduced aggregate demand. If income tax had been increased, for instance, the disposable income of households will have fallen. This will have led to a fall in consumption expenditure. The fall in aggregate demand is shown in Figure 3 by the shift to the left in the aggregate demand curve from AD_1 to AD_2. Economic growth, if it were measured by the short run change in GDP, will have fallen from what it would otherwise have been. In Figure 3, output actually falls from Q_1 to Q_2. Inflation will have moderated. In Figure 3, the price level actually falls from P_1 to P_2. Unemployment will rise from what it would otherwise have been because spending in the economy will not be as high. The current account position will be better than it would otherwise have been because there will be less demand for imports.

Data question

1. The government proposed to increase government spending in 2008-09 by more than taxation leading to a rise in government borrowing of £1.8 billion compared with 2007-08. Government spending was predicted to rise by £28.2 billion and taxation by £30 billion. In some areas, he announced spending increases to 2010-2011. For example, there would be additional spending of £14.5 billion on education, £900 million on science and £3.6 billion on transport.

2. The trade cycle is a regular fluctuation in GDP around a trend growth path. The trade cycle has four phases, boom, downturn, recession or depression and recovery. Figure 7 in the student's book shows the output gap. When there is a negative output gap, the economy is in recession. When there is a positive output gap, the economy is likely to be in boom. Figure 8 in the student's book shows rates of growth GDP. Boom years tend to be associated with high levels of economic growth whilst recessions are shown by low or negative growth.

Figure 12 in the student's book shows that in the fiscal years 1997-8 to 1999-2000, the government's budget surplus led to the government having a negative impact on GDP. During this time, a negative output gap was eliminated and a positive output gap emerged. Had the impact of fiscal policy on GDP been positive, economic growth would probably have been above its trend rate of growth and a positive output gap would have appeared much earlier. Therefore fiscal policy helped smooth out a potential unsustainable boom.

Between the fiscal years 2000-1 to 2004-5, a government budget deficit had a positive impact on GDP. Again this could be argued to have been counter-cyclical because a negative output gap appeared from 2001 with below trend growth in GDP. However, from 2005-6 onwards, the impact of changes in fiscal policy on GDP were estimated to be very small. At the same time, the output gap was estimated to have been almost zero with growth at around its trend rate.

Overall, then, it could be argued that changes in fiscal policy over the period 1997-2007 did help smooth out the effects of the trade cycle.

3. The changes in overall taxation and borrowing in the 2007 budget for 2008-9 were very small in relation to total GDP because the changes in government spending and taxation were very similar. The estimated impact on GDP shown in Figure 12 of the student's book was just 0.3 per cent of GDP. Therefore the changes will have had little or no impact on unemployment and inflation.

4. The Labour government has set itself two fiscal rules. One is the golden rule which states that government should only borrow money over the period of a whole trade cycle to finance investment. Current government spending over the period of one trade cycle should be exactly matched by revenues. The second is the public debt rule which states that the ratio of public debt to national income should be held at a 'stable and prudent' level, currently defined as less than 40 per cent of GDP.

The projections for national debt as a percentage of GDP made in the 2007 budget and shown in Figure 11 of the student's book show that national debt will be within the 40 per cent ceiling to 2012-13 even though national debt is rising.

The data for the golden rule is more difficult to read from the data and in particular Figure 10 in the student's book. The data do not give the exact starting point and ending point for the current trade cycle and so it is not possible to calculate whether the government budget surpluses of the end of the 1990s were greater or less than the government budget deficits of the first half of the 2000s. However, the data suggests that it is not immediately obvious that the government will meet its golden rule although if it fails to do so, the shortfall will not be that great.

36 Supply side policies

Question 1

(a) Tax rates may have an effect on incentives to work. The higher the marginal tax rate, the less of any increase in gross earnings that a worker will keep. Given that leisure has a value, the higher the marginal tax rate, the lower the cost of increasing leisure time at the margin. For instance, if a worker faces a marginal tax rate of 60 per cent, she may choose to work less hard and earn less than she could have done because the 40 per cent take home pay does not sufficiently compensate for the leisure time foregone.
(b) The studies suggest that there is only a weak overall link between tax cuts and the number of hours worked. The effects tend to be concentrated on small groups of workers. For instance, not surprisingly there was little effect on workers who could not vary their hours of work. The main effect was on 'the wealthy, rural workers, the middle aged and those without families' who were more likely to be able to work longer hours. C V Brown, in his study, found that the substantial increase in tax allowances in that year only increased the number of hours worked by 0.5 per cent.
(c) The implication is that increasing tax rates will have little effect on hours worked in the economy. Therefore, tax revenues will increase if tax rates are increased. This is true even between the 40 and 60 per cent tax rates since C V Brown found that there was little impact on incentives of the 1987 budget cuts in tax on higher rate tax payers. In Figure 2 in the student's book, A is likely to be at least 60 per cent if not higher.

Question 2

(a) The quality of the labour force is essential for the long term growth of the UK economy. An ever increasing level of skills will enable long run aggregate supply to rise, creating economic growth. In Figure 1, improvements in the quality of the labour force shift the long run aggregate supply curve from $LRAS_1$ to $LRAS_2$. This increases real output from OA to OB.
(b) In an advanced economy such as the UK, it is important that all workers have minimum levels of literacy and numeracy. The number of jobs available where such skills are not required has been shrinking over the past 50 years. A disproportionate percentage of the long term unemployed have very low skill levels. It is therefore inefficient for the UK to have workers unable to find jobs because of their low levels of human capital.
(c) The OECD argues that the UK tax and benefit system might be a disincentive to workers to acquire skills. It argues that there is very little difference between the net income after tax and benefits of intermediate level workers with some skills compared to low skilled workers. This has come about because the government has attempted to provide all workers with a minimum level of income after tax and benefits which has squeezed differentials at the bottom end of the pay scale. If there is little difference in net pay, there is little incentive for less academic students to stay on in education or to make efforts once in work to acquire more skills.

Figure 1

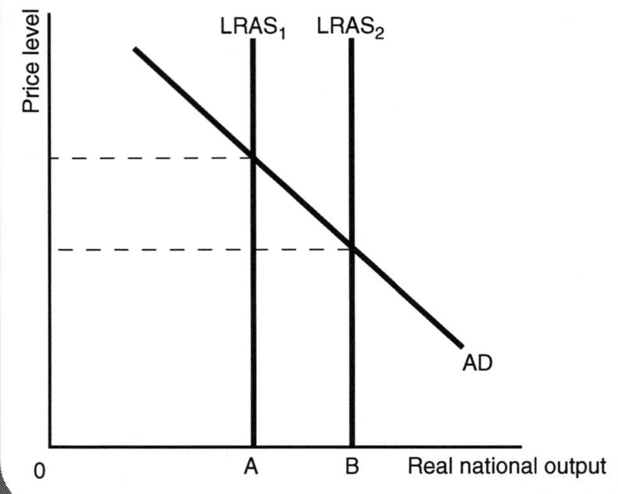

Question 3

(a) High company taxes are likely to discourage North Sea oil exploration and development. Company taxes effectively reduce the price that a company receives for producing a barrel of oil. For instance, if the price of oil were $60 a barrel, but there was the equivalent of a $40 a barrel tax on oil, the company would receive only $20 a barrel. This $20 would have to pay for all the costs of production and give the oil company a profit. Different oil fields have different costs. Some fields are too expensive to develop profitably. Others are very cheap to develop and operate and yield their owners high profits. When the price of oil rises, as it did between 2003 and 2006, more fields as yet undeveloped pass from being unprofitable to being profitable. Hence, the UK Offshore Operators Association is correct in saying that the extra 10 per cent tax on profits from North Sea oil fields imposed by the UK government in 2005 would lead to some marginal fields either not being developed or some existing fields not being given the investment to increase their output. The question is what proportion of potential production is actually affected by this increase in tax.
(b) Higher company taxes on North Sea oil profits will reduce investment in the UK oil sector. This will reduce long run aggregate supply of the British economy. The British government would probably argue that the reduction in investment will be minimal and therefore there will be effectively no reduction in long run aggregate supply. The UK Offshore Operators Association would probably argue that there will be a significant impact on the UK oil production sector and therefore there will be a significant impact on long run aggregate supply. Without further data, it is not possible to say who is correct on this issue.

Question 4

(a) Assistance from the government can increase aggregate supply in a variety of ways. One is direct spending on infrastructure projects. For example, the Northern Way business plan envisages spending £12 million on 'small but significant transport improvements'. This will increase the capital stock of the economy. A second way is by investing in capital in partnership with private enterprise. The £3 million earmarked for investment in a £6.5 million National Industrial Biotechnology Facility is likely to be a public/private sector partnership A third way is to fund ventures which will improve the human capital of the workforce. The Northern Way is planning to invest £15 million in 'centres of excellence in leadership, innovation and the skills for sustainable communities'.

Data question

1. The two candidates made a number of proposals. The left wing candidate, Segolene Royal proposed:

- a sharp rise in the minimum wage;
- an extension of the law to to give more workers the right to a basic 35 hour week;
- giving state-funding for young people to get their first job;
- the removal of a 60 per cent cap on income and wealth taxes;
- penalising companies which paid large dividends to shareholders;
- aid to companies in high unemployment areas.

The right wing candidate, Nicholas Sarkozy, proposed:

- cutting the 60 per cent cap on income and wealth taxes to 50 per cent;
- removing employer taxes on overtime pay for workers working the 35 hour week;
- the introduction of a more flexible contract of employment which would give employers more rights to sack staff;
- cuts in unemployment benefits;
- cuts in taxes for private investment in start up companies;
- cutting corporation taxes to average European levels;
- heavier taxes on companies which gave higher increases in dividends to shareholders than wages to workers.

Looking at four of these in more detail, a number could possibly increase France's growth rate. One of these is giving state funding to young people finding their first job. Young people can find it difficult to get on the employment ladder, particularly if they have relatively few skills. The danger is they become long term unemployed, representing a waste of a scarce resource. If these young people could become part of the long term labour force, the economy will have a higher income than would otherwise be the case.

Another policy is aid to companies in high unemployment areas. Again, if these areas have large numbers of long term unemployed, putting them back to work will increase national income.

A third proposal is giving employers more rights to sack staff. It could be argued that if more workers are sacked, this will increase unemployment and reduce economic growth. However, supply side economists would argue that France's labour laws impede the mobility of labour. They discourage firms from taking on workers because firms are worried that they then won't be able to get rid of them if economic circumstances change. Giving workers fewer rights in this area will encourage firms to take on more staff. Unemployment will fall and economic growth will rise.

A last proposal is the cuts in taxes for private investment in start up companies. Cuts in taxes might give greater incentives for investors to put money into start up companies. More start up companies leads to more output and jobs in the economy. Hence, economic growth will increase.

2. Segolene Royal's policies could be described as more interventionist. This is because her policies tend to limit the ability of markets to work. For example, raising the minimum wage or giving more workers the right to a 35 hour week reduces the power of the market to set free market equilibrium wages and levels of employment. Many of Nicholas Sarkozy's policies concern removing restrictions to the market. For example, reducing unemployment benefits, reducing top levels of tax and more flexible contracts of employment are all policies which will increase the power of the market.

However, not all of Nicholas Sarkozy's policies are free market in spirit. Imposing higher taxes on companies which give higher increases in dividends to shareholders than wages to workers is an interventionist policy.

37 Monetary policy

Question 1

(a) (i) Kevin Hawkins of the British Retail Consortium wanted a cut in interest rates to boost sales in the retail sector. The passage quotes Kevin Hawkins as saying that: 'The underlying position (in retail sales) is still weak and unlikely to improve unless and until there are further cuts in interest rates'. Lower interest rates would free up part of earnings because variable mortgage repayments would fall whilst they would also make the cost of borrowing for consumer durables cheaper.
(ii) Geoff Cooper wanted a cut in interest rates to boost sales in the market for housing, DIY and housing related expenditure. As Chief Executive of Travis Perkins, the builders merchant and owner of Wickes, the DIY/small builder chain of hardware stores, he wants to see more people moving house and making home improvements. Lower interest rates should stimulate the housing market.

Question 2

(a) (i) Wage increases may cause inflation. First, they increase aggregate demand, pushing the aggregate demand curve to the right. This is because wage increases give workers increased income which they spend. Second, wage increases cause an increase in costs to firms. Therefore the short run aggregate supply curve is pushed up and to the left.
(ii) Increases in the cost of materials and other inputs to firms are also likely to cause increases in prices. For example, the large increases in oil prices mentioned in the data will push up firms' costs. They will then attempt to pass on those cost increases to customers in the form of higher prices. This will shift the short run aggregate supply curve up and to the left, leading to a higher short run equilibrium price level.
(b) An easing of pressure on wages means that the rate of increase in wages is slowing down. This in turn means that aggregate demand is not increasing as fast, whilst aggregate supply is not falling as much. This reduces the rate of inflation. Equally if there has been an 'easing' of cost pressures on firms, this will slow down the rate of increase of prices. If this reduction in wages and cost pressures is greater than the Bank of England deems desirable, it can then step in and reduce interest rates. This will increase aggregate demand from what it would otherwise have been. Although inflation will then be higher, so too will the rate of increase in output. So long as the inflation rate is within the Bank of England target range, a cut in interest rates can benefit economic growth.

Question 3

(a) The UK economy was slowing in late 1998. The Bank of England felt that there was a 'continuous slowdown' whilst Kate Barker, the chief economic adviser to the Confederation of British Industry, stated that there was a danger of an 'outright recession'. This slowing of the economy led to an easing of inflationary pressures. Kate Barker argued that 'inflation pressure is minimal'.
(b) (i) The 0.25 per cent cut in interest rates will have increased aggregate demand. This is because cuts in interest rates boost consumption spending as households borrow more money. Hence equilibrium output will rise.
(ii) The cut in interest rates is likely to increase inflation. This is because aggregate demand will be greater than it would otherwise have been. Hence, the equilibrium price level will be higher.

Data question

1. The main trend in the CPI over the period 2002 to 2007 has been upward. In the first quarter of 2002, the rate of change in prices as measured by the Consumer Prices Index was 1.5 per cent. By the second quarter of 2007, it was 2.6 per cent. The main period of upward price inflation was from 4th quarter of 2004. Before then, inflation had fluctuated around the 1.4 per cent level.
2. The Bank of England uses interest rates to control inflation. When inflationary pressures build up, it increases interest rates. Equally when inflationary pressures are low, it cuts interest rates. Therefore there should be an inverse relationship between the two variables. This is indeed what is shown in Figures 5 and 6 in the student's book. At the start of the period, interest rates were at 3.5 -4.0 per cent and inflation was relatively low. As inflation increased, the Bank of England raised interest rates. By mid 2007, interest rates were 5.75 per cent.
3. The Monetary Policy Committee (MPC) was faced with a difficult decision in August 2007. Inflation in the economy, as measured by the CPI, had been rising and it was currently above the 2 per cent central target set by the government. However, there had been a small fall in inflation in the second quarter of 2007. Growth in GDP, household consumption and retail sales had also slightly fallen, indicating a possible weakness in growth of demand. On the other hand, the employment data would suggest rising demand with unemployment falling and the rate of change of employment picking up. In terms of costs, the rate of change of wages had fallen slightly whilst the value of the pound had risen helping to reduce imported inflation.

Overall, the evidence is mixed. If anything, it would suggest that inflationary pressures were easing. However, inflation was above its 2 per cent target and therefore the Bank of England would have been perhaps mistaken if it had cut interest rates at this point.
4. The MPC finds it difficult to know whether to change interest rates because different economic indicators give different pictures of what is happening in the economy. For instance, economic growth might be below trend, a sign of reduced inflationary pressures. On the other hand, import prices might be rising. This would be a sign of increased inflationary pressures. The MPC must therefore form an opinion on the balance of the evidence presented to it. It must decide which is the most reliable and which is the most important. Not surprisingly, members of the MPC are rarely unanimous in their decisions. In this case, at its August 2007 meeting, the Monetary Policy Committee decided to leave interest rates unchanged at 5.75 per cent.

38 Exchange rate policy

Question 1

(a) A rise in UK domestic interest rates with foreign interest rates remaining unchanged means that the UK becomes a more attractive place to invest money. Foreigners will put more money into savings accounts and interest bearing financial assets in the City of London.This will increase the demand for pounds as they exchange foreign currency for pounds to invest. Conversely, UK savers will now find it less attractive to save their money in foreign financial centres. Less money will flow out of the UK to buy foreign currency and hence the supply of pounds will fall. A rise in the demand for pounds and a fall in their supply on foreign exchange markets leads to a rise in the value of the pound.

The effect on the pound of a rise in interest rates is anticipated by financial markets. If they believe UK interest rates will rise, they will also believe that the value of the pound will rise. Actors in the financial markets then adjust their buying and selling to bring about the rise in the value of the pound before the underlying flows relating to saving have even started to change.This is what happened in December 2004 since in the article it was not even an actual rise in interest rates that prompted a rise in the value of the pound but a possible rise.

(b) When the South Korean and Japanese banks sell their own currency in exchange for US dollars, they increase the supply of their domestic currency on foreign exchange markets. An increase in supply then reduces the equilibrium price of their currency.

However, as with interest rates, there is also a speculative anticipation of what might happen. If markets believe that the sale of currency is a one-off, it might have little or no effect on the price because speculators anticipate the price will simply rebound almost immediately. If, on the other hand, speculators believe that the central banks will supply more currency for sale whenever the price of the currency threatens to rise, then they will tend to act as if the lower price is the equilibrium price.

Question 2

(a) All cheese exporters will have found selling into the US market more difficult following the rise in the value of the pound against the dollar in 2003.They faced making a difficult decision. If they kept the prices of their cheeses the same in pounds, then the price in US dollars would rise because it took more US dollars to buy £1 on the foreign exchange markets. A rise in the price of cheese in US dollars would result in lower sales because quantity demanded would fall. The exact impact would depend on the price elasticity of demand of US consumers for British cheese.The passage states that Neal's Yard Dairy, a UK seller of high quality cheese 'is partially protected because its US customers are less price sensitive than many.' However, if the article is correct that 'People go into a shop and spend the same amount on cheese', this implies that the price elasticity of demand for Neal's Yard Dairy cheese is (-) 1. On the other hand, the passage implies that commodity cheese manufacturers face a more difficult time with a higher price elasticity of demand for cheese. Summerdale International estimates that its global sales could drop from £3 million to £2 million in 2004 as a result of the higher value of the pound.This is a 50 per cent fall in sales value when the value of the pound rose 12.8 per cent between November 2002 and December 2003, from $1.56 to $1.79.

(b) The outlook was not all bleak though for UK cheese manufacturers.The euro had risen by even more against the US dollar than the pound.This meant that French, Italian and German cheese manufacturers had to put up their US dollar prices even more than UK manufacturers if they wanted to maintain their prices in euros. So UK cheese prices, although they went up in price in US dollars, did not go up by as much as continental European cheese prices.This meant that UK cheese was relatively more competitive to European cheese than before.

There was also another exchange rate effect. If the value of the euro rose more against the dollar than the pound, this must have meant that the value of the euro rose against the pound. So continental European cheeses exported to the UK should have increased in price in pounds, giving domestic UK cheese manufacturers a competitive advantage in the UK market.

Question 3

(a) The Japanese central bank between 1991 and 2004 had regularly intervened in the foreign exchange markets to sell Japanese yen and buy up US dollars. Selling yen for US dollars increased the supply of yen on foreign exchange markets and increased the demand for US dollars.Therefore the price of yen went down against the US dollar. It did this because the lower the price of the Japanese yen, the lower the foreign currency price of Japanese exports and the higher the yen price of imports into Japan. More exports and fewer imports boosted Japanese aggregate demand and contributed to higher GDP.

After March 2004, however, the policy appears to have changed. First, the Japanese economy was experiencing positive economic growth which it was hoped would continue rather than halt as in the 1990s. Second, the Japanese Central Bank was concerned about rising commodity prices. Japan is a major importer of commodities such as oil as it has few natural resources of its own.The lower the value of the yen, the higher the price in yen of commodity imports. Sharply rising commodity prices would be likely to feed through to either higher prices for goods and services made in Japan or lower profits for Japanese companies attempting to absorb the price increases, or some combination of both. High prices for Japanese goods in the export sector could lead to lower Japanese exports and thus a fall in aggregate demand.This would defeat the whole purpose of a policy aimed at stimulating economic growth. Hence, the Japanese Central Bank refrained from intervening in the foreign exchange markets to push down the value of the yen.

(b) Intervention in the foreign currency markets in 2003 and 2004 might have been responsible for some of the pick up in export volumes. In 2001, export volumes actually fell, due to the mild world downturn which started in that year. By 2004 export volumes were increasing at a rate of 15 per cent. Rising exports will have contributed to the increase in economic growth from 2002. So Figure 1 in the student's book might give some support to the view that exchange rate intervention achieved its objectives. However, clearly there were other forces at work which had perhaps an even greater impact on Japanese exports and therefore

Japanese economic growth.

Data question

Note: there was a misprint in the first impression of the 5th edition. This has been corrected in reprints. Questions 2 and 3 are as follows.
2. Explain how the fall in the effective exchange rate of the pound between 1992 and 1996 might have affected (a) export and import volumes, (b) average export and import prices, (c) the profitability of UK exporting firms.
3. What impact on the economic performance of the UK might the fall in the value of the pound against the euro have had between 2000 and 2007?

1. Three measures of the value of the pound are given in the data: the sterling effective exchange rate index, the value of the pound against a weighted basket of currencies; the value of the US dollar against the pound; and the value of the euro against the pound.

The trade weighted index shows the value of the pound substantially falling in value from September 1992, losing around 15 per cent of its value; but then from 1996, quickly regaining value and from, 1997, fluctuating within a range of an index value of 95 and 105. In terms of the US dollar, the US dollar was weak against the pound between 1990 and 1992, but then there was a substantial fall in the value of the pound against the dollar. The pound stayed weak against the dollar between 1992 and 2002, when a sharp appreciation of the pound too place. By 2007, the pound was as strong against the dollar as it had been for a time in 1990 and 1992, £1 exchanging for between $1.80 and $1.90.

In terms of the euro, there was a significant fall in the value of the pound against the euro from September 1992 to the end of 1995. Between 1996 and 2000, there was a substantial appreciation of the value of the pound against the euro, taking it to over 1.60 euros, but then the value of the pound fell back and by 2003-2007 it was trading in the range 1.40 to 1.50 euros.

The overall picture is one where the value of the pound remains relatively stable between 1990 and 1992, drops sharply from September 1992 and stays low to 1996, when it increases rapidly in value to around 2000 and then between 2000 and 2007 fluctuates within a relatively narrow range.

2.(a) There was a large overall fall in the effective exchange rate of the pound between 1992 and 1996, from a high of an index number of 98 to a low of 81.

In theory, a fall in the value of the pound is likely to have increased export volumes and reduced import volumes. This is because a fall in the value of the pound reduces the foreign currency price of exports but increases the pound sterling price of imports. For example, if the value of the pound is £1=$2, then cheese priced at £10 in the UK can be sold to the USA for $20. If the value of the pound falls to £1=$1, then the same £10 cheese can be sold to the USA for $10. The fall in the US dollar price will result in Americans buying British cheese.

Looking at Figure 2 in the student's book, what in fact happened between 1992 and 1996 was that both export and import volumes rose, with export volumes rising at a slightly higher rate than import volumes. The continued rise in import volumes is likely to have been due to increased demand for imports in the UK as incomes rose. But it could also have been due to importers keeping down UK prices of their products at the expense of their profit margins.

(b) In (a), it has already been explained how a fall in the value of the pound could affect prices. However, the impact on average export and import prices will depend on the marketing strategy of UK exporters and foreign firms selling imports into the UK. Taking the example of cheese, the UK cheese manufacturer exporting to the US could decide that, instead of reducing the dollar price of cheese to US customers, it will put up the price in pounds to export buyers. At its extreme, in the example in (a), it could decide to put up the pound price from £10 to £20. When the value of the pound falls from $2 to $1, the dollar price remains the same at $20. The UK exporter doesn't sell any more cheese into US markets but it increases its profit by £10. The change in the average price of exports will therefore depend on the mix of pricing strategies that UK exporters use. The more they respond to a lower value of the pound by raising the £ sterling price of their exports, the greater will be the average increase in the price of exports in £ sterling and the less will be the average fall in prices when measured in foreign currency terms. The same is true for imports. The more foreign companies choose to accept a cut in profit on each item sold for export to the UK, and the less they choose to accept a fall in sales volume due to higher UK prices, the less will be the average rise in import prices measured in £ sterling terms.

Looking at Figure 3 in the student's book, it is clear that UK exporters chose to increase their prices sharply following the fall in the value of the pound. Between 1992 and 1996, the value of the pound fell approximately 17 per cent on a trade weighted basis. Over the same period, the price of exports rose approximately 21 per cent. Importers too chose to raise their prices by approximately 26 per cent over the period. This would suggest that exporters chose a policy of increasing their prices and profit margins as the value of the pound fell. In contrast, importers kept their foreign currency prices the same which meant a rise in prices in pounds sterling for their products.

(c) UK exporters faced a difficult choice. If they raised their prices in £ sterling on exported goods, they could earn more profit per item sold but this would be at the expense of selling more and earning more profit by greater sales. If they kept their prices in £ sterling the same, their sales volumes would go up and they would earn more profit because they were selling more. But the profit per item sold would not increase. In practice, the decision about whether to raise prices would depend on a complex mix of the nature of the market into which they were selling and the relative costs of increasing production to allow for greater sales. A UK firm which enjoyed strong market power over its exports and which would find it costly to increase production would choose to increase its profits by raising its £ sterling price. A UK firm which was in a fiercely price competitive export market would be forced to maintain its £ sterling price the same and accept a lower foreign exchange price. Its sales volumes would rise, so increasing profit, but its profit per unit sold would remain the same.

Looking at Figure 3 in the student's book, the actual data for the UK economy would suggest that UK exporters chose to increase profits by charging higher prices rather than increasing sales volumes, whilst foreign firms exporting to the UK chose to increase their sterling prices to maintain their profits in foreign currency terms.

3. The economic performance of the economy can be considered in terms of economic growth, inflation, unemployment and the current account balance.

The fall in the value of the pound against the euro should

have boosted aggregate demand by increasing the value of exports and reducing the value of imports from what they would otherwise have been. This should have led to higher growth in GDP, although this might not have translated into an increase in the productive potential of the economy if investment failed to increase at the same time.

The fall in the exchange rate should have led to higher prices because the price of imports should have risen. Therefore there will have been a one-off rise in the inflation rate. However, unless the pound continues to fall in value, the inflation rate should then come down again in the longer term.

A boost to aggregate demand with more exports and fewer imports should lead to more jobs in the economy and therefore less unemployment.

In terms of the current balance, this should improve because export values will have increased whereas import values should have fallen compared to what they might otherwise have been.

However, the fall in the value of the euro against the pound was fairly small at approximately 7 per cent. This will have limited the effects of the fall. Moreover, the sterling exchange rate against the euro is only one of a number of important exchange rates for the UK economy. A better measure of the foreign currency impact is the trade weighted or effective exchange rate. Over the period 2000 to 2007, it fluctuated within a fairly narrow range. The rise in the value of the euro was offset by falls in the value of other currencies such as the dollar. Therefore, the overall exchange rate impact on the UK economy is likely to have

39 Production

Question 1

(a)
(i) x = 1.10 x 1.100.75 x 1.000.25 = 1.10 x 1.07 x 1.00 = 1.18. Hence the index of production increases by 18 per cent.
(ii) x = 1.10 x 1.200.75 x 1.000.25 = 1.10 x 1.15 x 1.00 = 1.27. Hence the index of production increases by 27 per cent.
(b)
(i) x = 1.10 x 1.000.75 x 1.200.25 = 1.10 x 1.00 x 1.05 = 1.16. Hence the index of production increases by 16 per cent.
(ii) x = 1.10 x 1.000.75 x 1.300.25 = 1.10 x 1.00 x 1.07 = 1.18. Hence the index of production increases by 18 per cent.
(c)
(i) x = 1.10 x 1.300.75 x 1.300.25 = 1.10 x 1.22 x 1.07 = 1.44. Hence the index of production increases by 44 per cent.
(ii) x = 1.10 x 1.500.75 x 1.500.25 = 1.10 x 1.36 x 1.11 = 1.66. Hence the index of production increases by 66 per cent.

Question 2

(a) Buying tyres from a supplier would be an example of a short run decision because most factors of production would remain fixed when this took place.
(b) The decision to close plants and make 30 000 workers redundant was arguably a long run decision. General Motors reviewed how it was using all its resources in North America and came up with a radical plan to downsize its operations. It could be argued that it was still a short run decision because the review did not include the operations of General Motors outside North America.
(c) A change from manufacturing petrol driven cars to cars powered by hydrogen is arguably a very long run decision. This is because the technology of the motor car is being changed.

Question 3

The question states that the fixed factors of production (brooms, mops, dusters, polish etc.) are to be combined with variable factors of production (the cleaners). It could be that 5 cleaners working together may clean your house in less than one fifth of the time it takes one cleaner. They might achieve this by cooperating together. However, it could be that even with 5 cleaners diminishing returns will have set in. Certainly by the time 20 cleaners are employed it is likely that output per workers would be lower compared to 1 cleaner being employed. The 20 workers are unlikely to have sufficient fixed capital (the brooms etc.) to keep themselves fully occupied all the time. With 1 000 cleaners in the house, the house would be too full of cleaners for any cleaning to be done. Total output would be zero.

Question 4

(a) Table 1

units

Capital	Labour	Total product	Average product	Marginal product
				8
8	10	1	8	
				16
10	2	24	12	
				18
10	3	42	14	
				18
10	4	60	15	
				10
10	5	70	14	
				2
10	6	72	12	

(b) Note that marginal product is plotted half way between the points on the horizontal axis.

Figure 1

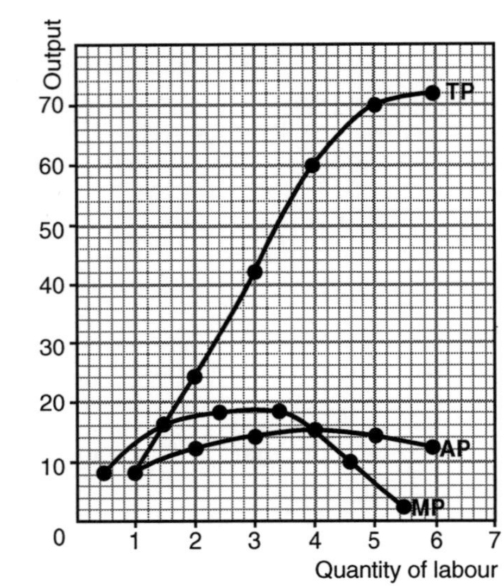

(c) (i) Diminishing marginal returns set in when 3 units of labour are employed.
(ii) Diminishing average returns set in when 4 units of labour are employed.

Question 5

(a) Increasing returns are experienced when the firm doubles its inputs of 1 unit of labour and 1 unit of capital, giving a threefold increase in output from 1 to 3 units. Equally, a 50 per cent rise in inputs from 2 units each of labour and capital to 3 units of each gives rise to increasing returns because output rises 150 per cent from 2 to 5.
(b) Constant returns are experienced when the firm increases its factor inputs from 3 units of labour and 3 units of capital to 4 units of labour and 4 units of capital. This 33 per cent rise in inputs is matched by a 33 per cent rise in output from 9 to 12 units.

(c) Decreasing returns to scale are experienced when the firm increases its factor inputs from 4 units each of labour and capital to 5 units each of both. This 25 per cent rise in factor inputs gives rise only to a 16.6 per cent increase in output from 12 to 14 units.

Data question

1. Overfishing is generally recognised to be a problem today. Too many fish are being caught for fishing stocks to remain at their present levels. In some cases, there is a danger that fish are being fished to extinction. Evidence for over-fishing comes from a variety of sources. In the most dramatic example, in the 1980s, the once plentiful fish stocks off Newfoundland were completely fished out and the fishery has still yet to recover. In the UK, in 2004, only 25 per cent of fish stocks were fished at a sustainable level. 75 per cent of fish stocks are still being overfished with the risk that the fish stock could be destroyed completely. The United Nations Food and Agriculture Organisation (FAO) in 2005 estimated that only 23 per cent of the world's fisheries were underexploited.

2. The problem of overfishing is an example of diminishing returns. The stocks of fish in a fishery are finite. The more boats are put into the fishery, the greater is likely to be the catch. However, the catch per boat is likely to be less if there are one thousand boats working the fishery than if there are one hundred (the principle of diminishing average returns). Every extra boat that is added will tend to reduce the amount of fish caught by each boat in the fishery. The addition to the total catch will also fall as each new boat is added to the fleet (the principle of diminishing marginal returns).

In UK fishing waters, the data in Figures 2 and 4 in the student's book would seem to point to diminishing returns. For instance, between 1982 and 1992, there was a substantial increase in the UK fishing fleet but fishing was at an unsustainable level. When the the number of UK boats fell from 1992, fisheries became more sustainable. Worldwide, the FAO estimates that 52 per cent of fisheries are being fully exploited and so adding more boats into these areas would lead to less and less being caught by each boat, an example of diminishing average returns.

3. There is a number of possible measures which the UK government could take to resolve the problem of overfishing.

One possible measure is to tighten the existing system of quotas on fishing catches. UK fishing policy is determined within the context of the European Union. At present, each country has a quota limit on the amount of fish that can be landed from its national trawlers. A, say, 25 per cent cut across the board in those quotas would help conserve fish stocks although the exact percentage reduction needed to restore the UK's fisheries is subject to disagreement. The fishing industry would be hit by these measures. Its income, however, would not necessarily go down by 25 per cent because the price of fish is likely to increase. For UK fishermen, the best outcome would be one where quotas were made more stringent on other EU boats but their quotas either remained the same or were even relaxed. This would allow UK fishermen to maintain their income and see some improvement in fish stocks. The main problem with this solution is that the existing quota system is fiercely disliked by the fishing industry. Tightening it further may be politically impossible. It would also be almost impossible to negotiate a settlement where the pain of extra quotas was only felt by non-UK fishermen.

A second solution would be to ban all fishing in a particular fishery. This would allow fish stocks to recover more quickly than if fishing continued. A ban would be particularly suitable if continued fishing on however small a scale could tip the fishery into complete destruction. However, a ban would hit fishermen and their livelihoods and could drive up the price of fish.

A third solution could be to place restrictions on the number of boats which were allowed to catch fish. Fewer boats would presumably catch fewer fish and hence fish stocks could be renewed. The scheme would be controversial to implement. If, for instance, it were decided to reduce the size of the fishing fleet, there would have to be some provision made for compensation to be paid to boat owners who lost their boats. The size of new boats would have to be restricted because there would be an incentive for bigger and bigger boats to be used. Those who retained their boats with a licence could benefit substantially if they could sell the licence to another boat owner, or sell the boat with the licence. In this situation, licences could become very valuable to those having them, whilst new entrants would face higher costs because they would have to buy a licence as well as a boat.

A fourth possible measure would be for taxes to be placed on fish sales. Taxes would raise the price paid by consumers and therefore quantity demanded would fall. The extent of the fall would be determined by the elasticity of demand for fish. If it were very low, large rises in the price of fish would have little effect on quantity demanded and hence fishermen could continue to sell large quantities of fish in the UK. However, taxes would be ineffective if they were only imposed by the UK. Fish would simply be diverted to other markets. The reduction in demand by consumers in the UK would slightly lower the price of fish, but UK demand is only a small fraction of demand throughout the EU and the rest of the world. Hence, there would be little impact on conservation and the fishing industry would be barely affected. If, however, the tax were imposed throughout Europe, the fall in quantity demanded would be much greater and therefore have more impact on the ability of the fishing industry to supply fish to the market. Even so, it is likely that EU fishing boats would find markets for their fish outside the EU. Prices might be lower but they might be attractive enough to keep the EU fishing fleet in business, with little effect on the amount of fish caught.

40 Costs

Question 1

(a) The accounting costs of her business were the costs which involved the payment of monies: namely, £18 000 for materials and £9 000 in wages making a total of £27 000.

Her economic costs included her accounting costs. But they also included:

- the opportunity cost of her premises - £10 000;
- the opportunity cost of her time spent in the business, which is half a teacher's salary - £15 000;
- the interest foregone on the capital tied up in the business - 5 per cent of £40 000, or £2 000.

Her total economic costs were therefore £54 000.

(b) On an accounting basis, given revenues of £60 000 and costs of £27 000, she made a profit of £33 000. However, on an economic basis, her revenues were only £6 000 more than her costs and hence her economic profit was only £6 000.

Question 2

Fixed costs are costs which do not vary with output. In the case of a restaurant, output could be measured by the number of meals served. Costs which Rachel Hughes could not vary with output would be the rent on the premises, interest payments on a loan and the cost of pots and pans.

Variable costs vary directly with output. Rice, cooking oil and VAT can all therefore be classified as variable costs.

Semi-variable costs are costs which can vary with output but only to some extent. For instance, the restaurant could open fewer hours if trade was poor. This would then reduce electricity bills and the cost of casual staff. Equally, Rachel Hughes could give herself a lower wage if business was poor.

Question 3

(a) Table 1

£

Output	Total fixed cost	Total variable cost	Total cost	Average fixed cost	Average variable cost	Average cost	Marginal cost
0	40	-	-	-	-	-	-
1	40	6	46	40.0	6.0	46.0	46
2	40	11	51	20.0	5.5	25.5	5
3	40	15	55	13.3	5.0	18.3	4
4	40	20	60	10.0	5.0	15.0	5
5	40	26	66	8.0	5.2	13.2	6

Figures rounded to the nearest decimal point.

Question 4

(a) - (d) (i) - (vii)
Table 2

£

Units of labour	Total physical product	Total fixed cost	Total variable cost	Total cost	Average fixed cost	Average variable cost	Average total cost	Marginal cost
1	20	200	50	250	10.0	2.5	12.5	12.5
2	45	200	100	300	4.4	2.2	6.7	2.0
3	60	200	150	350	3.3	2.5	5.8	3.3
4	70	200	200	400	2.9	2.9	5.7	5.0

Figures rounded to nearest decimal point.

Question 5

(a) Table 3

£

Units of labour	Total physical product	Total fixed cost	Total variable cost	Total cost	Average fixed cost	Average variable cost	Average total cost	Marginal cost
0	0	10	0	-	-	-		
1	8	10	2	12	1.25	0.25	1.50	1.50
2	24	10	4	14	0.42	0.17	0.58	0.13
3	42	10	6	16	0.24	0.14	0.38	0.11
4	60	10	8	18	0.17	0.13	0.30	0.11
5	70	10	10	20	0.14	0.14	0.29	0.20
6	72	10	12	22	0.14	0.17	0.31	1.00

Figures rounded to two decimal places.

(b)(c)(i)(ii) See Figures 1 and 2.

Figure 1

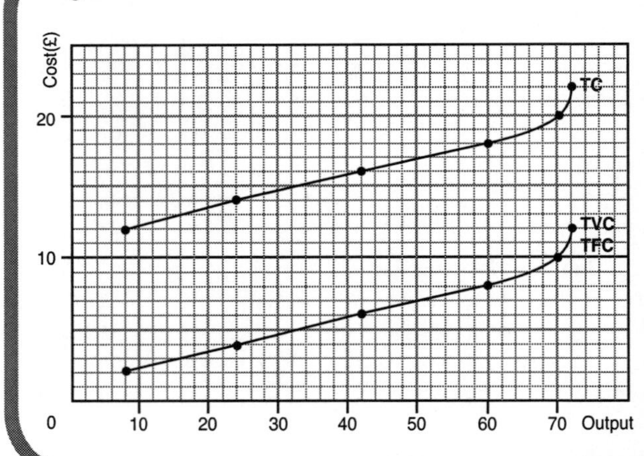

Question 6

(a) (i) Economies of scale exist for:
Firm A between 1 and 3 million units;
Firm B between 1 and 5 million units;
Firm C between 1 and 2 million units;
Firm D between 1 and at least 7 million units;
Firm E between 1 and 4 million units.
(ii) Diseconomies of scale exist for:
Firm A from 6 million units;
Firm B from 6 million units;
Firm C from 2 million units.

Figure 2

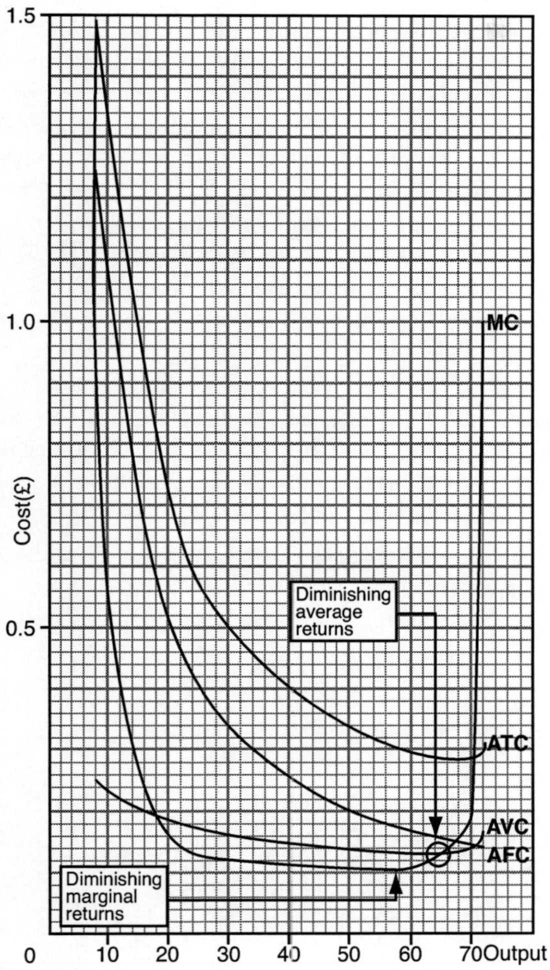

Firms D and E show no range of levels of output over which diseconomies occur.

(b) The optimum level of output occurs for:
Firm A between 3 and 6 million units of output;
Firm B between 5 and 6 million units of output;
Firm C at 2 million units of output.
It is not possible to determine whether the optimum level of output occurs at 7 million units of output for Firm D or between 4 and 7 million units of output for Firm E because higher levels of output might lead to even lower average costs. However, it is likely, at least for Firm E, that the optimum level of production occurs from 4 million units of output onwards.

(c) The minimum efficient scale of production occurs at:
3 million units of output for Firm A;
5 million units of output for Firm B;
2 million units of output for Firm C.
It is not possible to say whether it occurs at 7 million units of output for Firm D for the reasons put in (b). For the same reasons, it may occur at 4 million units of output for Firm E but this is not certain.

Question 7

(a) The merger of Boots and Alliance UniChem would lead to increased economies of scale in a number of different areas. First, there would be managerial economies. It should take fewer resources to manage the combined company than two individual companies. For instance, there should only be a need for one headquarters. There wi l only be one chief executive and one board of directors.

Second, there should be marketing economies. Some Boots products such as Soltan sun cream and No 7 make up will be sold through UniChem outlets for example.

Third, there should be technical economies of scale. If sales levels can be scaled up, average costs should fall. For example, there may be potential to merge some warehouse facilities, increasing the throughput of products through some warehouses and closing others. Some retail outlets may close if they are very near to another retail outlet.

Fourth, there should be buying economies of scale. The passage states that 'it hopes that its greater buying power will enable it to negotiate better prices from drug manufacturers'.

Overall, the merged business to generate £100 million in cost saving through exploiting the greater economies of scale presented by the merger.

Question 8

(a) There is likely to be a wide variety of sources of external economies of scale for food companies in North East Lincolnshire. One is infrastructure. The local airport, Humberside Airport, handles perishable products. The two local ports of Immingham and Grimsby handle 50 million tonnes of freight a year. Business parks such as as Europarc have been built with food processing in mind. The proposed extension to Europarc will include 'a network of shared-user waste, water recovery and energy generation facilities' aimed at food processing companies.

A second source of external economies of scale is likely to be the local labour force. A significant proportion of the local labour force will be employed in the food processing industry. Companies wanting to recruit new labour will therefore have a pool of labour used to this type of work from which to draw. The labour force is also likely to be the source of new start up companies. Individuals who have gained skills and expertise working for an employer will set up their own businesses, creating a dynamic effect on the local economy.

Local government can also be a source of external economies. Local government in the area will have more knowledge about the requirements of food processing than local government in areas where food processing is relatively unimportant. This means that local government in the North East Lincolnshire area is more likely to promote, initiate and approve schemes which are related to the food processing industry.

Question 9

(a) In 2002, GM sent in two senior US executives to Saab, the Swedish car company it owned. Their brief was to 'sort the company out' by reducing costs and selling more cars. Saab has a manufacturing plant at Trollhättan which was operating inefficiently. One source of inefficiency was overmanning - having too many workers employed for the amount of work available. Making part of the workforce redundant, combined with other efficiencies, the average number of hours it took to make a car was reduced from 50 to 30.

This can be shown on a diagram. In Figure 3, the short run average cost curve (SRAC) for the Trollhättan plant is shown. Given that the plant is now built, it will operate somewhere along that curve if production is efficient. The long run average cost curve (LRAC) shows average costs if all costs are variable. This curve shows how average costs would vary according to output if Saab started out from scratch with a greenfield site and a new labour force. In 2002, the company was operating

Figure 3

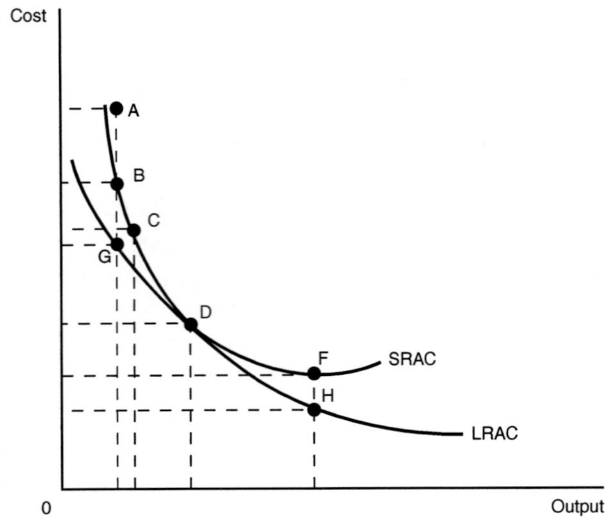

at the point A, within both its SRAC and LRAC curves. This is because it was operating inefficiently with too large a workforce. By making part of the workforce redundant and making other efficiency gains, it was arguably able to move onto its SRAC curve at the point B. Because the plant could not be changed, it was unable to cut costs further to move down onto its LRAC curve at the point G.

(b) Increasing production at Trollhättan, by building 'new, more attractive models', enabled Saab to cut short run average costs further. Fixed costs of production were spread out over a larger number of cars, so reducing average cost.

In Figure 3, this is shown by a movement down the SRAC curve from, say, B to C. The point C is still neither the short run or long run efficient point of production. GM wants to increase production further, possibly by building a small Cadillac at the plant 'to get it up to full working capacity'. Full working capacity is shown by the point D in Figure 3. This is the level of production for which the plant was built. In the short run, average costs could fall still further if production went beyond full capacity at the point F. However, at this level of production, an even lower average cost of production could have been achieved from a greenfield site at the point H.

Data question

1. Larger ships may enjoy larger economies of scale than smaller ships. The main reason is because they enjoy technical economies of scale. It is cheaper to build a large container ship per container (measured in the standard volume measure of a TEU) than a smaller ship. It is also cheaper to operate a large container ship. Fuel costs per TEU are lower, as are crew costs.

2. The average cost per TEU is likely to be lower for the voyage for the smaller vessel. This is because the 5 000 TEU vessel will be operating at the full capacity for which it was designed. In contrast, the larger 8 500 TEU vessel will be operating at far less than full capacity. But it will still have to have a full crew. The fuel cost of driving the larger ship will be higher than for the smaller ship. The insurance cost of the larger ship will be higher.

This can be shown on Figure 4. The long run average cost curve shows the average cost of running a ship (including an allowance for the initial cost of the ship) according to its size. The average cost of running a fully laden 5 000 TEU ship is OJ. The running cost of running a fully laden 8 500 TEU ship is lower at OK. In the short run, on the journey described in the question, the 5 000 TEU vessel is operating at maximum efficiency for which it was designed at the point A where its short run average cost curve is tangential to its long run average cost curve. However, the 8 500 TEU vessel is not operating at maximum efficiency. It is operating at the 5 000 TEU point on its short run average cost curve at the point C. Average costs are higher than for the 5 000 TEU vessel at OL.

A number of assumptions must be made to allow this conclusion to be reached. The two ships must be of roughly the same age, using the same technology available at the time of construction. The cost of fuel per litre for the two vessels must be the same. They must both be maintained to the same standard and they must be run as efficiently as possible in the circumstances. If the 8 500 TEU vessel were brand new and the 5 000 TEU vessel were 20 years old, it could be that even operating below capacity the 8 500 TEU vessel was more efficient than an old fully laden 5 000 TEU vessel.

Figure 4

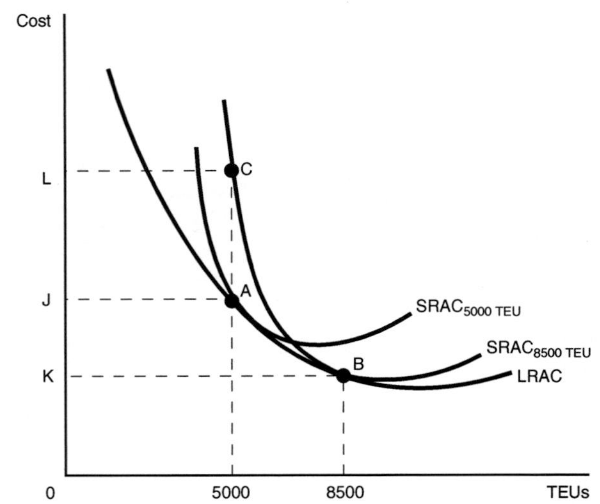

3. Diseconomies of scale in this case would occur when the average cost of operating container ships rises as their size rises. The article outlines a number of potential diseconomies of scale from using the latest very large container ships. One is that they will not be able to load and unload at many of the ports round the world because the ports cannot accommodate ships of this size. This means that if there is overcapacity on the routes on which they can operate, they may be forced to stand idle for part of the year. This will raise the average cost of operating these ships. The same problem arises if too many large ships are built to operate on even the restricted number of routes that can accommodate them.

Another problem is bottlenecks in loading and unloading at ports. Ports, such as Vancouver, and land transport operators, such as Canadian railways, will not necessarily be able to handle the new very large container ships efficiently. If these vessels have to wait in port too long to be loaded and unloaded, then their average cost of operation could be higher than for a smaller vessel where loading and unloading takes places far more quickly and the vessel can get to sea more quickly.

The article states that ship owners are confident that these will not be problems either in the short term or the long term. It is likely that ports will adjust, just as they have adjusted in the past to ever larger ships. However, the shipping industry has a history of building too many ships when there were boom times and then being left with too much capacity when demand for sea transport fell. A world recession is a major threat to the efficient running of very large container ships.

41 Revenues

Question 1

Table 1

Sales (million units)	Average revenue (£)	Total revenue (£)	Marginal revenue (£)
1	20	20	20
2	18	36	16
3	16	48	12
4	14	56	8
5	12	60	4
6	10	60	0
7	8	56	-4
8	6	48	-8
9	4	36	-12
10	2	20	-16

Data question

1(a)(i) 25 000 bicycles;
(ii) 30 000 bicycles;
(iii) 35 000 bicycles;
(iv) 40 000 bicycles.
(b) Figures 1, 2 and 3 are drawn from the following data.

Output	Total revenue (£)	Average revenue (£)	Marginal revenue (£)
25 000	10 000	400	
30 000	10 800	360	800
35 000	11 200	320	400
40 000	11 200	280	0

(c)
(i) -2.0. From £400 to £360, a fall in price of 20 per cent, quantity demanded increases from 25 000 to 30 000, a rise of 20 per cent. Price elasticity of demand is therefore -2.0 (20% ÷ 10%)
(ii) - 1.5. From £360 to £320, a fall in price of 11.11 per cent, quantity demanded increases from 30 000 to 35 000, a rise of 16.66%. Price elasticity of demand is therefore - 1.5 (16.66% ÷ 11.11%).
(iii) - 1.14. From £320 to £280, a fall in price of 0.125, quantity demanded increases from 35 000 to 40 000, a rise of 14.3 per cent. Price elasticity of demand therefore - 1.14.
2. Finchfield Cycles should cut prices on overseas sales rather than home sales. Assume that it cuts prices on both home and overseas sales by 10 per cent. Then quantity demanded would, assuming an elasticity of 4, rise by 40 per cent in overseas markets. In contrast, quantity demanded would, assuming an elasticity of 2, rise by 20 per cent in home markets. For a given price reduction, sales would rise more in overseas markets than home markets.

Figure 1

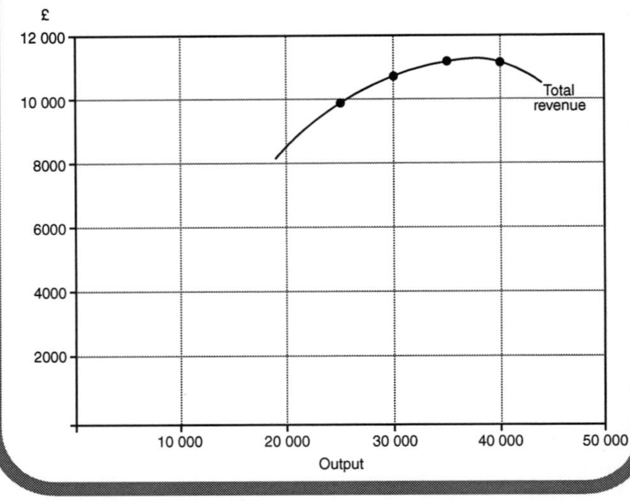

Figure 2

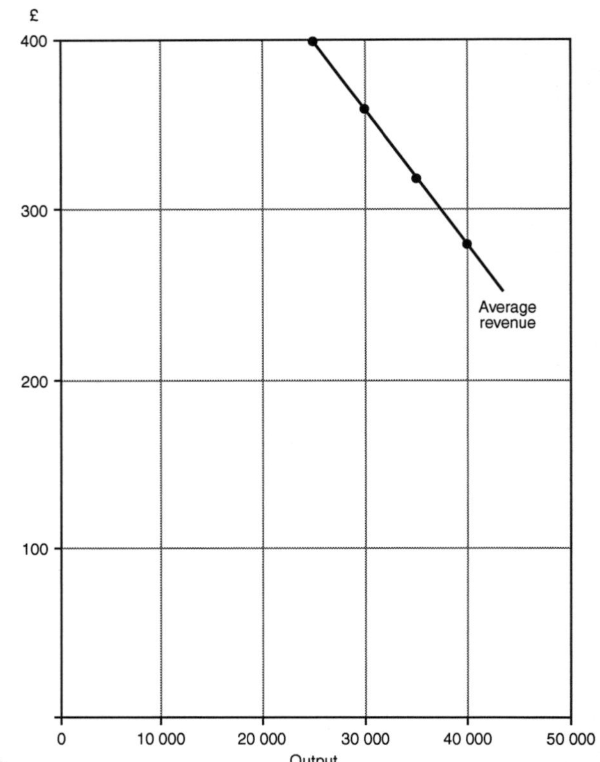

Figure 3

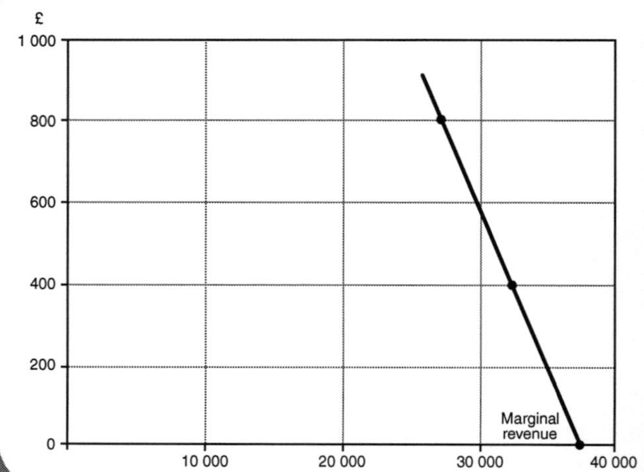

42 Profit

Question 1

(a) The accounting profit is the difference between accounting revenues and accounting costs. So:
Year 1 is £270 000 - £250 000 = £20 000
Year 2 is £310 000 - £280 000 = £30 000
Year 3 is £450 000 - £350 000 = £100 000

(b) The economic profit is equal to the economic revenue minus the economic cost. In this case, this is equal to the accounting profit minus the the difference between his previous salary of £70 000 and his current drawings from the business minus the interest foregone on the £50 000 of his savings. So:
Year 1 is £20 000 - (£70 000 - £30 000) - £5 000 = - £25 000
Year 2 is £30 000 - (£70 000 - £50 000) - £5 000 = £5 000
Year 3 is £100 000 - (£70 000 - £70 000) - £5 000 = £95 000.

(c) The normal profit of the firm is the profit that the resources used in the firm could have made in their next best occupation. The business person could have made £70 000 in his next best occupation and received £5 000 a year in interest. Hence the normal profit of the firm would have been £75 000.

Question 2

(a) (c) Table 1

Million units	£ millions				
Output	Total revenue	Total cost	Total profit	Marginal revenue	Marginal cost
1	10	8	2	10	8
2	20	14	6	10	6
3	30	20	10	10	6
4	40	30	10	10	10
5	50	50	0	10	20
6	60	80	-20	10	30

(b) 4 million units. Abnormal profit is £10 million. The firm will produce 4 million rather than 3 million units because normal profits will be higher.

(d) MC=MR at the profit maximising level of output of 4 million units. If the company only produces 3 million units, marginal revenue is greater than marginal cost. By expanding output by another million units, the firm can increase its profit. If the firm produces 5 million units, the marginal cost is greater than marginal revenue. By cutting back production by 1 million units, the firm could reduce its losses. Hence the point where MC=MR is the profit maximising level of output.

Question 3

(a) and (b)

Figure 1

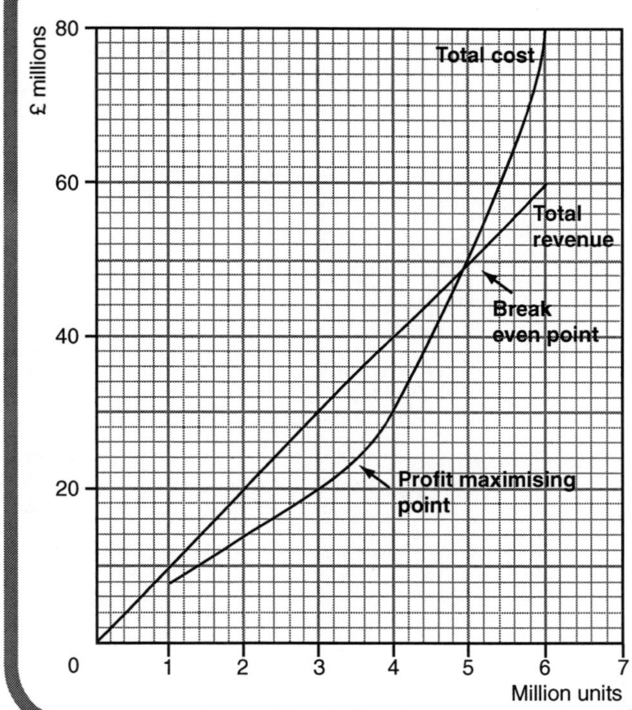

Figure 2

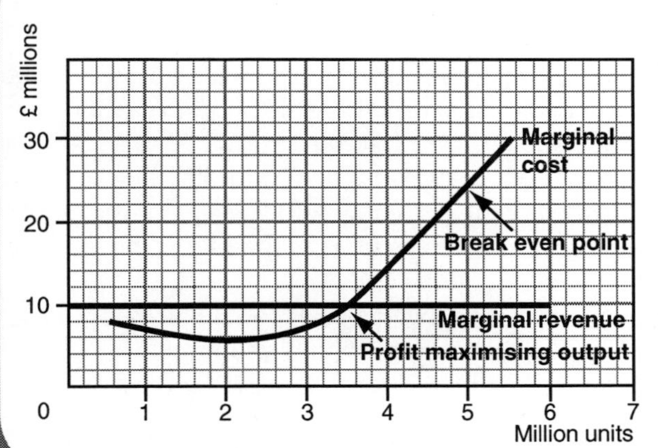

The profit maximising level of output in Figure 1 is 3.5 million units whereas in Question 2 it is given as 4 million units. The answer in Question 2 is an approximation, figures for an output of 3.5 million units not being given. Notice that total profit at output of 3.5 million units is approximately £16 million in Figure 1, greater than the £10 million profit at an output of either 3 or 4 million units.

Question 4

(a) 3 million units - where MC = MR = 6 million (at the highest level of output).

(b) 5 million units - where MC = MR = £20 million (at the highest level of output).

(c) 3 million units - where MC = MR = £10 million (at the highest level of output).

(d) 4 million units. The profit maximising level of output remains the same as in Question 2(b). This is because an increase in total cost of £5 million at each level of output has

no effect on marginal cost except on the first 1 million units produced. The profit maximising level of output remains at 4 million units because this is where MC = MR = £10 million.
(e) 5 million units. If total revenue doubles at each level of output, then so does marginal revenue. The profit maximising level of output is therefore where MC = MR = £20 million.

Question 5

(a) The total cost of producing 10 units is made up of the variable cost of £10 million (10 x £1 million) and the fixed cost of £10 million. With total revenue of £30 million, profit is £10 million (£30 million - £20 million) and therefore the firm will produce 10 units.
(b) The total cost of producing 15 units is £15 million of variable cost and £10 million of fixed cost. The firm will produce if it receives a revenue of £25 million because it breaks even at this level of output.
(c) The total cost of producing 20 units is £20 million of variable cost and £10 million of fixed cost. Although revenues of £22 million do not cover the total cost, the firm will still produce at this level of output because £22 million more than covers its variable cost of production. The loss is only £8 million (£22 million - £30 million) compared to £10 million (the fixed cost) if it shut down completely.
(d) The total cost of producing 25 units is £25 million of variable cost and £10 million of fixed cost. With potential revenues of only £20 million, the firm would choose to shut down the plant since it could not even cover its variable cost.

Question 6

(a) The total cost of producing 300 units is made up of £900 of fixed cost and £300 of variable cost. A 25 per cent mark-up would add £300 to the £1 200, making a total of £1 500. The price per unit would therefore be £5 (£1 500/£300).
(b) To break even the company would need to just cover its costs excluding profit. Therefore the break-even quantity sold would be 240 (£1 200 ÷ £5).
(c) In the short term the firm could sell 500 units (150 + 350) a week at £3. The total cost of production would be £900 of fixed costs and £500 of variable costs. Total revenues of £1 500 (£3 x 500) would therefore give a profit of £100. If it refused the order and sold just 150 units it would make a loss of £300 (revenues of £5 x 150 minus costs of £900 + £150). However, in the long term, if demand did increase to 300 units at a price of £5, it could make a profit of £300.

So the firm is faced with a choice. It could increase short term profit from -£300 to +£100 but it would then find it difficult subsequently to increase price to the original planned level of £5. There is no guarantee that the extra order of 350 would continue in the long term. If it were lost, the company would face selling low volumes at low prices. It might prefer to maintain the higher price of £5 and establish itself in the market, even though this means short term losses, for the sake of making a long term secure profit.

Data question

1. Marginal cost is the cost of producing an extra unit of output. The marginal cost of production at Baggeridge has risen because gas prices have risen. Fuel costs are a significant part of total cost in making bricks, particularly of the solid bricks that are made at the plant.
This can be shown on a diagram, Figure 3. The marginal cost curve has shifted upwards from MC_1 to MC_2 as a result of an increase per unit manufactured of AB in gas prices.

Figure 3

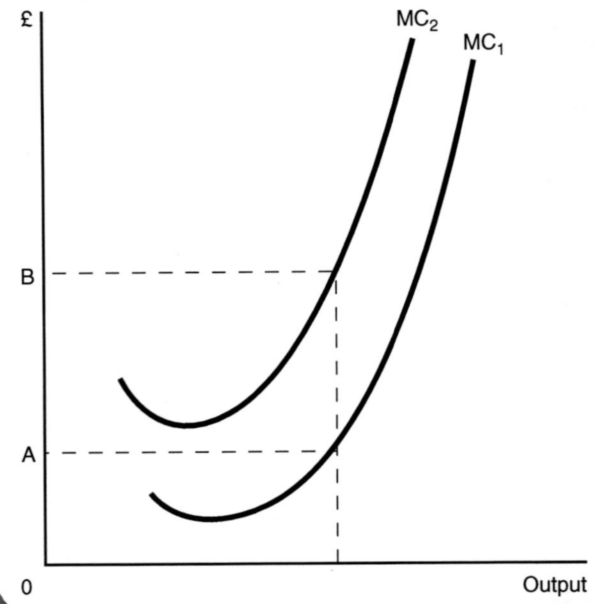

Figure 4

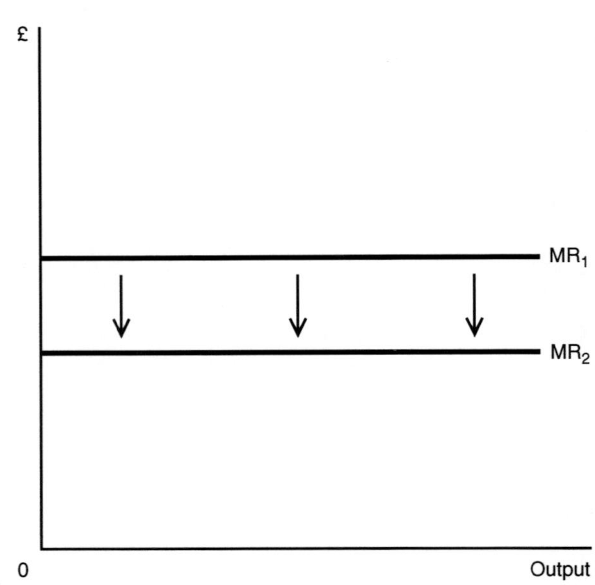

2. Marginal revenue is the revenue received from selling an extra unit of output. With demand for bricks falling, it is likely that the price the company can negotiate for the next order sold will be less per brick than before.

This can be shown in Figure 4. It is assumed that Baggeridge bricks is a price taker. So its marginal revenue curve is horizontal. When market demand falls, the marginal revenue curve of the company falls from MR_1 to MR_2. At any given level of output, the company now receives a lower price for its product.
3. With rising costs and falling prices, Baggeridge was operating the two factories at a loss. It said that 'we really can't afford to run these two factories'. So it chose to shut the two factories down temporarily. It must have been hoping that in the longer term either gas prices would fall or demand and prices for its product would rise.

The reason for the temporary shut down can be seen in Figure 5. The firm will profit maximise where marginal cost

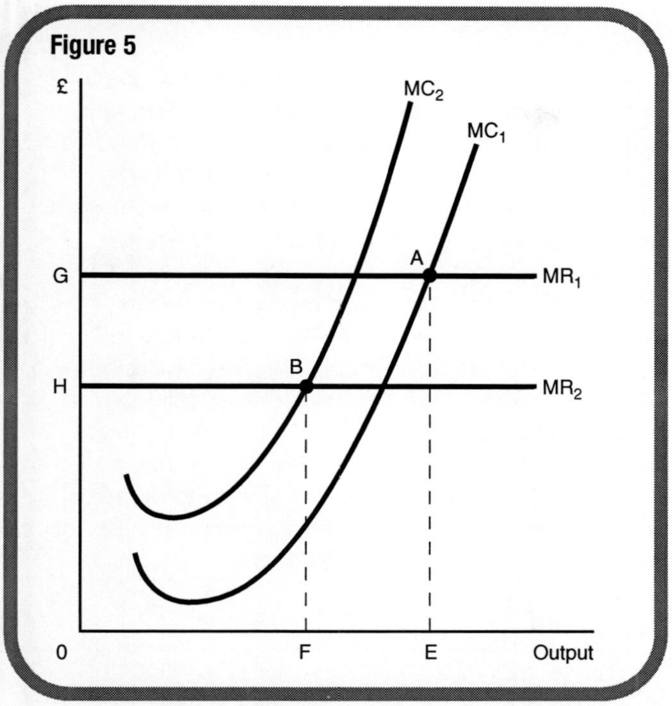

equals marginal revenue. Before gas prices rose and demand fell, the firm was operating at the point A at the intersection of MC_1 and MR_2. After gas prices rose and brick prices fell, the marginal cost shifted to MC_2 and the marginal revenue curve shifted to MR_2. The new profit maximising equilibrium where marginal cost equals marginal revenue is at the point B. Output has fallen from OE to OF whilst equilibrium marginal costs and revenues have fallen from OG to OH. FE represents the output of the two plants that have been shut down. OF represents the combined output of other Baggeridge plants.

43 Objectives of firms

Question 1

(a) The stakeholders of a firm are those groups which have an interest in its operation. The main stakeholders in Manchester United include the owners of the club, the shareholders; the creditors of the club; the management of the club; the players in the team; other employees of Manchester United; the fans; other football clubs and footballing associations; suppliers of materials and services to the club; sponsors of the club; buyers of services from the club such as Sky Sport; the local community around the Manchester United football ground; and the UK government.

(b) For some stakeholders in the club, the most important objective is likely to be profit maximisation. Many believe that the new owner of the club, Malcolm Glazer, is only interested in the club because of the profit it can generate. Equally, the creditors of the club, and in particular those who lent Malcolm Glazer the cash to help finance the purchase, will want the club to make enough profit for it to repay its debts.

For some stakeholders, the performance of the club is the overriding objective. So the fans are only really concerned with whether their team wins matches and trophies. As the example of Chelsea shows, they are only too delighted when an owner comes along willing to inject large amounts of capital in the club and runs the club at a huge loss in order to buy the best players.

For some stakeholders, arguably their own rewards are the main objective. For the players, for example, their main goal is to maximise their current earnings, and to maximise their future earnings by being part of a successful team. For other staff at Manchester United, getting their monthly pay cheque is the prime objective. For suppliers, their main aim is to earn revenue and profits from their contracts with Manchester United. Equally, those who buy services from Manchester United such as Sky Sport have their own financial gain as the main objective. Other football clubs and football associations want to use Manchester United for their own objectives, whatever those might be.

The local community and the UK government have different objectives. They have a wide range of sometimes conflicting objectives from job creation to promoting local and national pride to minimising the cost of the anti-social behaviour aspect of football.

Question 2

(a) Managerial theories of the firm argue that there is a divorce of ownership from control in large companies. The owners of the firm are a different group of people from those who run the firm. The result is that there is a conflict of objectives between the owners who wish to maximise profits and senior managers and directors who aim to maximise their own rewards even if this is at the expense of lower profits. Firms need to make some profit in order to survive over a period of time and this limits the ability of senior managers to maximise their own rewards. It leads to firms profit satisficing, making just enough profit to keep the owners happy and keep away predators who might want to takeover the company.

(b) The recent history of Compass described in the data could support managerial theories of the firm. The company had performed poorly in recent years, with profits down and its share price down. Yet the directors of the group awarded a large pension contribution into the pension schemes of the two most senior directors who were about to leave the company. If the firm had been a profit maximising firm, it would have minimised the payout to the two departing directors. To argue that the payments were justified because of their 'age and length of service' would suggest that the directors were more interested in maximising their own rewards than those of the shareholders. The payouts also seemed odd when, to bolster profits, the directors had announced only weeks before that they were reducing the pension entitlement of employees. However, from the perspective of a managerial theory of the firm, this made sense. By cutting employees' pensions, the directors could increase profits which would then enable them to make enough profit to keep the shareholders happy and give them, the directors, performance related bonuses.

Question 3

(a) Behavioural theories of the firm suggest that companies are controlled not, as in neo-classical theory, exclusively by shareholders, but by a variety of different and often competing interest groups. The data explain that during the 1960s and 1970s newspapers in the UK were controlled by a variety of different stakeholders. Editorial policy was in the hands of entrepreneurial owners, usually conservative in nature, who used ownership of the British Press not to make profits but to influence public opinion. Production was controlled in part by management, but also to a great extent by the workforce. Trade unions, for instance, controlled who was to be appointed to shop floor jobs. Consumers, on the other hand, exercised their preferences by rewarding with large sales those newspapers which provided few political facts but plenty of sexual titillation.

The balance of power changed in the 1980s. Soaring property prices and new technology meant that the rewards to shareholders of newspapers were now potentially much greater than before. Consequently they exerted much more pressure on management to cut costs and raise revenues. Trade unions and the workers they represented lost much of the power which they had used previously to extort as much as possible from the newspaper companies.

Today, it could be argued that behavioural theories of the firm fail to explain the behaviour of newspapers and that a more traditional neo-classical profit maximising model would explain better the decision making of British national newspapers. However, one interest group, the Conservative party, does seem to continue to exercise influence on Fleet Street. If national voting figures were anything to go by, the political spread of national newspapers should be much wider than it is today. The ability of newspaper owners to support the party of their choice is perhaps one reason why newspapers can go through difficult financial periods without them necessarily closing down. Owners are prepared to support them for longer than might be financially sensible to maintain their ability to form national opinion.

Data question

1. The stakeholders of a firm are those groups which have an interest in its operation. Nike has a number of stakeholders. The owners of the company, the shareholders, are one group of stakeholders. Another group is the directors and senior managers of the company such as Mark Parker, the CEO appointed in January 2006. The workers employed by Nike form another group of stakeholders. They tend to be relatively well paid, with many of the 24 300 being employed in the USA. Nike doesn't actually manufacture any of its goods. These are made by suppliers who form another group of stakeholders. The suppliers can also be distinguished from the workers of the suppliers who are mainly very poorly paid and living in Third World countries. Nike's immediate customers, the wholesalers and retailers who buy Nike products, are another group of stakeholders. Then there are the consumers who buy from the retailers. Pressure groups campaigning for better conditions for workers who manufacture Nike goods have been a strong stakeholder group. Governments, including the US government, also can be seen as stakeholders.

2. Bill Perez, quoted in the 2005 Nike Annual Report and Accounts, concentrated on defining the objectives of the company in terms of its growth. Success was about proving 'time and time again that it (the company) can continue to grow'. He talked about the importance of establishing two new brands, Starter and Converse, as' major players in the market'. He also talked about 'hunger': the company needed to hunger for success in the same way that the original founder of the company was 'hungry' when he was selling shoes out of the back of his car.

3. (a) The objectives of different stakeholders both conflict and coincide. Take the objectives of the owners and of the workers manufacturing Nike goods in the Third World. Nike's owners want the company to maximise profits. This can be achieved by paying as little as possible to Third World suppliers who in turn pay as little as possible to their workers. Those workers, however, want to maximise their pay. So the aspirations of Third World workers are in direct conflict with the goals of Nike shareholders.

Equally, the interests of pressure groups and Nike management also conflict. Pressure groups involved with Nike are concerned about the poor pay of workers manufacturing Nike products and about human rights abuses. Nike management arguably see these groups as a threat to their own goals of growing the market. Through campaigns, pressure groups can have a direct effect on sales. Therefore it could be argued that corporate responsibility becomes an exercise in damage control rather than a genuine desire to value the contribution of the stakeholders who are working for little pay to make Nike products.

It could also be argued that the interests of consumers conflict with those of shareholders and managers. The objectives of Nike the company relate to profit and sales. To sell Nike products, the company uses sophisticated marketing techniques. This includes trying to persuade consumers that by buying Nike products they are somehow being turned into athletes. Some Nike products are indeed used for sporting activities. Equally, much of the merchandise is used as a fashion statement and has nothing to do with sport at all. When Nike says that 'We feel lucky to have a genuine, altruistic reason to be: the service of human potential', this is marketing spin designed to alter consumer attitudes to their products. Nike is no different in its marketing approach from other consumer product companies. But arguably this conflicts with the interests of consumers who need to have correct information about products in making rational decisions about how to allocate their scare resources rather than distorted information supplied by marketing departments.

(b) It could be argued that the interests of shareholders and senior management and directors coincide. Shareholders wish to maximise their returns. Senior management wish to maximise their benefits too and this can be done by being 'hungry' for the success of the company through sales and profit growth. Mark Parker, in his press statement when he took over as CEO, stated that his objective was to 'continue delivering profitable growth for our shareholders' and 'delivering long-term value to shareholders'. However, it could be that senior management recognises that it has to make a satisfactory level of profit for shareholders but once this has been achieved, it can then pursue its own objectives of maximising returns to themselves.

44 Market structure

Question 1

(a) There is a large number of firms in farming, the legal profession, and grocery retailing. There are fewer firms in the provision of mobile phone services and air flights.
(b) Large firms predominate in grocery retailing, mobile phone services and air flights. In grocery retailing, the four largest supermarket chains have over 70 per cent of the market. In the provision of mobile phone services, Vodafone and a few other large companies dominate the market. In air flights, BA has the largest market share in the UK, but because of the cost of providing airline services, that market tends to be dominated by large firms.

Question 2

(a) In both the oil industry and in banking, the barriers to entry are large in many respects. In both industries, capital costs are high. A new entrant would have to put millions of pounds into any venture to enter the market. In terms of exploration and drilling for oil, economies of scale are not particularly large. Small oil companies have been as successful as large companies in finding and exploiting oil fields. In banking, in contrast, there are large economies of scale in retail or high street banking. The only entrants in recent years which have been successful in challenging the existing high street banks have been building societies which own chains of branches to rival the coverage of banks like LloydsTSB, or financial institutions which have used the new medium of the Internet to build a customer base. Banking has legal barriers. For a bank to operate, it must get a licence from the Bank of England. This will only be granted if the Bank of England is satisfied that the bank has enough capital to carry on trading in its sector of the market. Any attempted entry to the high street banking market would also encounter marketing barriers. Bank customers tend not to change banks. Hence, it is difficult for any new bank to gain a critical mass of customers in order to survive in the market place. Some building societies which have offered banking services have withdrawn from the market in recent years because of a failure to gain enough customers. It is also unlikely that all the new Internet banks will survive.

In contrast to oil and banking, food retailing has relatively low barriers to entry. The capital cost of buying a small local store is small. There are no legal barriers. Scale economies can be substantial in that the large supermarkets can buy at considerably lower prices than small corner shops. However, the local store might offset higher prices by offering a convenient location and, if necessary, opening longer hours. This may give a local corner store a potential natural cost advantage. Retail branding exists. However, the local corner shop can develop as strong a brand image in its area as the local Tesco or Sainsbury's. Even if a large firm wishes to enter the industry, again there are relatively few barriers to entry. As the example of foreign chains such as Aldi and Netto has shown, the giants of the supermarket trade can be challenged by companies prepared to spend the money on establishing chains of new supermarkets.

Question 3

(a) The benefit to Coca-Cola of owning the world's most valuable branded product is that it can generate sales and profits from the brand. In particular, because the brand is so strong, it can make much larger profit margins on Coca-Cola than on other drinks such as bottled water. Coca-Cola the drink has enormous economies of scale in marketing because so much of it is sold in comparison with other branded drinks. This partly explains why profit margins are so high. Another factor in high profit margins is the high price that can be charged for the drink. It has a lower price elasticity of demand than rival products.

One way of interpreting 'costs' is to explain the various costs involved in making the drink, such as preparation of the concentrate, bottling, distribution and marketing. Another is to talk about the opportunity cost of being so dependent for sales and profits on one single product. Other firms, particularly its main rival Pepsi-Cola, have developed multi-product strategies where sales and revenues come from a wide variety of products. The problem for Coca-Cola is that is uncertain whether its best strategy is to devote more resources to growing Coca-Cola the drink or diversifying into other product areas which have much lower profit margins.
(b) For consumers, one advantage of branded goods is that the goods are consistent in quality and can be easily recognised. So whether a consumer is in India, China, South Africa or the UK, Coca-Cola is the same identifiable product. Branded goods are also often better quality than non-branded goods. However, there are disadvantages to branded goods for consumers. Branded goods are typically more expensive than non-branded goods. Part of the higher price reflects the cost of producing a better quality product, but part is the higher profit margin that manufacturers of branded products can earn. Branded products also tend to be heavily promoted, distorting consumer perceptions about how they should allocate their scarce resources.

Question 4

(a) There are only two major civilian airline manufacturers in the world, Boeing and Airbus. They compete for orders from airlines and airline leasing companies. When Boeing gains an order, such as the $10 billion contract from Quantas Airlines in 2005, Airbus fails to get the order. Equally when Airbus gets an order such as for 150 planes for Chinese Airlines in 2005, Boeing loses the order. This means that the two companies are interdependent. When two firms are interdependent it means that the actions of one firm have a direct impact on the other firm. So the actions of Boeing have a direct impact on Airbus and vice versa.

Data question

1. Six key characteristics are:
- the number of firms in the industry;
- barriers to entry;
- barriers to exit;
- product homogeneity;
- knowledge;
- interrelationships within markets.

2. On the London to Paris route, there are a relatively small number of firms in the market. There is only one rail service, Eurostar which has 71 per cent of the market. There are several airline companies with Air France having the largest market share at 12 per cent. Finally there are a few coach companies which operate scheduled services.

For airlines and coach companies, barriers to entry are relatively low. With airlines, the main restriction is the availability of landing and take off slots at London's airports. However, barriers to entry for a rail company wanting to operate a rival to Eurostar are high. The sunk costs of buying rail equipment would be high. There are also legal barriers to entry.

Barriers to exit for coach and airline companies are relatively low. Coaches and aeroplanes can be used on other routes. The sunk costs of operating a rail service are likely to be much larger and so the barriers to exit for a rail company are much larger.

Within each mode of transport, there is relative product homogeneity. Whether travelling by Air France or British Airways, the service is essentially the same. However, there are a number of key differences between service providers. One is the start and end points of the journey. For a traveller living next to Heathrow airport, it might be more convenient to take the plane to Paris rather than going by Eurostar. On the other hand, most UK travellers find it more convenient to start their journeys in central London at St Pancras station rather than travel to one of London's airports. Another point of product differentiation is journey times. Most travellers find that door to door journey times are lowest for Eurostar. Travelling by Eurostar is also more comfortable than travelling by plane.

There is likely to be perfect knowledge within the market. Customers and producers can have access to the same information.

Because Eurostar has such a large market share, producers within the market are interdependent. If Air France expands its share of the market, it will have a direct effect on other producers with the market. The growth of Eurostar has driven some airlines, like bmi, out of the market.

3. It is unlikely that Eurostar will gain 100 per cent of the market on the London to Paris route for two routes. The first is that coach services are likely to always be cheaper than Eurostar. So travellers who are particularly price sensitive will continue to use coaches. Second there will always be some passengers for whom using an airport is more convenient than using the train. Those who live next to an airport, or who are seeking a connection from another airline flight, are likely to want to use air travel rather than catch a train.

However, Eurostar could continue to gain market share from its 71 per cent level in 2007. The example of other routes shows that high speed trains can decimate competitors. On the Brussels route, there are no direct flights any more. It could be that Eurostar will drive most of the remaining air services out of business. If this were to happen, Eurostar could have over 90 per cent of the market.

45 Perfect competition

Question 1

(a) One reason why farmers in the butter market could be said to operate in a perfectly competitive industry is because there are many firms in the market selling to a large number of buyers. As Figure 1 the student's book shows, there are wide fluctuations in the price of butter and therefore these many farmers have no control over the price they get for their butter. Hence farmers are price takers.

There is freedom of entry and exit to the industry. Farmers can move in and out of dairy farming.

Most butter is a standard product like oil or coal. The product is therefore homogeneous, a condition for perfect competition.

Buyers and sellers possess perfect knowledge of prices and production methods. These are widely available at little or no cost.

Therefore, the market for butter is a perfectly competitive market for most farmers. However, Figure 1 in the student's book shows that in the US the government will intervene to support the price of butter if it falls below around $2 300 a tonne. This means that there is a price floor in the market which would discourage farmers from leaving the industry if prices fell sharply. The larger the amount of government intervention in the market, the less perfectly competitive it becomes.

Question 2

(a) See Figure 1.
(b) (i) The effect on the market supply curve (a shift to the right) is so small that it cannot be shown on the diagram. Hence there will be no change in total quantity demanded or supplied.
(c) (ii) The demand curve for the individual firm will shift down as shown in Figure 1 (b).

Question 3

(a)

(£)

Output	Marginal cost	Total fixed cost	Total variable cost	Total cost	Average variable cost	Average total cost
2		100	100	200	50.0	100
	40					
3		100	140	240	46.7	80.0
	30					
4		100	170	270	42.5	67.5
	40					
5		100	210	310	42.0	62.0
	60					
6		100	270	370	45.0	61.7
	100					
7		100	370	470	52.9	67.1

(b) The firm's short run supply curve is the MC curve above the AVC curve, as shown in Figure 2.
(c) In the short run, the firm would cease production if the average price did not cover average variable cost. Hence it would continue in production if sales price per unit were £80, £70, £60, or £50 but would cease production if sales price per unit were £40 or £30.

In the long run, the firm would cease production if price did not cover average total cost. Hence, it would continue in production if price were £80 or £70, but would cease production if price were £60, £50, £40, or £30.

Question 4

(a) The combination of rising costs and rising demand means that the price of gold will increase. Rising costs means that gold mining companies are only prepared to supply newly mined gold at a higher price than before. Rising demand means that customers are prepared to pay a higher price for the same amount of gold as before.

Figure 1

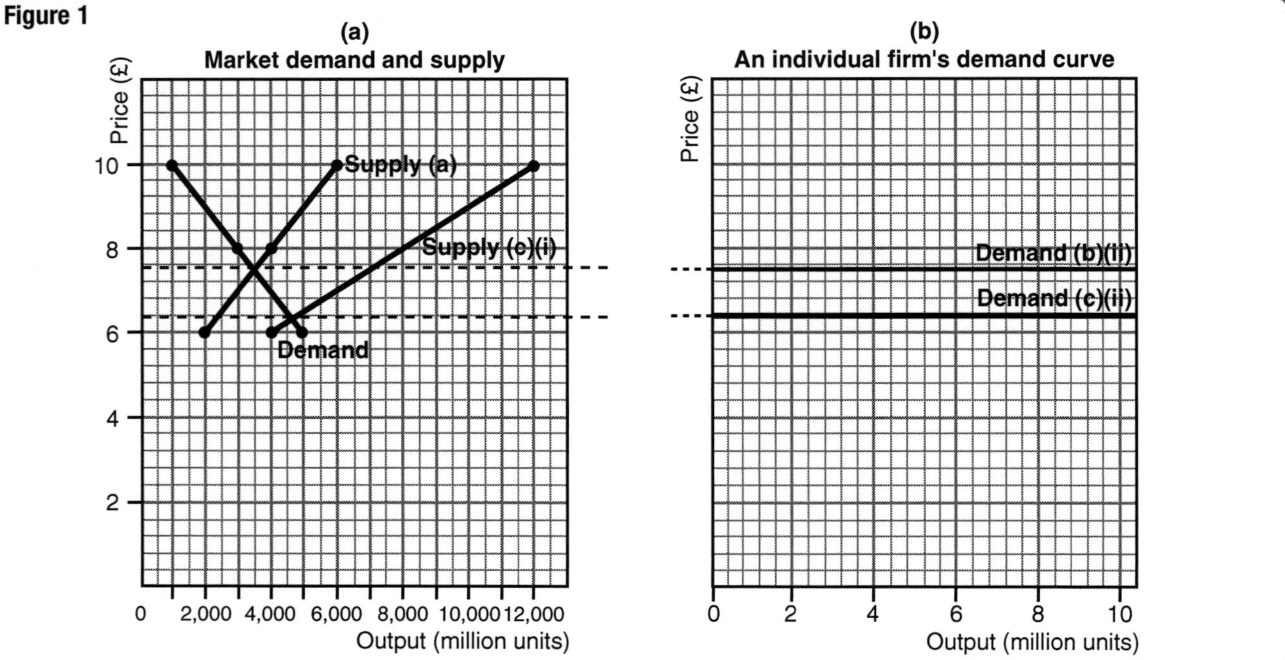

Figure 2

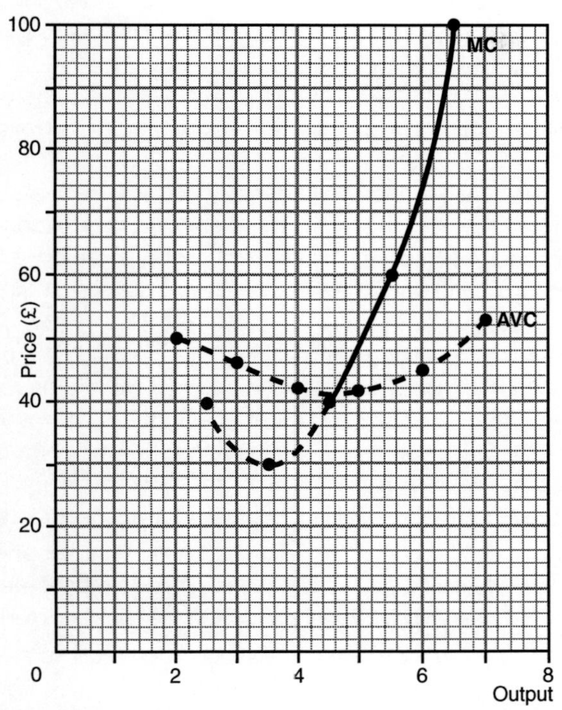

This can be shown on a demand and supply diagram in Figure 3. On the demand and supply diagram, rising costs shifts the supply curve from S_1 to S_2 whilst rising demand shifts the demand curve from D_1 to D_2. As a result, equilibrium price rises from OA to OB. On the perfect competition diagram to the right, the rise in equilibrium price shifts the marginal revenue = average revenue line upwards from MR1 to MR2. However, the firm also experiences a rise in costs, shifting both its marginal cost and average cost curves upwards. In equilibrium, the profit maximising firm produces where marginal cost equals marginal revenue. Initially this is at output OE. Because average cost equals average revenue at this output, the firm only makes normal profits. However, when both costs and demand rises, the new equilibrium output is at OF, where $MR_2=MC_2$. At this level of output, average revenue is above average cost by JB per unit. The firm therefore is making total abnormal profit of JHGB.

(b) The data states that the average cost of production for mined gold in 2005 was \$362 an ounce but gold prices were over \$500 an ounce. Ability to earn abnormal profit will therefore encourage gold mining firms to expand their output. Because many existing mines, particularly in South Africa, are mature and it is difficult to increase production from these mines, it means that gold mining companies will engage in exploration and development of new mines.

Question 5

(a) In a perfectly competitive market, the prices of factors of production will be bid up to a level where long run average costs are equal for all firms. The two vacant properties have very different lease payments. The one on the high street is much higher because the revenues that will be received by a retailer on the high street can be expected to be much higher than one tucked away on a side street off the high street. The difference of £30 000 a year in the lease reflects this difference.

Data question

1. Steel making is arguably a perfectly competitive industry. There is a large number of producers in the industry selling to a large number of buyers. There is freedom of entry to and exit from the industry. Firms can enter the steel market and set up new manufacturing plants and they can close down plants and leave the market if they so wish. Most steel production techniques are not protected by patents and there is widespread knowledge of the best production techniques. Therefore it can be argued there is perfect knowledge amongst steel manufacturers. There is also perfect knowledge among steel customers who are able to shop around for the best prices. Whilst there are many different types and grades of steel, steel is essentially a homogeneous product and steel manufacturers find it difficult to brand their products in any way.

Figure 3

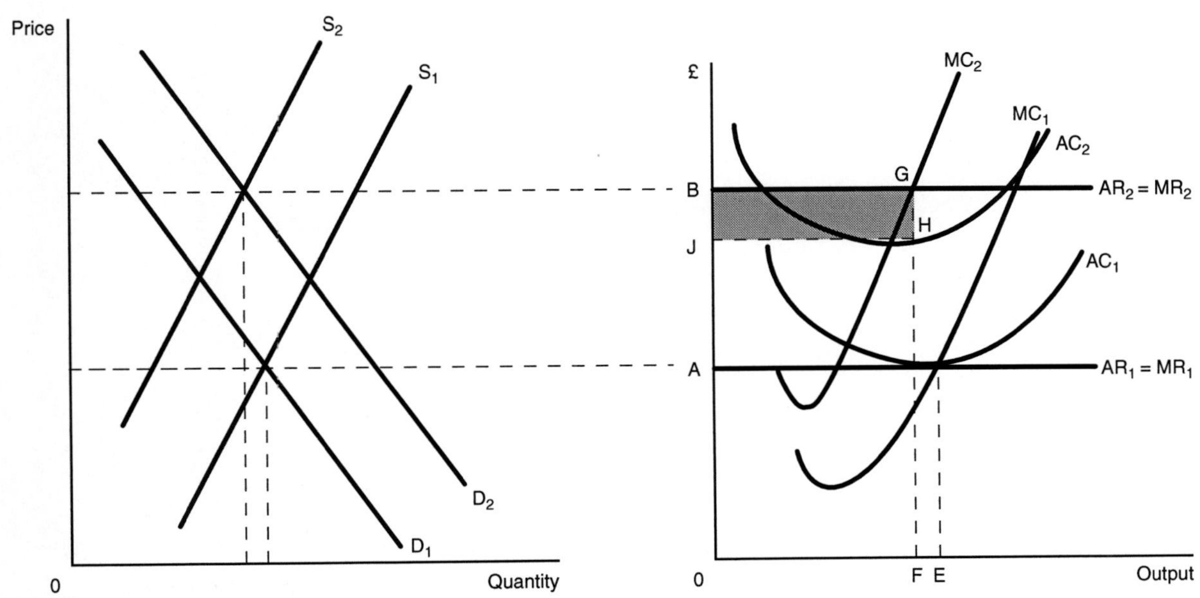

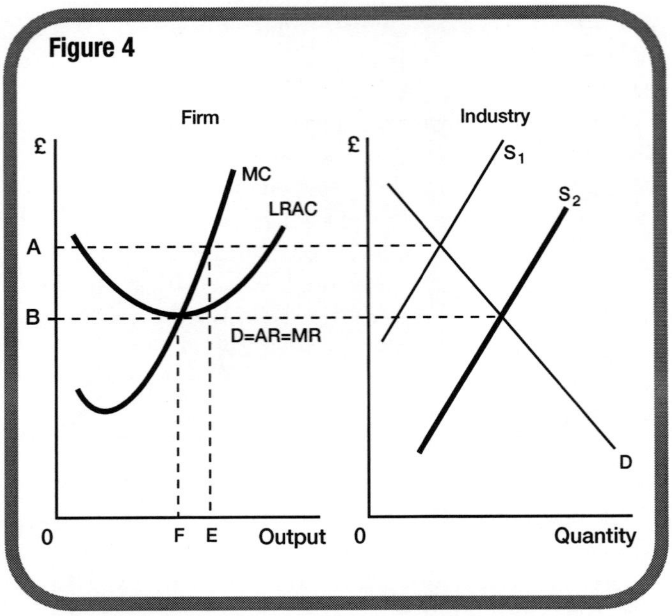

2. The long run impact on European producers of increased Chinese production will differ according to whether or not EU producers were earning abnormal profit in 2006. Assume they were making abnormal profit. The increase in Chinese production will lead to an increase in the world supply of steel, shown by the shift to the right of the supply curve from S_1 to S_2 in Figure 4. In 2006, an EU steel producer could charge a price of OA and, producing where marginal cost equals marginal revenue, its equilibrium level of output would be OE. It will make abnormal profit as AR is above LRAC. In addition, it would make normal profit since normal profit is included as a cost. In 2007, with extra Chinese production on the market, the world price might fall to OB. With lower prices, the EU steel producer would now only want to produce OF, a fall of FE. It would make no abnormal profit but would continue to make normal profit. The increase in supply is unlikely to have resulted in an exact price of OB. If the increase in supply led to a fall in price which was above OB, then the firm would continue to make abnormal profit, although it would be lower than at a price of OA. If the increase in supply led to a fall in price which was below OB, then not only would the firm not make abnormal profit but it would also also make less than normal profit. If the price fell low enough, and it didn't even cover its variable costs, then it would close down its plant.

3. (a) A tariff is a tax on imported goods. An EU tariff on steel would shift the supply curve of steel to the left for supply of steel in the EU. The result would be higher EU prices for steel. EU steel producers would therefore benefit. Not only would they receive a higher price for their steel but they would sell more steel. In Figure 4, assume that S_2 shows the supply of steel in EU markets. The equilibrium market price is OB where demand equals supply. A tariff is then imposed on imported steel which reduces supply to S_1. The new market price is OA. The individual EU producer then receives a higher price for its products than before the tariff is imposed. At a price of OA it is also willing to supply FE more steel. With higher prices and more output, its profits will therefore increase.

(b) EU steel consumers would lose out from the imposition of a tariff. The EU price of steel would rise following the imposition of a tariff. They would buy less steel at a higher price. Their costs would increase and this could reduce their profits.

46 Monopoly

Question 1

(a) (i) In 1986, British Gas held a number of monopolies. It was the monopoly transporter of gas down its pipelines in the UK. It was a monopoly supplier to industrial users and a monopoly supplier to households. It therefore held almost a complete monopoly of gas supplies, the only alternative being bottled gas suppliers like Calor.
(ii) By 1990, British Gas was still a monopoly transporter of gas to households and firms, and was a monopoly supplier of gas to households, but had lost its monopoly to supply gas in its industrial market. This was because the competition authorities had forced it to open up this market in 1988.
(iii) By 2004, British Gas had lost much of its monopoly power. It no longer owned the gas transport network which was controlled by Transco, a company demerged from British Gas in 1996. In both the industrial and household markets, it now faced competition from other suppliers for the supply of gas. The extent of the monopoly in the gas supply industry would depend upon what percentage of the market British Gas had managed to retain following the introduction of competition.
(b) In one sense, the gas industry was no longer a monopoly in that there was competition in both the household and industrial markets for the supply of gas. However, Transco retained a monopoly in the transport of gas. In the wider energy market, gas competed with other fuels such as electricity and oil. Transco was then just one carrier of fuel amongst many. Equally, British Gas was only one of many suppliers of energy.

Question 2

(a) Table 1

Output (units per week)	Marginal revenue	Total revenue	Average revenue
			£
0		0	0
	10		
1		10	10.0
	7		
2		17	8.5
	4		
3		21	7.0
	1		
4		22	5.5
	-2		
5		20	4.0

(b)(see Figure 1)
(c) Marginal revenue cuts the horizontal output axis when total revenue is at a maximum. Hence, marginal revenue is zero.

Question 3

(a) BT, in applying a complex tariff structure, is price discriminating in order to maximise profits. The elasticity of demand for calls is different for different users. So customers who want to phone from a fixed line to a mobile during the day from Monday to Friday are more likely to see that phone

Figure 1

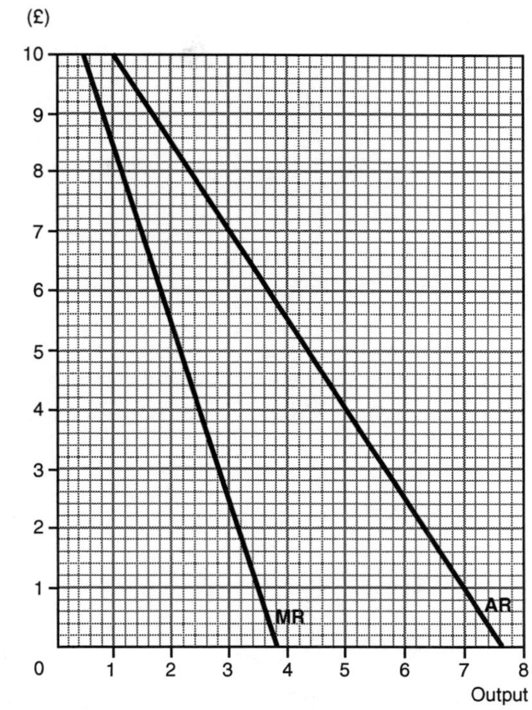

Figure 2

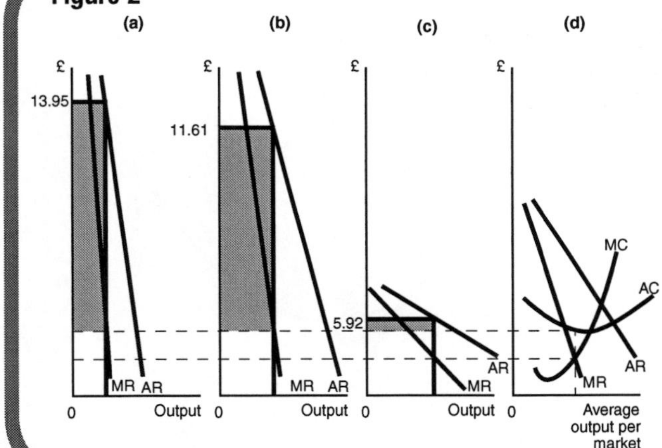

call as essential than if they were making a social call in the evenings or at weekends. So prices during weekdays are higher than in the evening or at weekends. Equally, there is greater demand for phone calls in weekday evenings than there is at weekends. Hence BT charges more for weekday evening calls than weekend calls.

Figure 2, which assumes that costs are identical throughout the day and week, shows why BT price discriminates in the market for fixed phone line calls to mobile phones. During the day Monday to Friday, when demand is least elastic, prices are highest as in diagram (a). During the weekend, when prices are most elastic, prices are lowest as in diagram (c).

Question 4

(a)(see Figure 3)
(b)(see Figure 4)

Data question

1. Motorway service stations are examples of local monopolies. This is because motorists on motorways do not have a choice of motorway service stations at which to stop in

Figure 3

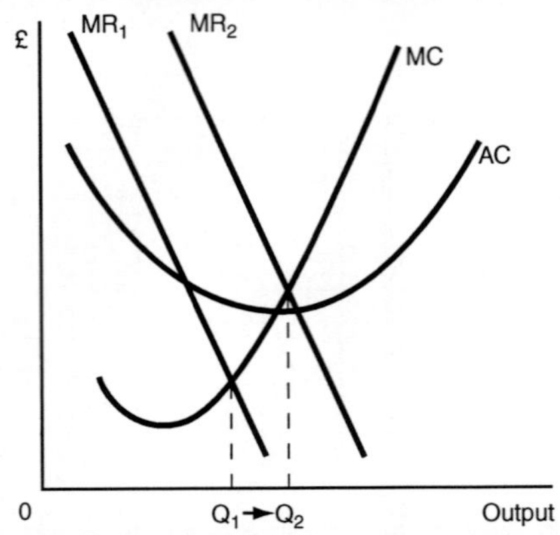

Figure 4

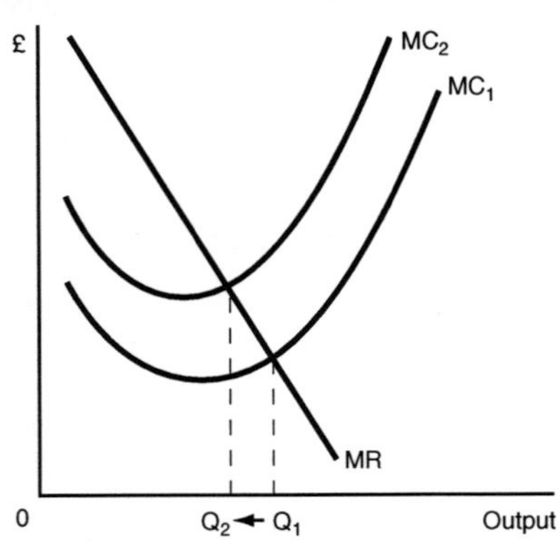

Figure 5

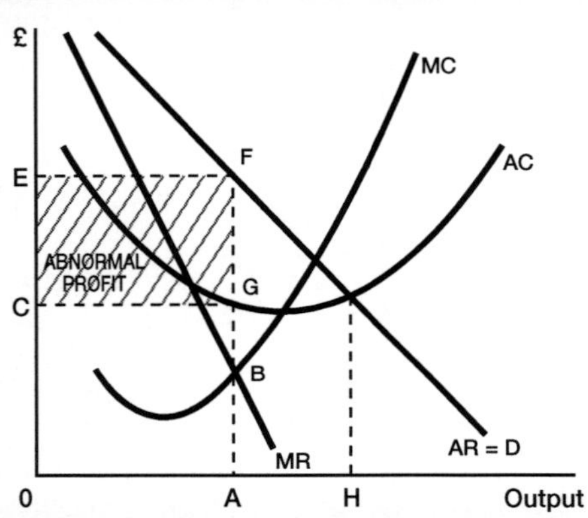

any single location. Service stations are spread out along motorways. They are only local monopolies because if motorists are prepared to travel to a different location, they can get the services that one motorway service station provides.

2. Supermarkets operate in a competitive environment. Competition drives prices down. In contrast, motorway service service stations have a local monopoly. They do not have to compete with other firms. Therefore their prices tend to be higher. This can be illustrated using a monopoly diagram. In Figure 5, the monopolist prices at OE at a level of output of OA where marginal cost equals marginal revenue. It then earns abnormal profit of CEFG. If the market were perfectly competitive, no abnormal profit would be earned. So production would take place where average cost equals average revenue at OH. Equilibrium price is lower and output is higher than under monopoly.

However, the situation is possibly more complex than just outlined. It could be argued that motorway service stations have higher costs than supermarkets. They don't enjoy the economies of scale of large supermarket chains. They also have to be open every day of the year, 24 hours a day. These factors would push the cost curves in Figure 5 upwards for motorway service stations and make prices higher and lower than indicated.

3. McDonald's can charge different prices in motorway service stations from its high street stores. Partly this is because it can split the market with little danger that consumers will go from the high price market to the low price market. So few travellers will seek out a high street McDonald's rather than stop at a service station when using the motorway. Second the price elasticity of demand of the two groups is different. Motorway service customers are less price sensitive partly because there is less competition at a motorway service area. This can illustrated using diagrams. In Figure 6, the motorway service market is shown in the left hand diagram. The equilibrium profit maximising price is at OG where marginal revenue in the market is equal to the marginal cost of production in both markets shown in the right hand diagram. The non-motorway service station market is shown in the middle diagram. The equilibrium profit maximising price is OH, lower than OG in motorway service stations.

4. Expanding sales at motorway service stations is likely to benefit consumers. On the one hand, it could be argued they will lose out because they will pay higher prices for products they could have bought elsewhere on the high street or at out of town stores. Motorway service stations may also have a much more restricted choice of items for sale than, say, a large hypermarket or a local high street.

On the other hand, consumers are relatively price conscious. They know that they are paying relatively high prices at motorway service stations but continue to buy despite the high prices. This would tend to indicate that they value the convenience of buying at a motorway service station. They are prepared to pay more because they don't want to make a separate shopping trip for a particular item.

Figure 6

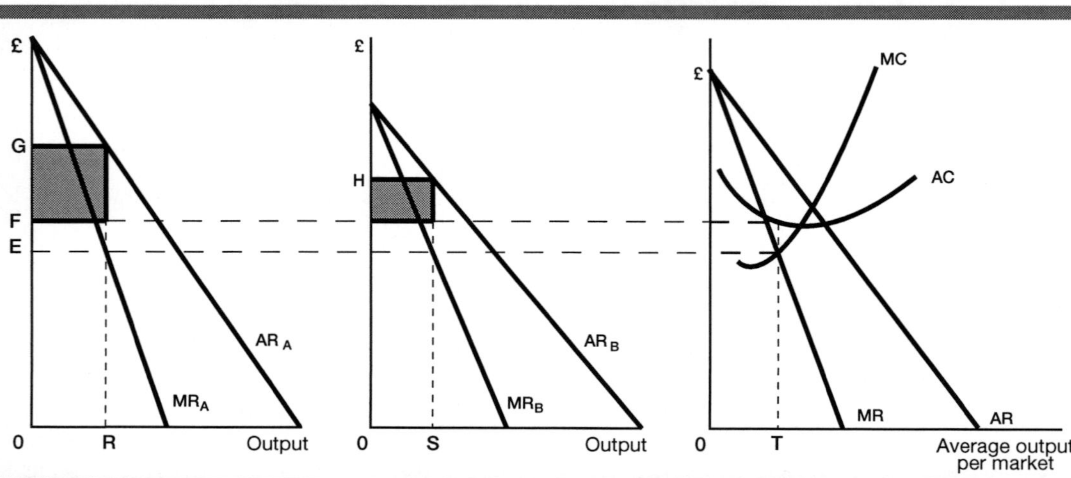

47 Oligopoly

Question 1

(a) Oligopolistic markets share a number of characteristics. First, there are only a few large firms in the market. In the market for chewing gum, there are two dominant manufacturers, Wrigley and Cadbury Schweppes. The rest of the market is split up between much smaller producers. In the US market, for example, the two largest manufacturers have nearly 80 per cent of the market between them.

Second, barriers to entry tend to be high. In this case, the main barrier to entry is marketing and distribution. Wrigley and Cadbury Schweppes have control of the main distribution channels in most world markets, making it difficult for competing firms to get their products on the shelves of retailers. This control is reinforced through advertising which creates a demand for their products from consumers.

Third, competition in oligopolistic markets tends to take the form of non-price competition. In the data, it gives two examples of non-price competition. One is buying up other manufacturers to gain market share. Instead of attempting to gain market share through lowering prices in the US market, Cadbury chose to buy up the US number two manufacturer Adams in 2003. The other example of non-price competition given is product development. Cadbury Schweppes hopes to gain market share by producing new products which will appeal to consumers.

Fourth, firms are interdependent. The actions of Wrigley have a direct impact on Cadbury Schweppes and vice versa. For example, if a new product from Cadbury Schweppes sells well, it is likely to take sales away from Wrigley.

Question 2

(a) Firms in an oligopolistic market tend not to compete on price. Instead, they engage in a number of different forms of non-price competition. It could be argued that the tinned vegetable market in the UK is not, in fact, oligopolistic. 70 per cent of the market is 'accounted for by own label products of the major supermarket chains'. Own label products tend to compete on price.

However, Bonduelle will not be competing on price. It has come up with a different product with different packaging to increase sales in the market. The product is different because it contains several vegetables rather than just one. The packaging is different because it is square rather than round and is a paper product rather than a tin can. By providing a different product, Bonduelle hopes to differentiate its product and be able to charge a higher price than competing own label products. This sort of behaviour is characteristic of oligopolistic markets.

Question 3

(a) De Beers raised prices and profits for diamond producers by controlling supply. Reducing supply to the market meant that the equilibrium price of diamonds rose. Higher prices also meant that producers could earn higher profits.

(b) There was an incentive for producers to move outside of the cartel because they could sell their diamonds onto the open market at a higher price than they could sell to the Central Selling Organisation. The CSO had costs such as maintaining a stockpile of diamonds which it recovered through paying lower prices for diamonds from producers. It also attempted to regulate fluctuations in price in the market which would sometimes have given other producers an opportunity to sell at a higher price.

(c) (i) In a period of rising demand, it would be difficult to persuade non-cartel producers to remain in the cartel because they can sell all their production at a high price.

(ii) The issue of 'blood diamonds' was causing De Beers increasing problems. It did not want a product which is associated with love, romance, weddings and special occasions to be tainted with negative images of war. To control the market before 2000, it needed to buy up these diamonds. Once the cartel was dismantled, it was no longer obliged to buy them and hence could project a 'clean' image to customers about buying De Beers diamonds. In the long term, it gambled that sales and profits would increase without the need to buy blood diamonds.

Data question

1. The UK national daily newspaper market is dominated by 7 newspaper companies - Trinity Mirror, News International, Express Newspapers, Telegraph Group, Independent Newspapers, Pearson and Guardian Newspapers.

Barriers to entry are very high. No national newspaper has had a successful launch since the Independent in 1986. The main problem for any new entrant is gaining a high enough circulation to cover costs. There is strong brand loyalty to existing newspapers and any newspaper which is threatened by a new entrant is likely to take retaliatory action, such as price cuts.

Newspapers are non-homogeneous. They are carefully positioned in different segments of the market using a mix of news, gossip, sport, competitions and free gifts to tempt customers.

Firms in the newspaper market are interdependent. Market share gained by one firm tends to be market share lost by another firm. For example, some of the extra 40 000 readers for The Independent and 60 000 readers for The Times when both adopted the tabloid format came at the expense of The Guardian which saw its circulation fall by 6.3 per cent.

2. In 2005, sales of The Guardian were falling. It could have reacted in a variety of ways. However, given that the national newspaper market is arguably oligopolistic, it chose not to respond by cutting its price. This could have sparked off a price war where all the newspapers engaged in the price war could have ended up worse off. Instead, it chose to respond to the new tabloid product innovation at The Times and The Independent by launching its own smaller format, the 'Berliner' format. This is smaller than a broadsheet but larger than a tabloid size. Non-price competition is a key feature of many oligopolistic markets, reducing the threat that competition will lead to losses amongst competing firms. Interestingly, The Times chose the launch of the new Guardian format to raise its cover price from 55p to 60p. The owners of The Times cannot have believed that a rise in price would have much impact on sales of the newspaper, reinforcing the point that in oligopolistic markets, firms do not compete on price.

Figure 3 in the student's book suggests that The Guardian made the right move in adopting the 'Berliner' format.

Between April 2005 and November 2007 its sales only saw a very small fall. Sales of other newspapers, except the Financial Times, fell by larger amounts. Non-price competition was therefore successful for The Guardian in what over the period 2005 to 2007 was a shrinking market for newspapers.

48 The kinked demand curve theory of oligopoly

Question 1

(a) Table 1

Output	Average revenue	Total revenue	Marginal revenue
1	49	49	
			45
2	47	94	
			41
3	45	135	
3	45	135	
			25
4	40	160	
			15
5	35	175	
			5
6	30	180	

(b)

Figure 1

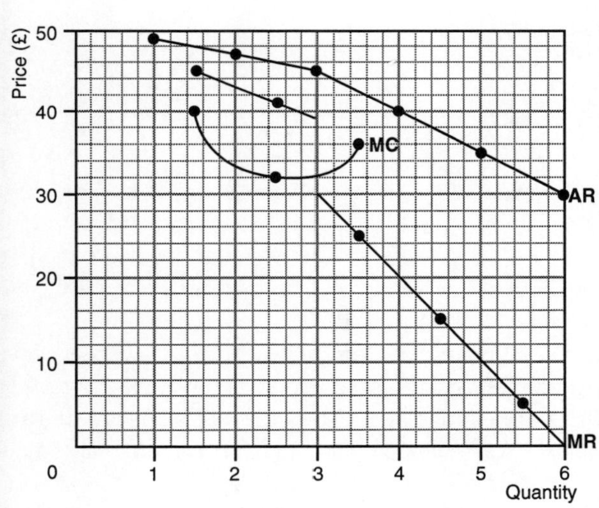

(c) The marginal revenue curve is discontinuous because the average revenue curve is kinked at an output of 3 units. This produces a large jump in marginal revenue at this level of output.
(d) See Figure 1.
(e) The firm is in equilibrium at an output of 3 units because this is the output where marginal cost equals marginal revenue and is therefore the profit maximising level of output.
(f) (i) and **(ii)** If marginal cost rose by £4 or fell by £2 at every level of output, the firm would continue to produce 3 units. This is because marginal cost remains equal to marginal revenue at this level as shown in Figure 1.

Data question

1. The airline market for flights to and from Romania and Bulgaria might be described as oligopolistic because there are only a few airlines on this particular route. Because there are only a few airlines, the firms are interdependent. The actions of one firm affects other firms in the industry. For example, the entrance of low cost carriers will lead to more price competition in the industry and a lower market share for existing carriers.
2. The kinked demand curve theory of oligopoly concludes that firms have different responses depending on whether their rivals cut prices or raise their prices. If they raise their price, a competing firm will choose not to raise its price in order to gain market share. If rival firms cut their prices, however, the firm will lower its prices too for fear of losing market share. The consequence of this is that the demand or average revenue curve is kinked around the current price level, P, as shown in Figure 2. So the entrance of budget airlines like Wizz-Air to the London-Bucharest market is likely to lead to British Airways cutting its airfare.

Figure 2

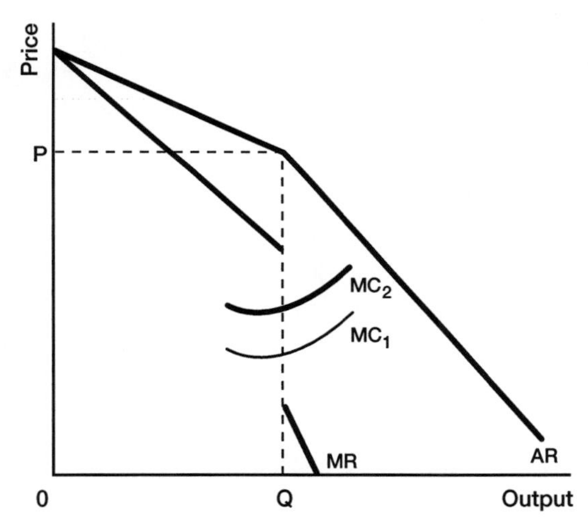

3. The kinked demand curve theory might be able to explain the behaviour of airlines once a number of lowcost carriers have entered the market. High cost carriers like British Airways will have reduced their prices to compete with the new low-cost carriers. A new price point will have been reached. Low-cost carriers will find it difficult to make further price cuts because otherwise they would make a loss. However, they will be reluctant to raise prices because they would fear new entrants to the market undercutting their prices.

49 Game theory

Question 1

The bank and building society deposit and mortgage market could arguably be described as a zero sum game. The gains of a group of players in the market, such as building societies, are the losses of the rest of the players in the market such as banks; and vice versa. For instance, Table 1 shows a hypothetical outcome for changes in interest rates on the market share of banks. Gains in market share by banks are automatically reflected in equal and opposite falls in market share by building societies. If both banks and building societies raise interest rates by the same amount, market share remains the same. If the banks are forced to raise interest rates by the Bank of England but the building societies keep their rates the same, then the banks will increase their market share by 10 per cent. If, on the other hand, the banks keep their rates the same but the building societies raise their interest rates, then the building societies will gain market share at the expense of the banks. Hence, Table 1 shows the banks losing 10 per cent market share in this example.

Table 1

		Banks	
		Raise interest rates	Leave interest rates unchanged
Building societies	Raise interest rates	0	-10 per cent
	Leave interest rates unchanged	+10 per cent	0

Because banks and building societies are playing a zero sum game and because no bank or building society can afford to lose market share, they tend to change their interest rates in line with one another.

Question 2

(a) Brand images have been established by American comic book publishers through a combination of promotion and production. In the case of Image Comics, for instance, it promoted its new range of comics heavily. It also created a new range of characters which appealed to comic buyers.
(b) Marvel Comics and DC were faced with a difficult situation when Image Comics set up as a rival in what had, up till then, essentially been a duopoly in the UK. If they had engaged in a price war, they might have driven Image Comics out of the market. However, they would have lost revenue in the meantime. They might also have found it difficult subsequently to raise their prices back up to their old levels. Each company might have been worried about the reaction of the other. If one had raised price, but the other had left its price constant, the firm which had raised price might lose market share.

The two existing firms, DC Comics and Marvel Comics, may also have been worried that a price war would not drive Image Comics out of the market. If consumers are not price sensitive, then a cut in price by the two established companies would have had little impact on sales of the new Image Comics' products. The cut in price would hit the revenues and profits of the two existing firms without having the desired effect of substantially reducing sales of Image Comics' products. Alternatively, Image Comics may have been set up with substantial reserves of money. It may have been prepared to tough out a price war with the two established firms. They would eventually have been forced to put back up prices to return to profitability and would have lost revenues and profits in the meantime without having achieved their desired objective of getting rid of the new competitor in the market.
(c) The 'going rate' for the job could be defined as the average pay for that job in the industry. When deciding what to pay, employers need to consider not just whether they can recruit new workers at that level of pay but also what would be the cost of disruption if certain workers left to take up positions elsewhere. For instance, assume that the going rate for an artist in the American comic book market was £20 000 a year. However, if one of the key artists in a company were to leave, it would cost £60 000 to recruit, train and wait for other artists in the department to fill the gap left by the departing artist. It would obviously be worth paying that artist more than the going rate to give him or her an incentive to stay with the company to avoid the £60 000 disruption cost.

In a different game scenario, the leaving artist may give a competitive edge to the rival company which he or she joins. For instance, assume that sales of comics fall by 2 000 a year as the result of the departure of the artist and rise by 2 000 at the company which he or she has joined. In this zero sum game, it would be worth paying the artist more than the going rate to prevent the loss of revenue which would be occasioned by his or her leaving.

Question 3

The 50 schools found it in their interests to collude on fees by swapping information about forthcoming fee rises. Consider a situation where schools do not collude and don't know what the fee increases will be at other schools. They might then set fees which were either higher than the average or lower than the average.

If increases in fees are consistently above the average, then the school risks losing a small proportion of potential new pupils. Because branding is strong, the loss is likely to be small but any loss of new pupils has an impact on marginal revenue. It also has a knock on effect because students lost at age 13, the entrance age for most top public schools, will reduce pupil numbers for the next five years. Five pupils lost with fees of £20 000 per year means a loss of revenues over five years of £500 000.

If increases in fees are consistently below average, a school will not necessarily gain any extra pupils. However, they will lose revenue from every existing pupil. Take a school of 500 pupils which sets its fees £500 below the average. This will lead to a loss of revenue of £250 000 in a single year. There is therefore a considerable incentive for schools to set their fees at the right level within the market.

This can be illustrated using game theory. In Table 2, School A has a choice between setting its fee increase of 10 per cent at the same level as other schools, or setting it below the average at 4 per cent. If it sets fees at the same new level as other schools, it gains 10 per cent in revenue. If it sets new fees at a level below that of other schools, it gains only 4 per cent. The outcome for all other schools is the same whatever choice School A makes, because the impact on their school numbers will be negligible. Quite clearly, it is in School A's interests to set its fees at the same level as other schools. It is an example of a dominant strategy. The easiest way to ensure for School A to ensure that it is setting its fees at the same level is to collude with other schools, for example by exchanging information. The conclusion must also be that it is in the interests of every public school to collude on fees.

Table 2

		All other schools
		Increase fees by 10%
School A	Increase fees by 4%	All other schools' revenue increased by 10% School A's revenue increased by 4%
School A	Increase fees by 10%	All other schools' revenue increased by 10% School A's revenue increased by 10%

Data question

1. Game theory is the analysis of situations in which players are interdependent. In 2002, Associated Newspapers had a near-monopoly of the London newspaper market. It had the only titles which cover the whole of London. However, it was vulnerable to a new competitor coming into the market to challenge that monopoly.

Given this threat, it had a choice. Either it cauld respond to a changing market and maintain its monopoly position but possibly be forced to accept lower profits than are currently made. Or it could continue with its current high profit strategy but risk a new entrant coming in and taking part of that market and profit away for the foreseeable future.

Associated Newspapers took the first choice. Associated Newspapers would like to publish one London newspaper. It could charge for this newspaper and would gain economies of scale compared to a situation where it published two or more newspapers. However, twice in recent years it has launched new newspapers. The first was a response to the success in other cities of a free newspaper published by a Swedish newspaper company. Associated Newspapers faced a credible threat that it would launch in London. It preempted this by launching Metro, a free newspaper distributed via the Underground network. The second was the justified fear that a lunchtime free newspaper could be launched. It decided to launch its own, Standard Lite, now called London Lite. It has saved on costs by using the same staff as the Evening Standard to make up this lunch time paper. There are also economies of scale across the three newspapers in selling advertising space and in printing.

The second choice would have been not to launch free newspapers but to sell only the Evening Standard. It then risked new entrants coming into the market taking market share away from the Evening Standard. In the short term, whilst there was no new entrant, Associated Newspapers could have earned higher profits. It might have continued to earn higher profits if no new newspaper appeared. But once a competitor came into the market, it was threatened with making lower profits. These profits would have been lower than the alternative of running its own free newspapers which cannibalised its own market.

2. Game theory can be used to understand the Evening Standard's reaction to a new entrant. If a new entrant came into the market to challenge the Evening Standard with a pay-for newspaper, one strategy the Evening Standard could use would be to lower its price. It is in its long term interests to drive the new entrant out of the market. Lowering the cover price of the newspaper in the short term would cost the company profits, but it would be better to lose some profit in the short term rather than substantial amounts of profit in the long term.

It should also be remembered that the cover price represents only one quarter of the current revenue of the Evening Standard. The other three quarters comes from advertising. Cutting the cover price of the Evening Standard in half would only lose the Evening Standard 12.5 per cent of its revenues, a loss which could be sustained in the short run.

How would a new entrant react to a price war? This depends on how much start up finance it has. If the owners of the new entrant have a large amount of financial capital which they are prepared to use to establish the paper in the long term, they are likely to match the Evening Standard's price cut to prevent it gaining a competitive advantage. This will be a very costly solution, however, because the new newspaper is unlikely to have the advertising revenues of the Evening Standard to stem its start up losses. A more likely scenario is the new start up will have limited finances. The Evening Standard can then outspend the start up and force it to leave the market.

The threat of a price war is a credible threat to any new entrant to the London paid-for newspaper market. This is the reason why there have been no new entrants in recent years despite the profits that the Evening Standard makes.

50 The theory of contestable markets

Question 1

(a) Clothing manufacturing is characterised by the existence of large numbers of relatively small firms. The vast majority of these produce unbranded products, making goods to order often from large retail chains. A few manufacturers own strong brands. Benetton and Levi are examples. Even these companies, however, tend to outsource production to other firms rather than produce all their own clothing in company factories. So branding is not a significant barrier to entry to the market. Nor are start up costs. It is relatively cheap in manufacturing terms to set up in the industry, operating a small firm. Given that manufacturing is often labour intensive in small firms, sunk costs are usually small. Hence there is freedom of entry to and exit from the industry. With arguably perfect knowledge in the industry, clothing manufacturing can be said to be a contestable market.
(b) Clothing retailers could also arguably be said to operate in a contestable market. It is relatively cheap to enter the market on a small scale and there is a large number of clothes retailers. However, chains such as Marks & Spencer and Miss Selfridge tend to take a larger proportion of the market than branded manufacturers. It could therefore be argued that clothing retailing is slightly less contestable than clothing manufacturing.

Question 2

(a) The inability of firms in an industry to lease capital equipment for short periods of time is likely to make the market less contestable. This is because it will force new entrants either to buy capital equipment which they might have problems reselling or lease for long periods. Consequently sunk costs are likely to be higher.
(b) High second hand prices for capital equipment are likely to make the market more contestable. This is because they make the existing costs for any unsuccessful new entrant lower than they would be if second hand prices were low.
(c) Heavy advertising by existing firms in the industry will make the market less contestable. Heavy advertising will create a considerable barrier to entry, making it difficult for any new entrant to gain a profitable share of the market.
(d) There are two contradictory tendencies in this example. On the one hand, a market in which a firm which has a natural monopoly has high barriers to entry. In the long term, only one firm can survive in a natural monopoly market. On the other hand, if the natural monopolist is highly inefficient, it may create an opportunity for a new entrant to raid the market, setting up in competition and exploiting the fact that the natural monopolist is charging high prices. So long as sunk costs are not too high, entrants will be attracted to and stay in the industry whilst the natural monopolist continues to be inefficient. It is likely that this competition will lead to the natural monopolist tightening its costs and becoming more efficient. The new entrant can then withdraw, having made short term profits.
(e) Patents will lead to a market being less contestable. If they are crucial to the manufacturing process, it will be impossible for new entrants to establish themselves unless they secure a licence to use the patents from the patent holder. This, however, may push up their costs to the point where they are unable to compete in the market.
(f) Government legislation which gives monopoly rights to a single producer in the industry will lead to a market being completely incontestable. Monopoly rights means that no other firm can enter the industry.

Question 3

(a) (i) Barriers to entry are likely to be low because Unilever is already a manufacturer of food, home, car and personal care products. It can probably at relatively low cost bring out versions of its products which are cheaper to manufacture and therefore can be sold at a lower price. More importantly, perhaps, Unilever also has excellent existing channels of distribution. Unlike a new start up company, it already sells large volumes of products to the large supermarket chains and other more specialist retailers. It has much more chance than a new start up that these retailers will put the new value products on their shelves. Once on those shelves, they have a chance that they will sell in sufficient volumes for the retailers to want to continue to stock them.
(ii) Barriers to exit are likely to be relatively low too. The new products are likely to be manufactured in the same factories and on the same production lines as existing products. It would be relatively cheap to withdraw a particular line. Unilever is already used to changing its product mix at the margins and failure of some lines would be a common phenomenon.
(b) Own label manufacturing is highly competitive. This is because it is relatively easy for new and existing firms to enter the market if other firms are earning abnormal profits. Supermarkets seek to pay the lowest price for goods. If they feel that an existing supplier is making too much profit on its contracts with them, they will both talk to other potential suppliers and negotiate hard with the existing supplier to bring the price down. Suppliers themselves are constantly talking to supermarket chains about increasing their sales to them. The result of this fierce competition arising from low barriers to entry is that manufacturers often find it difficult to make even normal profit.

Data question

1. The factors of production are land, labour, capital and entrepreneurship. Land is defined as natural resources such as the land on which an airport is built or oil fields from which oil is extracted and then turned into aviation fuel. Labour is workers such as airport staff, cabin crew and airline pilots. Capital is resources which are used up over a period to provide a flow of goods and services. These include airport facilities, offices of the airlines and the aeroplanes themselves. Entrepreneurs are individuals who take risks by combining the factors of production to produce goods and services. Examples of entrepreneurs include Richard Branson of Virgin Atlantic, and the US entrepreneurs who have launched Eos.
2. (a) There is a considerable price difference between transatlantic business class travel and economy class. It could be argued that economy class travellers, many of whom are tourists paying their own fares, are much more price sensitive than, for the most part, business people travelling in business class. The majority of the people in business class are not paying for their own travel. Their fares are paid by their employers. Where it is the firm who pays, business class travellers are completely insensitive to price. They want to

travel on airlines which offer them the most convenient services, the most comfort and the most air miles.

However, demand for business class travel is most likely to be slightly elastic. This is because if demand were inelastic, airlines could push up their prices. Although the number of passengers carried would fall, higher prices would still increase their revenues. Profits would increase not just because of the increase in revenues but also because costs would fall with fewer passengers.

(b) Eos is aiming to provide a superior service to the more established airlines such as BA and Virgin Atlantic. It is charging prices at the top end of business travel. Price elasticity of demand for its services is likely to be lower than that for Maxjet, which is aiming at the bottom end of the business class market. Maxjet is likely to appeal to more price conscious customers who don't want to fly economy class but are not prepared to pay the full price of a business class ticket.

3. The transatlantic air flight is not fully contestable. This is because there are significant barriers to entry to the market. The most important is the international treaty signed between the UK and the USA which sets conditions on what flights can be offered between the two countries. Many new entrants would like to fly from Heathrow Airport or Gatwick Airport but this is effectively impossible under the treaty. So new entrants are forced to fly from regional airports such as Stansted. This means that they cannot offer the same level of service as the more established airlines based at Heathrow or Gatwick. Competition is therefore limited.

There are other barriers to entry. One is financial. Eos has been formed with $87 million in equity finance. Airlines, therefore, cannot be started without considerable amounts of cash. Another barrier to entry is branding. Airlines like BA attempt to brand their services. It can be argued that brand loyalty is fairly weak amongst customers in some segments of the market, particularly at the bottom end. However, amongst many business class travellers, there is considerable brand loyalty. Some of this is due to air mile schemes which lock business class travellers wanting to collect air miles into travelling with one airline.

51 Other theories of the firm

Question 1

(a) (i) £2 400. If his costs were £2 000, Lee would add a profit margin of 20 per cent or £400, making a final price of £2 400.
(ii) £6 000. If his costs were £5 000, Lee would add a profit margin of 20 per cent or £1 000, making a final price of £6 000.
(iii) £9 600. If his costs were £8 000, Lee would add a profit margin of 20 per cent or £1 600, making a final price of £9 600.
(b) Lee may take the attitude that he should not revise his quote downwards because otherwise other customers may hear about this and attempt to push all his quotes down. Gaining a few pounds on this job might lose him thousands of pounds over all his future jobs. On the other hand, he may argue that there is very poor information in the market about quotes and this scenario is unlikely to happen.

Working backwards from his original £2 000 quote, this must have been made up of costs of £1 667 and a 20% profit mark-up of £333. Costs of £1 667 are above the £1 450 possible price. His costs are made up of variable and fixed costs. If his variable costs were greater than £1 450, then he probably wouldn't accept the quote. Not only would he not be making a contribution towards paying his fixed costs, but he would not even be covering his variable costs. On the other hand, it could be argued that part of his variable costs is his wages. If he were prepared to work for lower wages, he might be prepared to accept the job.

An alternative strategy might be to test whether the customer really has received another quote of £1 500. The customer may have simply invented this to make Lee accept a lower quote. Lee could try reducing his price by £100 and see what the customer says.

Question 2

(a)

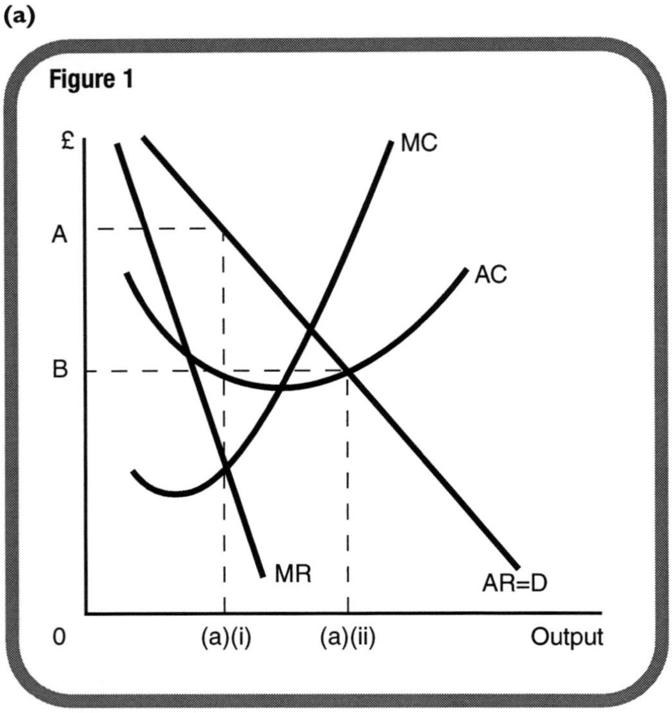

(b) Figure 1 shows that a monopolist which maximises profit will produce where MC=MR at output (a) (i) and price at A. If it now moves to being a sales revenue maximiser, subject to the constraint of making normal profit, it will produce where AC=AR at output (a) (ii) and price B. Hence output will be higher and price lower for a sales maximiser than for a profit maximiser.

Question 3

Behavioural theories of the firm suggest that the firm is controlled by a number of different groups (or stakeholders) rather than just the shareholders as in profit maximising models. In the case of Arcelor, those opposing Mittal Steel's bid for the company describe it in terms of its stakeholders rather than as a simple profit maximising company. For example, Thierry Bretton, France's Minister of the economy, finance and industry, said that the future of Arcelor was 'of crucial economic, industrial and social importance' and that its future 'must be taken into consideration by any government whose duty is to promote national growth'. Thierry Bretton clearly thought that the French state had a strategic interest in the company. Wolfgang Munchau, writing in the Financial Times, commented that Arcelor defined itself in terms of 'its size, measured in annual turnover, not profitability'. He also pointed out that Arcelor defined its goal to be 'a benchmark for economic performance, labour relations and social responsibility'. This would suggest that workers and local communities were as important, if not more important than making profit for its shareholders. Companies often make claims about their corporate social responsibility, putting customers first, or promoting their workers' interests, and yet their actions clearly show that they are profit maximisers. Without more information about the behaviour of Arcelor, it is difficult to say whether a behavioural model of the firm might more accurately describe the behaviour of Arcelor than a short run profit maximising model.

Data question

1. Phil Sawyer is using cost-plus pricing. He is taking the cost of the food ingredients and adding a mark-up to cover the fixed costs of operating the pub and to cover the profit. The mark-up is 200 per cent. So for a dish where the food ingredients cost £2.50, he would add £5.00 as the mark-up, arriving at a final price of £7.50. In practice, he then reduces this to £7.49 to give the impression that it is cheaper.
2. (a) If the wholesale price of fish doubles for a week, Phil Sawyer is unlikely to change his prices. This is because firms which use cost-plus pricing tend to maintain stable prices over a period of time to avoid confusing the customer. After all, if Phil Sawyer increased his prices for one week, and then brought them down, his customers might think that he was exploiting them during the week when prices were high. They might also react by not coming back, thinking that the new higher prices would be permanent. If Phil Sawyer did not want to 'lose' money by selling the fish at less than the 200 per cent mark-up, he could simply withdraw the fish from the menu and claim that it was 'unavailable' that week.
(b) If there is a downturn in the local economy and unemployment rises, then the demand for meals out in the local economy is likely to fall. Phil Sawyer will therefore see fewer customers coming to the pub. He could react by cutting his prices. However, if he uses cost-plus pricing techniques, he

is more likely to maintain prices and accept that he will serve fewer customers. The alternative could lead to a price war amongst local pubs where no one would gain because they would all be chasing the same pool of customers.

(c) If he has problems with overcrowding on a Saturday night, he is unlikely to increase prices just for the Saturday night. Instead, he will have to accept that he will have to turn customers away and lose potential business. To increase prices just for the Saturday night might give the pub a reputation for being expensive throughout the week and this could lose the pub custom.

(d) If overcrowding in the restaurant became a regular occurrence, he is unlikely to increase his prices. Instead, in the short term, he will have to expect customers to wait or he will have to turn customers away. In the long term, if the problem persists, he is likely to expand his premises and thus increase output. Alternatively, he could try to take his pub up-market, offering more expensive ingredients and thus charging higher prices. This would increase his profitability because the profit per meal served would be greater.

3. Organisational slack is inefficiency which arises because firms fail to minimise costs of production. Typically, organisational slack occurs in organisations where there are many different competing stakeholders, some of whom do not find it in their interests for the firm to minimise costs. For instance, workers employed by a firm would prefer to receive higher wages than the minimum needed to retain and motivate them even though this means that profits for the owners of the firm are reduced.

In Phil Sawyer's case, there is unlikely to be organisational slack. As the owner-manager of the pub, he is able to organise production in a way which will maximise profit. The data state clearly that he is very firm about new dishes that fail to sell. Unlike the chef, who probably would prefer more adventurous menus even if they did not sell as well or were not as profitable, Phil Sawyer is only concerned with the bottom line. This approach is likely to extend to every aspect of running the pub. Phil Sawyer will be attempting to minimise cost wherever possible.

52 Economic efficiency

Question 1

(a) This is an allocatively efficient level of output because prices = marginal cost at this level in both the goods sector and the service sector of the economy.

(b) (i) If only 2 million units of goods were produced, the price that consumers were prepared to pay for the last or marginal unit would be £8, whilst the marginal cost to society of production would be £4, as can be seen from Figure 1. At the same time, in the services market, the marginal cost of production would exceed price given that output would be greater than the original output of 4 million units. This must lead to a loss of efficiency. In the goods market, consumers now value the last unit produced more than the cost to society of producing that unit. In the services market, the cost of production of the last unit is higher than the value placed on it by consumers. Hence, efficiency could be increased by transferring resources from the services market to the goods market.

(ii) If only 2 million units of services were produced, then the value placed by consumers on the last item produced, £9, would exceed the marginal cost of production, £5, as can be seen from Figure 2. At the same time, in the goods market, production must now be more than 3 million units and hence the marginal cost of goods must be greater than the value placed by consumers on that good. This must lead to a loss of efficiency. In the services market, consumers now value the last unit produced more than the cost to society of producing that good. In the goods market, the cost of production of the last unit is higher than the value placed on it by consumers. Hence, efficiency could be increased by transferring resources from the goods market to the services market.

Figure 1

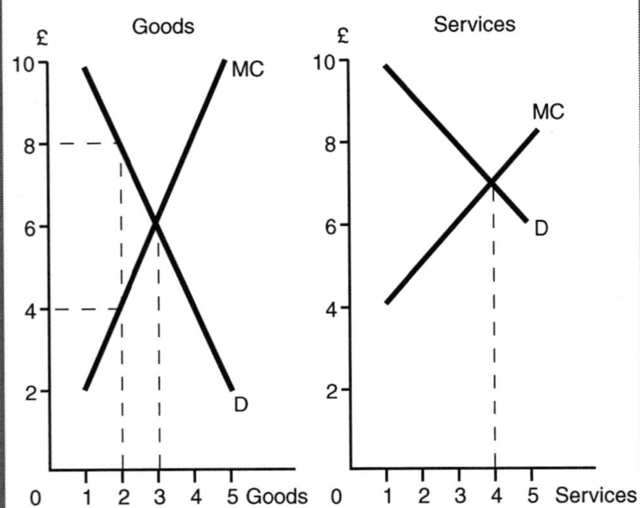

Figure 2

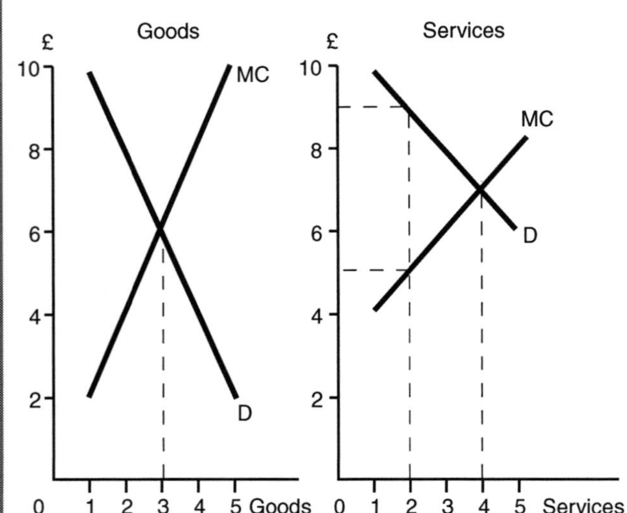

Question 2

In the short term at least, the world faces a trade-off between the size of the Brazilian rain forest and world production of beef. The more the rain forest is cut down, the more beef can be produced. This is shown in the production possibility diagram in Figure 3. Cutting down CD of the rain forest permits AB more beef to be produced. A ban on the felling of trees would not lead to any greater Pareto efficiency. This is because there would be losers as well as gainers. The losers would be beef ranchers in Brazil who would otherwise have expanded their herds. The gainers would be the rest of the world, who might benefit from a lessening of the impact of the greenhouse effect. Only if both Brazilian ranchers and the rest of the world gained (which would necessitate that production was taking place within the production possibility frontier and not on it) would a ban possibly lead to Pareto efficiency.

Figure 3

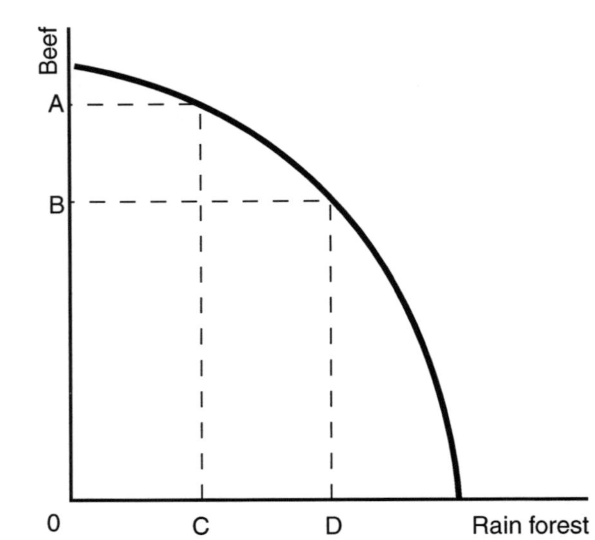

Question 3

(a) The thread cartel led to higher prices than if there had been competition in the market. Price was above marginal cost. The value that customers put on the product shown by its price was above the marginal cost of production and therefore there was allocative inefficiency. By reducing price and expanding output, marginal cost would have risen to the point where welfare was maximised where marginal cost equals price.

(b) Market failure occurs where there is a misallocation of resources. In this case, resources have been misallocated because too few resources have been devoted to the production of thread. Consumers through the price mechanism are indicating that they would prefer to have more thread produced at a lower price.

Question 4

(a) The transition from planned economy to free market economy has benefited the average East German citizen. Average incomes are now higher in real terms than before unification. However, some citizens are worse off. For instance, manual workers who had a job in 1989 but are now unemployed are unlikely to have benefited from unification. When employed in 1989, not only did they earn a wage, but they also enjoyed such benefits as free health care and subsidised housing. Today, they have to live on unemployment benefits and the package of goods and services provided free by the state has been reduced. The market mechanism may offer large quantities of high quality goods for sale, but for those East Germans on very low incomes, these are unaffordable in today's Germany. They therefore cannot benefit from the riches that the free market economy brings.

Data question

1. Retailers like Tesco and those on the Tottenham Court Road in London want to sell grey goods because they can make a profit out of these sales. In most cases, grey goods are sold at a discount to the official list price set by manufacturers. Customers want to buy grey goods from retailers like these because they can get them more cheaply than from official suppliers. In some cases, grey goods are goods which have not been launched in a market. Retailers with access to such grey goods can then sell them at a premium price to customers who want to be first into the market.

2. The legal banning of grey imports is likely to lead to allocative inefficiency in the market. In most cases, consumers will have to pay higher prices for many branded goods than they would otherwise have done. They will buy fewer goods and price will be above the marginal cost of production. In cases such as the Sony PlayStation described in the data, consumers are prepared to pay more for having access to goods which have not yet been officially launched. But by banning grey imports, these customers cannot cast their spending vote in the market. This leads to market failure.

3. Grey imports may threaten dynamic efficiency gains. For instance, the data quote Adidas as saying that exclusive dealing channels lead to products being 'consistently of high quality'. This is not a sound argument. Many products, such as food, are sold through non-exclusive channels and yet manufacturers maintain high quality. Equally, the data state that brand images are devalued through sales in supermarkets. This is likely to be true, but equally brands then become available to a much larger number of customers. Whether efficiency is raised by manufacturers being able to decide to whom to sell their product is debatable. However, the one argument which would support exclusive dealing channels is that of innovation. Such channels enable manufacturers to earn monopoly profits on their products. This encourages them, and their competitors, to innovate and produce new products on which they can earn more abnormal profits. This leads to a process of 'creative destruction' where one new product supersedes another. Without monopoly profits, there would not necessarily be the incentive to innovate and nor might there be the finance to do so.

53 Competition and efficiency

Question 1

(a) (i) Productive efficiency occurs when production takes place at lowest cost per unit. Productive efficiency is present, therefore, when a firm is operating at the lowest point of its average cost curve. Competition in the postal market might increase productive efficiency because firms with lower costs have a competitive advantage. They can either lower their prices and increase their market share or have higher profits than firms with higher costs. In the data, it states that 15 per cent of respondents to a survey about the postal market 'believed that competition had resulted insignificantly lower prices'.
(ii) Allocative efficiency is concerned with whether resources are used to produce the goods and services that consumers wish to buy. It occurs when resources are distributed in such a way that no consumers could be made better off without other consumers becoming worse off and when the price of a product equals its marginal cost of production (P = MC). Increased competition in the postal market is likely to have led to increased allocative efficiency. More choice in the market will have put pressure on Royal Mail to reduce prices. The overall size of the market may have grown because of falling prices and greater choice as economic theory predicts.
(iii) Dynamic efficiency occurs when resources are allocated efficiently over time. In the survey by Postcomm, one in five respondents had switched suppliers for at least some of their mail, showing the need for 'all postal operators to place more emphasis on customer service and innovation'. Improving customer service over time and innovation are examples of dynamic efficiency. So there is evidence in the postal market that increased competition has already led to increased dynamic efficiency.

Question 2

(a) A cartel is an organisation of producers which exists to further the interests of its members, often by restricting output through the imposition of quotas, leading to a rise in price. Producers organising together to restrict output is an example of an anti-competitive practice. Prices are raised by restricting competition in the market and so giving producers more power to set prices.
(b) The EU lift manufacturers restricted competition by coordinating their bids. This allowed them to allocate jobs amongst themselves, deciding whose 'turn' it was to win a contract and at what price.
(c) Market efficiency was impaired by the operation of the cartel. Prices were higher than they would have been if there had been genuine competition in the market. Output is also likely to have been lower. Therefore allocative efficiency is unlikely to have been present because price will have been set above marginal cost in order to maximise profits.

Data question

1. Anti-competitive practices are tactics used by producers to restrict competition in the market. In the example in the data, a number of airline companies had colluded to fix fuel surcharges on long-haul flights. By agreeing amongst themselves the size of the fuel surcharge, it prevented competitive forces from ensuring that some airlines set low fuel surcharges in order to win market share from rival companies.
2. These anti-competitive practices are likely to have raised revenue and profit for the airlines involved. By agreeing amongst themselves the size of the surcharge, it prevented competitive pressures from bringing down the surcharges at a later date. Hence, revenues increased. In theory, the fuel charges were imposed to cover the rising cost of fuel. In practice, the surcharges may have exceeded the rise in costs due to higher oil prices. In this case, profits of the airlines would also rise.
3. The cartels are likely to have led to inefficiency in the cargo and passenger airline markets. This is because the cartels allowed the airlines to charge a higher price than they would otherwise have been able to charge. Assuming they increased their profit through acting as a cartel, these anti-competitive practices will have led to allocative inefficiency. Price will have been higher than marginal cost. Prices will have been higher and output lower than if the market had been perfectly competitive.

54 Monopoly and efficiency

Question 1

(a) (i) If a multi-plant monopoly prices as in perfect competition and earns only normal profits, then it will price where AC = MC = AR, at the point V in Figure 1. With a multi-plant monopolist, the long run average cost curve is horizontal because it can add or take away plant, marginal plant, without changing average cost. Marginal cost is therefore equal to average cost. For normal profit only to be made, production must take place where AC = AR.

Figure 1

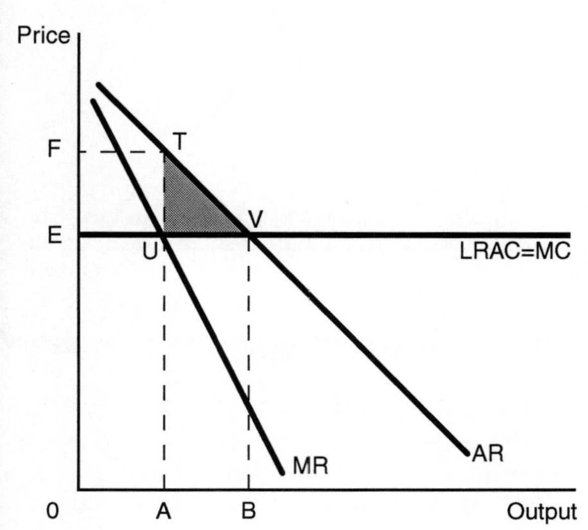

(ii) This would have resulted in an efficient allocation of resources. The company is producing at lowest average cost and is therefore productively efficient. It is allocatively efficient because it is pricing at marginal cost.

(b) (i) The figures suggest that there has been a considerable increase in profit. The two companies are now likely to be earning abnormal profit.

(ii) Resources are not now allocated efficiently. In Figure 1, a profit maximising firm would produce at OA, the level of output where MC = MR. It would then be able to earn abnormal profit of EFTU. Whilst the firm is still productively efficient, producing at lowest cost, it is allocatively inefficient selling at a price above the marginal cost of production.

(c) In Figure 1, the average costs of the nationalised monopoly in 1991 would have been above the LRAC line, indicating that it was productively inefficient. It would have priced on the AR curve where its actual average cost equalled average revenue, given that it was earning abnormal profit. This could have been between T and V or it might have been higher than T.

Following privatisation, costs fell. Hence the industry will have become less productively inefficient. On the other hand, it also pushed up prices to earn abnormal profit. If the 1994 price was above the 1991 price (i.e. the privatisation price was further up the AR curve in Figure 1 than the nationalised industry price), then privatisation will have led to greater allocative inefficiency. If it was below, privatisation will not only have increased productive efficiency, but allocative efficiency too.

(d) (i) Economic theory would suggest that, in a competitive market, new entrants would come into the market attracted by the abnormal profits being earned. Prices would then fall and abnormal profit would be eliminated.

(ii) It is likely to lead to a more efficient allocation of resources because competition will put further pressure on cost minimisation leading to productive efficiency. It is also likely to lead to less allocative inefficiency because price is likely to be nearer marginal cost.

Question 2

(a) Transco is a natural monopolist. It is a transporter of gas through its pipe network. Gas pipelines tend not to be fully utilised at any point in the day. More gas could be transported through the existing network of pipelines at very little extra marginal cost. Hence, Transco is unable fully to exploit economies of scale despite being the only firm in the piped gas transport market. This makes it into a natural monopolist. The same reasoning applies to both Network Rail and part of BT. With Network Rail, some of its track is fully utilised at peak times and at these times it is arguably operating at the bottom of its average cost curve. However, for most of the time, its network is underutilised and therefore it is a natural monopoly. For BT, again its land line infrastructure makes it into a natural monopolist. The most crucial area where its infrastructure is underutilised is between the local telephone exchange and the home or workplace of customers. This 'last mile' could take much more volume of traffic. Hence, BT is not operating at the bottom of its average cost curve.

(b) BT is not a natural monopolist in providing a telephone service to individual customers. Just as rail companies like Virgin pay Network Rail to run trains over its tracks, so companies like Cable & Wireless can pay the part of BT which is a natural monopoly to run telephone calls over those fixed land lines.

(c) According to C&W, British Telecom was putting unnecessary obstacles in the way of customers wanting to transfer from BT to C&W. In particular, BT was rejecting applications which did not conform exactly to the details on its database. As a result, 40 per cent of applications were being rejected by BT, an astonishing figure given that BT was able to send out bills to all those customers.

(d) BT wanted to minimise the loss of its customers to rivals. BT has had a long history of frustrating potential competitors making it difficult for them to enter the market. This is one of the reasons why it remains a dominant supplier of telecommunications services to households. By reducing the proportion of customers leaving, BT generates extra revenues and profits.

Question 3

(a) Patents give pharmaceutical companies a monopoly on particular drugs. This means that these companies are the only companies legally allowed to produce or sell these products (unless they have licensed their patents to another company). Patents are legal barriers to entry to the market.

(b) The process of creative destruction describes the process whereby one technology is replaced by another. In the pharmaceutical industry, drug companies cannot produce drugs which are under patent to another drug company. Instead, they attempt to find their own drug for a particular medical condition which is as good as, if not better than, the drug under patent. If they can find this drug, then they can become the market leader and enjoy monopoly profits.

(c) In one sense, patients would clearly be better off if new drugs did not have patent protection. Competition in the market would enable them to buy their drugs at much lower prices than patented drugs. On the other hand, loss of patent protection would mean that those pharmaceutical companies which engage in research into new drugs would not have the monopoly profits to finance that research. It would also act as a disincentive for them to spend any money on research into new drugs because immediately they launched the product, other companies would quickly find the chemical formula for the drug and sell their own versions at lower prices. This process can be clearly seen amongst drug companies which only sell generic drugs. Their research and development is solely to do with copying the drugs of other companies. In the short term, patients would benefit from lower prices. But they would also find that spending on research into new drugs would fall substantially.

Question 4

(a) The three markets were the software markets for operating systems, for media systems and for workgroup servers. There was interlinkage through Microsoft's operating system, Windows. Both the media software and the software for workgroup servers were built upon the operating system.
(b) Microsoft wanted to develop monopolies in these markets for two reasons. One was that in the short term, they would be able to gain monopoly profits from selling the software. The second was that each new application built upon Windows could help reinforce Microsoft's long term monopoly position by creating major barriers to entry. The more applications ran on Windows, the less would competitors be able to compete in the market.
(c) The European Commission attempted to control Microsoft in a number of ways. One was to order it to unbundle its Media Player software from Windows and to offer a version of Windows without Media Player. The second was to order Microsoft to give competitors enough source code for those competitors to be able to build new software applications which could be run on Windows. The third was to fine Microsoft E497 million for abusing its virtual monopoly over the PC desktop market in Europe.
(d) Competition might have been more effectively promoted if Microsoft had been broken up into competing companies. One way to do this would have been to break Microsoft up into, say, four companies each having copyright on the existing version of Windows. Then each company would be given individual products which Microsoft currently sells. For example, one company might be given copyright over Media Player software. The companies would then develop new, possibly incompatible versions of Windows, but also attempt to break into their competitors markets by making their own versions of other products. This might have promoted competition but there are two problems with this solution. One is that Microsoft is a US company and the European Commission did not have the power to break Microsoft up into competing companies. Only US competition authorities could do this. Second, it could be argued that the Windows operating system is a natural monopoly and that consumers would be worse off if incompatible versions of Windows became commonly available on the market.

An alternative would have been for the European Commission to have effectively set up some sort of regulatory authority to monitor Microsoft's practices in Europe. Like regulatory bodies in the UK, it would have the power to set maximum prices for sale of Microsoft software in the EU and to prevent Microsoft from engaging in uncompetitive practices. This would preserve the advantages of having a single operating system in wide use but would limit the ability of Microsoft to exploit the consumer.

Data question

Figure 2

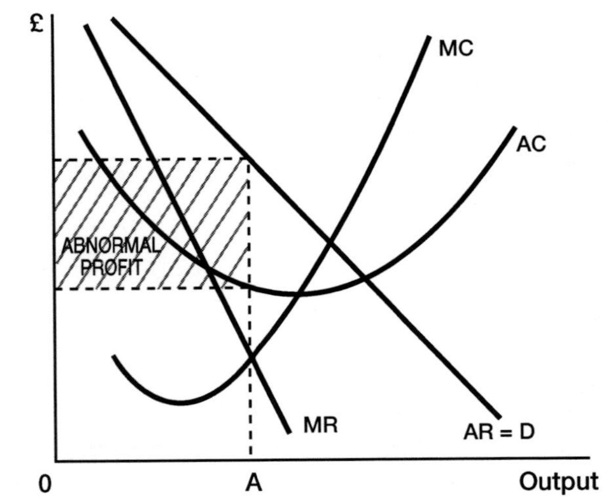

1. A firm is a pure monopolist if it has 100 per cent of the market. BAA could be considered to be a local monopolist because it owns most of the key airports in Southern England. By owning Heathrow, Gatwick and Stansted, it has '80 per cent of the flights and 90 per cent of the passengers leaving the south-east and East Anglia'. It can protect its monopoly with high barriers to entry because it is impossible to increase capacity in the short to medium term. New entrants cannot open new airports or build new runways because of the difficulty of obtaining planning permission.
2.(a) A monopolist such as BAA is likely to be a profit maximiser. In Figure 2, it produces OA output because this is where marginal cost equals marginal revenue. But at this level of output it is neither productively efficient or allocatively efficient. It is productively inefficient because it is not producing at lowest average cost at the bottom of its average cost curve. It is allocatively inefficient because it is not producing where price (or average revenue) equals marginal cost. Its prices are greater and its output lower than if it were operating efficiently.

It could be argued that BAA is a multiplant monopolist. Each airport is a different plant with each capable of operating independently. If this were the case, as shown in Figure 3, it would be productively efficient but allocatively inefficient. There would be productive efficiency because it would be producing at the lowest point on its average cost curve. However, it would be allocatively inefficient because it would not be producing at the point V where price equals marginal cost. Instead, it would produce output OA where marginal cost equals marginal revenue, the profit maximising level of output.
(b) Dynamic efficiency occurs when resources are allocated efficiently over time. BAA is likely to be dynamically inefficient because it fails to invest sufficiently over time. It will choose to earn higher profits now rather than invest for the future

Figure 3

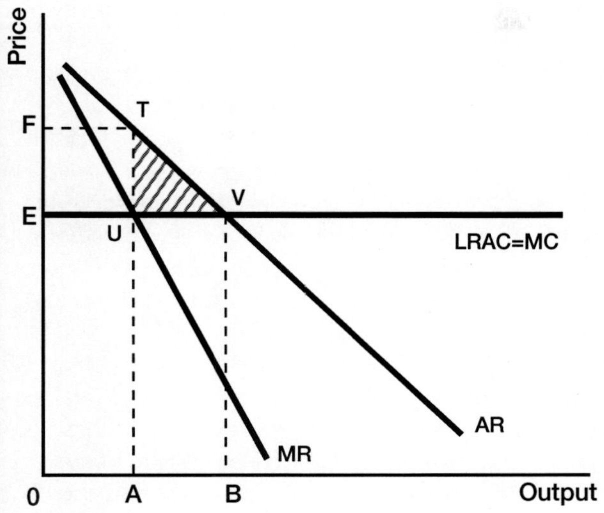

because it is a short term profit maximiser. The data states that 'Heathrow is starved investment' and argues that the three airports owned by BAA are 'money machines'. It then states that 'the absence of competition means BAA has little if any incentive to expand capacity or to improve facilities.'

3. The data suggest that the solution to the problem of inefficiency at Heathrow airport would be to break up BAA's monopoly in the south of England. If each of the three airports currently owned by BAA were owned by independent companies, there would be an incentive for each company to attract as many passengers as possible. To do this, they would have to offer better facilities and more reliable services. Any airport which failed to improve would see its passenger numbers fall. It would have a profit incentive to minimise costs because reducing cost with a given revenue would yield higher profit. Expanding passenger numbers would get the airport nearer the allocatively efficient point of production. There would also be greater dynamic efficiency because firms would have to invest to create the better services demanded by passengers in a competitive market. Abnormal profit would fall to pay for the increased investment.

On the other hand, it could be argued that each airport has a local monopoly. A passenger flying from Gatwick will be flying from there because Gatwick is convenient to get to for the passenger or because it is offering a particular destination at the right price. Most passengers could not choose instead to fly from Heathrow or Stansted. Breaking up BAA's monopoly, on this argument, would do little to improve efficiency. Instead of there being one monopolist , there would be three.

However, whilst for many passengers, each airport is a local monopolist, for a minority there would be a choice. If Heathrow lost just 10 per cent of its passengers to Gatwick and Stansted because they began to offer a better service, then this would severely hit the profits of Heathrow. It only requires a relatively small percentage of passengers to switch for there to be a significant impact on revenues and profits. Therefore, competition could possibly increase efficiency.

55 Growth of firms, mergers and efficiency

Question 1

(a) A significant proportion of the hotel industry is comprised of small firms. Barriers to entry are relatively low. For the price of a large house, a couple can set themselves up in business. If trade initially is slack, one partner can have an outside full time job and they can live off the earnings from that job. Economies of scale are relatively low. The unit costs facing a small hotel are unlikely to be much higher than that of a chain. Indeed, they might be lower if the chain has to pay higher wages to unionised staff. There is likely to be less organisational slack in a hotel owned and managed by the same person. Chains of hotels are more likely to find it difficult to control costs. Small hotels can offer a more personalised service, accommodating individual needs more easily. A well run small hotel may also offer lower prices if costs or profit margins are lower.
(b) Despite all these advantages, large chains of hotels are common and have a significant share of the market. One important factor which might favour chains in the future is the consumers' desire to purchase a guaranteed minimum standard of service. When booking a non-chain hotel for the first time, the consumer is uncertain exactly what standard of accommodation is being purchased. Chains of hotels can provide a greater guarantee of quality. Chains are also in more of a position to enter new markets and invest heavily in new facilities. For instance, hotels with swimming pools and other leisure facilities, or low-cost no-frills accommodation, are two market niches which have been developed by chains in recent years.

Question 2

(a) easyJet could be argued to have increased productive efficiency in the economy. By offering low fares, not only have its passengers enjoyed low prices, but the competition from easyJet has forced other airlines such as British Airways to cut costs. It could also be argued to have increased allocative efficiency. In some instances, before 1995, some airlines were able to exploit consumers by pricing at above marginal cost. easyJet, through rigourous price competition, eliminated the abnormal profit made by some airlines. easyJet has also contributed to dynamic efficiency. Its own operations and the competition which it has created have led to a much greater variety of routes being offered with far more passengers using aeroplanes than in 1995.

Question 3

(a) Horizontal merger - Wm Morrison and Safeway are both retailers in the grocery and general store markets.
(b) Vertical and horizontal merger - Greene King as a pub operator merging with Laurel, another pub operator, is an example of a horizontal merger. Greene King as a brewer merging with Laurel is an example of a vertical merger.
(c) Vertical merger - Ford is a manufacturer of goods whilst Kwik-Fit is a retailer/fitter of car parts.
(d) Conglomerate merger - British American Tobacco is a cigarette manufacturer whilst Farmers Group is an insurance company.
(e) Horizontal merger - Pete & Johnny and Pepsi are both manufacturers of soft drinks.

Question 4

(a) Procter & Gamble could have chosen to develop its own brands to rival those of Gillette. However, as the owner of some of the largest brands in the world, it knows that it is very difficult to launch new brands successfully. It is even more difficult to challenge highly successful brands already in the market. With no certainty that any brand development would have been successful against Gillette, however, much money was thrown at the development, it made far more sense to merge with Gillette.
(b) The merged company would have benefited from a number of economies of scale. The main economy of scale would be in marketing. By pushing the new company's products down one distribution channel instead of two, average costs would fall. The new company would also be able to get better prices for its products from the giant supermarket chains because of the volumes it would now sell. Equally, it would be in a better position to negotiate 'better marketing deals and secure prime spots for their store displays'.

Data question

1. (a) Ford buying Kwik-Fit was primarily an example of a vertical merger. Ford, a manufacturer of cars, was buying forward in its supply chain. However, it could be argued that it was a horizontal merger because Ford already owned an after-sales chain called Rapid-Fit in the UK. This was in direct competition with Kwik-Fit.
(b) CVC and PAI are both private equity companies. These companies buy other companies from which over time they hope they can extract value by selling them at a higher price than they bought them. They achieve this by improving the profitability of the companies. The companies that they buy can be from a wide range of industries. As such, CVC or PAI buying Kwik-Fit would be an example of a conglomerate merger.
2. (a) Ford decided to buy Kwik-Fit as part of an expansion strategy. It wanted to become a 'leading consumer services business'. This meant moving downstream from car manufacturing to providing a range of services to customers. These included offering traditional dealer network services. They also included offering repair services such as those offered by Kwik-Fit.
(b) CVC and PAI were interested in buying Kwik-Fit because they could see an opportunity for making a capital gain by buying the company at a lower price and selling it on some time later at a higher price.
3. (a) Ford bought Kwik-Fit for £1 billion and sold it for £330 million. Clearly it failed to make a success of the company. It failed to tackle productive inefficiency, production at lowest average cost. When CVC Partners took over the company, it closed some loss making sites. Part of the problem with these sites is likely to have been low revenues, but equally, average costs are likely to have been too high because of a lack of throughput of customers. The company was also allocatively inefficient, failing to deliver products at the right price that customers wanted. CVC Partners in contrast managed to find new customers over and above those that came because of the growth in the economy. Ford failed to deliver dynamic

efficiency because it failed to put the resources in to grow the business. Instead, almost as soon as it bought Kwik-Fit , it decided on a change of strategy which emphasised going back to its core business of vehicle development and production.

(b) CVC, in contrast, increased Kwik-Fit's economic efficiency. It raised both productive and allocative efficiency for the reasons described above. It also expanded the firm leading to dynamic efficiency.

56 Technological change

Question 1

(a) Production costs of the new Tata car will be lower than the production costs of a standard European model of car. Fixed costs will be lower partly because the cost of research and development has been lower. Tata has used 'lower-cost Indian engineers and out-of-the-box solutions to research and development.' Variable costs will also be lower partly because labour costs are lower but also because the specifications of the car are much less than an EU car. For example, the cheapest model is powered by a 600 cc engine whereas the smallest EU engines tend to be around 1000 cc.

These differences in costs can be shown in Figure 1. The average cost curve of the Tata, AC_1, is lower than the typical EU car, AC_2, because of both lower fixed and variable costs. The marginal cost curve MC1 for the Tata car is also lower because the cost of producing an extra vehicle is lower.

Figure 1

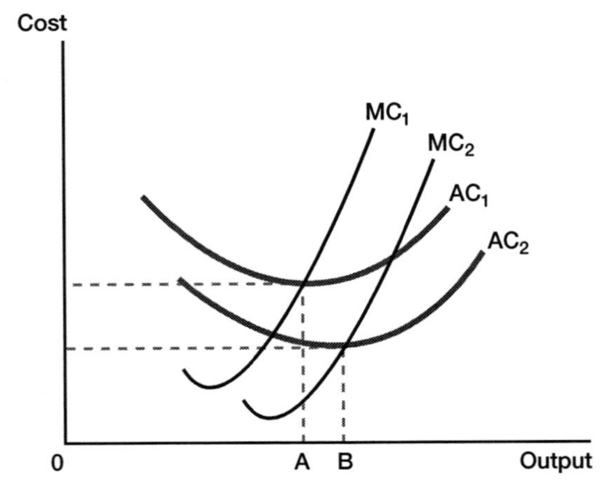

(b) The price paid to Tata for the car must equal the average cost of production if it is to make normal profit. The average cost is made up of average fixed cost and average variable cost. As output increases, average fixed cost falls. This initially contributes to a fall in total average cost. Initially, average cost is likely to be above average revenue because of high average fixed costs. But as production increases, average cost will become equal to average revenue. This point could be reduced at 250 000 cars.

(c) In India where the car will be produced, labour costs are a fraction of those in the EU. On the other hand, the cost of capital is likely to be the same. If Tata can buy machinery at low prices, for example, so too can EU producers by buying from the same source as Tata. Therefore Tata is likely to use far more labour intensive methods of production. Because labour is so much cheaper, it will substitute labour for capital, thus reducing its costs compared to a situation where it uses more capital.

Question 2

(a) (i) The barriers to entry to the mobile phone handset market are relatively high. First, the costs of designing and producing a mobile phone are significant, particularly for a new entrant which will have set up costs. Second, there are high marketing barriers. Mobile phones need either to be adopted by mobile phone telecommunications companies such as Vodaphone or Orange, or stocked by mobile phone retailers such as Carphone Warehouse. Both of these channels tend to stock only mobile phones from established mobile phone manufacturers such as Nokia or Motorola.

(ii) Barriers to legal music downloads are also very high. The cost of setting up a download site is relatively low. However, for it to be legal, the owners of the site must have negotiated an agreement with the copyright owners of the music to sell the music on the site. Even large companies such as Apple have had difficulties negotiating such agreements. Moreover, Apple with its iTunes site has 'gained some monopoly power over the market'. Its technology is easy to use. There are a number of major companies which have already challenged the dominance of iTunes and failed. It would be even more difficult for a new entrant to gain even a small share of the market.

(b) The iPhone was a new entrant to the market in 2007. It will therefore have increased the number of firms in the industry. If the iPhone proves to be a commercial failure, it will have little effect on the structure of the market. However, if it is successful, it could take a significant share of the market. This might drive other firms out of the market making it less rather than more competitive. The iPhone could also increase the proportion of phones sold in the market that have strong brand images. Again this would tend to reduce rather than increase competition in the market. A successful iPhone is likely to increase barriers to entry to the market because competitors will find it difficult to copy its technology.

Data question

1(a) Wal-Mart is the world's largest retailer, selling $400 billion of merchandise in 2008 from 6 500 stores. Technology can profoundly affect the way in which a firm like Wal-Mart operates. Its methods of production are different from the local corner store. For example, a small corner store owner might go to the cash and carry to pick up stock. The stock is then put on the shelves with a marked price. At Wal-Mart, stock is tracked electronically. Customers pick up items from the shelves. The items are scanned using a bar-coding system at the check-out. The computer then subtracts those items from the stock in the store. It then automatically contacts suppliers to deliver fresh stock to the store through the 'continuous replenishment system'. Electronic data interchange means that invoices are issued automatically to Wal-Mart by suppliers. The Wal-Mart system means that the company knows exactly what is in stock at any one time and in which store. Stock is reordered as and when needed. Therefore stock is minimised to the advantage of Wal-Mart. Overall, technology has allowed Wal-Mart to develop less labour-intensive methods of production, with capital in the form of computer systems, replacing labour.

(b) New technology can reduce costs, typically by reducing labour inputs and cutting waste. In the case of Wal-Mart, its computer systems have eliminated much of the need for workers to track stock as it passes through the supply chain. Wastage is reduced because stock is only delivered to a store as and when it is needed. Perishable products like fresh vegetables, meat and bread are more likely to be sold than thrown away because they pass their sell by date in the store. Stock is also reduced in stores to exactly the right level. Reducing stock levels in the system saves Wal-Mart cash because less stock is held overall in the supply chain. Its average cost curve is therefore lower than many of its rivals.

(c) The supply of goods and services is affected by new technology. In the case of Wal-Mart, new technology has allowed it to supply the same amount of goods at a lower price to its customers. It has also given it the information to put stock into individual stores which exactly mirror the spending patterns of customers in that store. For example, a store in New England might have more affluent customers than a store in Chicago. By tracking the spending patterns of customers in an individual store, goods can be put onto the shelves which customers most want to buy. New technology also affects Wal-Mart's supply chain. Its suppliers, for example, produce new products using the latest technology. This can be anything from the latest in television technology to the latest in materials in fishing rods.

2. New technology has radically altered the structure of the retail markets in which Wal-Mart operates. Before Wal-Mart, retail markets were typically highly fragmented. Technology has since given major supermarket chains an ability to deliver a greater range of products than typically found in a local shop at a much lower price. The result has been that concentration ratios in these retail markets have risen substantially. In the UK, for example, the four largest supermarket chains, which include Asda owned by Wal-Mart, now dominate the retail grocery market. The largest supermarket chain, Tesco, sells over 12 per cent of all retail sales in the UK.

With supermarkets now dominant, it means that their markets are oligopolistic. The actions of one supermarket impact on sales of other supermarkets. There are also substantial financial barriers to entry for any firm which wishes to challenge the supermarket chains. Wal-Mart entered the UK market not by setting up its own chain of stores but by buying Asda.

3. New technology can give a firm a competitive edge over its rivals in a number of ways. New technology, as in the case of Wal-Mart, can lead to greater productive efficiency. Average costs can fall. Wal-Mart has used its cost advantage over rivals to open stores across the USA and the world.

New technology can also give firms an advantage in terms of product. For example, the Apple iPod and iTunes have allowed Apple to dominate the markets for MP3 players and Internet downloads of music. New products have allowed Proctor & Gamble, suppliers to Wal-Mart, to compete more successfully against rivals in the market.

However, as the data states, new technology can often fail. RFID tags have proved to be a step too far for most suppliers of Wal-Mart. The cost of introducing the system has been too high in comparison with the benefits that it gives suppliers. Equally, most new products launched will either fail or sell poorly. For every iPod, there are thousands of examples of failed new products. The introduction of new technology can actually hinder a firm. In the case of Wal-Mart, its concentration on the introduction of RFID tags meant that its rivals were able to out-compete Wal-Mart in new areas such as Internet retailing. Like all economic agents, firms have limited resources. If they choose to back the wrong technologies, their rivals which choose the right technologies will gain a competitive advantage.

57 Public versus private sector provision

Question 1

(a) The Labour Party placed a strong emphasis on nationalisation in its 1945 Party Manifesto. It argued that many industries were fragmented, either into small firms which failed to achieve economies of scale, such as the coal industry, or into local monopolies, such as the railway companies, which had failed to invest sufficiently under private ownership. Nationalisation would give the economies of scale necessary for the efficient running of these industries. Nationalisation would cut out the wasteful advertising and promotion associated with competition, whilst giving industries the money and the incentive to undertake research and development. Private ownership was also associated with poor management. Public ownership would enable the best management to be appointed which would oversee a modernisation of production methods. Overall the Labour Party argued that nationalisation would provide better quality services at a lower price.

Question 2

(a) (i) Productive efficiency was increased because nationalised industries did not produce at lowest average cost. Privatisation tended to lead to a fall in both average costs and prices. For example, over the twenty year period to 1999, electricity prices fell by 24 per cent and gas prices by 35 per cent in real terms. It is likely therefore that privatisation contributed to allocative efficiency where price equals the marginal cost of production.
(ii) Privatisation has increased the amount of choice available to customers. Whilst some privatised industries such as water remain monopolies for domestic customers, in gas, electricity and telecommunications there has been a significant increase in the amount of choice of provider. Even in rail, whilst part of the network is still a monopoly, there is limited competition between different rail companies on other parts of the network.
(iii) Innovation has increased. Whilst many utilities such as gas, electricity and water provide a product which cannot be changed over time, others such as rail companies and telecommunications companies can bring innovative products to the market. On the railways, for example, much of the pre-privatisation rolling stock has been replaced with more comfortable and reliable rolling stock. Even in water, the large investment programme could be argued to be innovative as it seeks to improve water quality, reduce pollution and reduce inefficiencies such as water leakage.

Question 3

(a) There is a variety of ways in which a government can control privatised utilities. One is to use regulation to control the behaviour of privatised utilities which retain monopoly powers over their market. For example, in the UK, regulatory authorities such as Ofgem for the gas and electricity industries and OFCOM, for telecommunications have been set up with powers to set prices, as shown in the third of the extracts in the data, and investigate anti-competitive practices. They have the power to fine companies if they breach the rules, as shown in the first of the three extracts in the data.

Another way of controlling privatised utilities is to break them up into competing companies. For example, both the gas and electricity industries were broken up by the government to create competition.

Third, governments can create competition in the industry by allowing new firms to enter the industry. BT was not broken up on privatisation but competitors have been allowed into the industry. In the last extract in the data, BT's regulator, OFCOM, was being urged to encourage consumers to take advantage of that competition given that BT still held 70 per cent of the residential market.

Question 4

(a) There are two main ways in which private sector involvement can benefit NHS patients. In the short term, the private sector can be used to treat patients when there are bottlenecks in the NHS system. So the private sector can be used to provide one-off reductions in waiting lists for example.

In the longer term, however, the private sector can provide competition for NHS trusts and hospitals. If private sector companies are more efficient at treating patients, they will take work away from NHS hospitals and trusts. This will provide an incentive for NHS hospitals to improve their efficiency by cutting costs and improving services.
(b) Public sector unions oppose contracting out because experience shows that contracting out leads to lower pay, fewer workers employed and an increase in the workload for those workers that keep their jobs. Private contractors can undercut the NHS by increasing productive efficiency. However, this can come at the expense of the workers in the industry.

Data question

1. Since 1953, there has been a dramatic fall in the number of passengers travelling by bus. In 1953, there were nearly 16 billion bus journeys made per year. by 2006/7, this had fallen to less than 5 billion. However, there has been some increase since 1998/1999. This has mainly been made up of increased bus use in London.

In contrast, the number of passengers using air transport has dramatically increased. Since 1985, the number of passengers leaving and entering the UK on international flights has increased from 53 million to 185 million whilst those travelling on domestic flights has increased from 9 million to 23 million.
2. Deregulation is the process of removing government controls from markets. The local bus market was deregulated in 1986. This meant that companies were free to compete on local bus routes. In London, deregulation took a slightly different form. Bus companies had to bid for the right to gain a monopoly on a particular route. Both in London and outside London, unprofitable routes were put out to tender and the bus company offering to run the route for the lowest subsidy won the contract.

In the airline market, deregulation within Europe has meant that EU airlines since 1997 are free to fly to whichever destination they wish. However, particularly popular airports such as London Heathrow have a lack of capacity and this limits the ability of airlines to gain landing and take off slots.
3. Superficially, it might seem as if deregulation in the air passenger market has been far more successful than deregulation in the bus market. Air passenger numbers have been growing whilst the number of bus passengers has been

declining. However, the EU airline market was only deregulated in 1997 and air passenger numbers have been climbing since well before that time. Equally, whilst bus deregulation occurred in 1986, the downward trend in bus travel was present thirty years before then.

The broad trends in travel numbers would have been present with or without deregulation. Bus travel is arguably an inferior good. As incomes rise, people choose to travel by car or by rail rather than bus. Air travel, in contrast, has a high income elasticity of demand. As incomes rise, households spend a significant portion of their rising income on holidays which use air travel.

Deregulation, however, can also be judged against other criteria. Both air and bus deregulation have led to some customers having greater choice of company from which to buy the service. Both deregulations have led to an increase in the number of services being provided to customers on some routes.

However, both have in some ways failed to meet other aims. It is arguable whether bus deregulation has helped to reduce traffic congestion. Indeed, some argue that it has increased it because there are now more half empty buses on the road. For air transport, if deregulation has encouraged greater use, then this leads to greater environmental problems. It could be argued both for buses and air transport that greater government control would provide a more sustainable and environmentally friendly package of transport modes.

58 Environmental market failure

Question 1

(a) Asbestos is a problem because it causes serious illness in workers exposed to the material. It takes between 15 and 40 years for the illness to develop, by which time many workers have left their original jobs. The two main diseases which workers can develop are mesothelioma, a type of cancer, and asbestosis, a scarring of the lung tissues. The problem for companies which employed the workers is that they have to pay compensation to the workers, again many years after the original contact with asbestos.

(b) The marginal private cost of using asbestos to a company is the cost of the material and wages of the workers used to manufacturer or make product from the material. On top of this is the compensation firms have to pay out to victims of asbestos. However, the data states than many workers die before they receive compensation because of the slowness of dealing with the claims. Once dead, the workers lose their right to compensation. This means that firms are not paying the full social cost of their use of asbestos.

This can be shown in Figure 1. The marginal private benefit of using asbestos is shown by the downward sloping demand curve. The marginal private cost without any compensation being paid is shown by MPC_1. With compensation, the marginal private cost curve shifts upwards to MPC_2. However, this is still not the full marginal social cost because not all workers receive compensation. As a result, the equilibrium cost to companies rises from OA to OB but is still the full equilibrium marginal social cost of OC.

(c) (i) Allocative inefficiency can take place where price, or marginal benefit, does not equal marginal social cost. In this case the marginal social cost of use is greater than the marginal social benefit. In Figure 1, equilibrium marginal social cost is OC. However, even with compensation, it is OB. Price of OB is less than marginal social cost of OC and hence welfare gains can be made by using less asbestos to a level where marginal social cost equals marginal social benefit. This did not take place in Britain in the 1960s because few realised the medical problems that asbestos caused among workers. In China today, employers are likely to know the medical problems that asbestos can cause workers in later years. However, they are choosing to ignore these problems because either there is no regulation on the use of asbestos or the regulations are being ignored. Chinese firms using asbestos must not believe that they will pick up the bill for compensation in decades to come.

(ii) The welfare loss to society from the use of asbestos are the triangular areas on Figure 1 FGH and EGJ. The marginal private cost to firms if no compensation is paid is MPC_1. The welfare loss from the use of asbestos is then EGJ, the difference between marginal social cost and marginal social benefit at each point of output. If compensation is given but the compensation does not reflect the full social cost, the marginal private cost curve is MPC_2. The welfare loss is lower at FGH but it is still present. The welfare loss would only be eliminated if price were to equal marginal social cost. In China today, the welfare loss is high because firms are unlikely to have to pay compensation in the future. In Britain in the 1960s, the welfare loss turned out to be lower at FGH because at least some of the workers affected were compensated at a later date.

Figure 1

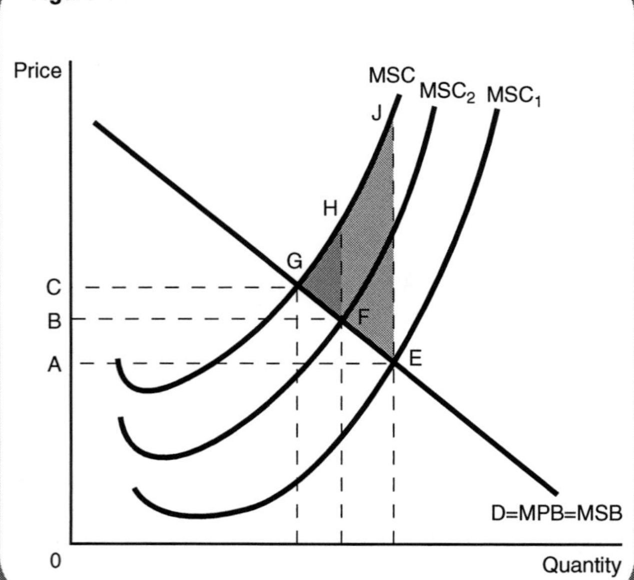

Question 2

(a) Carbon emissions arise when petrol is used in a car or gas is burnt to heat a house. These carbon emissions cause a negative externality because they contribute to global warming which is having a negative impact on our climate. A negative externality occurs when social costs are greater than private costs. The private costs of burning carbon fuels is the price customers pay for fuel. The social cost is this private cost plus the cost of externalities such as the costs arising from global warming.

(b) Burning fuel which leads to global warming has distributional effects. This is because those burning the fuel are not necessarily the ones who will be affected most by global warming. Those burning most fuel tend to live in rich developed countries. However, they impose costs on the most vulnerable in poorer developing countries who suffer from drought or floods caused by global warming. There is therefore a redistribution of the cost from those who create it in rich countries to those who burn little fuel but suffer the consequences.

(c) Economic theory would suggest that there will be a misallocation of resources when externalities are created. One method of internalising the externality is for governments to raise taxes to pay compensation to those who suffer. However, this is a relatively crude way of dealing with the problem because those who are taxed are not necessarily the ones who create the externality. If income tax were raised, for example, to deal with environmental problems, there is no direct link between earned income and the cost of individual environmental problems. It would be better if the tax were specifically focussed on the activity creating the externality. For example, the tax on sending waste to landfill is a better way of dealing with the problem of the disposal of waste than a rise in VAT on all goods and services.

Equally, there are other ways of dealing with externalities apart from tax. Methods such as regulation and permits are alternative policies which may have more efficient outcomes. Equally, economic theory suggests that eliminating the externality might be achieved if those who suffer the effects of the externality paid those who created it to stop their activities.

Figure 2

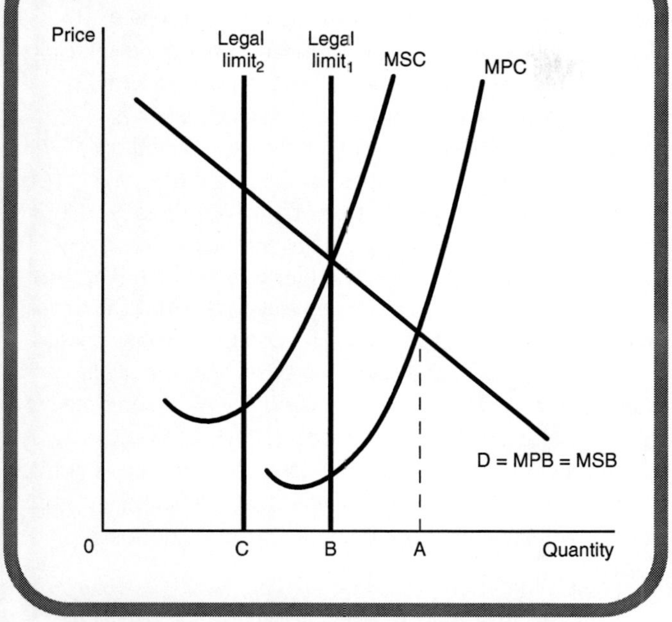

Figure 3

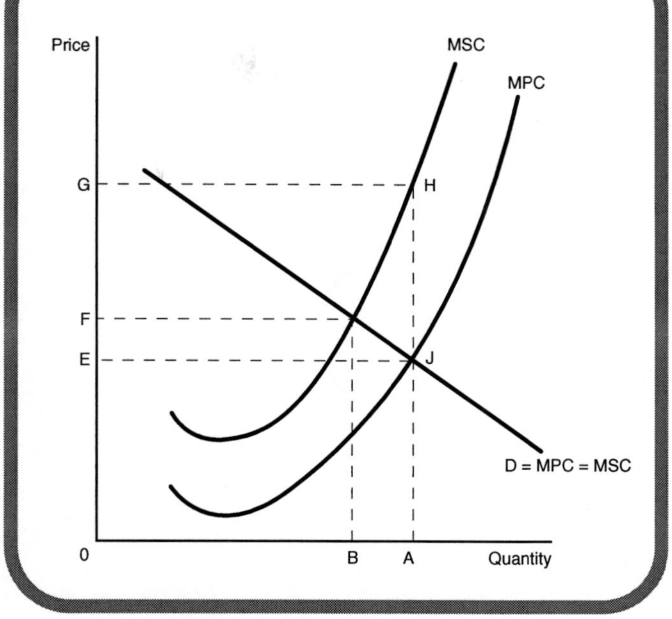

Question 3

(a) The Royal Commission on Environmental Pollution has suggested that there should be a 'no spray zone' of five metres round fields to protect the health of bystanders and those living near sprayed fields. This is because there is evidence that pesticides can cause a variety of illnesses such as respiratory irritation to immune disorders.

(b) Economic theory would suggest that the marginal social cost of an activity should equal its marginal social benefit if welfare is to be maximised. In Figure 2, if no controls on the use of pesticide are used, farmers will equate the marginal private cost of use with their marginal private benefit, shown by the demand line. As a consequence, OA of pesticides will be used. However, the socially optimal level of use is at OB where the marginal social cost equals the marginal social benefit. If regulation, such as a ban on spraying within a five metre zone, could achieve this, then welfare would be maximised. In practice, it is very difficult for governments to set the legal limit at exactly the right level because of a lack of information. Farmers have responded to the proposals of the Royal Commission on Environmental Pollution by saying that the regulation would be too strict. They are arguing that the new regulation would put the legal limit to the left of the social optimal level of OB at OC. At this point, too little pesticide would be used. Without a lot more evidence, it is difficult to say whether farmers are right in their assertions or not.

Question 4

(a) The externality in this case is being internalised because the company is having to pay for the cost of the clean up and for the court costs incurred in the prosecution. In Figure 3, the marginal private cost of the firm's activities are shown by the curve MPC. However, these are less than the marginal social cost. The company failed to monitor their drainage system, no doubt saving them cash in the short term but leading to the spillage. In Figure 3, the equilibrium output for the firm not taking account of the externalities was OA. If all costs were taken into account, it would be OB. The price of their activities would have to rise from OE to OF to take full account of their social costs. The cost of the clean up could be represented by the area EGHJ, the value of the externalities at output OA which is HJ times the level of output. However, it should be noted that whilst the company was fined £60 000 on top of costs incurred, no compensation was paid to those who suffered. These included those living on canal boats at Ocker Hill moorings. Their distress might have been smaller or greater than the £60 000 fine. If it was greater, the full cost of the externality would not have been internalised.

Question 5

(a) Transport for London is proposing to put a tax on heavy vehicles which do not comply with EU emissions standards entering the greater London area within the boundaries of the M25. This would mostly apply to vehicles built before 2002 because vehicles built after this point tended to conform to the new stricter standard. If the tax were imposed, it would internalise some of the externality created by older heavy vehicles. This can be shown in Figure 4. The marginal private benefit to owners of older heavy vehicles is shown by the demand curve. Equilibrium output without a tax is at OA where the demand curve intersects the marginal private cost

Figure 4

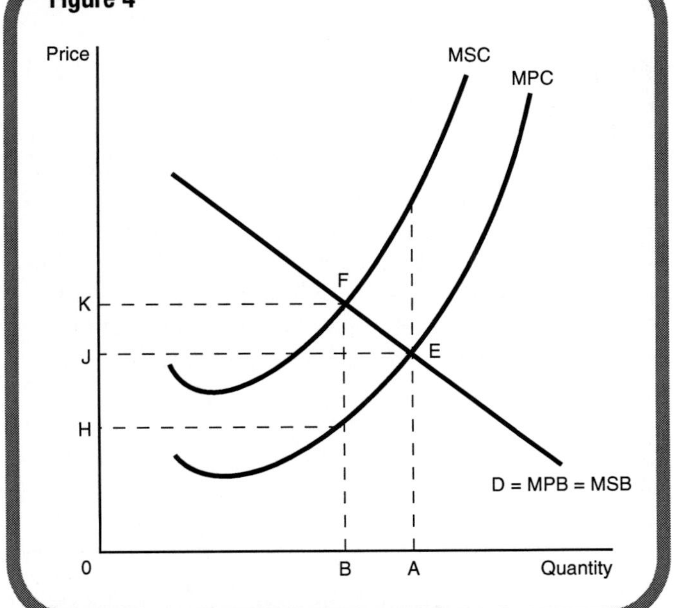

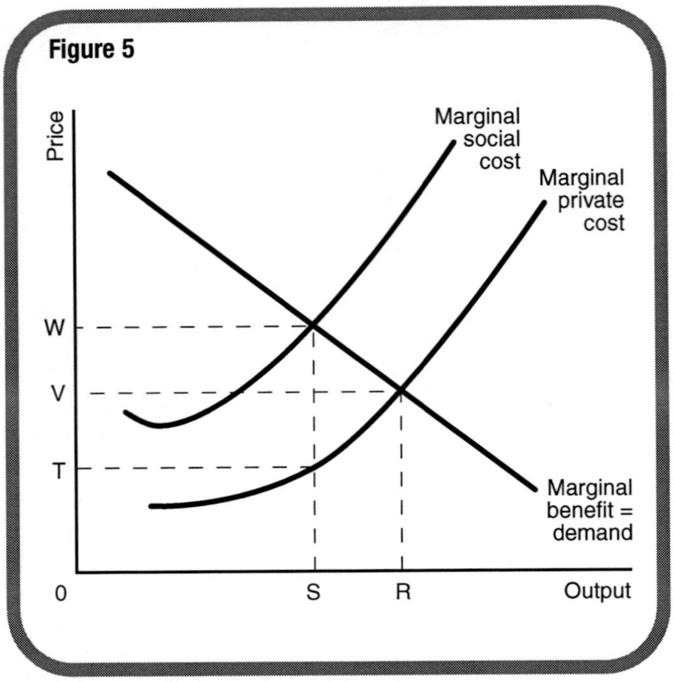

curve. However, the socially optimal level of output is OB where the marginal social cost curve intersects the demand curve. At an output level of OA, EFG of welfare is lost because production is too high. By raising a tax of HJ per unit to bring marginal private cost up to the level of marginal social cost, this welfare loss would be eliminated.

(b) The Confederation of Passenger Transport is arguing that the marginal private benefit to coach and bus operators is less than the marginal social benefit. This is because bus and coach companies are a key part of the London tourist industry, bringing visitors in from outside the capital, for example, to watch West End shows. If the tax were imposed, coach operators would have to raise their prices, fewer visitors would come to London and tourism would suffer. However, this is not an argument against imposing the tax. Transport for London is arguing that coaches built before 2002 impose externalities on the people of London. The point of a tax is to raise the price to customers and so reduce output. Any externalities which occur because of tourism should be taken account of when setting the tax. What the coach operators could argue, however, is that the tax is too high and leads to too great a fall in output below the socially optimal level of output.

Question 6

(a) A pollution permit is a licence given, usually by government or a government agency, to pollute the environment in a particular way. Without the permit, the firm or country would not be allowed to create pollution of this type. For instance, in the EU there is a system of pollution permits issued by governments to companies designed to control emissions. Permits can be traded between firms to ensure that there is an efficient allocation of resources in pollution reduction.

(b) Figure 5 shows a situation where the marginal private cost of production is lower than its marginal social cost. Welfare would be maximised if production could be cut back from OR to OS where the marginal private and social benefit equalled the marginal social cost. Under a system of regulation, firms in an industry would be given maximum pollution levels without any regard to cost of compliance. For instance, two similar sized firms would probably be given the same limits. However, it might be far more costly for one firm to comply than the other, perhaps because it is using much older plant.

Assume there are two firms, A and B, both emitting 150 units of pollution each at present. The government wants to cut this by one third and issues pollution permits of 100 units of pollution. It will cost Firm A, which has old plant, £10 million to reduce pollution by 50 units. It will cost Firm B, which has new plant, £2 million to reduce pollution by 50 units and £3 million to reduce it by a further 50 units. With a rigid system of regulation it will cost society £12 million (£10 million from Firm A and £2 million from Firm B) to reduce pollution by 100 units. With pollution permits, it would pay Firm A to buy a 50 unit pollution permit from Firm B for any price less than £10 million. Firm B will be prepared to sell so long as it covers the cost of modification of equipment, which is £3 million. Firms A and B will therefore find it mutually acceptable to trade the permit so long as it is priced between £3 million and £10 million. For society, the cost of reducing pollution by 100 units is £5 million, the amount it costs Firm B to reduce pollution from 150 units to 100 units. The net gain to society of a permit system compared to regulation is then £7 million (£12 million - £5 million).

Data quesiton

1. (a) Social costs and benefits include both private costs and benefits and positive and negative externalities. The social costs include the actual cost of building houses but should not include the actual cost of the building land. The social cost of building land may well differ from its actual cost. It may be lower than at present because planning laws artificially raise its price. It may be higher because it does not take account of the damage to the environment or to others who live in the local area. The private benefits are the benefits received by those living in houses. The social benefits would also include the benefits that are gained when people live together in a community. For example, a city like London gives external benefits to its population because there is such a wide range of attractions on offer from shopping centres to museums and art galleries to swimming pools. These are not necessarily available in a small village in the north of Scotland. As the Swiss example in the data shows, there can be benefits to local inhabitants of having more people living locally.

(b) Bigger houses tend to occupy more land. Hence their social cost must include not just the extra cost of building a bigger house but also the associated costs of damage to the environment. The social benefits include the private benefit that living in a bigger house gives to people.

2. Many argue that building large housing developments on greenbelt land creates negative externalities. This is because the social cost exceeds the private cost of development. The externalities created include damage to the environment. This can be shown in Figure 6. If only the marginal private cost and benefits are considered, equilibrium output of new houses would be OA. However, the marginal social cost of new housing is higher than the marginal private cost. The socially optimal level of output is OB. As a result there is a loss of welfare of GHK, if OA houses are built.

3. Others have argued that planning restrictions have led to a misallocation of resources with too few houses being built. The planning system artificially forces up the price of building land because land with planning permission to build residential houses is in such limited supply. In the data it states that the ratio of the price of building land in the South East of England to agricultural land is 300:1. However, the value that individuals put on agricultural land is relatively low compared to other uses including building. Using some agricultural land for further

Figure 6

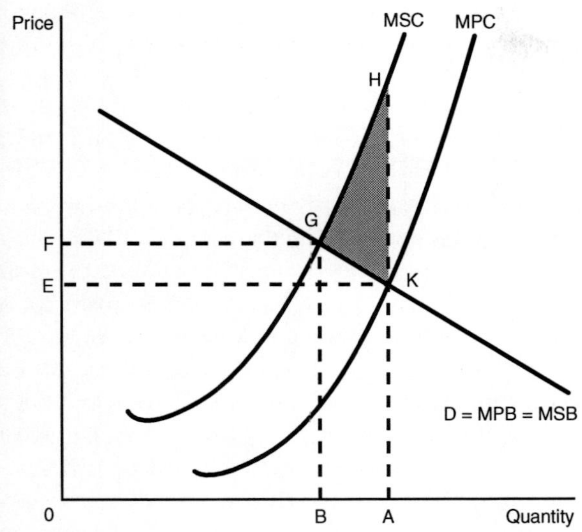

Figure 7

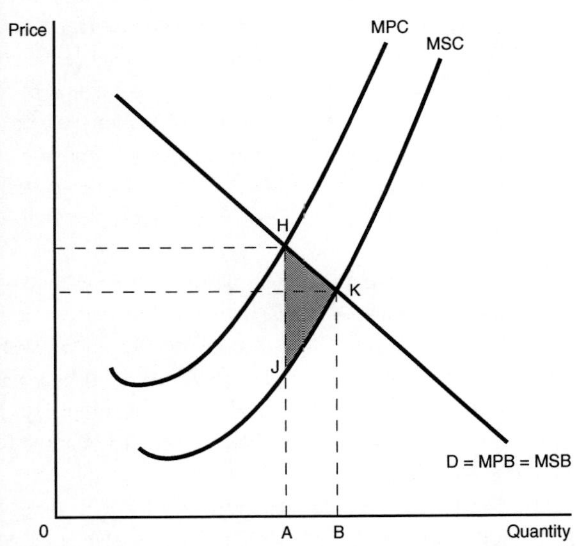

building would reduce the price of building land and bring it closer to its actual social cost.

This can be shown in Figure 7. The marginal private cost curve is above the marginal social cost reflecting the fact that planning has artificially driven up building land prices to above their marginal social cost. As a result, there is AB too little building land used to achieve an optimal allocation of resources. The welfare loss is the triangle HGK.

4. It is unlikely that an optimal allocation of resources would be achieved if all planning laws were removed. It could lead to houses being built on areas such as privately owned public spaces even though people put the very high value of £10.8 million per hectare on such land. Equally, planning laws are needed to prevent one householder building a new house or extending an existing house in a way which would considerably reduce the value of their next door neighbour's house.

However, it could be argued that there would be considerable net social benefits from releasing some land for building which is currently agricultural and within the green belt . As the data shows, there is considerable pent up demand for both more houses and larger houses. The UK has a housing stock which is 'among the oldest, pokiest and most expensive in the developed world'. Although pressure groups like CPRE (the Campaign to Protect Rural England) are correct in saying that new house building creates costs above simple building costs, it can be argued that they vastly overestimate the externalities involved. On this argument, CPRE is simply an example of 'middle-class Nimbyism'. Their supporters want to 'benefit from living in a nice house and a pleasant environment but nobody else is allowed to benefit from a similarly nice environment down the road from them'. These rural middle-class Nimbys are gaining substantial positive externalities at the expense of the 80 per cent of the UK's population who are 'imprisoned' within overcrowded urban areas. CPRE and other similar groups could then be argued to be supporting a highly inefficient allocation of resources which gives substantial benefits to the constituency which they represent. Making a few per cent more of Britain's land mass available for residential building could then be argued to be highly desirable and could lead to the elimination of the market failure currently present in the housing market.

59 Cost-benefit analysis

Question 1

(a) Social costs include both private costs and externalities. The main private cost which will be paid by those building the bypass will be the cost of construction put at between £210 and £405 million. However, there will be other costs which will be classified as externalities because they will not be paid for through construction or maintenance. These include the loss of 'natural land' and the destruction of wildlife habitats. Increased numbers of cars on the road will 'increase air pollution and reduce air quality'. They will also generate increased volumes of greenhouse gases, contributing to global warming. Friends of the Earth argue that the bypass will increase congestion, not reduce it. If congestion is increased, then there will be a cost to motorists in terms of longer journey tlmes taken.

The main social benefits will be felt by industry and probably motorists. Despite the arguments of the Friends of the Earth, the bypass is likely to reduce congestion in the Aberdeen area and reduce journey times. This will benefit local industry which will save on transport costs. However, it is also likely to attract more industry to the area, creating new jobs and increasing prosperity. For private motorists, journey times are likely to be reduced.

(b) The private costs to the Scottish Executive, and Aberdeen and Aberdeenshire Council will be the building and then the maintenance of the bypass. The private benefit might be lower maintenance costs of roads inside the bypass as their usage falls. If industry is attracted to the area, the two organisations might benefit from higher tax revenues, assuming that tax revenues can be seen as a 'benefit' for a government body.

Question 2

(a) (i) The private cost is the cost you pay. So the short term private cost of the meal will be the £4.99 you paid for it. However, if the meal is part of a very unhealthy diet, it is likely to contribute towards long term private costs for you. For example, it might contribute to 'increased illness, to lost days of work' and ultimately to 'premature death'. Such meals are associated with higher incidence of diabetes, high blood pressure and heart disease. The most obvious sign that the long term private cost is greater than £4.99 will be if you suffer from obesity.

(ii) The externalities of the meal are the costs others have to pay because you have consumed the meal. It could be that as a result you have to receive health care which more healthy taxpayers have to pay on your behalf. It could be your work colleagues have to cover for you whilst you are away ill. Your family and friends will also suffer from having to look after you when you are ill.

(b) A shadow price is a price put on an item which is an estimate of its full social cost. Economists believe that putting a monetary price on something helps to arrive at effective decision making. In the case of obesity, if the monetary cost of obesity were low, then it would not be a major problem. However, if it is high, then it is an issue which society should address. One key cost of obesity is early death. Economists are interested in trying to put a price on early death. What value should be put on a reduced average life expectancy of, say, five years for individuals who are obese? This price then needs to be fed into any calculation about the cost of overeating and poor diets. For example, what is the social cost of a fast food meal? If it is much more than the menu price, this would suggest that the government should intervene, for example by internalising the externality and placing a much higher tax on it.

Question 3

(a) Benefits differ across time because a rate of return needs to be taken into consideration. In this case, one way to take future costs into account is to project costs forward. The rail link will cost £200 million today if it is to last 50 years, but only £100 million if it lasts 25 years. So, if it were built for just 25 years, £100 million could be saved on the cost today. We can then project that figure forward and calculate how much it would be worth if it were invested at 10 per cent per annum. At 10 per cent, it would be worth £1 083 million (£100 million x 1.125). The cost in twenty five years of then repairing the link is £900 million. So the cost of repair in 25 years' time is less than the value of £100 million saved by not building it for 50 years initially if the saving had been invested at 10 per cent per annum. Hence, it is cheaper to build it for 25 years and repair the rail link than build it for 50 years.

A second way of arriving at the same answer is to project the figures backwards. The £900 million it will cost to repair the link in 25 years is worth only £83 million today (£900 ÷ 1.125). Hence, it would be cheaper to build the rail link to last 25 years and then repair it (total cost £100 million plus £83 million) than build it for 50 years (total cost £200 million).

These calculations ignore any other costs incurred in the rebuilding of the rail link such as delays to passengers at the time.

(b) If we project forward, the £100 million saved by building the link for only 25 years would be worth £339 million (£100 million x 1.0525) in 25 years' time if the rate of interest were 5 per cent. This is much less than the £900 million it will cost to repair the link for the second 25 years of use. Hence, it will be cheaper to build it for 50 years rather than 25 years with a repair for the second 25 years.

A second way of arriving at the same answer is to project the figures backwards. The £900 million it will cost to repair the link in 25 years is worth £265 million today (£900 ÷ 1.0525). Hence, the present cost of building the rail link which only lasts 25 years and then rebuilding it is £365 million (£100 million plus £265 million). This exceeds the £200 million cost of building it today to last for 50 years. Hence, at this rate of discount, it would be cheaper to build it for 50 years.

Data question

1. Social costs are the costs to society of an economic activity. It is equal to the costs incurred by the producer, the private costs, plus external costs (negative externalities), which are costs not paid for by the producer. For example, those using Heathrow Airport have to pay for the cost of running the facility. This includes the wages of staff, the cost of buildings and runways and the land itself. These are therefore private costs. However, the owners of Heathrow Airport do not pay local residents for the noise pollution the airport creates. Noise pollution therefore is a negative externality.

Social benefits are the benefits to society of an economic activity. It is equal to private benefits plus external benefits (or positive externalities). The private benefits of Heathrow Airport are the benefits which accrue to those who pay to use the services of the airport. So passengers who buy airline tickets to fly from Heathrow receive private benefits. No positive externalities are identified in the data. However, these could include the benefits of beautiful architecture of the new Terminal 5 building to visitors to the airport who are not flying.

2. (a) In a cost-benefit analysis of extending Heathrow airport, the analysis would include both private costs and benefits as well as positive and negative externalities. Examples of private costs would include the cost of buying extra land, constructing new buildings and the extra operation costs of an expanded Heathrow airport. Examples of private benefits would include the revenues generated from airport fees, representing the value that passengers place on using the airport. External costs would include noise pollution to local residents. Positive externalities might include a shadow price put on faster journey times or a more reliable service for passengers.

(b) Wider damage to the environment might not be included as monetary values in the cost-benefit analysis. For example, damage to local wild life or destruction of plant species on land used to build the new runway might not be included. It could be very difficult to place a monetary value on air pollution, especially if there is not consensus about what levels of extra air pollution will occur.

3. If the cost-benefit analysis shows that the proposed extension has a positive net present value, it means that the measured social benefits over time are greater than the measured social costs. Benefits and costs will include both private benefits and costs and externalities which have been given a monetary value. Benefits in the future will have been discounted back to their present value using a rate of interest or discount.

However, not all costs and benefits will be included in this because some costs and benefits are not quantifiable. For example, the data mentions the problem of climate change. It is unlikely that the impact of climate change will have been included in this cost-benefit analysis because its impact is as yet uncertain and difficult to quantify. Local residents may suffer increased road traffic congestion as a result of the extension to Heathrow which may not be included as a cost in the analysis.

Without knowing the exact nature of the costs and benefits not given a monetary value in the cost-benefit analysis, it is difficult to say whether the scheme should go ahead. However, Greenpeace would almost certainly argue that the environmental damage caused by the extension would create costs which would far outweigh any positive net present value. The business community would probably argue that the unmeasured costs and benefits are small and likely to be less than the positive present value. Hence, they would argue the scheme should go ahead. Without more information, it is difficult to know which side is correct in its thinking.

60 The demand for labour

Question 1

(a) Real capital per employee has increased in all industries between 1978 and 2006. However, it has increased in some industries more than in others. For instance, in mining, quarrying, electricity, gas and water, the increase was 463 per cent, whilst in construction it was only 64 per cent. In contrast, the increase in real gross capital per employee was 88 per cent in in transport and communication, 152 per cent in finance and business services, 127 per cent in manufacturing, and 147 per cent in distribution, hotels, and restaurants.
(b) Economic theory suggests that a rise in the real cost of labour compared to capital would lead to more capital intensive production. For instance, if the cost of capital remains constant, but wages go up 83 per cent, there will be an incentive for firms to install machinery to do the job of some of the workers. This indeed is what is suggested in Table 1in the student's book. The amount of capital used per employee has increased in every industry.

Question 2

(a) (b) Table 1

per week

Number of revenue product	Total physical product (units)	Total revenue workers £	Marginal product £
1	10	100	100
2	24	240	140
3	36	360	120
4	44	440	80
5	50	500	60
6	53	530	30

(c) The firm will employ up to the point where the weekly wage per worker (the marginal cost of labour) equals the marginal revenue product of the last worker employed. For instance, if the weekly wage were £60, then the firm would employ the first worker because her MRP is greater than £60. The same is true of the second, third and fourth workers. The MRP of the fifth worker is £60. The firm will therefore neither gain nor lose by employing that worker. Hence, the profit maximising level of employment is either 4 or 5 workers. The answers to this question are therefore:
(i) 4 or 5 workers;
(ii) 5 or 6 workers;
(iii) 2 or 3 workers;
(iv) 3 workers.

Question 3

(a) Table 2

Number of workers employed	Number of units produced and sold per week	£ Price per unit	Total revenue product	Marginal revenue product
1	10	15	150	150
2	24	14	336	186
3	36	12	432	96
4	44	11	484	52
5	50	10	500	16
6	53	9	477	-23

(b) The firm will employ workers so long as their marginal revenue product exceeds or is equal to their wage. Hence:
(i) 4 workers;
(ii) 4 workers;
(iii) 3 workers;
(iv) 3 workers;
(v) 2 workers;
(vi) 2 workers.

Question 4

(a) The elasticity of demand for labour on a North Sea oil rig is likely to be relatively low. Oil production in the North Sea is already very capital intensive. The proportion of labour cost to capital cost is therefore low. Hence rises in wage costs will not have as much of an impact on total cost as in more labour intensive industries. It is also difficult to substitute capital for labour in the North Sea. Due to the dangers involved, what can be automated and mechanised has, on the whole, already been done. The tasks performed by workers are those that are difficult or impossible to automate. Again, difficulty in substituting capital for labour tends to lower the elasticity of demand for labour.

Data question

1. (a) Marginal revenue product is the value of the physical addition to output of an extra unit of a variable factor of production. It is equal to the physical product of labour times

Figure 1

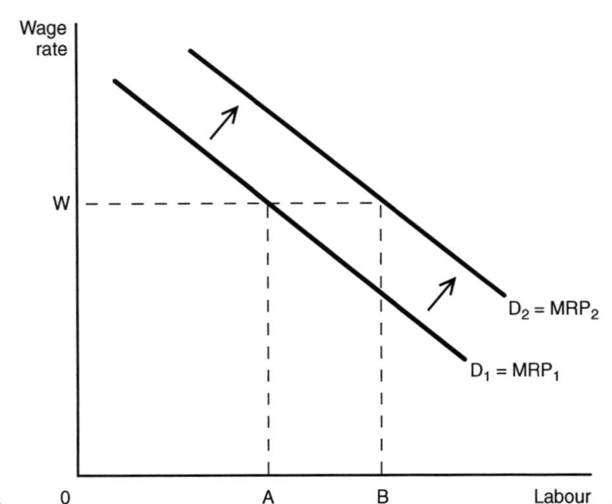

the price of what a worker can produce. In 2005, the demand for accountants rose because governments introduced new reporting and regulatory requirements on businesses. Firms needed more accountants to deal with the volume of work this created. The data describes this work as 'lucrative' for the big accounting firms. They were almost certainly able to push up the price of jobs given the tight market for accountants. Higher prices for jobs meant that the marginal revenue product of labour increased.

(b) The demand curve for accountants will have shifted to the right, showing an increase in demand for accountants. In Figure 1, at a wage rate of OW, accountancy firms demanded AB more accountants.

2. There is a number of determinants of elasticity of demand for labour. One is the availability of substitutes. For legal reasons, firms have to use qualified accountants to audit their accounts. They also need accountants to draw up accounts. Some work can be automated. However, certainly in the short run, there are no really good substitutes for accountants. Hence this would suggest that the demand for accounts is price inelastic.

A second factor is the elasticity of demand for the product. Again, for legal reasons, companies have to use outside firms of accountants to audit their books. The product is this external audit. The elasticity of demand for the product is therefore very low because the work has to be done for the company to continue in business. With a low elasticity of demand for audits, the elasticity of demand for accountants is likely to be low.

A third factor affecting elasticity of demand for labour is the proportion of labour cost to total cost. The wages of accountants form the single largest cost for accountancy firms. Accountancy is a highly labour intensive service. this would suggest that the elasticity of demand for accountants should be relatively high rather than low.

Overall, it is likely, therefore, taking these three factors into consideration that the demand for accountants is less elastic rather than more elastic.

61 The supply of labour

Question 1

(a) The data give little support to the idea that the supply curve for labour is backward sloping. For both females and males, the supply of labour was greater in 2007 at the end of the period than in 1992 at the start of the period.

However, the proportion of economically active males aged 50-64 did decline between 1992 and 1995 despite rising wages. It could be argued that this showed that men were substituting leisure, in this case probably early retirement, for work because of better pay. However, the fall in the activity rate probably had more to do with high levels of unemployment which discouraged males from seeking work than with high wages.

Question 2

(a) Workers in general were found by Professor Brown to be unaffected by changes in taxes. He found 'no evidence that tax cuts encourage people in unemployment either to work harder or to work longer.' However, workers on average earnings, if anything, worked less when given tax cuts according to the report.

This can be explained using the concepts of income and substitution effects. When a worker receives a tax cut, the cost of leisure time rises because workers can now buy more goods and services if they work. Therefore, they will tend to work longer hours, in the same way that if bread falls in price, more bread will be bought. However, work is arguably an inferior good. The higher the income of workers, the fewer hours they wish to work. Hence, cutting income tax will have the opposite effect to the substitution effect. The income effect will be negative.

Figure 1

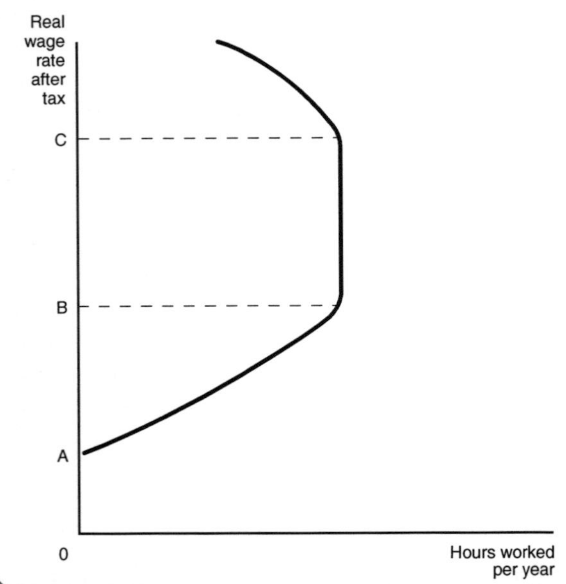

For a male on average earnings, the data state that the negative income effect of a tax cut will be slightly more important than the positive substitution effect. Hence male workers on average earnings will, if anything, slightly reduce their hours of work in response.

This can be shown in Figure 1. The supply curve of labour is at first upward sloping, then vertical and finally backward bending. The real wage rate on the vertical axis is assumed to be the real wage rate after tax has been deducted. The government commission found that in general, workers were on the vertical part of the supply curve between wage rate B and C i.e. a rise in real wage rates after tax caused by a tax cut had no effect on the number of hours worked. However, breaking the labour force down, male workers on average wages were on the backward bending part of the supply curve above the point C i.e. a cut in tax which raised real wage rates led to a slight fall in the number of hours worked.

(b) In contrast, for female part time workers, the positive substitution effect is greater than the negative income effect. Therefore a cut in income tax will lead them to work more hours. In Figure 1, female workers, particularly part time female workers, were between the wage rate A and B on the upward sloping part of the supply curve.

Question 3

(a) The marginal cost of labour is derived from the following figures.

Table 2

£ per week

Number of workers employed	Wages per worker	Total wages	Marginal cost per worker
			200
100	200	20 000	
			240
200	220	44 000	
			280
300	240	72 000	
			320
400	260	104 000	

Figure 2

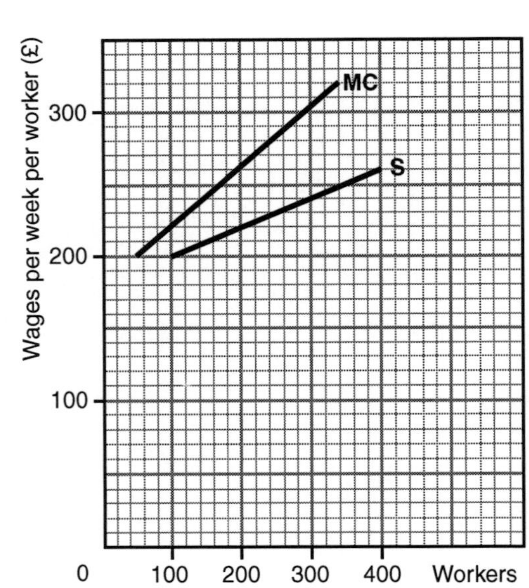

(b) The supply curve and the marginal cost curve would both be horizontal at a wage rate of £200 per week.

Question 4

(a) Most adults in the population could successfully become shelf stackers or checkout assistants. However, only a minority have the ability or training to become managers of supermarkets. In the 50+ age group few would want, even if offered, to undergo training to become a manager. However, many, particularly those who have taken early retirement, would be prepared to work part time in demanding jobs in supermarkets. Hence supermarkets are likely to offer a lower percentage increase in wages for shelf stackers, etc. if they wish to increase employment of these workers than if they wanted more managers (i.e. the elasticity of supply of shelf stackers in the 50+ age bracket is higher than that for managers).
(b) A recession leads to higher unemployment in the economy. As a result, the number of people applying for a job, all other things being equal, is likely to increase. Some firms chose to reduce pay rates in the recession and yet still found that they had more applicants than before the recession started. This is an indication that the elasticity of supply has increased.

Question 5

(a) The data show that, as the real average earnings of women have risen, from £174 in 1971 to £429 in 2007, so the supply of women in the UK employment market has increased from 9.0 million to 13.4 million. This would support the theory that the supply curve for labour in an economy is upward sloping, with more workers offering themselves for employment as the wage rate increases.
(b) Many would argue that the increase in real earnings of women is only one factor which explains the increased participation of women in the labour force in recent years. Another factor is the fall in the real price of labour saving devices. Seventy years ago, the cost of a washing machine or hoover, for instance, was so high that it was out of the reach of ordinary workers. Women traditionally had to stay at home to perform household tasks in a highly labour intensive way. Today, the washing machine, the dishwasher, the microwave oven and ready prepared meals have transformed the lives of women because these innovations have enabled them to reduce significantly the time taken to maintain a household.

Social attitudes too have changed. It is likely that women today, unless looking after children, should work. Few might argue that a woman should drop her career if she has children so long as there is suitable provision to have them looked after. Whether or not it can be argued that social attitudes have changed simply because the rewards to women working have increased so substantially is a debatable point.

Data question

1. Ethnic minority workers have distinct labour force characteristics when compared with white workers. For instance, Figure 15 in the student's book shows that unemployment for all groups of ethnic workers is higher both for males and females than for white workers. In 2004, the unemployment rate for white males averaged just under 5 per cent. For Bangladeshi males it was nearly three times that level at 13 per cent.

Figure 16 in the student's book shows that white workers in 2001-2004 earned more per week than all other minority ethnic groups apart from Indians and Chinese. It also shows that the position of white female workers is less favourable compared to females from ethnic minority groups than males. White females workers earn less on average per hour than Chinese, Indian, Black mixed, Black Caribbean and Pakistani females workers.

Figure 17 in the student's book shows that white male British workers were most likely to be in full time employment. For females, white British workers were second most likely to be in full time employment, behind Black Caribbean female women. However, both male and females British workers were most likely to be in work, whether full-time or part-time.

Figure 19 in the student's book shows that white workers are not necessarily more likely than those from ethnic minority groups to hold positions of managers, senior officials and professionals. Chinese and Indian males are most likely as a proportion of their ethnic group to hold these types of position. Black Caribbean and Black African men are least likely to hold them. The situation is similar for women, although the differences between ethnic groups are less marked.

Figure 20 in the student's book shows that in 2003, white workers, whether male or female, did not have better qualifications than workers from minority ethnic groups. Some ethnic groups had better qualified workers than white workers. Chinese workers were particularly well qualified.

Table 8 in the student's book shows that white workers had higher employment rates than any other minority ethnic group across all age ranges. The minority ethnic group which most approached white workers was Indian workers.

2. (a) Table 8 in the student's book shows that employment rates for workers from ethnic minority groups can be significantly lower than for white workers. However, total supply must also include workers who offer themselves for work but who fail to get a job. If the unemployment rates shown in Figure 15 are included, then the difference in supply between ethnic groups is much reduced. Even so, workers from many minority ethnic groups have lower labour force participation rates than whites, as shown in Figure 17. One reason for this might be that they are discouraged from even seeking work because of high levels of unemployment among workers from their ethnic group. Pakistani women in 2002-2005, for example, had an unemployment rate of 19 per cent. This must have discouraged other Pakistani women from even thinking about getting a job.
(b) One reason why workers from ethnic minorities are less likely to be in employment than white workers is discrimination. Figure 18 in the student's book shows that 22 per cent of the population did not think it wrong to discriminate against Black/Asian workers whilst another 25 per cent thought that it was 'usually wrong' and therefore sometimes right. another reason might be wage rates. Figure 16 in the student's book shows that some minority ethnic groups tend to earn lower pay than whites. This may be a disincentive for them to take on a job rather than receive benefits for being unemployed.

3. There is a wide range of measures which could be adopted to help improve the position of workers from ethnic minorities in the labour force.

One major area for improvement lies in the field of education and training. As has already been discussed, ethnic groups differ widely in this area. Any programmes therefore need to be targeted towards those ethnic groups which seem to be most disadvantaged. Pakistanis and Bangladeshis, for instance, seem to be particularly disadvantaged in both qualifications and training received. Raising levels of human capital amongst selected ethnic minority groups will then help them gain better jobs and make their equality of opportunity comparable to that of white workers.

Workers from ethnic minorities also need to be given greater access to the labour market. Discrimination is one factor which hinders their progress. Continued efforts through the use of the legal system and through education of employers will help to continue to reduce discrimination. It could also be argued that there should be positive discrimination in favour of workers from ethnic minority groups. For instance, employers could be forced to impose quotas on employment of staff. However, compliance is a major problem with any form of quota unless there are fierce penalties built into the system. It can also demotivate white staff who in turn feel discriminated against.

The greater acceptance of female workers in general in the workforce will help attract more female workers from ethnic minorities to participate in the labour force. Greater accessibility of child care facilities will be another important factor in attracting female workers from ethnic minorities into work.

62 Wage determination

Question 1

(a) (b)

Figure 1

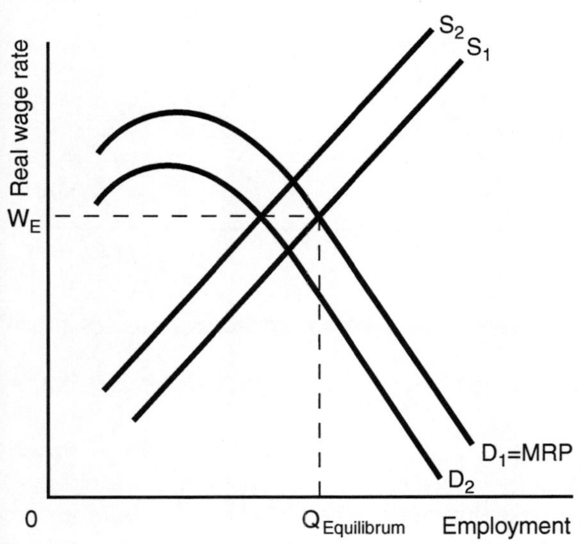

(c) (i) a shift to the left in the demand curve from D_1 to D_2; **(ii)** a shift to the left in the supply curve from S_1 to S_2; **(iii)** a shift to the left in the demand curve from D_1 to D_2; **(iv)** a shift to the left in the demand curve from D_1 to D_2; **(v)** a shift to the left in the supply curve from S_1 to S_2 and a shift to the left in the demand curve from D_1 to D_2.

Question 2

(a) In an increasingly globalised economy, the labour markets of different countries are increasingly having an impact on each other. Just as in the UK, the labour market in the South East of London is affected by what happens in the labour market in London, so what is happening in the labour market in China is increasingly affecting what is happening in the labour market in the UK or the USA. The USA is losing low skill and unskilled jobs to China mainly in the manufacturing sector. That means that there is less demand for these types of workers in the USA. Less demand but the same amount of supply results in falling real wages in industries such as the hospitality industry in which Miguel works. In contrast, in China real wages are likely to rise over time. As more jobs are created in China, the demand for Chinese workers rises. Higher demand means a higher equilibrium wage.

This can be shown in Figure 2. In the US labour market, lower demand for unskilled workers is shifting their demand curve back to the left, resulting in a fall in the equilibrium wage rate from OA to OB. In the Chinese market, an increase in demand for unskilled labour is pushing their demand curve to the right. This raises the Chinese equilibrium wage from OE to OF. Eventually, if the world economy creates a perfect labour market, the equilibrium wage rate in the USA will equal that in China.

Question 3

(a) The earnings of a worker in a market are determined by the forces of demand and supply. On the demand side, the four workers are likely to have different marginal revenue products. Mike Sellers, the 19 year old sales assistant, for instance, is likely to have a far lower MRP than, say, Addo Tower, the 49 year old finance director. Partly this is because of age. Mike Sellers will have far less experience than Addo Tower. Mike Sellers is also likely to be less productive than Petra Ellis, the 29 year old personnel assistant. She is likely to be able to perform a much wider range of tasks than Mike Sellers.

On the supply side, Addo Tower and Geena Miles are likely to be far more qualified, and therefore in shorter supply, than the other two workers. Mike Sellers lives in West Wales, an area of relatively high unemployment, and this factor has almost certainly helped depress his wages. Addo Tower's wages in contrast are likely to have been boosted because he lives in London a relatively low unemployment and high earning area of the country.

Figure 2

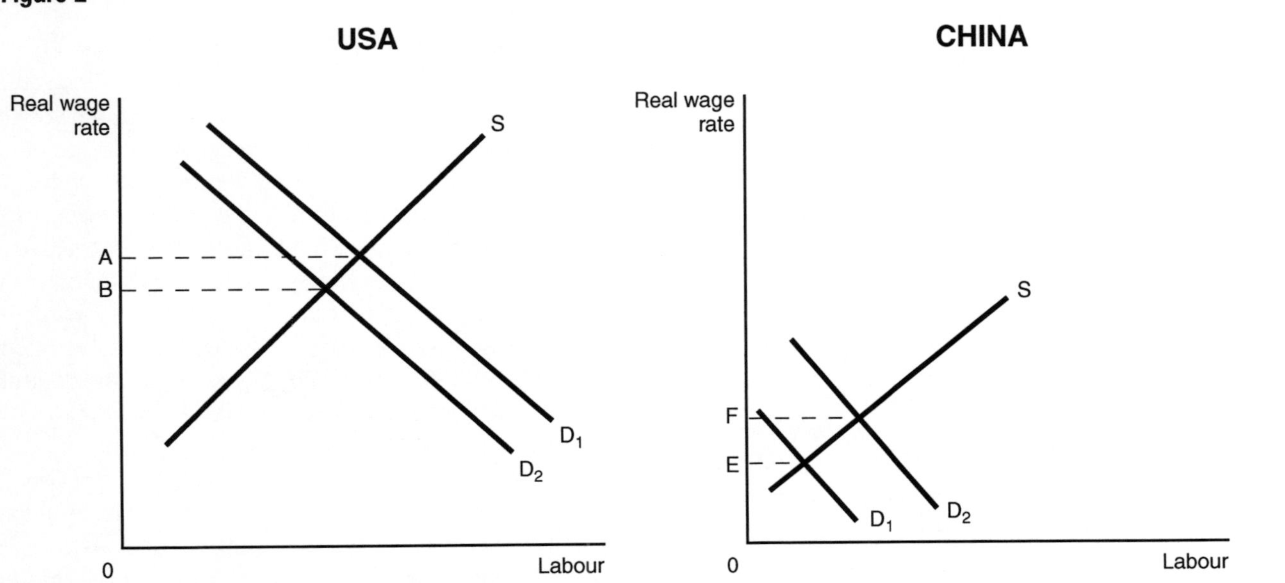

Question 4

(a) The marginal revenue curve is plotted from the following data.

Table 1

Number of workers employed	Total revenue product (£ per month)	Marginal revenue product (£ per month)
		700
1	700	
		600
2	1 300	
		500
3	1 800	
		400
4	2 200	

(b) (i) 1 worker; **(ii)** 3 workers; **(iii)** 3 workers; **(iv)** 0 workers; **(v)** 2 workers.

Figure 3

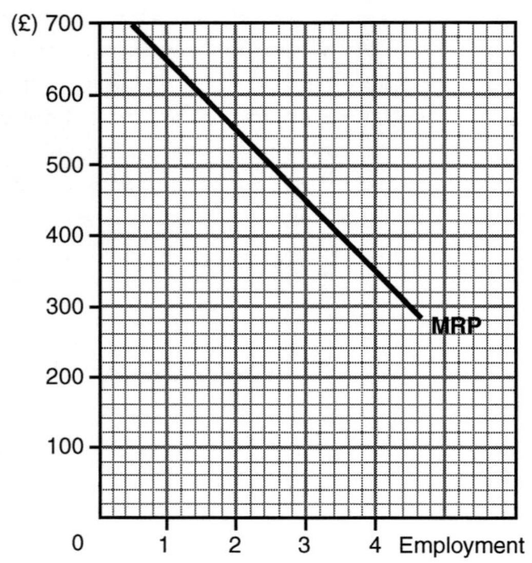

Question 5

(a) See Figure 4.
(b) In the labour market for teachers, it can be argued that the teacher unions are so weak that effectively a monopsony employer faces a competitive supply of teachers. In Figure 4, the equilibrium wage would therefore be OE and employment would be OA.

If individual bargaining were to take place, employers would attempt to pay individual teachers the minimum needed to retain them in the job. This minimum is shown by the supply curve of labour. So some teachers would be employed for very little. The OAth worker would have to be paid OE in Figure 4. If employment were OB, marginal teachers would have to be paid OF. The marginal cost of employing extra labour would not be shown by the MC curve but by the supply curve line. This is because employing an extra teacher at a higher rate of pay does not mean that existing teachers have to be paid any more under individual bargaining. The total cost of employing OB workers is therefore the triangle OHB, the sum of the minimum amounts that teachers are prepared to work for.

Under national wage bargaining, the total wage bill would be OEJA. Under individual bargaining, OA workers could be employed for just the triangle OJA. If employment were to remain the same, the government could save money. However, what if the government chose instead to use the savings per teacher on employing AB more teachers? So long as the AJHB, the extra cost of employing OB teachers rather than OA teachers, was equal to or less than OEJ, the savings on changing to individual bargaining, the government would not have to spend more money employing more teachers and might indeed be able to save money.

Figure 4

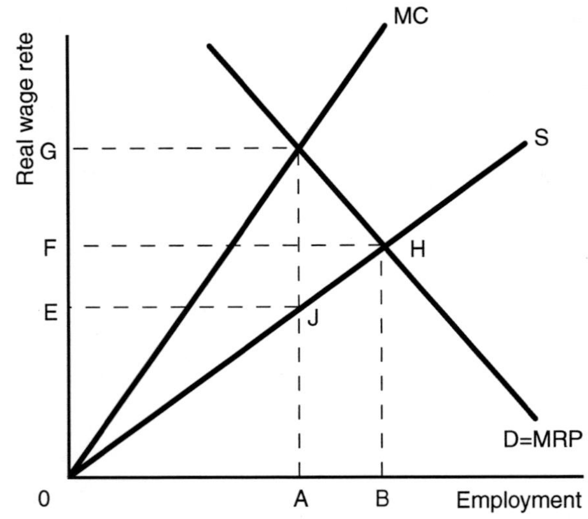

Data question

1. Wages differ between regions. In April 2007, male workers in London and the South East of England were paid the highest average wages whilst Wales, the North East and Northern Ireland had the lowest average wages. These regional differences are broadly the same both for male and female workers.

Unemployment rates are highest in the West Midlands and the North East. They are lowest in the South West and the South East.

2. A number of factors may account for why there are differences in average earnings between regions. One is the marginal revenue product of labour in a region. The workforce in the South East has above average human capital per worker. Table 6 in the student's book gives one indication of this. It shows that, apart from Scotland and Northern Ireland, the South East produced more highly qualified 16-19 year olds than other regions. With above average human capital per worker, the region can expect its workers to be paid more highly because they are more productive. This is illustrated in Figure 10 in the student's book where London, the South East and the South West all have above UK average levels of productivity (output per hour worked).

A supply side factor is the difference in the cost of living between regions. Housing costs are higher in the South East than in the other regions of the UK as can be seen in Figure 9 in the student's book Workers are therefore only prepared to supply themselves for higher wages.

Another factor influencing wage rates is levels of unemployment in a region. The higher the level of unemployment, the greater will be the number of applicants for any job, all other things being equal. With greater supply of workers, employers will be able to pay lower wages than in areas of low unemployment. Hence, the areas of the country which have had low unemployment in recent decades, such as the South East, have the highest average wages, whilst high unemployment regions like Northern Ireland and the North East have the lowest average wages.

3. One way of reducing the earnings gap is to make the balance of demand for and supply of workers more equal between regions. On the demand side, the government needs to encourage job creation in areas of high unemployment. It also does this through its regional policy, giving grants, for instance, to key firms which move into a region or expand their plant. The government also receives EU monies for regional regeneration. However, the persistence of the gap between the regions suggests that more could be done. Giving more regional aid, for instance, might increase the rate of new job creation in depressed areas.

On the supply side, the government could encourage workers to move from high unemployment areas to low unemployment areas. As Table 5 in the student's book shows, this is happening to some extent anyway. The South East and the South West, with relatively low unemployment rates, have seen an influx of people since the 1980s whilst high unemployment areas such as the North West have seen net emigration. Encouraging migration between regions poses problems, however, for government. Faster growing regions such as the South East already feel that their population is too large for the land area available. They don't want to have to build new houses or accept more cars on their roads. Poorer regions, on the other hand, complain that it is the most educated and entrepreneurial of their workers who leave to seek work in richer regions. It then becomes even more difficult to attract new firms to set up in their regions, or get workers to set up their own firms. Depopulation leads also to a waste of scarce resources. In some parts of the UK, houses are being pulled down because landlords cannot find tenants for them. Schools are not full. The road network has considerable spare capacity. Whole communities can go into a spiral of decline as young people leave and are not replaced. So encouraging migration between regions has many disadvantages.

The earnings gap between regions is not just caused by imbalances between the total demand for and supply of labour. It also occurs because workers in different regions have different levels of human capital. Workers in the South East, for instance, on average are more educated and trained to a higher level than workers in the North East. Equalising levels of human capital between regions is therefore very important to equalise average earnings. The government could increase levels of spending on education and training, focussing the increases on areas of low income. This is a long term solution. There may be little effect for 10-20 years. However, without a better educated workforce, employers will not be prepared to pay higher wages compared to the current average.

Equalising the cost of living between regions would also help equalise wages. One key difference between regions is the cost of housing. The government could substantially reduce house prices in the South East if it relaxed planning controls on the building of new houses. This would be fiercely resisted by existing home owners and residents who would not want to see the prices of their houses fall or see further development near where they live. Environmental groups too would object, claiming that the South East was being overdeveloped. Governments have therefore tended not to alienate voters by authorising large housing schemes in the South East.

63 Trade unions

Question 1

(a) Economic theory suggests that in a competitive labour market, trade unions will raise wages but lead to lower unemployment. In Figure 1, the equilibrium wage rate without unions is OA. However, with unions, it is raised to OB because it negotiates higher wages with employers. However, at a wage rate of OB, the supply of labour increases from OF to OG whilst the demand for labour from employers falls from OF to OE. The result is a fall in employment from OF to OE, and EG unemployment is created. So Wal-Mart might be correct in saying that its anti-unionisation policy creates jobs compared to supermarket chains which allow trade unions to represent their workers.
(b) Wal-Mart's rivals are likely to be at a competitive advantage by employing unionised labour. If trade unions lead to higher wages in those firms, they will have higher costs. This means that this will either have to charge higher prices compared to Wal-Mart or earn lower profits which can affect long term investment in the business. One of the keys to success of Wal-Mart has been its very low prices which other competitors have found difficult to match.

Figure 1

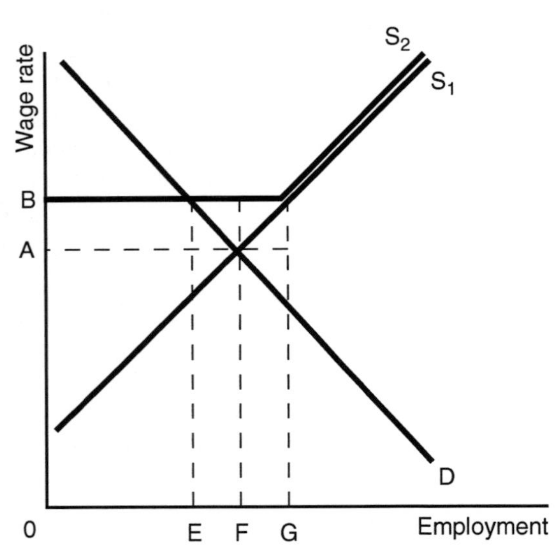

Question 2

(a) (i) 5 workers - the firm would employ workers up to the point where the marginal cost of employing an extra worker equalled the marginal revenue product of labour.
(ii) £7.
(b) 6 workers - again where MC=MRP.
(c) In an industry where many employers face monopoly trade unions, neo-classical theory suggests that trade unions will increase wages in the industry but at the expense of employment. However, if a trade union faces a monopsonist buyer of labour, the trade union may increase employment in the firm from what it would otherwise have been.

The data in Table 1 in the student's book help us understand why this is the case. In a non-unionised firm, the marginal cost of employing extra workers increases as shown in Table 74.1 in the question. For instance, the marginal cost of employing the fifth worker is £10 but of employing the sixth worker is £12. Compare this with a situation where the firm is unionised. The trade union will negotiate a minimum wage for its members, although the firm is free to pay above this rate if it so wishes. In Table 1, the firm can hire up to 6 workers at this minimum wage rate of £8. The minimum wage rate then becomes the marginal cost of employing an extra worker over the range 1 to 6 workers. In Table 1, the marginal cost for a firm of hiring 5 or 6 unionised workers is actually below the marginal cost of hiring 5 or 6 workers if there is no trade union. Hence, employment can be higher in a unionised firm than in a non-unionised firm if that firm is a monopsonist.

Question 3

(a) Most nurses work for one employer, the National Health Service. The government, through NHS Trusts, is therefore essentially a monopsonist, a single buyer of labour. Equally, most nurses belong to one of a small number of trade unions which act as monopoly suppliers of labour to the industry. In theory, nursing trade unions should be powerful negotiating bodies, able to take on the monopsonist they face. In practice, nurses have tended to refuse to take strike action because this would damage the interests of their patients. This has weakened their industrial power.

In the short term, the supply of nurses is relatively inelastic. Small changes in demand can therefore have a considerable impact on the bargaining power of nurses.

The hairdressing industry is fiercely competitive, with large numbers of small firms attempting to survive in the market place. Because there are so many firms and the product they sell is relatively homogeneous, hairdressers tend to be price takers, facing a very elastic demand curve. The more elastic the demand curve for the product, the more elastic is the demand for labour in that industry. Hence trade unions have little opportunity to increase wage rates in individual firms. If they had success in pushing wages up by, say, 10 or 20 percent in one firm, that firm would find it very difficult to pass on the increase to customers in the form of higher prices. Given that hairdressing firms on the whole do not earn abnormal profits because the industry is so competitive, a rise in wages in one firm could well force it out of business.

Another important factor in the hairdressing industry is that there are relatively few employees in each firm and trade unions find it much more difficult to recruit and organise labour in industries where workers are relatively dispersed. Moreover, many employees are relatively young and therefore are likely to be less militant than older workers.

Question 4

(a) Employers are likely to gain from increased productive efficiency. The train unions in both cases are offering training packages for workers which is likely to make them more productive. Unionisation could also lower costs for employers if it becomes cheaper to deal with labour issues such as consultation with the workforce or recruitment of staff.

Data question

1. Trade unions exist to protect the interests of their members. One key role for a trade union is to negotiate on

Figure 2

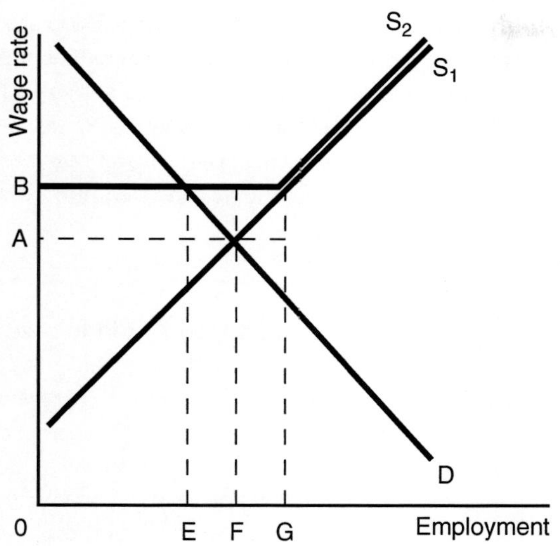

behalf of its members with management - collective bargaining. For instance, it might negotiate over pay or over working conditions as in the construction industry or the printing industry described in the data. Trade unions might have to defend their members' pension rights as happened with the Public and Commercial Services Union. Trade unions also act as pressure groups attempting to change government and management policy in their favour.

2. Economic theory would suggest that trade unions push up the wages of their members but employment falls as a consequence. In Figure 2, trade unions entering a competitive labour market succeed in changing the supply curve from S_1 to S_2. OB represents the minimum wage that trade unions allow their members to work for. Without unions, wage rates were OA and OF workers were employed. After the entry of trade unions, wages are now OB and AB represents the size of the union mark-up. Employment falls to OE and hence EF jobs are lost. Unemployment rises more by EG because FG workers now want to work in the industry attracted by the higher wage of OB.

The report quoted in the data from the Centre of Economic Performance suggests that the size of the union mark-up, shown in Figure 9 in the student's book, was 14 per cent in 1993 for all workers but this had fallen to 6 per cent by 2000. The Report also estimates that females, part-time and manual workers benefit particularly from being members of trade unions. 'The pay differential between women and men, black and white workers' has narrowed.

Economic theory suggests that trade unions create unemployment because higher wages reduces the demand for labour. Trade unions would argue that the negative effect on employment of modern unionism is likely to be small and might even be positive. This is because trade unions are key to helping employers negotiate improvements in working practices with the workers they represent. By operating in partnership with management, trade unions can help bring about lower costs and thus greater productive efficiency by persuading workers to be more flexible. In return, workers expect employers to share some of the productivity gains made through higher wages. Making firms more competitive creates jobs rather than reduces them.

Trade unions would also argue that partnership helps reduce the risk of strike action and the costs that are associated with it. Negotiation and partnership lead to a committed workforce where strike action is unlikely. This will have positive effects on employment as firms become more competitive.

3. Critics of trade unions argue that they impair economic efficiency. By pushing up wages, they increase costs to firms and make them less competitive. Employment is lower than it would otherwise have been and there is allocative inefficiency in the labour market because price no longer equals marginal cost. Free market economists would therefore advocate further restrictions on the activities of trade unions. For instance, it could be made illegal for them to support strike action on behalf of their members.

However, it could be argued that trade unions have an important role to play in a modern industrialised economy. By representing the interests of workers, they prevent workers being exploited by employers, particularly in markets where employers are monopsonists. In such markets, employment and wages are lower than they would otherwise be in a free market. Trade unions, by pushing up wages, help remove market failure rather than increasing it. Trade unions also help improve efficiency by making it less likely that workers will strike. They are an important way in which management ensures that workers are motivated and do not feel aggrieved by their actions.

64 Labour market failure

Question 1

(a) Three barriers to mobility are mentioned. One was the position of working spouses. Not only can a geographic move by one partner lead to the loss of the job and therefore earnings of the other partner, but it can also lead to a long term disruption in that partner's career. The result could be that the two partners taken together suffer financially in the long term from the geographic move of one of the partners.

A second barrier is family. Parents are anxious to ensure continuity of education for their children which moving would disrupt, whilst some have strong family roots in a local area which they are reluctant to break.

A third barrier is the workings of the house market. In the first half of the 1990s, with a slump in property prices, it became very difficult to sell houses. Workers were very reluctant to move without having some chance of selling their existing houses.

(b) In a perfect market, factors of production are free to move to earn their highest reward. For instance, if the marginal revenue product of a worker in one occupation were £60 000 and in another only £40 000, then firms in the former industry would be able to offer a high enough salary to persuade the worker to work in the occupation where society values the worker most highly. If there are barriers to mobility, then the market will function imperfectly. In this example, all other things being equal, there would be inefficiency if the employee worked in the £40 000 occupation because his or her productivity would not be maximised. Another inefficiency arises from unemployment. It could be that firms in one region need workers but can't find them whilst in another region there is considerable unemployment of that type of worker. The economy as a whole could produce more if barriers to mobility were removed such that either workers could move to where there are jobs or firms could move to where there are unemployed workers.

Question 2

(a) The theory of segmented labour markets suggests that labour markets are not homogeneous. In a dual labour market, workers in the formal sector have permanent full time jobs. They have careers, receive training and are valued by their employers because they are likely to remain with the employer for some time. In the informal sector, workers are typically part time or on short term contracts. They are not seen as having a clear career and are not worth training from an employer's point of view because they are unlikely to fill positions of responsibility or remain with the firm for long.

Wages in the formal sector of the economy are likely to be higher on average than in the informal sector. Firms are prepared to pay more for permanent full time workers than temporary or part time staff. What's more, in a period of rising unemployment, firms will tend to shed their informal sector workers first. They will also seek to secure maximum cost economies by cutting or not increasing wages of informal sector workers. However, they will be reluctant to lose their permanent formal sector workers and will be more likely to increase real wages.

The data would tend to confirm this. In the four industries in the data with above average proportions of full time workers, wage increases between 1990 and 1993 were above the national average. In the four industries with above average proportions of part-time and casual workers, wage increases over the same period were below the national average. In the case of distribution and repairs, average wage increases were below the rate of inflation, i.e. real wages fell over the three year period which saw a nearly doubling in unemployment.

Question 3

(a) The 48 hour working directive is likely to add to costs for employers where working more than 48 hour weeks is a relatively common feature. For example, for NC Engineering, workers installing and servicing machine tools can sometimes work more than 48 hours a week because of travelling. For farmers, at the height of the harvesting season, some of their labourers work more than 48 hours. To get round the directive, such employers will have to hire more workers or cut back on production, both of which could lead to higher average costs for employers. In Figure 1, the supply curve of labour shifts to the left in a labour market where working more than 48 hours is relatively common. This is because those workers who used to supply more than 48 hours per worker can no longer do so. As a result, the equilibrium wage rate will rise from OA to OB and there will be a fall in quantity demanded from OE to OF.

Figure 1

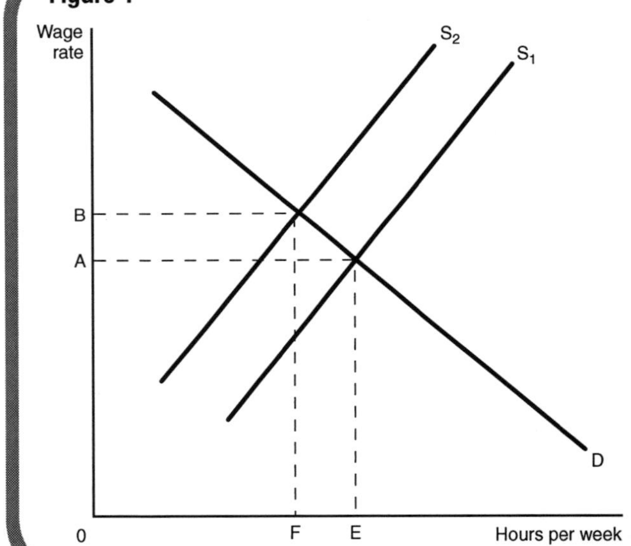

Data question

1. Employment rates in labour markets in the 'Rhineland model' and the 'Mediterranean model' are relatively low because levels of employment protection are relatively high. In Figure 10 in the student's book, all the countries in these two models have an OECD measure of strictness of employment protection legislation at or above 1.5. If employers find it difficult to make workers redundant or close down plants, they are less likely to employ people. High levels of employment protection tends to lead to less labour intensive production methods.

2. Poverty is higher in countries adopting the 'Anglo-Saxon model' for two reasons. One is that unions tend to be weak and therefore fail to raise wages at the bottom end of the pay range. Second, benefits for being out of work are relatively low. This not only puts those unemployed into poverty but also it tends to increase the number of workers in low paid jobs since they wouldn't have taken those jobs if unemployment benefits had been higher.

3. France and Denmark are part of the the 'Rhineland model' and the 'Nordic model' respectively. Greece and the UK are part of the 'Mediterranean model' and the 'Anglo-Saxon model' respectively. Countries in the Rhineland and Nordic models have greater equality in terms of income than countries in the Mediterranean model and the Anglo-Saxon models. One aspect of market failure is inequality of income and therefore countries like Greece and the UK can be said to be suffering from market failure in the way their economies are structured.

Equally, the Nordic and Anglo-Saxon models tend to produce higher rates of employment. It could be argued that high levels of employment protection seen in countries in the Rhineland and Mediterranean models lead to market failure because too few people are employed. The protection does not allow labour markets to clear. Hence employment tends to be lower whilst unemployment tends to be higher.

65 Equality and equity

Question 1

(a) In 1970, wages and salaries accounted for over three quarters of household income. By 2005-06, this had fallen to approximately two thirds. Self-employment income has increased slightly as a proportion over the thirty five year period. The main increases, though, have been in non-earned income - investments, annuities and pension and social security benefits.

(b) Inequalities have increased between 1970 and 2005-06. Partly, this is due to increasing inequality in wages and salaries, not shown by the data. However, the growth in non-earned income provides some clues to the reasons why inequalities have grown. The growth of social security benefits would suggest that there are a larger number of relatively poor households in the economy. Investment income, in contrast, is likely to be concentrated amongst more affluent households, indicating that there is a larger number of these in the economy too.

Question 2

Note: in the first impression of the fifth edition there is a misprint. This has been corrected in reprints. The Top fifth for 2002-03 should be 40 not 41.

(a)

Figure 1

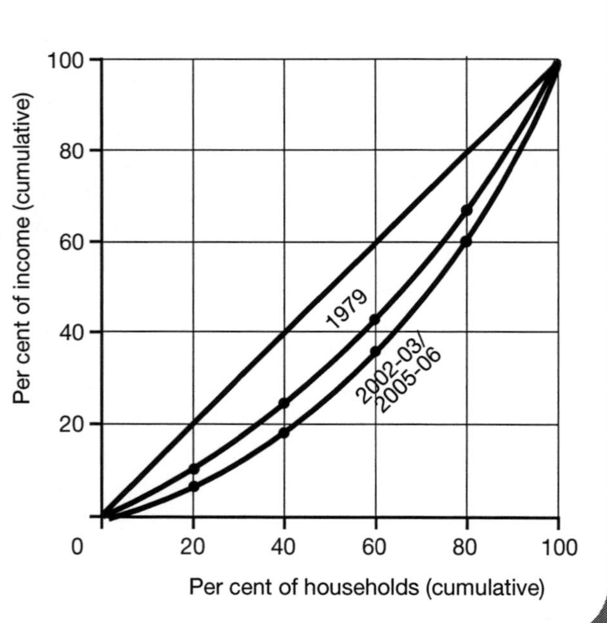

(b) The distribution has become less equal, shown by an outward shift in the Lorenz curve. In 1979, for instance, the bottom fifth of households by income received 10 per cent of all income. By 2005-06, this had fallen to 7 per cent. In contrast, the share of the top 20 per cent of households had risen from 35 per cent to 40 per cent.

Question 3

(a) In 1971, average weekly earnings of women were 55.6 per cent that of men. By 1981, this had increased to 65.0 per cent and was 76.3. per cent by 2007. It could be argued that horizontal equity between men and women has therefore improved over time, although the large earnings gap remaining between men and women was evidence that horizontal inequity still remained in the 2000s.

However, there are differences in employment patterns between men and women which might account for differences in wages. For instance, full time women workers, on average, work fewer hours than full time men. The result is that when hourly wages rather than earnings are compared, the gap between men and women is reduced. In 1971, women earned 63.5 per cent the hourly wage of men. By 2007, this had improved to 83.1 per cent.

Another factor which might account for the difference is the level of skill and experience of male and female workers. On average, female workers have less work experience than males because females still traditionally leave work in their 20s or 30s to look after children. This reduces their level of human capital compared to males.

Overall, it is likely that horizontal equity has improved over time between male and female workers. It is also true that male and female workers are not homogeneous and that the existence of wage differentials does not necessarily show that there is any horizontal inequity in the market.

(b) The 1970s saw the enactment of two major pieces of legislation which helped the position of women considerably. The Equal Pay Act 1970 made it illegal to pay women less than men if they were doing the same job. The Sex Discrimination Act 1975 guaranteed women equality of opportunity in the workplace. These two Acts are likely to have given a considerable boost to women's pay relative to male earnings. During the 1980s, momentum was maintained with a number of pioneering decisions from the European Court of Justice which helped the position of individual groups of women. Women have had greater opportunities for education and training. They have also reduced the average period of time spent out of the workforce to bring up children, ensuring that less human capital is lost.

Question 4

(a) The scheme whereby a few disabled people received cars whilst the vast majority received nothing could be said to be horizontally inequitable. Disabled people in the same position were not treated equally. Therefore, the change to Mobility Allowance could be argued to have increased horizontal equity in the UK.

(b) The provision of cars for disabled people could be argued to have been allocatively inefficient. If all markets in the economy were perfectly competitive, then price would equal marginal cost in each market. However, in the market for cars adapted for the disabled, it need not necessarily have been the case that the value placed on the car was equal to its marginal cost of production. For instance, a car might cost £7 000, but a disabled person might only be prepared to pay £2 000 for a car. If it is given free to him, then he will take it because the marginal private benefit of £2 000 far exceeds the marginal private cost to the individual of taking possession of the car, which is zero. However, the marginal social cost of £7 000 far exceeds the marginal private benefit of £2 000. Hence, the change to Mobility Allowance, where all disabled people were given an allowance to spend as they like, is likely to have increased efficiency in the economy.

Data question

1. (a) Figure 6 in the student's book shows the types of household that are likely to be poor. In the bottom quintile, nearly 60 per cent of households are ones where no one is in work. Either they are of working age below 60 (the yellow bar) or they are retired (the orange bar). In the next to bottom quintile, these two groups account for 42 per cent of households with a larger proportion of retirement households included. In terms of life changes, losing your job and becoming unemployed, going from having a job to being inactive perhaps because an individual is now looking after a child, or retiring are likely to lead to relatively low incomes. The data also suggest that splitting a household is likely to lead to lower incomes for the new households created. So separation between partners or husband and wife and children who leave home is likely to create lower incomes. So too is looking after children when a parent leaves their paid employment to become a full time carer.

(b) In Figure 6, it can be seen that 92 per cent of households in the top quintile have at least one person in the household working (blue plus the red bars). Being in work and gaining a highly paid position or being successfully self employed is therefore almost a necessity to become a high income household.

2(a) Horizontal equity is the identical treatment of identical individuals or groups in society in identical situations. It is difficult to assess from the data whether horizontal equity exists in the UK. For instance, Figure 6 in the student's book shows different households and their incomes. Those with a full time job in in the top quintile will have a different job to those with a full time job in the bottom quintile.

However, Figure 7 would suggest that horizontal equity does not exist between men and women. At no stage in their lives do women earn on average as much as men. On the other hand, it could be argued that women still take time out to look after children and that this could account for the disparity in earnings. Women work on average fewer hours than men and the occupations that men and women typically have can be very different.

Table 6 would also suggest a lack of horizontal equity. Children from different ethnic groups have different chances of living in low and high income households. For example, 60 per cent of children of Pakistani/Bangladeshi origin live in households in the bottom quintile by disposable income compared to 23 per cent for white children. In contrast 18 per cent of children from an Indian ethnic background live in householders in the top quintile by income distribution compared to a national average of 13 per cent. Overall, children are more likely than adults on average to live in low income households.

(b) Vertical equity exists when there is different treatment of individuals or groups to promote greater equity. The evidence in the data for vertical equity is indirect. Figure 6 shows quintiles of households by disposable income. The UK tax and benefit system imposes higher levels of tax on high income households than on low income households. Low income households also receive more benefits. This helps to reduce income inequalities. Equally, in Figure 7, women are more likely to receive benefits and pay lower taxes than men because their average incomes are lower.

3. The increase in the number of private pensions since the mid-1980s would initially suggest that poverty would be reduced over the next 50 years. Pensioners tend to be in low income groups and form the largest single group in the bottom fifth of households by income.

However, whilst individuals might have been saving harder for their retirement, the state since 1981 has been reducing the value of the basic state retirement pension as a proportion of income. It is still increasing it in line with inflation, which would suggest that absolute poverty will not increase. By not linking it to wages, it could be that relative poverty has risen. The latest pension reform proposals agreed after the Turner Commission Report will restore the link between the basic state pension and earnings from around 2012. This should take some pensioners out of poverty who would otherwise have fallen into poverty over the next 50 years.

Another problem is that the return on private pensions is uncertain. It could be that, over the next 50 years time, the savings of workers about to become pensioners are worthless, perhaps because of high inflation. Or the rate of return could have been less than the increase in wages for workers so that relative to wages, average private pensions have fallen.

The most worrying problem, however, is that many companies have been downgrading or abolishing the final salary pension schemes. These are schemes where both employer and employee put in money and the scheme then pays out a proportion of salary on retirement as a pension depending on how many years of contribution have been made. There were two main advantage of these schemes. One was that a significant proportion of workers offered membership of the scheme took it up. The second was that companies paid contributions into the scheme on behalf of their employees. When final salary schemes are replaced by personal pension schemes in companies what typically happens is that fewer workers join the scheme and less is paid into the pension by both employer and employee. Young workers in particular are not paying into any form of pension scheme because they feel they cannot afford to save.

The future of pensions in the UK is extremely uncertain. The outlook for those currently under 30 is not particularly bright because not only are they failing to pay into pension schemes but they will also have to pay higher taxes to pay for more generous state pensions for their parents' and grandparents' generation.

66 The redistribution of income and wealth

Question 1

(a) In the UK, everyone has the opportunity to buy the make and model of car they wish, subject to an income constraint. In this sense there is equality of opportunity in car ownership. However, it could be argued that there is no equality of opportunity because everyone's income is different. Low income households do not have access to private cars because they cannot afford to buy and run them. Equally, most individuals would want to own a car which they think is better than the one they have, but are unable to do so because of lack of income.

The same arguments could be used when considering access to the road system. With tolls, there would be equality of opportunity for everyone to use the road system subject to an income constraint. At present, with access to free roads, there is no income constraint on use. Imposing tolls would therefore reduce equality of opportunity. However, the new situation would only make road use comparable to car use.

(b) (i) Cutting the basic rate of income tax by the amount raised in new road taxes would lead to some redistribution of income. Heavy road users would probably lose, as would commuters who use their car to travel into busy urban centres. They would pay more in road tolls than they would receive through the cut in tax. Another small group of losers would be low income households who did not pay income tax at the basic rate of tax, but who did own a car and used it on congested roads. Winners would be those households which paid income tax at the basic rate but did not use their car much at peak times or did not own a car. Middle income pensioner households, for example, are likely to be major gainers.

It should also be remembered that a cut in the basic rate of income tax will give more benefit in money terms to high income households than to low income households. An individual earning £25 000 a year will benefit more than one earning £10 000 a year if both do the same amount of mileage on tolled roads.

(ii) Using the new road taxes to subsidise public transport would make motorists worse off in income terms, whilst making those who use public transport better off. Some motorists would switch from cars to public transport and they too would be better off. Those who continued to use the roads would get some benefit in the sense that their journey times would presumably be faster with fewer cars using the roads.

Question 2

(a) Most of the tax changes had the effect of making the distribution of income more unequal. The income tax cuts tended to disproportionately favour high income earners against lower income earners. The higher income earners saw their marginal tax rates fall from 83 per cent to 40 per cent, and they shared the same cuts in the standard rate of tax as lower income earners. The cuts in income tax rates of course did not help the millions of households who earned so little that they paid no income tax at all.

The VAT increases are likely to have hit low income households more. VAT is often argued to be a regressive tax because high income earners save a large proportion of their income compared with low income households. Certainly, the imposition of VAT on household fuel is likely to have hit low income households disproportionately because fuel forms a much larger share of household spending of low income groups compared to high income groups.

The change in the rating system to the council tax will also have transferred income from the less well off to the better off. High income earners were gainers because they tend to live in properties which saw their tax cut. Low income earners living in owner occupied property tended to see their tax increase because they lived in low value properties.

The reduction in value of tax relief on interest on mortgages is likely to have hit young households with large mortgages more than older households with small mortgages. The value of the tax relief was also worth less as a proportion of income to high income households than medium and low income households because there was a £30 000 limit on tax relief. Removal is therefore likely to have hit high income households less.

The introduction of the two types of tax credit will have helped alleviate child poverty in households where one member of the household is working. As such, it should make the distribution of income more equal.

Question 3

1. An indirect tax is a tax levied on goods or services, such as value added tax or excise duties.

2. Indirect taxes are regressive according to the data. This is because, as incomes rise, households pay a smaller proportion of their income in indirect taxes. The top fifth of households by disposable income paid 14 per cent of their income in indirect taxes. The bottom fifth of households paid 29 per cent of their income in indirect taxes, more than twice as much.

Question 4

(a) (i) Large cuts in income tax rates on the better off would, on a logical basis, seem to lead to large cuts in the proportion of tax paid by them. If, for instance, the tax liability of an individual earning £100 000 a year falls from £60 000 to £40 000, then the share of his income paid in tax falls.

(ii) The proportion of total tax paid by high income earners actually increased in the 1980s. In 1976-77, for instance, the top 10 per cent of income earners paid 35 per cent of all income tax paid. By 1991-92 this had risen to 42 per cent. For the top 1 per cent of income earners, the proportion increased from 11 per cent to 15 per cent.

(iii) Large falls in income tax rates for high income earners can paradoxically lead to increases in the proportion of total tax collected from them. One reason is that high rates of tax encourage evasion and avoidance. There is a greater incentive not to declare income if the marginal rate of income tax is 83 per cent rather than 40 per cent. There is also a greater incentive to spend time, effort and money to get round paying tax, for instance by moving offshore or employing accountants to devise tax avoidance schemes.

Another reason is that high rates of tax discourage income generating activities such as work. If the marginal rate of tax is 83 per cent, an individual may not consider it worthwhile working long hours or taking on more responsibility. Hard work, enterprise and risk taking are then not undertaken and tax revenues are consequently less. On the other hand, lower rates of tax encourage people to work hard and earn money.

Hence, tax revenues can rise despite a fall in tax rates.

Economic welfare is likely to have risen following the tax cuts. Partly this is because less tax avoidance on the part of the rich will have meant that lower income earners will have had to pay less in tax to fund the same level of government spending. Partly it is because wealth generation will have contributed to new jobs and greater prosperity throughout the economy. It could be argued, though, that very little of this new wealth 'trickled down' to lower income groups but remained concentrated amongst the very rich. Hence, reducing the top rate of tax helped increased inequalities of income and wealth.

(b) (i) Abolishing the tax allowance on mortgage payments meant that those with mortgages had to pay more in tax. Those with mortgages are more likely to be found in the upper half of the income distribution than the lower half, where renting is more common. Hence the increase in the proportion of tax paid by the top 50 per cent of income earners from 85 per cent to 88 per cent between 1990-91 and 1997-98 might be explained by the abolition of mortgage tax relief.

Equally, though, it could be argued that abolition particularly hit the 'next 40 per cent' group in Table 1 in the student's book those who were in the 50 to 90 per cent of the income range. Yet they saw their share of income tax liability fall from 45 per cent of the total to 40 per cent over the same period. However, it must be true that their share of income tax liability would have been even lower by 1997-98 if mortgage relief had not been abolished.

(ii) The abolition of mortgage relief probably led to an increase in economic welfare. Subsidising the purchase of homes by those who could already afford to buy will have increased rather than reduced inequalities in society. There is also an argument that, given the highly inelastic supply of houses in the short term, subsidies simply helped to push up the prices of houses rather than making them more affordable. The benefits of tax relief went to those selling houses and not to those buying or trading down. Neither one of these groups was likely to be poor.

Question 5

(a) Margaret Thatcher made a number of points in defence of the greater inequalities seen in the 1980s. Fist, she argued that whilst the gap between the 'haves' and the 'have nots' had increased, all had still benefited, even the poorest. She gave the example of a married man with two children in the lowest decile of earnings who had seen his earnings increase by 12.5 per cent over the decade.

She then implied that those who had benefited the most were those who had done so through 'their own endeavours and initiative'. The benefits of lower taxes had gone to those who were creators of wealth in society and therefore, by implication, they justly deserved their new found prosperity.

These wealth creators did not just create wealth for themselves. They also created wealth for society. In particular, in creating wealth, they were producing the resources through which 'poverty can be assisted'. For instance, those with high incomes not only paid more in tax at the end of the 1980s than at the beginning of the decade, but they also contributed a larger proportion of tax than before. Hence, they could hardly be accused of not paying their fair share of the kitty.

Finally, she saw her policies not in terms of enlarging inequalities, but in terms of enlarging opportunities. Opportunity and the ability of individuals to prosper were far more important than any consideration that the gap between rich and poor might have substantially increased.

Data question

Reducing poverty

The characteristics of poverty in the UK

Poverty can be defined in a number of different ways. Absolute poverty occurs when individuals do not have the resources to be able to consume enough necessities to survive. Absolute poverty today in the UK is very rare and occurs mainly because individuals do not take advantage of the safety net provided by the state. Relative poverty is defined as relative to existing living standards for the average individual. Relative poverty by definition exists in any society where inequality exists. Relative poverty in the UK is arguably much greater today than it was in the early 1960s. Then, approximately 13 per cent of individuals had an income which was 60 per cent or below that of median (average) income. By the early 1990s, this had increased to over 20 per cent before falling back a little to 16 per cent by 2004/05.

On a slightly different measure of income inequality, the Joseph Rowntree Foundation estimated that in 2005-06, 13 million people were living in poverty. Of this 13 million, 3.8 million were children.

Think tank proposals for alleviating poverty

Members of the think tank put forward a wide variety of proposals for dealing with the problem of poverty. The first was increasing the minimum wage to £8.00 an hour. This would help the low paid in employment. However, much of the benefit would accrue to richer households because the main beneficiary of a rise in minimum wages would be female workers. Many female workers live with a male who is also working and therefore their household is not particularly poor. Moreover, raising the minimum wage would do nothing for retired households or for the unemployed. Some economists would further argue that minimum wages would lead to job losses amongst the low paid as they are priced out of work. Raising wages might also push low paid workers into paying further income tax and National Insurance contributions whilst receiving less in benefit. Hence, any gross increase would be much reduced as a net increase, the problem known as the poverty trap.

Raising the state pension and benefit limits by £50 per week will tackle the problem of poverty amongst a large number of the poor in the UK. However, it is by far the most costly solution to the state of all the proposals because there are so many pensioners and because the increase would be substantial. Moreover, a minority of pensioners are relatively affluent, in receipt of occupational pensions, and therefore do not need this increase to raise them out of poverty. It could be argued that a means tested benefit would be less costly.

Raising child benefit by an average of £15 per week per recipient would give a considerable boost to alleviating child poverty. An estimated 3.8 million children live in households below the poverty line. However, it would be enormously expensive to the state because child benefit is a universal benefit, paid to households irrespective of income. Most of the money paid out would go to households which did not need the cash. Hence, the money could be argued to be misdirected. Making child benefit into a means tested benefit to get round this problem would lead to other problems. The take up of means tested benefits is far less than 100 per cent.

It would stigmatise households who received the benefit. It would be costly to administer and make the problem of the poverty and unemployment traps worse.

Raising the Job Seekers' allowance by an average of £50 per week per worker would help the newly unemployed. However, the newly unemployed are unlikely to be in poverty unless they were already in poverty when they had a job. Most workers who find themselves out of a job will maintain their standard of living by drawing on savings, taking on modest borrowing and cutting out all non-essential spending. It could raise the numbers unemployed because it will encourage unemployed workers to spend longer searching for the right job. It will also have no effect on the longer term unemployed over six months because the Job Seekers' allowance is only given to the unemployed for the first six months.

Cutting the standard rate of income tax by 2p in the pound is unlikely to have any direct effect on poverty. The poor pay little or no tax. Almost all the direct benefit of this would accrue to the better off in society. It could be argued, however, that it would encourage the better off to work harder and be more entrepreneurial. They would create jobs for others and this would lead to a 'trickling down' in income to the poor. Unfortunately, the data would suggest that there is no trickle down effect in practice. In the 1980s, for instance, when there were substantial tax cuts for the better off, the relative position of the poor deteriorated and they received little of the benefit from a growing economy.

Providing free 24 hour nursery care and creche facilities would be of particular benefit to low income households with a mother and small children where the parent was either in work or wanting to work. For those in work, it is likely to save money in child minding fees. It could also help them to move from working part time to working full time. For those not in work, it could provide them with an opportunity to take on work. It would, however, be an expensive solution, with most of the benefit accruing not to those in poverty but to better off women already in work.

Cutting all benefits to workers able to work but not in work would, in the short term, increase poverty. It could be argued, however, that this would provide a powerful incentive for them to get jobs. The cycle of dependency would be broken and individuals would be forced to assume responsibility for themselves instead of relying on a nanny state for benefit. Whilst there might be some element of truth in this, it is highly likely that poverty would increase as a result of this move. The jobs that workers would be forced into would be very low paid, most below current benefit levels. They might be in work but they would be worse off.

Increasing government spending on education and training by 10 per cent could have some impact on the unemployed if it were channelled towards training for those out of work. However, it would be more likely to have an effect on poverty in the long term if it raised education levels, particularly of those children who live in poorer households. These children are more likely to become poor themselves than children raised in better off households. The higher the educational level of an individual, the less likely he or she is to become unemployed or to take a low paid job. The danger with the proposal is that the money spent would have little impact on raising educational standards or giving better training to more people. The cost of education per child would rise with no increase in output.

Another proposal

Another proposal would be highly radical. This would be for the state to give everyone in the UK a benefit large enough to take everyone out of absolute poverty and reduce relative poverty. It would end the means testing of benefits and lead to a high level of security for individuals. It would have three major drawbacks. It would be very expensive, requiring much higher levels of direct tax than at present. Basic tax rates might have to be at, say, 40 or 45 per cent. This in turn might prove to be a major disincentive to work, leading to lower economic growth. Third, the transition from the present system, where many individuals have paid National Insurance contributions to secure a right to a benefit, to the new system where those individuals would lose those rights, would prove difficult. There would be many losers as well as gainers and, as the example of the poll tax showed, individuals do not like large government imposed changes to their incomes.

An evaluation of these proposals

One of the difficulties of dealing with poverty is that it has many causes. Solutions which address one aspect of poverty may do nothing to help alleviate other forms of poverty. For instance, measures to reduce poverty amongst the unemployed will do nothing to help pensioners or single parent households where the parent does not wish to work. Equally, it should be remembered that there is considerable movement from year to year between deciles of income. A household which sees a sharp drop in income from, say, unemployment may quickly recover its earning position.

However, poverty seems particularly concentrated amongst the elderly and those without jobs. Measures which would provide higher incomes for low income pensioners and more jobs for those without work would seem best placed to help reduce poverty. The problem with all the solutions put forward is that they are either too costly or would not necessarily lead to the creation of more jobs. Economists are divided about how to create jobs, some arguing that the direct creation of jobs through an increase in aggregate demand is required, whilst others argue that only supply side measures will bring about a long term increase in real jobs. The most promising measure would possibly be the increase in the state pension, not by £30 which would be too costly but, say, by £10 or £15, or the restoration of the link between pension increases and wage increases.

67 The business cycle

Question 1

(a) The UK economy went into boom in 1978 and the early part of 1979. Growth was high at a little under 3 per cent, unemployment was falling, whilst demand pressures in the economy, resulting from high investment for instance, caused the current account on the balance of payments to fall into deficit. By 1980, the economy was plunging into recession. Output fell by 2 per cent, investment began to fall whilst unemployment rose to 1.6 million. The current account on the balance of payments moved sharply into surplus, reflecting a fall in demand pressures in the economy. The bottom of the cycle was reached some time in 1981. Output was still falling in that year, investment expenditure fell again, whilst nearly 1 million workers were added to the unemployment figures. The economy then began to recover. Output grew by 1.7 per cent in 1982, the first increase since 1979. Investment was slightly up on 1981 levels, reflecting renewed business confidence, whilst the current account surplus fell, reflecting a slight increase in domestic expenditure. Unemployment, however, was still rising, but unemployment tends to lag behind other indicators of the cycle.

Question 2

A major world recession would result in exports from the UK falling. This would significantly reduce aggregate demand in the UK and push the UK economy into recession. Eventually, economic forces would stabilise the economy at the bottom of a slump and then begin to pull it into a recovery phase.

Question 3

Note: in the first impression of the fifth edition there is a misprint. This has been corrected in reprints. The figures for Change in gross domestic product at market prices should be

Change in gross domestic product at market prices	
1994	*35.7*
1995	*25.4*
1996	*24.8*
1997	*28.4*
1998	*31.6*
1999	*29.6*
2000	*38.1*
2001	*24.7*
2002	*21.9*
2003	*30.1*
2004	*36.4*
2005	*21.2*
2006	*33.5*

(a) For a multiplier effect to be present, changes in investment would have to be correlated with changes in national income. All the changes in investment, apart from 2003, were positive and all the changes in the GDP were also positive. However, it is difficult to see any other correlation between the two variables. For example, in 2005 when the change in gross fixed capital formation was just £3.0 billion, GDP grew by £21.2 billion. In 2006, when gross fixed capital formation grew by the much larger £16.4 billion, GDP increased by only £33.5 billion.

(b) There is a little more evidence for the accelerator theory of investment than for the multiplier from the evidence. For example, the year when the change in investment was lowest in 2003 was associated with large increases in GDP in 2001, 2002 and 2003.

(c) The multiplier-accelerator model suggests that the multiplier and accelerator interact to lead to upward increases in both investment and GDP. However, in the data, there is not enough evidence to support or refute the theory. More sophisticated econometric models would have to be used to determine whether there was any link.

Question 4

(a) Expenditure on stocks and work in progress is part of investment in the economy. A rise in expenditure on stocks and work in progress will therefore produce a rise in aggregate expenditure and vice versa. The change in stocks and work in progress in 1980 was -£3.4 billion, and accounted for over half the fall in GDP that occurred in that year. Given that there is likely to have been a multiplier effect on national income of the change in stocks and work in progress, it can be seen that this change must have been a major determinant of the 1980 recession. In 1981, stocks and work in progress fell £3.2 billion, at the same time as GDP fell by £3.1 billion. Again, this provides evidence that changes in inventories contributed to the recession of the early 1980s. By 1982, the change in stocks and work in progress was still negative, but national income began to increase again. There must have been increases in other expenditures to account for this. By 1983, both changes in stocks and GDP growth were positive again. Overall, the data lend support to the hypothesis that business cycles can be inventory led.

Question 5

(a) In 1929 and the early part of 1930, there was, according to Friedman and Schwartz, a small decline in the money supply. However, this decline accelerated considerably as a consequence of a wave of bank failures starting in late 1930. When customers lost confidence in their banks, they attempted to withdraw their deposits, substituting them with currency (i.e. dollars). This had two effects. First, it forced more banks into bankruptcy because they did not have the cash reserves to pay their deposit holders, and this in turn reduced the money supply by the amount the deposit holders lost in the aftermath of the bankruptcy. Second, banks were forced to increase their reserve ratios of cash to deposits. They now needed to hold more cash for every dollar of deposit they held before 1930, in case depositors demanded their deposits back. This meant that they were unable to lend out such a large proportion of their deposits as before. Therefore the money supply fell because there was less borrowing in the economy than before.

(b) The problems of the American banking system led to a significant fall in the money supply, exogenous to the US economy. This fall led to excess demand for money. As a result, spending fell as both households and businesses attempted to restore their money holdings. For some, who lost all their savings in the banking crisis of 1930-31, it was a catastrophe, because their incomes depended upon their savings. For others, losing their savings meant that they had to start all over again trying to save for old age, for instance. This fall in spending then had a multiplier effect on the economy with others losing their jobs and hence losing their income and their ability to spend. The Great Depression resulted.

Data question

1. The four phases of the business cycle are boom, downturn, recession or depression and recovery.

In a boom, economic growth is relatively high, unemployment is low and there are inflationary pressures in the economy. The Japanese economy was in boom in the late 1980s and early 1990s when growth in GDP rose to a high of over 6 per cent in 1988.

In a downturn, GDP growth falls, unemployment rises and inflationary pressures are reduced. In the early 1990s, the Japanese economy went into a downturn with economic growth falling to almost 0 per cent by 1993.

In a recession or depression, economic growth is either very low or is negative. Unemployment rises whilst inflationary pressures fall. Arguably, much of the period from the early 1990s to the early 2000s were years of depression for Japan. Although there were spikes in economic growth, the economy returned twice in 1998 and 2002 to negative or virtually zero economic growth rates.

In a recovery, economic growth begins to recover whilst unemployment begins to fall and inflationary pressures build up. The Japanese economy was arguably in this recovery phase from 2003 to 2005.

2. (a) Economic growth, unemployment and inflation are linked in the business cycle. When the economy is in its recovery phase, economic growth is rising. This should lead to falling unemployment because the rise in GDP leads to more demand in the economy. Equally, more demand in the economy leads to greater demand-pull pressures. At the top of the cycle, high economic growth is leading to more falls in unemployment but greater inflationary pressures. When the economy goes into recession and growth in GDP is falling, unemployment will tend to rise and inflationary pressures will begin to fall. In a depression, low or negative economic growth leads to rising unemployment and low inflation because aggregate demand is weak.

(b) Japan's experience clearly shows these links. In the late 1980s when the economy was in boom, unemployment fell but inflationary pressures began to mount up. During the mid 1990s and early 2000s when the Japanese economy slipped in and out of a prolonged depression, the unemployment rate rose from just over 2 per cent in 1991 to over 5 per cent by 2002. Inflation fell over the period from a high of 3 per cent in 1991 to a low of -1 per cent in 2002. In the recovery phase from 2002, economic growth was positive whilst unemployment fell and inflation rose.

3. Bank of Japan intervention can affect the course of the trade cycle. By lowering interest rates, the Bank of Japan can stimulate aggregate demand because interest rates affect both consumption and investment. In the 2000s, the data states that the Bank of Japan had a zero interest rate policy. This means that the equivalent of bank rate in the UK was 0 per cent. Unfortunately, the zero interest rate policy couldn't prevent the Japanese economy going back to almost zero growth in 2002. This shows the limitations of monetary policy. If interest rates are already zero, the central bank cannot cut them further. The business cycle must then be controlled through other means such as active fiscal policy.

68 Economic growth and welfare

Question 1

(a) GDP measures the output of the economy which is traded. However, output is only one amongst many factors which contribute to a nation's standard of living.
(b) There are many other factors which should be included. For example, the Measure of Domestic Progress (MDP), produced by the New Economics Foundation, suggests that 'social and environmental costs, including the damage done by crime, the depletion of natural resources, and pollution such as emissions of greenhouse gases' should be included in measures of quality of life. Important too are political freedoms, the social and cultural environment, the working environment and freedom from fear of violence. Recent work on happiness suggests that factors such as levels of education and quality of relationships are important.
(c) The MDP suggests that 1976 was the 'best on record for the quality of life in Britain'. However, 'those old enough to remember 1976 might be surprised that this was the best year for Britain's overall affluence'. The problem is that the MDP only takes a selective number of variables and leaves other crucial variables such as levels of inflation and unemployment out of the index. By concentrating on some social and environmental costs, the index has distorted the real picture of what life was like in 1976. GDP per capita is obviously not a perfect measure of the standard of living either. However, at least it does not pretend to be an accurate index of the quality of life in the UK unlike the MDP.

Question 2

One obvious difference in the two kitchens is the amount of capital equipment in each. There is very little equipment in the turn of the century kitchen, whereas today's kitchens have a wide range of labour saving devices. Looking more closely, there are two other important differences. Less equipment, no running water and no electricity meant that people at the turn of the century had to work much harder and longer to perform simple household tasks, such as cooking and washing, than people today. It was also less hygienic and less pleasant. There would be few people who would want to return to housing conditions commonly found at the turn of the century and therefore, in this respect, economic growth has been highly desirable.

Data question

Note: in Table 4 there is a misprint in the first impression of the 5th edition. This has been been corrected in reprints. The Retail Price Index for 2006 should be 981 and not 907 as printed.

RISING LIVING STANDARDS

Introduction
Living standards, for the most part, have improved since the 1970s. From an economic viewpoint, the most important statistic is the rise in real incomes per head of the population. This rise in income enabled governments to spend more on behalf of citizens and it gave greater after tax spending power to individuals. However, the period also saw the deterioration of a number of key variables, such as a rise in obesity and greater congestion on motorways.

The economy
The economy grew in size between 1971 and 2006. GDP at current prices rose 22.8 times whilst prices rose 9.8 times. In real terms, the value of GDP in 1971 at 2006 prices was £564.1 billion (£57.5 billion x 981 ÷ 100). The real increase in GDP over the period was therefore 131 per cent. In per capita terms, income at 2006 prices increased from £10 091 to £21 616, an increase of 114 per cent.

This increase in income helped increase the spending power of households. The volume of of domestic household expenditure on goods and services more than doubled over the period. Not surprisingly, ownership of consumer durables also increased. The number of households owning a washing machine increased from 65 per cent to 95 per cent, whilst those with a land line telephone increased from 35 per cent to 92 per cent. Many products such as mobile phones, CD players and home computers simply didn't exist in the early 1970s. Others, such as tumble dryers or dishwashers, were available in the US market but were so uncommon in the UK market that surveys recorded that no households in the UK possessed these items .

Higher incomes allowed the government to spend more on services. In education, for instance, there was a fall in the pupil/teacher ratio from 22.6 to 1 in 1970-71 to 17.1 to 1 in 2006. The numbers in higher education exploded from 620 000 in 1970-71 to 2.49 million in 2006.

Economic progress was not without its drawbacks, however. Britain's roads became more congested. In 1971, the average daily flow of motor vehicles on motorways was 28 500. By 2005, this had climbed to 75 500. Water and energy consumption have grown, which has caused environmental problems. However, a range of air pollutants such as sulphur dioxide and nitrogen oxides have seen reductions, mainly because of the decline of heavy industry in the UK.

The benefits of growth were unequally distributed. Medical practitioners saw their real gross weekly earnings nearly double. But manual workers such as caretakers, bricklayers or carpenters have not been as fortunate. Waiters and waitresses actually earned less in real terms in 2005-6 than in 1971. There was also a growth in unemployment. Job security was less in 2006 than in 1971.

Society
Economic factors are not the only ones which contribute to the standard of living of individuals. Society has changed since the 1970s.

The number of divorces has increased, with more adults and children in one parent homes. Some would argue that this is a positive sign with fewer people locked into unhappy marriages. Others would argue that it shows the break up of family life and that children brought up in single parent families experience more problems than children brought up in the traditional married household.

Abortions have increased from 63 400 in 1971-72 to 199 019 in 2006. Some see abortion as murder. They might argue, therefore, that this increase is undesirable. Others, however, might argue that it reflects greater freedom of choice, in particular for women, and this choice has improved their living standards.

Women have increasingly entered the workforce, although much of the increase since 1971 has been in part-time employment. This has increased household income. However, its impact on the family has been much debated. Some would argue that children brought up by working mothers are likely to suffer more problems in later life than those brought up by the mother who stays at home. Others disagree.

The structure of the population has changed. Death rates are falling. There are now more old people and fewer young people than in 1971. This has helped drive social security spending. It has also increased demand for services related to the elderly.

Recorded crime was approximately the same in 2005/06 as in 1981 although it peaked in the mid 1990s. This could be seen as an indication of the increasing breakdown of society in the 1980s and 1990s. Alternatively, it could be argued that the level of crime was little different. Increasing affluence and greater expectations of good behaviour led to an explosion in its recording. Equally, some argue that changes in recorded crime tend to be correlated with the number of 14-25 year old males in the population since they are the main perpetrators of crime.

Obesity has risen over the period. Rising incomes mean that food is affordable to all in society, even those on relatively low incomes. Obesity rates rose alarmingly over the period 1993 to 2003, doubling for males and nearly doubling for females. On the other hand, the incidence of smoking has declined, more so for men than for women.

The next 20 years

GDP is likely to carry on rising over the next 20 years. Many economists would argue that this will bring with it an increase in our standard of living. We will be able to afford to buy more goods and services. Our increased taxes will pay for better hospital care and better schools. What's more, technological advance will enable us to buy not just better quality products but also new products yet undreamt of. Communication will continue to be revolutionised by the Internet and mobile phone technology. The Caribbean could become as affordable to the average family as the Costa del Sol.

However, some would argue that the future is much more bleak. At its extreme, some have argued that we are facing an environmental catastrophe. If global warming, the thinning of the ozone layer or a series of nuclear accidents don't destroy us, then the economy will self destruct through the overuse of non-renewable resources and growing amounts of all types of waste. Like the Easter Islanders, we will destroy our global village through over exploitation of natural resources. Others would argue that the breakdown of the family and rising crime will destroy our social fabric. We will have our television sets and cars but live isolated lives, afraid to go out but also afraid of the burglar coming in. During the day, our roads will be clogged with cars. At night, the streets will be deserted but for people roaming around terrorising the ordinary citizen.

In another vision, the benefits of economic growth will go almost entirely to the better off. The rich will live in secluded areas, employing security guards to protect themselves. The average citizen will be no better off. The poor will become worse off. This underclass will be trapped in a cycle of economic deprivation where the lack of economic opportunities will lead to neglect of education and training which in turn leads to unemployment and no chance of advancement. The only way out for these communities will be crime and terror.

On balance, the more optimistic scenario is likely to prevail. Rising GDP will enable most people to consume more whilst allowing for greater social spending and a cleaner environment. Social values are unlikely to break down, even if more people are prepared to admit to having difficulty living up to those social values. However, if a minority of the population fail to share in this growing prosperity, it is debatable as to whether it can be claimed that the UK is 'better off' today.

69 The economics of happiness

Data question

1. GDP is a monetary measure of the output of goods and services of an economy. It therefore attempts to aggregate what is produced in a single denominator, a currency such as pounds, euros or dollars. For example, the GDP per head of the population of Bhutan in 2005 was $5 620 measured at purchasing power parities. For the UK, this was £35 580, over six times as much. GDP doesn't measure all outputs. For example, it does not include the value of housework or child rearing when no money changes hands for these services. In Bhutan, where there will be a significant subsistance agricultural sector, GDP will not measure the output of food grown and consumed by households. Nor does GDP measure the utility of outputs. For example, it cannot compare the utility (or welfare or happiness) of £10 spent on food compared to £10 spent on clothes.

'Happiness', in contrast, measures the well being or welfare of an individual or group of individuals. Bhutan, although a low income country, came 8th in the world in a study of happiness conducted by the University of Leicester. The UK, with its GDP over six times greater than Bhutan, came 41st out of 178 countries. This illustrates that happiness is not necessarily associated with the production and consumption of goods and services, measured by GDP. Instead, happiness is determined by a wide variety of factors. In Bhutan, for example, the term 'Gross National Happiness' is, according to a 1998 declaration by the prime minister of Bhutan, associated with sustainable and equitable socio-economic development, conservation of the environment, preservation and promotion of culture and good governance.

2. Maximising growth in GDP has its advantages as a main policy objective. It is a clear and measurable goal. Rising GDP can also be associated with improved health care and education, rising consumption of a variety of private sector goods and services as well as increased resources for preservation of the environment. High economic growth also tends to be associated with some measure of good governance. Countries which have very poor governance tend to have relatively low economic growth rates at best and shrinking economies at worst.

However, the evidence suggests that high income countries do not necessarily have the highest levels of welfare or happiness. In a 2005 survey, for example, 45 per cent of Bhutanese adults reported being very happy compared to only 30 per cent for US citizens. This is despite the average US citizen having a much higher income than the average Bhutanese citizen. This evidence supports the Easterlin Paradox which states that, having attained a certain level of GDP, further increases do little or nothing to increase levels of happiness.

Therefore, it makes more sense for the government of Bhutan to pursue a goal of maximising growth in happiness rather than growth in GDP. The problem with this aim is that it is not clear how it can be achieved. The 1998 definition by Bhutan's prime minister, Jigmi Thinkley, is not necessarily correct. Adrian White, the author of the the University of Leicester study, stated that countries with good access to healthcare and education tended to be at the top of happiness scorings. Good healthcare and education systems tend to require high levels of GDP to finance them. Bhutan's citizens, for example, would probably report higher levels of happiness if infant mortality rates in the country fell significantly or there was less tuberculosis prevalent in the population. Increased life expectancy might also increase happiness levels.

So, maximising economic growth is probably not a good policy goal for Bhutan's government. However, given the poverty of the country, achieving some levels of economic growth is likely to lead to increased levels of welfare. However, economic growth should not be achieved at the expense of those indicators which contribute to existing happiness.

70 Unemployment and the Phillips curve

Question 1

(a) Mr Robert Quinn was probably cyclically unemployed, put out of work by the downturn in construction in London. However, it could be argued that he was frictionally unemployed because he was likely to get another job soon, or that he was suffering seasonal unemployment given that he was made redundant in February, traditionally a poor month for employment in the construction industry.
(b) Mr David Kimber was probably cyclically unemployed, although as with Robert Quinn, it could be argued that he was frictionally or seasonally unemployed.
(c) Mr Kirpal Singh was probably voluntarily unemployed, suffering from real-wage unemployment. He could have retained his job at Harrods but chose not to because the net rewards to the job, which were influenced not only by pay but also by the travelling involved in the job, were not great enough.
(d) Ms Susan Morrison had been through two jobs, the first one of which she had quit because she felt she was underpaid. She too was therefore voluntarily unemployed. She could get a job if she were prepared to work for less.
(e) Ms Patricia Jones had resigned from a previous job because she felt underpaid. She was therefore voluntarily unemployed, suffering from real-wage unemployment.
(f) Similarly, Mr Peter Vaas had resigned because of low pay and therefore could be argued to be voluntarily unemployed.

Question 2

(a) The article suggests that unemployment is mainly involuntary rather than voluntary. It gives a number of pieces of evidence which would support this conclusion from a survey of 6 000 employed and unemployed workers.
'Only 12 per cent of the unemployed said they expected pay above that of the average of their employed counterparts.' The unemployed, on the whole, are not asking for wages above the 'going rate'. 88 per cent were willing to work for wages at or below current average wage rates.

It stated that '77 per cent of the unemployed were willing to take a job even if there were no financial necessity, compared to 66 per cent of those in jobs'. This would indicate that the unemployed place a greater value on working for working's sake than those in work.

45 per cent were prepared to undertake training whilst 40 per cent were prepared to move area. A significant minority of the unemployed are prepared to increase their level of human capital and suffer the disruption of moving area to find a job.

Question 3

(a) With inflation running at 2.8 per cent per annum, workers would have needed a 2.8 per cent pay rise to have maintained the real value of their earnings. The wage increases in the data were between 3 and 4 per cent. If the rate of inflation had been 0 per cent, it is likely that the wage increases would have been lower. To give the same real rate of increase, the wage settlements would have been in the 0.2 to 1.2 per cent range.
(b) In contrast, if inflation had been running at 15 per cent, the negotiated wage settlements would have led to substantial falls in real earnings for the workers. Hence, it is likely that they would have negotiated for wage increases over 15 per cent. Lecturers, for instance, would have been looking for a pay increase of 18 per cent.

Question 4

(a) A short run Phillips curve would show that as the rate of inflation rises, so the the level of unemployment falls and vice versa. This relationship is shown over the period 1988 to 1994 when falling unemployment was at first associated with rising inflation but then falling inflation was associated with rising unemployment. However, through the rest of the period 1996-2006, there was no pattern to changes in inflation in relation to changes in unemployment.
(b) (i) The NAIRU is the non-accelerating inflation rate of unemployment. It is the level of unemployment at which inflation will neither increase nor decrease.
(ii) For the NAIRU to have fallen, lower unemployment levels have to be associated with the same rate of inflation. There is no evidence that the NAIRU changed during the period 1988-1994. Changes in unemployment were inversely correlated to changes in inflation. However, the NAIRU seems to have been falling between 1994 and 2006. A two thirds fall in the number of people out of work has been associated with fluctuating levels of inflation in the narrow range 1.3 to 3.4 per cent.

Question 5

(a) A range of problems is identified in the data including poor psychological health and greater risk of marriage break-up. The unemployed found it harder to find employment than those in jobs because they were less likely to mix with those in work and partly because of this had less access to information about jobs.
(b) The problems of the unemployed impose high costs on the rest of society. For instance, marital breakdown creates one parent families which often have to be supported by the state and whose members can be psychologically damaged themselves by the break up of the family. Psychological stress will often be accompanied by treatment on the NHS, pushing up costs to the taxpayer.

Data question

Why unemployment?

Recent trends in unemployment
Unemployment, shown in Figure 12 in the student's book showes a cyclical pattern over the period 1970-2007. At the start and end of the period, ILO unemployment was between 4 and 5 per cent of the labour force. In between, three significant peaks can be distinguished in 1977-78, 1984 and 1993. These were lagged responses to the three deep recessions of 1974-76, 1980-82 and 1990-1992.

All regions of the UK experienced a similar cyclical pattern of unemployment. However, some regions fared better and some worse over the time period compared to the national average. Scotland and the North East were above average whilst the South East was significantly below average.

The possible causes of unemployment
Unemployment rose and fell throughout the period 1970-2007. At its highest in 1986, it was nearly three times its level in 1970 and 2007. A way of trying to understand why there has been this change in unemployment is to consider the

different causes of unemployment.

One type of voluntary unemployment is frictional unemployment. This might have changed because unemployment benefits have risen or fallen, enabling workers to search longer for the right job or forcing them to take a job sooner than they would wish. Levels of frictional unemployment can also be changed by the amount of help the government gives to get people into jobs. Schemes like the New Deal, for instance, place great stress on equipping the unemployed with search skills and encouraging them to apply for jobs. The data give no evidence to suggest whether or not such strategies have been successful in reducing unemployment.

There is likely to have been some structural unemployment throughout the period. Unemployment in the 1950s and 1960s was much lower than that experienced since that period. Figure 13 in the student's book shows that employment in manufacturing declined from 7 million in 1978 to 3 million in 2007. Many workers who lost jobs in manufacturing will have found it difficult to get jobs in the growing service sector. Equally, there was a considerable shake out of labour from primary industries such as coal mining which will have contributed to structural unemployment. The regions that were worst affected were those outside of the South East of England. It could be argued that the difference between unemployment rates between regions like Scotland and the North East represent the level of structural unemployment in these regions throughout the period.

Figure 17 in the student's book shows employment rates for workers by ethnic group. Non-white ethnic groups tend to have employment rates below that of white workers, and the gap is significantly larger for Pakistani and Bangladeshi females than for males. Lower employment rates are likely to reflect high unemployment rates. Another cause of unemployment could then be discrimination in the workplace against workers from minority ethnic groups. Equally, a number of factors such as where in the UK minority ethnic groups live and their educational backgrounds could explain the increased unemployment rates.

Real wage unemployment could have been caused by a number of factors. One would be the strength of trade unions. The 1980s and 1990s saw a diminution of the power of trade unions following trade union 'reform'. This decline in power is reflected in Figure 18 in the student's book which shows that days lost in strikes had fallen almost to zero by the early 1990s from quite high levels in the late 1970s and has since remained at very low levels. Trade union reform might help account for the rapid fall in unemployment after 1986 and again after 1993 following the two major recessions at the start of the 1980s and 1990s. Real wage unemployment could also have been caused by the existence of minimum wages, high tax rates and too high benefit rates.

However, it is clear from Figure 12 in the student's book that a significant influence on unemployment between 1978 and 1998 was the trade cycle. The two large recessions of 1980-82 and 1990-92 led to very large rises in unemployment. Equally, the subsequent booms in the economy led to substantial falls in unemployment rates. Evidence for this cyclical pattern is reinforced by Figure 15 in the student's book which shows the pattern of skilled labour shortages over the period.

Conclusion

The evidence from the data shows clearly that much of the unemployment in recent times has been caused by a lack of demand in the economy. The three major recessions of the mid-1970s, early 1980s and early 1990s saw large increases in unemployment. However, this does not help explain why unemployment was higher in these two decades than in the 1950s and 1960s. It could be argued that structural unemployment caused by declining manufacturing industry was the most important underlying factor which pushed up unemployment rates from the 1970s. It could be that government policies which reduced trade union power, and reduced marginal rates of income tax helped to bring down involuntary unemployment after the mid-1980s. However, it is unlikely that any one single factor can explain the changes in unemployment since 1978. A mixture of factors is likely to have been responsible.

71 Inflation and deflation

Question 1

(a)

Year	% inflation
1	10.00
2	8.75
3	5.60
4	2.15
5	4.00
6	4.30
7	6.76
8	9.78

In year 1, the inflation rate is 10 per cent, calculated by (10 x 0.3) + (10 x 0.7). In year 2, it was 8.75 per cent, calculated by (5 x 0.25)+(10 x 0.75). Years 3 to 8 are calculated in a similar way i.e. (% increase in price of food x weighting of food) + (% increase in price of all other items x weighting of all other items).

(b)

Year	RPI
1	100.00
2	108.75
3	114.84
4	117.31
5	122.20
6	127.25
7	135.85
8	149.14

In year 1 the price index is 100. In year 2 the price index can be calculated by Year 1 RPI x (1 + Year 2 inflation rate ÷ 100) = 100 x (1 + 8.75 ÷ 100) = 108.75. In year 3 the price index can be calculated by Year 2 RPI x (1 + Year 3 inflation rate ÷ 100) = 108.75 x (1 + 5.6 ÷ 100) = 114.84.

Question 2

(a) The General Index of Retail Prices is constructed in part from the results of the Expenditure and Food Survey. Figures for expenditure of the average household in the UK are used to form the weights in the Index. However, it is possible to construct other price indices, for instance by constructing weights based not on average expenditure but on the expenditure of particular groups of people. This is what economists do when they calculate the various pensioner indices, the one in Table 3 in the student's book being based on average expenditures of the two person pensioner households found in the Expenditure and Food Survey.

(b) The pensioner household receives pension increases in line with changes in the General Index of Retail Prices. But their cost of living is going up in line with the Pensioner Index. So wherever the General Index rises faster than the Pensioner Index, the pensioner household is better off and vice versa.

(i) From the data, it can be seen that an increase in real purchasing power occurred in all but one of the periods shown - 1977-1981, 1982-1986, 1987-1991, 1997-2000, 2001-2004 and 2005-2006.

(ii) A decrease in real purchasing power occurred in the period 1992-96.

Question 3

(a) The demand-pull theory of inflation suggests that inflation is caused by excess demand in the economy. If planned expenditure rises above the full employment level of income, then equilibrium income must rise, but the rise will be in nominal and not in real terms because the economy is already at its full employment level. The excess of planned expenditure over that needed to produce full employment at stable prices is known as the inflationary gap.

(b) One of the problems in the data presented is that it is not possible to gauge what was the full employment level of income over the period 1970 to 1978. However, when unemployment fell and the growth rate of the economy increased, it is likely that the economy moved towards its full employment level and vice versa. The nearer the economy is to full employment, the more likely it is that demand-pull inflationary pressures would build up and therefore the more likely there is to be inflation in the economy.

What can be seen from the data is that the rise in inflation in the first half of the 1970s is matched to some extent by a fall in unemployment and a rise in the rate of growth. 1973 in particular saw a sharp fall in unemployment and particularly high growth. This then fed through to increases in prices over the next two years. The rise in unemployment and the negative growth rates of 1974 and 1975 then helped to squeeze inflation out of the economy from 1975.

The data would indicate that there is no simple relationship, if indeed there is one at all, between growth of the economy, unemployment and inflation. Perhaps there were other factors at work which could explain why inflation continued to rise in 1975, for instance, when unemployment was rising and output falling. The time lags involved are also unclear from the data.

Question 4

(a) The pensioner on a fixed income lost 2.8 per cent of her purchasing power in 2005 and 3.2 per cent in 2006.

(b) The saver saw a real loss of 0.8 per cent on her savings in 2005 and a real loss of 0.7 per cent in 2006.

(c) It is not possible to say whether the taxpayer was worse off in 2006 than in 2005 because there are no figures to compare the fiscal year year 2005/6 with 2004/5. However, in April 2006, the increase in tax allowance was 2.9 per cent, roughly the rate of inflation for 2005. Hence the income taxpayer will have been neither better off nor worse off in real terms.

(d) It is not possible to say whether the mother was worse off in 2006 than in 2005 because there are no figures to compare the financial year year 2005/6 with 2004/5. However, in April 2006, the increase in child benefit was 2.6 per cent, roughly the rate of inflation for 2005. Hence the mother will have been neither better off or worse off in real terms.

Data question

1. Inflation is a sustained rise in prices over a time period. For instance, if average prices in an economy rise by 2 per cent over a year, then the annual rate of inflation is 2 per cent.

2. The data show five different ways in which inflation is measured in the UK. The RPI, the Retail Price Index, measures prices for the average household. The government uses the Expenditure and Food Survey to construct a picture of average household spending. It then gives weights to each item of expenditure. For instance, if food is 15 per cent of total expenditure whilst expenditure on household energy is 10 per cent, then increases in food prices will be given one and a half times the importance of increases in household energy when calculating the index. Not all items are included in the average. For instance, corsets and men's cardigans are no longer in the index because expenditure on these items is too small a percentage of the total. Sample prices are collected once a month and used to calculate the average price level in that month.

RPIX is the RPI minus expenditure on mortgage repayments. It is sometimes useful to exclude mortgage repayments because the government uses changes in interest rates to control the rate of inflation.

RPIY is the RPIX minus indirect taxes such as VAT. Again, the government may change the rate of indirect tax for economic reasons and it may be clearer to exclude them from the inflation figure to see the underlying rate of inflation.

The fourth measure of inflation shown in the data is the two pensioner household index. The RPI measures inflation for the average household. However, no such household exists in practice. It is sometimes useful to calculate averages for groups of households, such as one pensioner households, single parent households or two adult two children households. The two pensioner household index is an example of such a measure.

The fifth measure of inflation shown is the CPI. This is calculated from the same data as the RPI. However, unlike the RPI which excludes high income households and pensioner households which derive at least three quarters of their total income from pensions and benefits, the CPI includes all households. However, the CPI excludes various items of expenditure related to housing. The CPI also uses a different method of averaging than the RPI. The CPI uses a geometric mean whilst the RPI uses an arithmetic mean.

3.(a) A pensioner who retired in 1989 on a fixed private pension will have seen his income fall each year in real terms since that year. The inflation rate, as measured by the two person pensioner household index, fluctuated by between 7.5 per cent in 1990 and 1.1 per cent in 2000. His real overall income will not have fallen by as much as the inflation rate because part of his income, the state retirement pension, was index linked. The larger the proportion of his income that has come from his fixed company pension, the larger will have been the fall in his real income during the year.

(b) A UK 'technofreak' is likely to have suffered less from inflation as officially measured than others. This is because the Retail Price Index finds it difficult to cope with changes in technology. Cars, for instance, tend to improve technologically over time. Yet this is not reflected in the Retail Price Index. If a manufacturer increases prices by 5 per cent for an entry level car model but also slightly improves the specification, the RPI will simply record the 5 per cent increase. Technological improvements have been particularly noticeable with computers, where the power of computers has risen enormously over the past twenty years but this is not captured in official inflation statistics. Mobile phones were not even in the index in 1989.

(c) A food shopper in Brazil suffered greatly from inflation in the early 1990s. With hyperinflation at the time, shoppers were forced to spend their earnings immediately or risk seeing much of it decline in value. They found it difficult to know what a good price was for a product since it was continually going up. Hyperinflation made it difficult to shop around because so much information needed to be collected each time a purchase was made. 'Shoe leather' costs were therefore very high.

72 The quantity theory of money

Question 1

(a) £20 (MV=PT, so 200 x10 = P x 100).
(b) £40 (MV=PT, so 400 x 10 = P x 100).
(c) The price level, P, will fall to £26.66. (Since MV=PT, so 400 x 10 = P x 150).
(d)(i) 150 (the value of T, the level of money national income PT divided by the price level P).
(ii) £4 000 (P x T, £26.66 x 150).
(e) 15 (M/P = 400/26.66).

Question 2

(a) The velocity of circulation has not been constant over time. The velocity of circulation of M0 increased over the period 1970 to 1992 from 13 to 32 before falling to 29 in 2004. For M4, the velocity of circulation fell from 1.9 to 1.6 and then rose back to 2.0 in the 1970s, fell sharply in the 1980s to 1.2 and fell slightly in the 1990s and 2000s to 1.0.
(b) The rise in the velocity of circulation of M0 can be attributed to the rise in use of bank instruments and money substitutes in payment for goods and services. Instead of households receiving a wage in cash, and then spending the cash over the week, households tended to receive payment into a bank account. They then used cheques, debit cards and credit cards to make major purchases. Cash was obtained in relatively small amounts and spent quickly. Hence, as more and more people have acquired bank accounts and various types of cards over the past 30 years, the velocity of circulation of cash has risen. The stagnation of M0 from 1992 might indicate that the change in the way that people make payments has stabilised and that using cash to pay for goods is now a constant percentage of rising income.

Part of the fall in the velocity of circulation of M4 in the 1980s can be attributed to an increasing tendency to pay workers monthly rather than weekly. Workers then keep much larger amounts of money on average in bank and building society accounts to pay their household bills. Equally, the growing use of credit cards has led many households to keep money in bank and building society accounts and pay back the credit card company in full just once a month. This has the effect of slowing down the velocity of circulation of money.

Anther factor which might explain the fall in the velocity of circulation of M4 in the 1980s was the financial deregulation which took place at the time. Changes in the law and Bank of England regulations meant that banks and building society were able to increase their lending to customers. Households used this opportunity to borrow more money but did not necessary spend it all (i.e. they increased their holdings of money in relation to income). This then led to a fall in the velocity of circulation of M4.

The stagnation of the velocity of circulation of M4 since the early 1990s may indicate that these factors have worked their way through the economy and that markets are now in equilibrium with households and businesses holding a constant amount of money in relation to income.

Question 3

(a) In the short term, there may be no link between changes in the money supply and the other two variables, economic activity and inflation. This is because growth in the money supply may simply reflect a growth in the demand for money. In 2005, for example, growth in broad money was high at 12.6 per cent but the Bank of England said this was possibly due to non-bank financial organisations 'choosing to hold more of their wealth in cash or liquid deposits'. If this were the case, the money would not be spent and so there would be no change in economic activity or inflation.

On the other hand, the Bank of England suggested that an alternative explanation was these non-bank financial organisations were building up a stock of money to spend on assets in the future. If the money were spent on, say, shares or bonds, then the money would leak out into the economy. It would then get spent, raising the level of economic activity. Then demand-pull inflationary pressures could begin to appear, especially if the economy was near, at or above its full employment level.

In the long term, any prolonged period of monetary growth over and above the rate of growth of economic activity would be inflationary. The demand for money cannot increase indefinitely and so at least some of the growth in the money supply would leak into higher spending which would be likely to cause inflation.

Data question

1. Throughout the second half of the 1980s, the money supply measured by M4 grew by between 12 and 19 per cent per annum. Given that real GDP was only growing at between 2 and 6 per cent, this was a very high level of monetary growth. Some of it represented an increase in the demand for money. If the demand for money rises at any given level of GDP, then the velocity of circulation of money will fall. Throughout the period 1985-1992 shown in the data, the velocity of circulation of M4 did indeed fall. However, it did not fall far enough to prevent a build up of inflationary pressures in the economy. High monetary growth at first stimulated economic activity, pushing the annualised growth of real GDP up from 2 per cent in the first quarter of 1985 to 6 per cent by the first quarter of 1988. However, this level of growth in real GDP was unsustainable, pushing the economy out beyond its long run production possibility frontier and creating a large positive output gap. The result was a build up of inflationary demand-pull pressures. Inflation, after falling in 1986, began rising again in 1988 and eventually rose from 4 per cent in the first quarter of 1988 to over 10 per cent by the third quarter of 1990.

The rise in interest rates from May 1988 led to a fall in money supply growth from the first quarter of 1990. Its very rapid fall was reflected in a rapid fall in both the rate of inflation and the rate of economic growth.

The period 1985-1992 gives clear support, therefore, to the hypothesis that changes in the money supply affect inflation through the monetary transmission mechanism.

73 Taxation

Question 1

Excise duty on tobacco is a significant source of government revenue. It is a tax on volume sold rather than on value. Over time the real value of the tax per packet of cigarettes will decline if there is inflation in the economy (the process known as 'fiscal drag'). Hence, the government must increase duty in line with inflation if the real value of the tax is to be maintained.

However, the government may also have other objectives apart from raising revenue. It can be argued that tobacco is a demerit good, one which if left to the free market forces would be overconsumed. The higher the tax on cigarettes, the lower is likely to be the consumption and hence the lower the costs to society of tobacco abuse.

Another consideration might be the control of inflation. An increase in tobacco duties will feed through to an increase in the Retail Price Index. Hence a government may not increase tobacco duties as part of its short term anti-inflation policies.

Finally, the government may wish to take into account that excise duties are regressive, the burden of the tax falling disproportionately on the lower paid. A rise in tobacco duties will, all other things being equal, make the distribution of income in the economy less equal.

Question 2

(a) Income tax is a direct tax because it is levied directly on the individual earning income.
(b) National Insurance contributions are a direct tax because they are levied directly on workers and employers.
(c) Inheritance tax is a direct tax on the estate of individuals who die and leave money.
(d) Corporation tax is a direct tax, levied directly on companies on the level of their profits.
(e) Capital gains tax is a direct tax, levied directly on individuals who make a capital gain on transactions.
(f) The council tax is an indirect tax because it is levied on the value of property.
(g) VAT is an indirect tax because it is levied on most goods and services purchased in the UK.
(h) Excise duties are indirect because they are levied on a limited number of goods such as tobacco or petrol and the tax is removed indirectly from income only when it is spent.

Question 3

(a) According to Adam Smith's canons of taxation, there are advantages and disadvantages to collecting revenues for lighthouses, buoys and beacons through general taxation rather than through light dues.

With both taxes, the timing of collection and the amount to be paid is clear and certain. Equally with both taxes the means of payment and the time of the payment is convenient to the taxpayer.

However, the cost of collection of the £73 million used to pay for lighthouses is likely to be lower if collected through general taxation than if collected through light dues. This is because the cost of collecting an extra £73 million, for example by raising income tax rates, would be negligible since income tax is already collected. However, there must be some administrative cost in collecting the £73 million through light dues.

On the other hand, it could be argued that light dues are better at collecting taxes according to the ability to pay of the individual taxpayer. If taxes are collected through extra VAT, for example, this will hit both poor and rich. If light dues are used, they are collected from ships and shipping companies which are able to pay to absorb these costs. Because shipping benefits most from the service, it is more equitable that light dues are used rather than general taxation.

It could be argued that light dues are not compatible with foreign tax systems since in other EU countries apart from Ireland and Greece, lighthouses are paid for out of general taxation. It could also be argued that as a result, other EU ports such as Rotterdam or Hamburg have an unfair competitive advantage compared to UK ports. However, given that other port costs are lower in the UK, it is unlikely that there would be an inefficient transfer of resources away from the UK to the Continent as a result despite the predictions of the Independent Light Dues Forum.

Overall, given that there is a long history of light dues and there is no obvious evidence that they have distorted the allocation of resources to date, it would probably be better to retain them rather than switch to general tax funding.

Data question

1. The current income tax system has a number of different marginal rates of tax, increasing as the income of the taxpayer rises. So a taxpayer pays nothing on around the first £5 000 of income, and then pays 10 per cent, 22 per cent and finally 40 per cent on success tranches of income. This means that the average rate of income tax increases as income increases but never reaches 40 per cent because the first £X of income is taxed at 0 per cent, 10 per cent and then 22 per cent. This is illustrated in Table 79.4 in Economics. The average rate of income tax for the average £100 000 plus income earner is 33.4 per cent.

A flat tax has the same structure but there are only two rates of tax. One is 0 per cent because income earners would be able to earn £X free of tax. Then a second rate of tax would be applied to all subsequent income.

2. Those in favour of flat taxes argue that they would lead to greater efficiency. They argue that lower marginal rates of tax for high income earners would cause them to work harder and be more entrepreneurial. At the bottom end of the income range, those on low incomes would also gain if the tax allowance, the proportion of income on which no tax would be paid, were increased substantially. Again, this would encourage them to work harder and so they too could end up paying more in tax. Proponents of flat taxes point to high growth countries like Hong Kong and Estonia where flat taxes exist and argue that flat taxes were a key reason why these countries have grown fast. So the argument is that if it works for Estonia, it must work for the UK.

Those in favour of flat taxes also argue that tax revenues could increase compared to the present system. First, higher rate taxpayers would be less likely to evade and avoid paying taxes. Secondly, lower rates of marginal tax would 'make the UK more attractive to foreign investors'. They would then pay more tax. Again, pointing to the example of Estonia, it introduced a flat tax and was able to pay off its national debt. Therefore, this must be possible for the UK as well.

However, there are major problems with these arguments. One is that there would be very few gainers from a flat tax.

The vast majority of taxpayers would end up paying more in income tax. The incentive effect would be confined to a very small group at the very top of the income range and those taken out of paying tax at the bottom end. If lower taxes really do provide incentives to work, and there is little or no evidence that this is the case for the UK, then a flat tax would disincentivise most UK workers.

Another problem is that the details of the tax discussed by the Adam Smith Institute - a tax free free allowance of £12 000 followed by a flat rate of 22 per cent - would initially cut income tax revenues by one third, or £45 billion a year. It would be fanciful to think that the incentive effects of the tax would somehow increase income tax revenues over time by £45 billion. Inevitably, unless the government were to significantly increase its borrowing and therefore the National Debt, other taxes would have to rise.

As for equity, a flat tax would almost inevitably lead to a less equitable distribution of tax. As Table 4 in the student's book shows, with a flat tax rate at 22 per cent, every taxpayer gains, but the biggest gainers would those at the top end of the pay scale. For example, for those earning £7 500 - £9 999, they currently pay an average rate of tax of 5.1 per cent. Under the Adam Smith proposals they would pay no tax, saving them a maximum of £510 (£9 999 x 5.1 per cent). Those earning £20 000 - £29 999 currently pay an average tax rate of 15.4 per cent and would pay 11.4 per cent with this flat tax. This would save them a maximum of 4 per cent of tax or £1 200 (£29 999 x 4 per cent). But those earning more than £100 000 would see their average tax rate fall from 33.4 per cent to a maximum approaching 22 per cent. This is a minimum fall in tax of 11.4 per cent. Take someone earning £200 000, the saving in tax would be at least £22 800 (£200 000 x 11.4 per cent). Most would make modest savings but very high income earners would make very large savings in tax.

In practice, a flat tax rate would probably be set to bring in the same amount of revenue as at present. At this point, as Table 4 in the student's book shows, the average tax rate would have to be 18.2 per cent because this is the current average tax rate for all taxpayers. The marginal rate of tax for high income earners would inevitably fall from its current 40 per cent under a flat tax. The data suggests that it might fall to 30 per cent. This would mean that at least 28.5 million taxpayers would be worse off whilst possibly 2 million taxpayers would be better off. The 2 million would be individuals at the top end of the income distribution. The 28.5 million would be below them. The result would be a significant shift of the tax burden from the rich to the poor leading to greater inequality.

74 Government spending

Question 1

(a) Currently the transport infrastructure of the UK is barely sufficient to meet transport needs. Road congestion is estimated to cost companies £20 billion a year alone, with the cost to private motorists. Improved transport infrastructure might at least prevent this cost from increasing. There is also a danger with the current infrastructure that foreign firms will be deterred from investing in the UK. This would lower GDP and mean fewer jobs in the UK. Britain's international competitiveness could also suffer. Improved transport infrastructure might avert at least some of these problems.
(b) Revenues raised from road pricing would come from both the private motorist and from commercial vehicles. Already, congestion is costing companies an estimated £20 billion a year. To increase efficiency, therefore, it would seem sensible to spend at least part of the revenues on reducing congestion for commercial vehicles. However, private motorists also suffer costs from current congestion and therefore it would seem equitable to devote part of the resources raised to improving the road network for their use. Some would argue that revenues should be used not for the private motorist but for public transport as has happened with the Congestion Charge in London. Improving public transport might have greater social benefits than improving the road network for the private motorist because externalities such as emissions and noise pollution would be reduced.

Question 2

(a) Figure 1 in the student's book shows various models of state/private sector provision of goods and services. Kilmarnock Prison would be in box D where the state pays for the service but it is produced by the private sector.
(b) The Scottish Prison Service would have contracted out the prison on cost grounds. A private sector company should have been more productively efficient, producing at lower average cost, than a similar state run prison. The quality of service should have been the same because the contract should have laid down minimum standards of service expected. In practice, opponents to the privatisation of the prison have not complained about the price that Premier Custodial Group have charged. Instead they are complaining about the quality of service, such as letting inmates use drugs and alcohol.

Question 3

(a) The experience since 1979 suggests that contracting out a public service, or the threat of contracting it out, leads to greater productive efficiency. Public services have often proved to be supplied at too high a cost. The competitive process leads to lower costs for the same quality service. Allocative efficiency is unlikely to be changed if the contract specifications lay down that the contractor must provide the same quality service as before. Similarly, there should be no effect on equity.

However, allowing libraries to operate in a free market system is likely to have considerable effects on both allocative efficiency and equity. At present, library users consume to the point where their marginal private benefit is zero because the service is free at the point of use. However, there is a positive marginal cost to society of providing the service. Hence, it could be argued that allowing a private firm to charge a price per book loan or per borrower would bring about allocative efficiency because marginal private benefit and marginal private cost would then be equal.

On the other hand, public libraries were founded on the principle that there were significant positive externalities in providing them. Allocative inefficiency would then occur if marginal social benefit, including the positive externalities, was higher than the current marginal social cost of providing commercially run services. In fact, experience from other countries shows that, unless there is a free or heavily subsidised service, private firms do not find it profitable to provide such a service. Hence, except in major cities, there is no library provision.

There would also be a significant impact on equity. With fees being charged for use, there would be a redistribution of income from current taxpayers. If, in addition, most areas lost the use of their local library service, present users would be denied access to libraries. It could then be argued that there would be vertical inequity. The rich could still afford to use national library services or buy books. Most, including the elderly who tend to fall into low income groups, would no longer be able to use the service.

Data question

1. Since 1997, there have been substantial increases in NHS spending. After growing at between 2 and 3 per cent from 1997-98 to 1999-2000, growth and forecast growth in spending jumped to between 6 and 10 per cent per year between 2000-01 and 2007-08. The peak year for increase in spending was 2003-04.
2. Two types of equity can be distinguished. Horizontal equity is the identical treatment of identical individuals in identical situations. Vertical equity is the different treatment of people with different characteristics in order to promote greater equity.

There was some degree of horizontal equity in the NHS before the government made such large increases in spending. However, extra funding has helped improve the degree of horizontal equity. For example, waiting list times have fallen and more operations have been carried out. Before 2000, patients would wait different times to be seen and have an operation. Because waiting lists have fallen substantially, the difference in waiting times between patients has narrowed. Equally, before the increases in spending, the UK lagged behind other European countries in the proportion of GDP devoted to health spending. By 2007-08, this difference in funding had been eliminated.

Vertical equity may also have improved. Extra resources are being devoted for example to caring for the elderly, a particularly expensive and growing area for the NHS. The elderly have far more needs than those, for example, aged 20-30. New drugs coming onto the market are also being funded, allowing either better treatment for some individuals or providing new therapies for diseases which before doctors found hard to treat.

Efficiency in the NHS can be measured by using productivity figures comparing inputs and outputs. The data states that the Office for National Statistics (ONS) has found that productivity in the NHS has been falling over time. This is despite policies such as the introduction of competition in the service and the use of the private sector to compete with the public sector. However, every extra £1 spent has yielded fewer and fewer services. ONS admits that its measures are too crude because they fail to capture increases in the quality of service. Higher spending has allowed the quality of services to improve considerably. For example, productivity calculations can't capture falls in waiting lists. Yet long waiting lists were a matter of grave concern to patients at the start of the 2000s.

Ultimately, the government at the start of the 2000s wanted to bring about a step change both in the volume of services and the quality of the service provided. There is general agreement that this has happened. However, some argue that the government has not had value for money for the huge sums poured into the NHS since the early 2000s and that the service is more inefficient than before. Others argue that the money has not gone into the right areas and that equity has not improved.

3. Those who already use private health care, which tends to be the relatively well off, would like to see more private health care being used, for example by cutting taxes and cutting the spending on the NHS. However, cuts in taxes are likely disproportionally to benefit the better off. Those in lower income brackets would then find it hard to afford top-up care.

The NHS is increasing its use of private health care providers anyway. It is putting contracts for work out to the private sector in order to bring down costs or cut waiting lists. This is arguably a better use of resources than giving money to individuals who would not get the buying economies of scale enjoyed by the NHS.

It could also be argued that health spending is a merit good. If left to free market forces, it would be underconsumed. One reason for this is information failure. Spending on health is more costly for the elderly who tend to have low incomes. Under the present system, there is a transfer of resources from those of working age who pay most tax but tend to be relatively healthy compared to old people. It is a form of insurance organised by the state. However, if left more to free market forces, people of working age would be unlikely to set aside enough in savings to pay for their treatment in old age. Those of working age do not have sufficient information about old age to make rational choices about saving. Lowering taxes and spending on the NHS to allow taxpayers to top-up private health care would lead to market failure.

On the other hand, it is argued that individuals know best about how to spend their money. Forcing individuals to buy certain goods and services through the tax system is bound to lead to a loss of welfare.

It can also be argued that the NHS is inefficient at providing health care. Cutting back spending to allow taxpayers to buy more private health care would lead to an increase in the quantity of more efficient private sector services. However, there is no evidence that private health care is more efficient than public health care provision. The United States, with the largest health care system in the world, spends over half as much again of its GDP on health services than the European average but is frequently criticised for its high costs.

75 Fiscal policy and demand management

Question 1

An automatic stabiliser is an economic mechanism which reduces the impact of changes in the economy on national income. Fiscal stabilisers occur where spending and tax revenues automatically change to reduce the magnitude of changes in national income. Active fiscal policy is the deliberate manipulation of government expenditure and taxes to influence the economy.

(a) This new higher band is an example of active fiscal policy because it is designed to reduce the quantity demanded of very high petrol consumption cars.

(b) This is an automatic stabiliser because the active fiscal policy measures of changes in tax rates have been stripped out from the increase.

(c) This is active policy designed to improve the quality of education.

(d) This is an automatic stabiliser because it arises from changes in a component of aggregate demand.

Question 2

(a) Tax cuts without a corresponding cut in government spending will increase aggregate demand in the economy. This could destabilise the economy if the output gap were zero or positive. Tax cuts would then lead to an an unsustainable boom in the economy with increased inflationary pressures and an unsustainable fall in unemployment. The current account balance would also be likely to deteriorate. As with any unsustainable boom, the economy would quickly go into recession, producing a boom and bust cycle.

(b) Cutting both taxes and government spending in theory should have little impact on aggregate demand. Therefore it should have no effect on aggregate demand and should not lead to an overheated economy. It can be argued that, in the short term, it would actually lead to aggregate demand falling. If government spending is cut by £10 billion, for example, aggregate demand will fall by £10 billion. However, if income tax were cut at the same time by £10 billion, households would not necessarily spend all that £10 billion initially. Households might decide to save part of that £10 billion. This would mean that consumption would not rise by the £10 billion to counter the £10 billion fall in government spending. The result would be a fall in aggregate demand. It could be argued that this is a problem of time lags. There will be a different impact on aggregate demand depending on what taxes are cut and the exact timing of the reactions of taxpayers to these cuts.

Question 3

(a) What the graph shows is that the government has been too optimistic about the budget surplus or deficit in its forecasts since the 2002 budget. For example, in its 2002 budget, it forecasted a budget surplus of nearly £10 billion for 2006-07. In its 2003 budget, it had revised this down to £5 billion. By the 2006 budget, the forecast for 2006-2007 was a deficit of £7.5 billion.

(b) The government has steadily revised downwards its forecasts for public borrowing. Public borrowing is broadly government spending minus taxation. One explanation for the downward forecasts is that the government has engaged in active fiscal policy, raising public spending. Another is that economic growth has been slower than forecast. This reduces forecast levels of aggregate demand and incomes, which in turn means that tax revenues will be lower because of the workings of automatic stabilisers.

(c) The reason why the author is not worried is because the actual outcome is likely to be little different from the forecast. Inevitably, forecasts of variables such as public borrowing are wrong because public borrowing is the difference between two very large numbers, government spending and government receipts including taxes. For the forecast to be inaccurate by a few billion pounds is well within margins of error. Small variations are therefore nothing to be concerned about.

Question 4

(a) The data compare how three other countries have performed relative to the UK between 1995 and 2004. Productivity in the UK is likely to have increased over the period. The data shows whether these three countries have increased their productivity more than or less than that of the UK.

Germany's productivity has increased at a slower pace compared to the UK. In 1995, productivity was 11 per cent higher than that of the UK. By 2004, it was the same. The same falling trend of productivity compared to the UK has been experienced by France over the period. In 1995, productivity was 22 per cent above the UK. By 2004, this was only 11 per cent. For the USA, the picture is more complicated with productivity relative to the UK fluctuating between 1995 and 2004. However, in 1995, US productivity was 30 per cent higher compared to the UK but by 2004, it was only 28 per cent higher.

(b) Extra funding for capital expenditure in school buildings will play a small but important role in supporting growth in the supply side of the economy. In terms of the five 'key drivers of productivity', it will clearly increase the stock of physical capital of the economy. In the long term, it will help to raise skills levels by contributing to better education of children. It could be argued to support science and innovation through science education and through enterprise education. More generally, a better educated workforce could be one which is more entrepreneurial and one which increases the ability of the economy to adopt innovation. Better school buildings, of course, might do none of these things. However, it is equally true that poor school buildings make it more difficult to deliver education because facilities, such as for science education, can be out of date; and time spent in school can be less efficiently used if buildings are ill suited to the needs of 21st century education.

Data question

1. An automatic stabiliser is an economic mechanism which reduces the impact of changes in the economy on national income. Fiscal stabilisers occur where spending and tax revenues automatically change to reduce the magnitude of changes in national income. Active fiscal policy is the deliberate manipulation of government expenditure and taxes to influence the economy.

Figure 8 in the student's book shows government estimates of how automatic stabilisers and active fiscal policy has combined to help reduce fluctuation in the economy. When the output gap, the difference between actual GDP and trend

GDP, was positive, as between 2001-2002 and 2003-2004, both automatic stabilisers and active fiscal policy helped reduce the level of GDP from what it might otherwise have been. When the output gap was negative, between 2002-03 and projected 2008-09, automatic stabilisers and active fiscal policy were for the most part increasing GDP from what it would otherwise have been.

2. The government's golden rule states that 'over the economic cycle, the government will borrow only to invest and to fund current spending'. The sustainable investment rule states that 'public sector net debt as a proportion of GDP will be held over the economic cycle at a stable and prudent level; other things being equal, net debt will be maintained below 40 per cent of GDP over the economic cycle'.

These two rules are important for the long term economic stability of the UK. Take a scenario where the government consistently borrows more for current expenditure than it receives. Over time, the National Debt will then increase. At some point, this increase becomes unsustainable. The government is no longer able to afford to make debt repayments and has to resort to one of two ways of reducing or eliminating the debt. One is to generate hyperinflation to reduce the real value of the debt. The other is to default on the debt. Both routes have been tried by countries over the past two hundred years and both routes create chaos in the economy, reducing their ability to grow over time.

The other scenario is that the government consistently receives more than it spends and thus provides a deflationary impact on the economy. Such measures can then lead to the economy having a permanent negative output gap. Not only is unemployment much higher than it need be, but such an output gap will discourage investment and so reduce the long run growth potential of the economy.

Relatively small deviations from the golden rule are unimportant from an economic viewpoint. If the government has borrowed an extra 1 per cent of GDP over the trade cycle, it will make no difference to the long run performance of the economy. Equally, whether 40 per cent is the right ratio of the national debt to GDP is debatable. Most EU countries have debt ratios larger than this. However, 40 per cent should bring about long run macroeconomic stability and so is a not unreasonable target to set.

3. Arguably, fiscal policy has been 'prudent' since 1997 and has helped create a healthy economy. The economy has grown in each successive quarter since 1997, which contrasts very strongly with the boom and bust business cycles of the 1970s, 1980s and early 1990s. Volatility in GDP has also been lower than in most other industrialised economies.

Fiscal policy has also been used in conjunction with monetary policy to reduce output fluctuations. Monetary policy and fiscal policy have worked together to deliver both low inflation and strong growth.

Macroeconomic stability helps create the conditions for high growth. 'Stability allows businesses, individuals and the government to plan more effectively for the long term, improving the quality and quantity of investment in physical and human capital and helping to raise productivity.' Economic theory would suggest that instability makes it more difficult for businesses to plan output and investment. In a highly volatile economy, some businesses may be cautious and afraid that there will be a sudden unexpected downturn in the economy. They then may abandon investment projects. Equally, businesses may invest only to find that there is a slump in the economy and their production falls rather than rises. This capital expenditure may then be wasted. Human capital too may deteriorate in a slump in the economy. Workers may lose their work skills by being unemployed for long periods of time. In contrast, macroeconomic stability creates a climate of relative certainty where economic actors can plan and have some reasonable expectation that those plans will turn into reality. This encourages investment.

It can be argued, then, that fiscal policy since 1997 has been successful. On the other hand, it could be argued that the government has not faced the difficult economic conditions that occurred in the 1970s and 1980s. The golden rule and the sustainable investment rule have not been put to the test to see whether they would stand up to very difficult economic conditions. Whether the monetary turmoil of 2008 will show that the government has deceived itself into thinking that it has been a successful manager of the economy remains to be seen.

76 Supply side policy issues

Question 1

(a) Figure 1 in the student's book shows the productivity of the US, French and German economies relative to that of the UK. Over the period, output per hour worked rose 36 per cent in the UK. Output per hour worked in the other three economies rose but by less than 36 per cent since the relative differential between them and the UK fell over the period. However, given that the rank order between the countries was the same at the end of the period as at the start, Figure 1 would indicate that all three countries had similar growth rates in labour productivity over the period.

(b) Increasing the level of education and skills in the workforce is likely to raise their productivity. A person educated to degree level is likely to be able to produce more per hour in monetary terms than someone with no qualifications. A skilled electrician is likely to be able to produce more per hour in monetary terms than an unskilled building labourer.

Investment in infrastructure increases the amount of capital per worker in the economy. This is likely to raise average GDP per hour worked. For example, building a new motorway will increase the productivity of the transport sector. Building a new school will, in the long term, contribute to better educational skills on the part of the workforce, increasing labour productivity.

Tax and regulations affect incentives. Poorly targeted taxes can reduce the willingness of people to work or firms to set up, expand and make profits. Too much regulation stifles the ability of firms to produce and innovate. It increases their costs and makes them less productive.

Competition and market frameworks are important because competition spurs on firms to increase their productivity. In a competitive market, firms which fail to compete effectively could be forced to leave the market. Where there is little or no competition, a vital incentive to maximise productivity is missing. Monopolists, for example, can be 'lazy' and inefficient.

Public sector efficiency is important too. If the public sector is inefficient, then average productivity in the UK will be lower than it would otherwise have been. Public sector inefficiency can also impact on the private sector. For example, an inefficient public sector will mean that taxes will have to be higher to pay for the inefficiency. Higher taxes might discourage private sector workers and firms from working, investing and innovating. This would then lower private sector productivity.

Question 2

(a) According to the data, the elasticity of supply of labour for women is higher than that for men. It argues that 'men's labour supply is more rigid' in contrast to women who are 'responsive to increase(s) in after-tax wages'. This can be shown in Figure 1. The supply of male workers is wage inelastic, shown by the fact that the supply curve would hit the horizontal axis if fully drawn. The supply of female workers is wage elastic, shown by the fact that the supply curve would cut the vertical axis if fully drawn.

The elasticity of supply of men differs from that of women because men traditionally have few alternatives to paid work. It has arguably in the past been socially acceptable for women not to work, for example, because they are bringing up children or simply running the home.

Figure 1

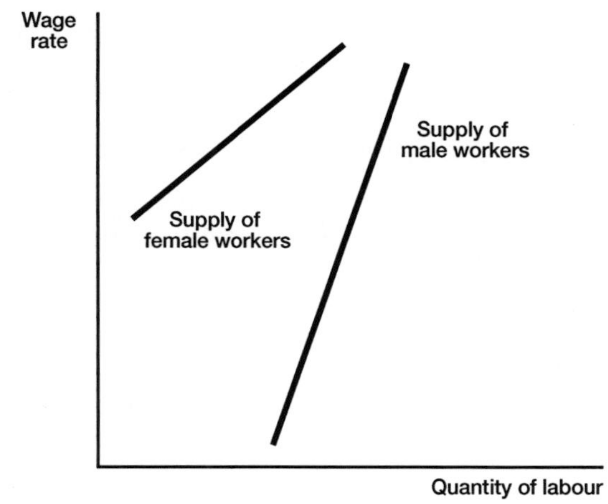

(b) Assume that the standard income tax rate for men were 25 per cent but only 15 per cent for women. According to the data, men would work roughly the same hours whether their income tax rate were 25 per cent or 15 per cent. Men's labour supply is more rigid, and so an increase in taxes would not reduce their labour supply by much, if at all.' In contrast, women are influenced in the number of hours they work by their marginal tax rate. Lowering tax rates would increase the participation rate of women i.e. the number of women in the workforce. If the tax rate were 25 per cent, fewer women would go out to work, or more would choose to work part-time rather than full-time compared to a situation where the income tax rate were 15 per cent. Therefore, increasing the tax rate for men and reducing it for women would see hardly any men drop out of the labour force but a significant number of women join the labour force. The supply of labour would therefore increase, making this a successful supply side policy.

Question 3

(a) Immigration can reduce inflation and increase economic growth because it increases the supply of labour to the economy. In Figure 2, increased immigration has shifted the long run supply curve of the economy from $LRAS_1$ to $LRAS_2$. This shift shows economic growth because real output is LM higher than it would have been without the immigration. It has also reduced prices in the economy form ON to OP. In a dynamic economy where inflation is positive, immigration reduces inflation from what it would otherwise have been.

Figure 2

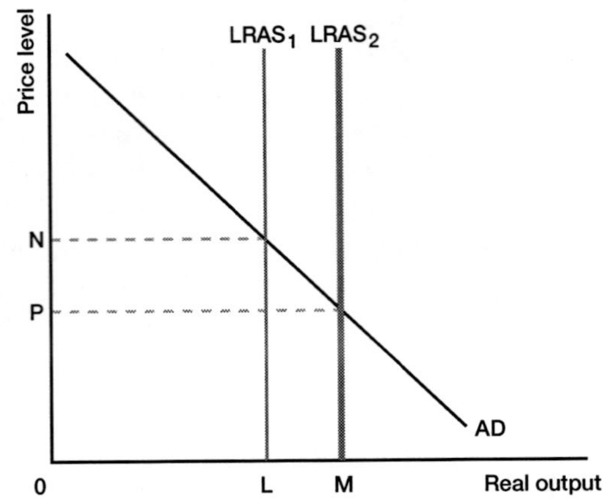

(b) Supply side policies which increased flows of immigrants into the UK will increase the supply potential of the economy. More workers in the economy means that more can be produced. However, they will not necessarily increase labour productivity. Assume there are 10 workers in the economy and total output is £100. Then output per worker is £10. If an extra immigrant worker is added to the working population and total output increases to £10.50, then the supply potential of the economy has risen by £0.50 but output per worker has fallen to £9.55. If the output of the average immigrant worker is below that of the existing workforce, labour productivity will fall. It would equally fall if the immigrant workers created an equal amount of unemployment and output per worker were defined as output per worker employed or unemployed. For labour productivity to rise, either immigrant workers would have to have higher average productivity than the original workforce. Or they would have to release workers from the existing labour force to go into higher than average productivity jobs.

Data question

Note: in the first impression of Economics 5th edition there is a misprint. This has been corrected in reprints. Question 1 should refer to Figure 6.

1. Figure 6 shows the UK, and therefore Northern Ireland, has the lowest corporate tax rate amongst the countries shown apart from the Republic of Ireland. At almost 25 per cent in 2005, this compares to 25 per cent for France, 28 per cent for Canada, 29 per cent for the USA and 32 per cent for Japan and Germany. The Republic of Ireland, in contrast, had an effective average corporate tax rate of 11 per cent.

2. The Executive of Northern Ireland certainly see lowering corporate tax rates as a supply side policy. They would argue that lowering corporate tax rates in Northern Ireland will increase the amount of investment in the province. It would increase incentives for UK, including Northern Ireland, firms to increase their investment. It would also attract foreign investment. For Northern Ireland, a lower corporate tax rate might, for example, attract new investment from the Republic of Ireland or might prevent investment going south of the border and be retained in Northern Ireland.

3. The Northern Ireland Executive and entrepreneurs like Sir Anthony O'Reilly believe that lowering corporation tax rates in the province would be a highly effective supply side policy. Figure 7 shows that about 50 per cent of international business executives when surveyed agreed. However, there were a number of other factors which they rated as being even more important when considering investment decisions. Transport and infrastructure, labour costs, potential productivity increases, telecoms infrastructure and the legal and regulatory environment were all more important. This would suggest that lowering corporation tax rates is not likely to be the most effective supply side policy change that the government could make. More effective would be measures to improve transport and infrastructure within the province perhaps by direct investment or providing incentives for the private sector to invest. Cutting red tape, or lowering taxes on the employment of workers, could prove more effective.

However, Figure 7 suggests that cutting corporate tax rates would be more effective than other supply side measures such as improving access to local financial investors, availability of land and support from public authorities.

77 Money, its supply and demand

Question 1

(a) All of these items in the two photographs are to some extent a store of value and a standard for deferred payment. The ten pound note, the cheque, the shares and the gold bar are most obviously so. But the painting, if an original, and the collector's set of stamps can act as a store of wealth too. All suffer from the fact that they will change in value over time. The five pound note and the cheque will decline in real value due to inflation. The other assets could go up in value or equally they could go down, depending upon market demand and supply for that asset in the future. These fluctuations in price also make these assets a poor unit of account.

Only the bank note and the cheque could be considered a medium of exchange in the UK today. It would not be possible to buy groceries in a supermarket with an oil painting or gold bullion, for instance.

In conclusion, only the bank note and the cheque possess the four functions of money to any great extent although they are not as good a store of value as some of the other items. The others cannot be said to be money, if only because they are such a poor medium of exchange.

Question 2

(a) Only the bank note and to some extent the cheque would be widely accepted as a means of payment for goods and services. All the assets apart are portable. There is no indication on the photograph of the size of the ingot, but if it were in scale with, for instance, the ten pound note, it would be far too heavy to carry around to use for everyday transactions. All of the assets are to some extent durable over time and should survive if used infrequently for a number of years. The gold bullion is perhaps the most durable of the assets. The painting is not divisible, whilst the other assets are to some extent. For instance, the ten pound note can be divided into 10 pound coins, whilst the gold ingot could be split into two. All are limited in supply with the possible exception of the painting. If it is a reproduction, then any number can be produced if it were to act as money. Finally, the cheque and the share certificate would be relatively easy to forge. The other assets would be more difficult to forge, although if the painting were a reproduction, there would be little point in forgery!

Question 3

(a) Emma Higgins possesses £20 in cash. In addition, she has £200 in her bank account to which she can gain access through her cheque book. Therefore she has at least £220 in money.

The deposit in her building society account too could be seen as money. It is likely to be withdrawable on demand and therefore can be converted immediately into cash. Hence, it could be argued that she has £470 in money.

Another of her assets, according to the data, is a £50 000 stake in her house. However, her house is not money in that it is not a medium of exchange at all. Equally, the £50 worth of goods she bought cannot be used as a medium of exchange and therefore cannot be regarded as money.

Her mortgage, her overdraft facility and her credit card limit are examples of credit and are not assets at all. Therefore they could not be included in her money holdings.

Question 4

(a) (i) The opportunity cost for Kim Yip of holding £250 in cash is probably the interest forgone on holding money in a building society account. Building society account deposits are easily accessible and maintain their nominal value over time. Hence building society deposits are a better substitute for cash than, say, shares where neither of these is the case.

(ii) The opportunity cost of holding British Telecom shares is probably the dividends and capital gains to be made from holding other shares. Alternatively, Kim Yip could hold more government bonds, in which case he is forgoing the benefit of a market rate of interest of 7 per cent.

(iii) The opportunity cost of owning a £70 000 house is perhaps less obvious than with financial assets like cash or shares. The financial capital tied up in the house is only £30 000 because he has a £40 000 mortgage. He would also need to rent somewhere to live if he did not own his own house, and the value of the rent would have to be deducted from any income he gained from the £30 000. For instance, he could put his £30 000 in government bonds earning 7 per cent. The opportunity cost, each year, would then be £2 100 (7 per cent of £30 000) minus his rent. Alternatively, he might choose to spend it all. The opportunity cost would then be the benefits gained from the expenditure minus the rent he would have to pay.

(b) The demand for money curve is downward sloping. As interest rates rise the demand for money falls, as it becomes more attractive to exchange money for an interest bearing asset. Therefore Kim is more likely to use the £250 cash to purchase government bonds. Kim might also compare the rate of return on his other assets and decide whether to sell these assets and use the cash to invest in government bonds. So, for example, he may decide that the new interest rate of 10 per cent on government bonds is more attractive than the 3 per cent dividend on British Telecom shares.

Data question

Prospects in the UK market for money

Money and money substitutes

For some time, the death of money has been predicted. Money substitutes, like credit cards, will take the place of money in transactions. Assets which are classified as money must fulfil four functions to some degree. They must act as a medium of exchange, readily acceptable as payment for goods and services. They must be a unit of account. This means that money acts as a measure of value. If a hamburger costs £3 and a theatre ticket costs £30, then 10 hamburgers have the same value as one theatre ticket. They must act as a store of value, so that if money is kept as money it will be valuable tomorrow and not just today. They must finally act as a standard for deferred payment. They must be able to transfer debt from one time period to another.

Money substitutes, in contrast, fulfil some but not all of these functions. Characteristically they act as a medium of exchange but, for instance, are not a store of value. A credit card is acceptable in a wide range of transactions. However, it cannot be a store of value because by the very nature of a credit card it is a way of borrowing money that an individual does not possess.

The changing market

The demand for notes and coins continues to rise. In 1995 in the UK, there were £21 billion in circulation. By 2007, this had more than doubled to £48 billion.

However, the number of transactions using cash has been in decline since 2000 whilst the number of non-cash transactions has been rising. Money substitutes such as automated payments, credit and charge cards and debit cards all saw increases in numbers of transactions exceeding 100 per cent between 1995 and 2005. Only cheques have seen a fall in their usage as other forms of money substitutes have become more popular.

The future

The future for a manufacturer of bank notes and plastic cards is bright. There is a growing demand for bank notes and plastic cards as consumer spending increases. The largest increases are likely to be in demand for credit cards and debit cards. Whilst we are a long way from a cashless society, the increase in the proportion of transactions using cards has in no way come to an end. It can be expected that more individuals will have and use cards in the future.

This has implications for the money supply. If more transactions are carried out using credit cards rather than cash or drawings from bank or building society accounts, the need to keep money in cash or in accounts will diminish. Households may decide instead to put their money into non-monetary financial assets such as shares. Hence, the growth in the use of money substitutes is likely to lead to lower growth in the money supply than would otherwise have been the case.

78 The rate of interest

Question 1

Figure 1

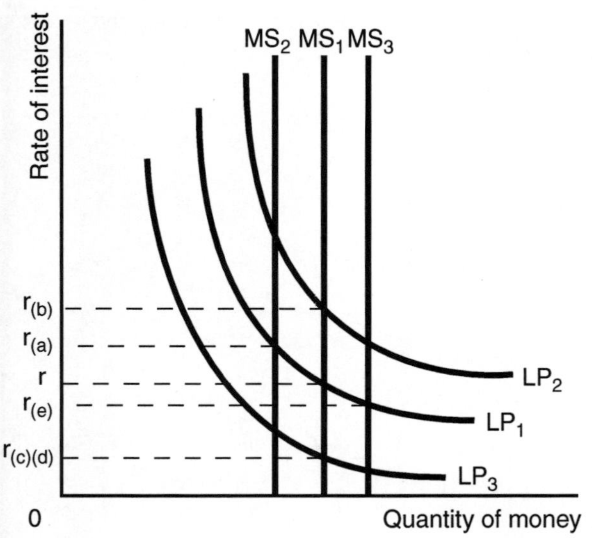

Question 2

(a) The risk of default is one major factor which determines interest rates. Banks are more likely to go bankrupt than the UK government. Hence, interbank rates of interest for money loaned for one year at 6.04-5.96% are slightly higher than the equivalent UK government gilt edged stock rates at 5.3%. Equally, mortgage interest rates of 6.49% are lower than unsecured personal loans of 10.0%. If a borrower defaults on a mortgage, the lender can repossess and then sell the property which has been given as security. The same is not true for an unsecured loan.

The length of loan is another aspect of risk. The longer the loan, the more likely it is that there will be a default on the loan, or interest rates may change, altering the market value of the security. Hence the longer the loan the higher should be the rate of interest. In the interbank market, for instance, the interest rate was 5.8-5.72% for overnight money, 5.95-5.87% for one month and was 6.04-5.96% for one year.

Administrative costs are another factor in differentiating interest rates. The higher the cost of administering a loan, the higher the rate of interest is likely to be on a loan. For instance, it costs far more to administer a Barclaycard Platinum credit card or Miss Selfridge Account Card than an authorised overdraft per pound borrowed. Hence the rate of interest on a credit or store card is higher than on an authorised overdraft.

Some differences in interest rates occur simply because one lender wants to earn a higher profit than another. For example, it could be that the issuers of the Miss Selfridge Account Card seek higher profits than the issuers of the Barclaycard Platinum credit card, given that the interest rate on the former is 29.9% whilst on the latter it is only 14.9%.

Question 3

(a) Nominal interest rates are likely to be higher, the higher the rate of inflation in an economy. Compare two countries, both with nominal interest rates of 5 per cent, but one with zero inflation and the other with 20 per cent inflation. In the first, savers are able to make a real return of 5 per cent by saving. In the other, they are losing 15 per cent per year. Savers are unlikely to carry on saving in the long term if they are continually losing money. In the higher inflation economy, savings will fall. On the other hand, there will be a large demand for borrowed funds because borrowers will see the value of their borrowing fall by 15 per cent each year. Demand for borrowed funds will exceed the supply of savings. Hence interest rates will rise. If there is equilibrium in the zero inflation economy between savings and borrowing, it would indicate that nominal interest rates would have to rise to 25 per cent in the high inflation economy to return the money markets to equilibrium.
(b) The data in Figure 6 in the student's book would give considerable support to this hypothesis. There is a clear positive correlation between inflation rates and interest rates for all three periods shown. As inflation increases, so too do nominal interest rates.

Data question

1. (a) The real rate of interest is the difference between the nominal interest rate and the inflation rate. For instance, if interest rates were 10 per cent and the rate of inflation were 4 per cent, then the real rate of interest would be 6 per cent.
(b) Real interest rates were positive from 1981 to 2006 with interest rates above inflation. In 1980, all three measures of the rate of interest were below the inflation rate and so real interest rates were negative.
2. There is a variety of factors which might account for why some interest rates are higher than others. One is risk of default. The government is the safest borrower in the UK. A bank or building society is more likely to default. Hence, short term government borrowing, shown in the data by the Treasury Bill yield, tends to offer a lower rate of interest than short term borrowing by banks or building societies, shown by bank base rates, all other things being equal.

Another factor is the length of time money is borrowed. The data show two interest rates on government borrowing. The government securities data is for 20 year borrowing, whilst the Treasury Bill data is for 3 month borrowing. In theory, the longer money is borrowed, the higher should be the rate of interest. This is because lending money long term is less flexible than lending short term. It also exposes lenders to greater capital risks if they are able to sell their loan to another party. For most of the period 1980-2006, long term government interest rates were higher than short term interest rates. The main exceptions were the period 1988-91 and 2005-2006 when markets judged that short term rates would fall quickly and allowed short term rates to be above long term rates as a consequence.

A third factor determining interest rates is administrative cost. The higher the administrative cost associated with the loan, the higher the rate of interest is likely to be. The data does not provide evidence which would illustrate this. It would be necessary to compare, say, credit card interest rates with interest rates on large bank loans.

A fourth factor is expectations of future changes in interest rates. British government securities are less volatile than bank base rates because of this factor. When short term interest rates are very high, markets expect interest rates to fall in the future. Hence, this expectation is built into the yield on long term loans. Equally, when short term interest rates are very low, markets expect interest rates to rise and this tends to lead to longer term interest rates being above short term interest rates. As already explained, this expectations factor can be seen during the period 1988 to 1991.

All these factors ultimately affect the demand and supply of funds in each money market and it is the interaction of demand and supply which determines the rate of interest in each market.

3. Economic theory would suggest that higher inflation would be reflected in higher interest rates. If inflation is high and interest rates low, real rates of interest will be negative. This will discourage saving but encourage borrowing, leading to disequilibrium in the market. Only when real interest rates are positive is equilibrium is likely to be restored. The period 1980 to 1999 would suggest that economic theory is correct. The period started off with high inflation rates and high interest rates. When inflation subsequently fell, so too did interest rates. The rise in inflation in the late 1980s coincided with a rise in interest rates whilst the fall in inflation in the 1990s saw a fall in interest rates.

79 The operation and limitations of monetary policy

Question 1

(a) The Bank of England might have cut interest rates in November 2005 because inflationary pressures seemed low whilst there was a risk that economic growth might falter.

Economic growth might fall below the Bank of England's forecast because of weakening consumption expenditure. This is the most important component of aggregate demand. Consumption is weakening partly for three reasons. High oil prices were forcing consumers to spend more on motoring but this was probably denting consumer confidence about the ability of households to maintain their spending. There was increasing slack in the labour market, which probably meant that unemployment was rising, hitting both actual consumption and consumer confidence. Finally high levels of existing household debt meant that households could be unwilling to take on more debt particularly to buy consumer durables. Falling consumption growth would also mean that saving would rise.

If the rise in aggregate demand is weakening, this will reduce demand-pull inflationary pressures in the economy. Hence, despite cost-push pressures from higher oil prices, the outlook for inflation was good and the Bank of England could cut interest rates to give a mild boost to spending.

Question 2

(a) Economic theory would suggest that there is an inverse link between the rate of interest and the money supply. In Figure 1, the rate of interest is initially r_1. In equilibrium, the money supply must therefore be M_1. If the rate of interest rises to r_2, there will be a movement back up the demand for money curve. The new equilibrium level of the money supply must be M_2. Hence a rise in interest rates leads to a fall in the money supply.

In practice, there may be lags between changes in interest rates and changes in a particular measure of the money supply such as M4. In Figure 2 in the student's book, the rise in interest rates from mid-1988 to 1989 could be argued to have led to the fall in the rate of growth of the money supply from the beginning of 1990. Equally the cuts in interest rates from the end of 1990 would eventually have led to the fall in the rate of growth of the money supply bottoming out in 1992 or 1993.

Figure 1

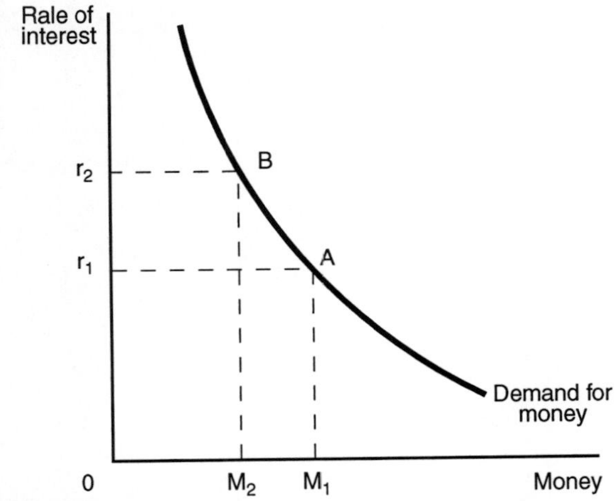

Question 3

(a) A Chancellor cannot simultaneously control the level of the money supply, the rate of interest and the exchange rate. He or she can only control one of these three and then has to allow the other two to find their own level.

In 1987, Nigel Lawson found that he could not control both the exchange rate and the rate of interest. Free market forces were driving the exchange rate upwards, which he considered undesirable. To reduce the value of the pound, he was forced to reduce interest rates. A reduction in interest rates reduces the attractiveness of London as a centre to place funds. The relative rate of return in, say, Frankfurt or New York will now be higher. Hence, British investors will move some of their funds abroad, increasing the supply of pounds onto the foreign exchange markets, whilst foreign investors will move less of their funds into the UK, thus reducing the demand for pounds. An increase in supply and a fall in demand for pounds will lower its price. The converse is also true, as Nigel Lawson found in 1989. To prevent a fall in the exchange rate, the Chancellor can increase interest rates.

Changes in the rate of interest will have a direct effect on the growth of the money supply. A rise in interest rates will, assuming that the liquidity preference schedule remains the same, have to be associated with a fall in the money supply. Therefore, Nigel Lawson had to increase interest rates in 1988 to 'brake the rise in the money supply'.

There is also a direct link between changes in the money supply and the exchange rate, although this is not illustrated in the passage. Between 1987 and 1989, the exchange rate of the pound was determined primarily by free market forces. However, between 1990 and 1992 the UK was a member of the ERM, the Exchange Rate Mechanism of the European Monetary System. The pound was fixed in value against other currencies in the ERM. The Bank of England pegged the value of the pound on a day to day basis by buying and selling currency. When the Bank of England buys or sells pounds, this has a direct impact on the money supply. Purchases of pounds (selling foreign currency) will reduce the money supply and raise the exchange rate, whilst sale of pounds (to purchase foreign currency) will increase the money supply but lead to a fall in the exchange rate.

Question 4

(a) (i) According to the revised series, the rate of growth of average earnings was falling from a peak of 5.3 per cent at the start of the year to 4.2 per cent at the end of the year.

(ii) The Bank of England should have cut interest rates on this evidence because growth in average earnings is a key indicator of growth in aggregate demand. If wages are rising fast, it is likely that labour markets are overheating due to excess demand in goods markets. If wage increases are slowing, then so too are inflationary pressures.

(b) (i) The proposed new series in 1997 showed wage rises fairly constant at the start of the year and then rising from less than 4 per cent to over 5.5 per cent by the end of the year. This was the opposite of what the revised series showed.

(ii) If the Bank of England had used the proposed new series, it would have been under pressure to increase interest rates.

The upward movement in increases in wage rates would have been a sign that the economy was overheating and therefore growth in aggregate demand needed to be curbed.

Data question

1. A rise in interest rates is likely to lead to a fall in GDP for a number of reasons. The rise in interest rates leads to a number of changes in money markets. Banks and building societies will put up their interest rates on loans and mortgages. Rising interest rates tend to have a downward effect on the price of assets such as stocks, shares and houses, reducing consumer wealth. Rising interest rates also hits confidence in the future of the economy making consumers and firms more cautious. This then feeds through into spending in the real economy.

The rise in interest rates will lower household consumption and investment by firms. Households often buy consumer durables on credit. Raising interest rates means that repayments become more expensive and this discourages households from taking on further debt. For firms, if interest rates rise, the cost of borrowing for investment projects rises too and profitability falls. This reduces the amount firms are willing to spend on investment.

Reduced asset prices will make households and firms less wealthy. They will then spend less. Equally, the fall in confidence in the economy will hit spending.

A rise in interest rates is also likely to increase the value of the pound because the demand for pounds from foreigners to invest in the UK rises, whilst the supply of pounds falls from UK investors who now prefer to keep their money at home. A rise in the value of the pound makes exports more expensive to foreigners and imports cheaper for UK buyers. As a result exports fall and imports rise from what they would otherwise be.

A fall in consumption, investment and exports with imports rising leads to fall in aggregate demand. This is turn leads to a fall in demand pull inflation. The rise in the exchange rate also leads to a direct fall in import prices. This reduces cost-push inflation.

The passage states that the effects of interest rate changes are lagged. GDP falls over a period of around 5 quarters whilst inflation only begins to fall in the second year following an interest rate rise.

2. The Bank of England has to weigh up the relative importance of current rising aggregate demand which is leading to a rise in inflation with the potential impact of the recession in the USA on the UK economy. The recession in the USA is likely to affect the UK in two ways. First, UK exporters will find it harder to sell into the USA. Second, recession could well have an impact on confidence in the economy. John Maynard Keynes called this 'animal spirits'. UK households and firms may fear that the recession will be exported to the UK and cut back on their consumption and investment plans. There may be a more direct impact if share prices in the USA have fallen sharply and this had led to a fall in share prices on the London Stock Exchange. If household wealth falls, this will lead to lower consumption.

If the rise in current inflation is large, the Bank of England will probably push up interest rates despite the deep recession in the United States. However, if the rise in inflation is only a few 0.1 percentage points above its target, then the Bank of England may well leave interest rates alone. This is because it would assume that the recession in the United States would have sufficient effect on UK aggregate demand to bring UK inflation back to its target rate of growth. It could even be that the Bank of England would cut interest rates if it felt that the US recession was deep enough to put the UK into recession too.

3. The Bank of England faces a number of problems in implementing policy. First, it often doesn't have completely accurate statistics at its disposal to say where the economy is at present. GDP figures can easily be revised by 1 per cent or even more for instance. Moreover, the statistics often fail to show a coherent picture of the economy and where it stands at present. Some indicators might be pointing to a recession, others to a boom and yet others to somewhere in between.

A further problem is that the models that economists use are not always accurate. Partly this is because they fail to capture all the changes currently going on in the economy. Partly it is because economies are always changing and what has happened in the past is not a completely accurate guide to what will happen in the future.

Implementing policy may also change the way in which the economy works. Goodhart's Law states that if the authorities attempt to manipulate one variable which had a stable relationship with another variable before, then the relationship will change or break down.

The Bank of England is therefore faced with a difficult task in implementing policy. However, its record since it gained independence in 1997 has been good. Either this shows that it has been particularly good at its task or that the conditions in the economy have been so benign that it would have been difficult not to have succeeded.

80 The limits of government policy

Data question

1. The government argued in 2006 that it had 'increased stability by creating a more certain and predictable environment for private sector decision makers'. Private sector decision makers are individuals, households, entrepreneurs, voluntary bodies such as charities and firms that are not owned by the state. The most important elements of the economic environment which the government claims is now more stable could be argued to be the rate of economic growth, the rate of unemployment, the rate of inflation, the rate of interest, the level of taxation and government spending and the exchange rate. In particular, the government would claim that the economy is no longer moving in the boom and bust economic cycles of previous decades. Inflation has fallen to very low levels and unemployment is at its lowest for several decades. Interest rates are low too, reflecting low inflation. As for the exchange rate, the data says that 'since the introduction of the euro in 1999, the volatility of sterling's effective exchange rate has been under half that of the euro and around a third that of the US dollar'.

2. Monetary policy can be used to reduce volatility in the economy. In 1997, the government gave the Bank of England its independence. It charged it with responsibility for maintaining low and stable inflation, and having achieved that to support the government's other policy objectives, including those of growth and employment. The government decided on a target of growth in the RPIX of 2.5 per cent plus or minus 1 per cent, which was changed in December 2003 to the growth in the CPI of 2 per cent plus or minus 1 per cent.

The Bank of England achieves this through changing interest rates. If it believes the economy is at or above its productive capacity and that the growth rate is such that the positive output gap will get even larger, then it tends to increase interest rates. This reduces aggregate demand by cutting consumption and investment and, through the exchange rate effect, reducing exports and increasing imports. In Figure 1, aggregate demand is shifting over time from AD_1 to AD_2. Increasing interest rates shifts the aggregate demand curve back from AD_2 to AD_3. This reduces the rate of inflation from what it might otherwise have been.

If, on the other hand, the economy is below its productive capacity, the Bank of England will maintain low interest rates and allow the growth rate to be above its trend rate. This will increase aggregate demand from what it would otherwise have been and shift it nearer to the full employment level of economic activity.

Policy is now forward looking. The Bank of England makes frequent small adjustments to interest rates in an attempt to keep the economy on a course where output is equal to productive capacity and therefore the output gap is zero. If inflationary pressures seem to be building up, the Bank of England will raise interest rates to forestall any rise in the actual inflation rate, and vice versa.

3. It can be argued that the period 1997-2006 was relatively benign years economically. There were shocks to the UK economy including the dot-com boom, a large rise and fall in equity prices in the late 1990s and early 2000s, and large rises in oil prices from 2003, but these proved relatively easy to absorb.

However, a deep and prolonged recession in the USA coinciding with a stock market crash might be much more difficult to manage. The Bank of England might be forced to reduce interest rates to such a low level to stimulate demand that further cuts were impossible. This is the liquidity trap situation. If interest rates were zero and the economy was still in recession, the government could be forced to used fiscal policy to revive the economy. Its rules - the golden rule and the sustainable investment rule - might then have to be abandoned.

On the other hand, a deep recession in the USA might have limited impact if GDP in the rest of the world and particularly the EU remained relatively buoyant. Equally, it could be that the new present arrangements for controlling output in the UK economy might be more robust than the policies pursued in the 1970s, 1980s and early 1990s. They might be able to smooth out an economic shock more smoothly than, say, at the time of the first oil crisis in 1973-74. Certainly, the economy is in much better shape than at any time since the early 1960s, with fast growth and low inflation. This gives the government a far sounder base from which to counter a supply side shock such as a recession in the USA.

Figure 1

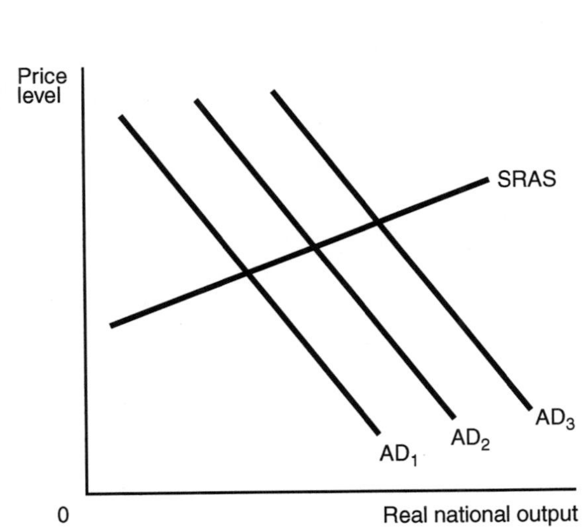

81 Globalisation

Data question

1. Globalisation can be defined as the integration of the world's economies into a single international market rather than many local or national markets. Globalisation involves not just creating world markets in trade in goods and services. It is also about creating a global market for capital and for labour. For example, the UK is buying increasing quantities of goods such as odometers or pencil erasers from China. Chinese companies and its government are buying legal services from the UK. Companies like Samsung, the south Korean electronics manufacturer, move their factories from country to country pursuing the goal of cutting their costs in order to remain internationally competitive. Firms like the Spanish company Santander Central Hispano are buying up foreign firms in order to expand their presence globally. What is not in the data is the increased flows of people across national borders as the world's labour market becomes more fluid.

2. Globalisation is taking place because capitalism has become the world's dominant model of organising economic resources.

Consumers are seeking out the lowest cost products for any given quality of product. Consumers prefer to buy an Isle of Wight pencil eraser which is priced at 20p rather than 50p. They are prepared to pay a price premium if the jeans they want are in the shops now and not in three months time.

Firms are responding to these pressures by focusing on costs and quality. If a UK retailer can buy a pair of jeans made in China for £1, they would prefer to do this rather than pay £3 to a UK manufacturer for the same quality. However, as the example of Primark shows, sometimes firms are prepared to pay higher prices if they can get earlier delivery. Globalisation gives firms a much greater choice about where to source goods and services.

Owners of factors of production can also exploit globalisation. China has been growing at around 10 per cent per annum for the past three decades as firms move production to China to take advantage of cheap labour. Workers in China are prepared to work long hours for low pay because for many the alternative is to stay in rural areas working on farms for longer hours and lower pay. Governments in Eastern Europe are luring companies to locate there not just because of the low wage advantage they offer but because land prices are low. Equally, the UK is highly successful at attracting inward investment because of the quality of its workforce, its English language medium and its membership of the EU.

3. The UK is clearly losing comparative advantage to other countries in certain industries. For example, it can no longer compete with low labour cost countries in the production of most textiles or other low value products. However, the law of comparative advantage states that even if one country has an absolute advantage in the production of all goods and services, its trading partners will retain comparative advantage in the production of some of these goods and services. This is because it pays to trade so long as the opportunity cost of producing goods and services is different. Firms in the UK have responded to increasing globalisation by moving up market into higher value products. Services in particular have been highly successful in recent years. The UK managed to increase its world share of services from 6.5 per cent in 1993 to 8 per cent by 2003, a significant achievement. The UK has a comparative advantage in the production of a number of services such as financial services, research and development and legal services.

The UK has been one of the more successful developed economies in recent years, particularly in Europe, enjoying strong economic growth. The current account balance on the balance of payments has deteriorated in recent years but this balance is the difference between two very large numbers representing exports and imports. The UK is having to adjust to a new world where labour costs in countries like China and India are very low. However, this presents opportunities for the UK economy as well as threats. So long as the UK economy remains flexible and able to change the composition of exports over time, it will remain competitive overall against countries such as China, Slovakia and the USA.

82 World trade

Question 1

Absolute advantage

	Cars	Computers
(a)	UK	France
(b)	UK	France
(c)	France	UK
(d)	UK	France
(e)	France	UK

Question 2

(a) In the UK, the cost ratio of meat to bread is 2:4, whilst in France it is 3:4. Therefore:
(i) England has a comparative advantage in the production of meat whilst;
(ii) France has a comparative advantage in the production of bread.
(b) Before trade took place, total meat production in the two countries was 58 units whilst total bread production was 46 units. If England uses all its resources to produce meat, it can produce 60 units of meat (total man hours available 300 ÷ cost per unit in man hours 5), whilst France can produce 50 units of bread (200 ÷ 4). Therefore the two countries could produce 2 more units of meat and 4 more units of bread if both specialised fully and then traded.
(c)

	Cost ratio of meat to bread		Comparative advantage	
	UK	France	UK	France
(i)	5:10	10:10	Meat	Bread
(ii)	35:70	30:70	Bread	Meat
(iii)	5:10	5:10	Neither country has a comparative advantage	
(iv)	5:10	5:10	Neither country has a comparative advantage	
(v)	5:10	4:10	Bread	Meat
(vi)	15:30	10:30	Bread	Meat

Question 3

(a) (i) England; **(ii)** Portugal and Chile; **(iii)** Chile; **(iv)** England.
(b) (i) England; **(ii)** Portugal; **(iii)** Chile; **(iv)** England.

Question 4

(a)

Figure 1

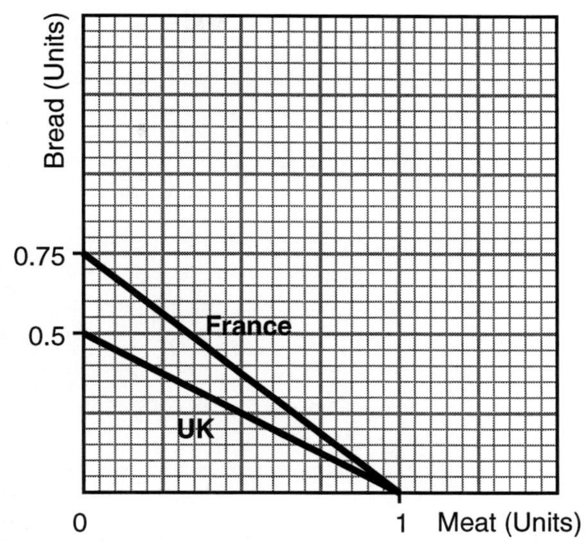

(b) Both countries will find it advantageous to trade if the price ratio lies between the two lines, that is between price ratios of 1 unit of meat to ½ unit of bread and 1 unit of meat to ¾ unit of bread. This means that neither country would simultaneously find it advantageous to trade at any of the price ratios in the question. At best, if the price of meat to bread were 1:½, England would be indifferent about whether to trade (it can produce meat and bread at this price ratio domestically anyway) whereas France would find it advantageous to produce bread and exchange it for English meat.

Question 5

(a) There are two possible reasons why consumers buy imported brands. The first is that the locally produced substitutes are not of the same quality. One reason why brands become internationally successful is because they appeal to a wide variety of consumers and provide consistent quality. The second is that imported brands are heavily marketed. The marketing usually carries messages that people who drink the brand are successful in some way. Drinking expensive imported brands therefore acts as a status symbol for the consumer.
(b) Sales of premium drinks fell heavily during the Asian crisis in the countries affected. The manufacturing companies could have responded by cutting prices. In the short term, this might have made the products more competitive compared to local

drink brands. However, in the long term it could have severely damaged the image of the brand. Drinks like Johnnie Walker whisky or Martell cognac are examples of non-homogeneous goods. Consumers in the Far East drink these products because they are different from locally produced brands. Their price elasticity of demand is likely to be relatively low. Hence, a high price strategy is likely to maximise revenues and profits. Cutting prices will harm their image and risks reducing the brand to a commodity product where price is the most important consideration when consumers buy.

Data question

1. The UK has lost comparative advantage in production of easy to manufacture, low skill products to countries such as China and Poland. This is because wage and other costs are much lower in these countries. In Poland, for example, wage costs are one quarter those in the UK. Combined with low transport costs, this gives these countries a competitive advantage in these mass manufactured goods. In contrast, China and Poland do not have sufficient technology and skilled labour to compete against the UK in specialised manufactured products. Hence, despite having much higher wage costs and charging much higher prices, the UK is competitive in these markets.

The theory of comparative advantage states that trade between countries will be beneficial if the relative costs of production differ between goods. The ratio of the cost of production of mass manufactured, low technology goods to low volume but high technology work is much greater in China than it is in the UK. Hence, China should specialise in producing high volume, mass manufactured goods whilst the UK should specialise in low volume, high technology products.

2. As countries such as China become more developed, their costs of production will rise. For example, labour costs will rise and the price of land and factories will go up. They will also acquire more advanced technology as well as a more skilled labour force. Because successful developing countries such as China and Poland are growing more quickly than mature economies such as the UK, the gap between both costs and manufacturing capability will narrow between them and the UK. It might take Poland 30 years and China 70 years to catch up with the UK. When this happens, the costs of production in these countries will be very similar. Inevitably, the UK will lose comparative advantage in some of its existing high technology manufacturing industries to Poland and China. Equally, there will be countries which will still be less developed and have lower wage costs. On current trends, it is difficult to see many African countries catching up with the UK in terms of development over the next 100 years. The UK will then retain a comparative advantage viz a viz these countries in high cost high technology products.

83 Trade policy

Question 1

(a) Equilibrium price is 50, whilst equilibrium quantity demanded and supplied is 75.
(b) (i) 90; **(ii)** 60; **(iii)** 30.
(c) (i) 10; **(ii)** 10; **(iii)** 20.
(d) If the government imposed a tariff of 40 per unit, the price of imports including the tariff would rise to 60. This is above the equilibrium price if the domestic market were supplied completely by domestic producers. Therefore, imports will be zero, quantity demanded will be 75, all of which will be supplied by domestic producers.

Question 2

(a) A tariff is a tax imposed on goods being imported into a country. Tariffs are also known as duties or customs duties or import duties. For example, in 2001, the US government imposed a tariff of between 8 and 30 per cent on steel being imported into the USA. This will have increased the import price to US customers of steel of between 8 and 30 per cent.
(b) Tariffs are used to protect domestic industry. The US steel industry was in favour of tariffs because it made imported steel more expensive. It could therefore charge higher prices to its US customers and gain a larger market share. US steel buyers were against the tariff because they now had to pay higher prices for steel.

This can be shown in Figure 1. The US demand for steel is shown by the demand curve, D. If there were no foreign trade, US steel manufacturers would supply along the supply curve SDomestic. However, if there is trade, assume the US could buy any amount of steel at a price of P and the world supply curve is SWorld. At a price of P, US steel buyers would buy ON of steel. JN of this would be imported and OJ would be supplied by domestic steel manufacturers. The US government now imposes a tariff of PQ. The price of imported steel therefore rises to OQ. As a result, US steel buyers cut back their purchases to OM. Of this, KM is imported and JK is supplied by domestic US manufacturers. The outcome is that as a result of the tariff, US steel manufacturers sell JK more steel and the price they receive for all the steel they sell rises from OP to OQ. Their revenues increase from OJVP to OKWQ. However, US steel buyers suffer because they now have to pay PQ per unit more for their steel.

Figure 1

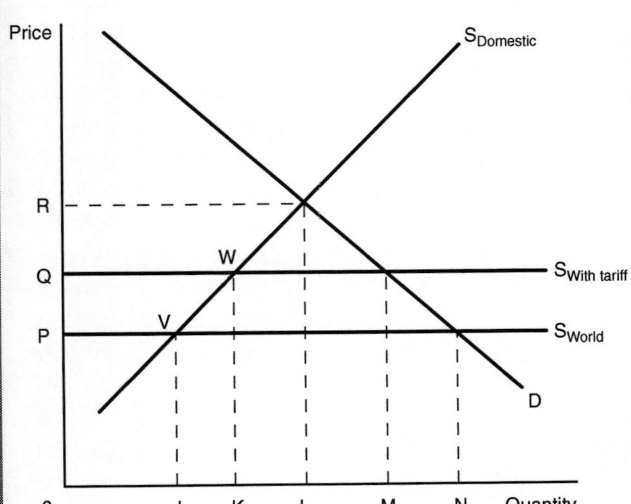

(c) The main beneficiaries of continued steel tariffs would have been the US steel industry. It would have been able to continue to sell more steel at a higher price to US steel buyers. Those buyers would have continued to lose because if tariffs were abolished, they could buy more steel at the lower world price of steel. However, continued tariffs could also have affected a number of US industries if the EU had implemented its threat to impose tariffs on imports from the US into the EU. The EU had singled out a number of products for retaliation including Florida fruit juice, motor cycles farm machinery, textiles and shoes. US manufacturers of these products would have seen demand fall because the EU price with tariffs would have been higher than before.

Question 3

(a) (i) Dumping is the sale of goods at less than cost price by foreign producers in the domestic market.
(ii) Duties on imports are a tax on imports. They are also called tariffs, or customs duties or import duties.
(b) European shoe manufacturers are arguing that Chinese manufacturers are dumping shoes onto the EU market. This means that they are selling their shoes below the full cost of production. Because they are dumping, the Chinese are able to charge very low prices and have gained considerable market share. Chinese shoe exports to the EU increased 700 per cent between January and July 2005. The result is that European manufacturers, including those in Italy, have suffered from falling sales. The Italian shoemaking association forecast that the Italian industry could lose 40 000 of its 101 000 jobs because of the imports.

However, it is unlikely that Chinese manufacturers are dumping shoes. They simply have much lower costs of production that European manufacturers. Those lobbying for trade restrictions simply want to maintain the output and profitability of their industry by attempting to keep as many Chinese shoes out of the EU market as possible.
(c) Europe is likely to be a major loser from the imposition of duties on Chinese shoes. European consumers would be denied the ability to buy cheap Chinese shoes. Instead they would have to buy more expensive shoes made within the EU. The welfare loss would be considerable. Admittedly, EU shoe manufacturers including those in Italy would be gainers. Profits and jobs would be maintained. However, the gain to shoe manufacturers and workers of restricting trade would almost certainly be far less than the gain to EU consumers if there were free trade in shoes.

Question 4

(a) The article states that countries such as the USA and Japan and trading blocks like the EU are blocking food imports by imposing 'excessively strict hygiene standards'. This means that they impose hygiene standards which are beyond what is necessary to ensure that the food is safe to eat.
(b) EU farmers benefit from such bans because it keeps out cheap foreign imports. This means that prices in the EU are then much higher which benefits farmers.
(c) There are two groups who are likely to be net losers. One

is consumers in the countries imposing the bans. For example, EU consumers pay much higher prices than they would otherwise do for the food they eat because of these bans. Second, farmers in agricultural exporting countries lose out because they are unable to export their products to countries imposing the bans. As a result, demand for their products is less and they receive a lower price for their produce from other customers.

Data question

1. (a) Before 2005, there were quotas on the imports of textile products into the main consumer countries such as the USA and Japan and trading blocks such as the EU. By restricting supply, the equilibrium price paid by consumers was higher. This had the same effect as if a tax were placed on imports.

This can be shown in Figure 2. Supply by high cost producers in developed countries like the USA or UK is shown by the supply curve S. These countries could without any trade barriers import an unlimited amount of textile prices at a price of OR. The supply curve for imported goods is shown by the line SWorld. With no protectionist barriers, demand would be OJ. Of this, OF would be supplied by suppliers in developed countries. The rest, FJ, would be imported from cheap labour countries such as China. Assume that quotas are placed on imports of textiles from low cost countries. Only GH is allowed to be imported. As a result, prices in developed countries increase from OR to OS. This is the equivalent of placing a tax of RS on imported textiles.

(b) Placing quotas on goods raises their price and forces consumers to buy from more expensive sources. The cost of textile quotas to US consumers alone before 2005 was estimated to be $70 billion annually. In Figure 2, the price per unit rises from OR to OS following the imposition of quotas. Without quotas, US consumers would have spent OR, the world price, times OJ, the quantity demand. Therefore total spending would have been OJTR. After the imposition of quotas, US consumers now have to pay OS per unit and buy OH. Total spending is therefore OHVS. The $70 billion could be the difference between these two areas. However, it is more likely to have been calculated by looking at the difference in the total cost to US consumers of buying OH, the amount bought with quotas. OH bought without quotas would cost a total of OR x OH. With quotas, it is OS x OH. The $70 billion then becomes the difference in the two areas, RWVS.

(c) Quotas saved jobs in high cost countries because production in high cost countries was higher with quotas than without. In Figure 2, producers in high cost countries produced OG with quotas but only OF without quotas. Therefore, with quotas they produced FG more textile products. The extra jobs in high cost countries were generated from FG of production.

(d) Low cost countries lose out from quotas because they are limited in what they can export. This means lower production and fewer jobs. In Figure 2, without quotas, low cost countries could export FJ. With quotas, they only export GH. The loss in sales, estimated to be $40 billion, is the difference between the area FJTY and GHVX. The loss in jobs of 27 million comes from the loss in potential production of FJ minus GH.

2. The reimposition of textile quotas on imports from China would be of most gain for EU textile producers and EU textile workers. EU textile firms could charge higher prices and sell more products as a result. EU textile jobs would be preserved through this protectionist method. However, there would almost certainly be some gain for low cost countries such as Bangladesh which now have no quota barriers to their exports to the EU. They would be able to pick up some of the orders which the Chinese were not able to fulfill because of the reimposition of quota barriers.

Figure 2

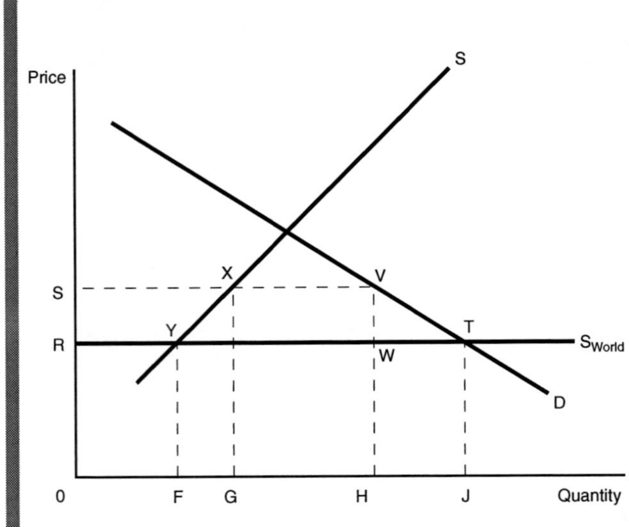

The losers would be Chinese textile manufacturers and their workers and EU consumers. Chinese textile manufacturers would not be able to sell as much into the EU. However, it should be noted that the effect of quotas is to raise the prices that importers receive for what they do sell. Chinese manufacturers could charge higher prices for the goods sold within their quota. EU consumers would also lose out because they would now have to pay higher prices for the textiles they buy.

The scale of the gains and losses can be seen from US estimates of the cost of quotas. The data states that 'each job saved in the US textile industry by quotas is estimated to have cost consumers an average of $170 000 a year'. The data also states that the elimination of all quotas (not just on Chinese imports) on textiles would see 15 per cent of jobs in the textile industry go in the UK and 13 per cent in Germany.

3. (a) China is currently highly competitive in many types of manufacturing industry which require relatively low skills. Textiles is an example of this. Chinese manufacturers are competitive because they can deliver the right quality garments at very low prices. However, the Chinese don't have complete superiority in the market. China is a long way away from markets in the EU. Goods coming from China by boat take an average of 22 days to arrive. Some EU retailers including Zara and Primark have developed business models which require very fast response times to consumer demand. By carefully looking at trends, they aim to get high fashion clothes into their shops within weeks of spotting surges in demand. This gives low cost manufacturers closer to the EU such as Turkey a competitive advantage over the Chinese.

(b) The Chinese economy is growing very rapidly. Over the past two decades, it has doubled its GDP every seven years. If this trend continues, wages in China will inevitably rise. This will erode their price competitiveness in low skill industries such as textiles. Inevitably, poorer countries such as Bangladesh will begin to win orders at the expense of Chinese manufacturers whose costs are rising faster. It could be that Chinese textile manufacturers in twenty years will be relatively uncompetitive on world markets because of high labour costs. China will have moved on to making more value added products which allow it to compete with much higher wages.

84 Balance of payments issues

Data question

1. (a) Foreign direct investment (FDI) can help the growth of the Chinese economy in two main ways. One is that FDI increases the resources available to an economy. If a UK company invests £10 million in setting up a Chinese company, then an extra £10 million of resources is available to the Chinese economy. In the short term, the investment boosts aggregate demand and national income. In the longer term, the company will produce goods and services which in themselves will also increase national income. Another way in which FDI can help the growth of the Chinese economy is that often FDI is associated with transfers of knowledge and technology. Working for a Western company can sometimes lead Chinese workers to set up their own companies in the same line of business. On a larger scale, existing Chinese companies can copy Western production techniques if they can see them in action in China.

(b) Growth of the Chinese economy in 2007 was fuelled by exports. As a result, China's current account surplus in 2007 was 12 per cent of its GDP. If China has a large surplus on its current account, this must mean that other countries have a deficit. The main deficit country, as can be seen in Figure 5 in the student's book, was the USA. Hence, Chinese growth in exports led to global imbalances.

2. Global imbalances could be corrected in two main ways. One is for surplus countries like China to revalue their exchange rates to make their exports more expensive and their imports cheaper. Deficit countries like the USA would also devalue their currencies making their exports cheaper and their imports more expensive. At some exchange rate, countries could achieve a balance on their current account. An alternative would be for deficit countries to reduce their incomes and so reduce their demand for imports. If the USA went into a deep recession, its purchase of goods from countries like China would fall, pushing its current account into balance.

3. Global imbalances threaten the economic security of all trading countries round the world. For example, if borrowers in the USA defaulted on some of their international loans, the holders of those loans in countries like China and Saudi Arabia would lose money. So it is in the interest of lending countries to ensure that borrowing countries do not borrow so much that they are unable to repay their loans. However, in the short term, countries like China and Saudi Arabia which have large current account surpluses are under no pressure to act. In contrast, continued large deficits by the USA may make it increasingly difficult for the US to borrow funds from abroad. So long as lenders are willing to make loans to US borrowers, a US deficit is not a particular problem. But if foreigners became reluctant to lend to the USA, then there could be an international financial crisis. Such crises have affected South Asia, Latin America and Russia over the past twenty years and led to world recessions. Therefore, there is more pressure on the US to correct its deficits than on countries with surpluses to reduce their current account surpluses.

85 Government policy, the balance of payments and exchange rates

Question 1

(a) The revaluation of a currency leads to domestic exporters facing a choice. They can either maintain their foreign currency price and reduce their price in their own currency terms, thus reducing their profit margins. Alternatively, they can keep their domestic currency prices the same but then charge higher foreign currency prices. Or they could do some combination of the two - reducing domestic currency prices by less than the percentage devaluation and making up the difference with higher foreign currency prices. In the passage, Chinese textile manufacturers are likely to absorb the increase themselves accepting lower profit margins but keeping foreign currency prices the same. In contrast, in the Chinese electronics industry, manufacturers 'are more likely to pass on the price increase to their customers'.
(b) If the foreign currency price remains the same, there should be no effect on export volumes. However, any rise in the foreign currency price will lead to a fall in export volumes. The exact amount of the fall will depend upon the price elasticity of demand for exports. The data implies that the price elasticity of demand for Chinese textile manufacturers could be quite high because buyers can easily substitute Chinese exports with exports from other countries such as India or Bangladesh.
(c) Revenues would fall whichever pricing strategy was adopted. If foreign currency prices were maintained, volumes would not fall but domestic prices would go down, resulting in lower revenues. If domestic prices are maintained, leading to a rise in foreign currency prices, volumes will fall, again leading to a fall in revenues.

Question 2

(a) The short term impact on imports of a depreciation of the pound might be different from its long term impact. In the long term, a depreciation should lead to a rise in import prices in pounds but a fall in export prices in foreign currency terms.
In the short term, however, importers may not put up their prices. As the Bank of England says, this may be because 'many of their contracts are fixed for set periods'. A firm selling goods to the UK, for example, may have agreed to supply 100 000 items over a twelve month period at a price of £1 per item. The depreciation of the pound in the middle of the contract means that the foreign firm will receive less of its currency in return for the pounds it receives from its British customers. Equally, the Bank of England suggests that importers haven't change their prices 'because of the cost of changing their price lists'. Changing prices is not necessarily costless and foreign firms may only change their prices once or twice a year to keep down costs. A third explanation put forward by the Bank of England is that importers may be unsure whether the depreciation of the pound is permanent. Importers don't want to be changing prices and possibly losing contracts if one month later, the change in the value of the pound is reversed.
(b) If there is a depreciation of the pound, import prices are likely to rise. This will increase inflation in the UK, according to Andrew Smithers in the article. The Bank of England could react by raising interest rates. This in turn will lead to lower spending, for example on consumer and investment goods by households and firms. A fall in aggregate demand could then lead to 'bit of a recession' with rising unemployment.

Question 3

(a) A cut in eurozone interest rates relative to US interest rates should lead to a fall in the value of the euro against the US dollar. If the euro falls in value, the number of euros that an exporter like Heineken will receive for each US dollar will go up. Hence, European exporters will be better off following a depreciation of the euro. Not all European exporters will choose to keep their foreign currency prices the same and so increase their profit margins. Many exporters will choose to reduce their foreign currency prices in order to make their exports more price competitive, raising export volumes.
(b) A cut in eurozone interest rates, which is likely to lead to a depreciation of the currency, is likely to lead to an increase in the value of exports and a fall in the value of imports. Hence the current account balance, which is export values minus import values, will improve. Export and import values are the volume of exports and imports times their average price in the domestic currency. When the currency depreciates, both exporters and importers can choose whether to maintain their prices and volumes, or change their prices and therefore volumes, or some combination of both. For example, Heineken in the data tends to maintain the US dollar price of its exports to the USA even when the euro changes in value. A fall in the value of the euro would mean that its average price of exports to the USA in euros will rise when maintaining a constant dollar price for its products. Higher average prices times the same volume sold means that the value of Heineken exports to the USA will rise. Or take the example of a US company exporting to the eurozone. When the value of the euro falls, it decides to keep its US dollar prices the same and therefore its prices in euros will rise. Higher euro prices will lead to a fall in sales. Depending on the elasticity of demand for imports, import values will either increase (if demand is inelastic) or fall (if demand is elastic).

Question 4

(a) A letter of credit is a form of loan used in international trade. An importer is less likely to buy foreign goods if credit is not available. The Bangladeshi measure effectively limited loans to 50 per cent of the value of imported goods. Hence, fewer imports will have been bought by Bangladeshi businesses, and this in turn will have led to an improvement on current account.
(b) With fewer imports, the supply of takas onto the foreign exchange market will have fallen. This fall in supply will then have raised the equilibrium price of the taka from what it would otherwise have been.

Data question

1. Over the period 1996 to 2001, there was a significant appreciation in the effective exchange rate of the pound. The value of the pound climbed sharply between 1996 and 1998 from an index value of 82 to 105, before falling back slightly to 101 at the end of 1998, and then stabilising in value in the range 105 to 109. Against the US dollar, the pound was broadly stable between the end of 1996 and 1999, but then fell to 2001. Against the euro, the pattern was broadly similar to the effective exchange rate.
2.(a) In the short term, the J curve suggests that the current

account will deteriorate. In Figure 1, this is shown by the movement from A to B. The deterioration occurs because of the different response times of export and import values. In the short term, it is assumed that importers raise their domestic prices in line with the devaluation. A 10 per cent devaluation leads to a 10 per cent rise in the price of imported goods, for instance. In the short term, demand for goods and services is inelastic. Hence, the value of imports rises. With export values unchanged, the current account deteriorates.

(b) In the long term, the current account will improve. This is shown by the movement from A to C. In the long term, the demand for imports is less elastic than in the short term. Hence, some substitution of imports will occur, reducing the import bill from B. The demand for exports will rise because exporters will have had the time to find new markets and stimulate existing markets. Hence, export values will rise. Assuming that the price elasticities of demand for exports and imports are greater than one, the rise in value of exports will more than outweigh any possible rise in value of imports (imports values could fall of course). Hence, the current account position will improve.

Figure 1

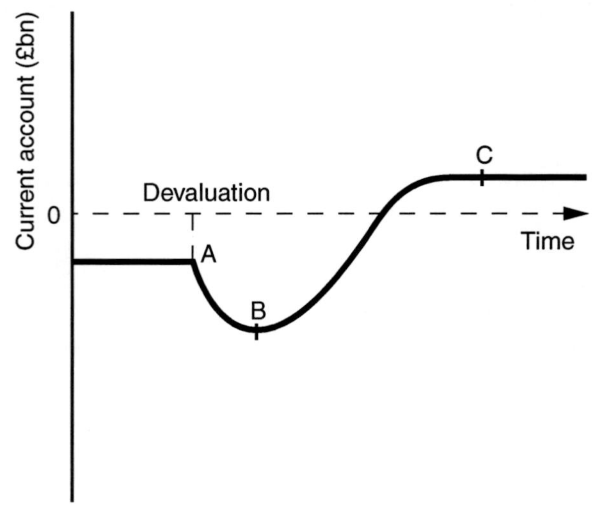

3. The sharp rise in the value of the pound between 1996 and 1998 should, if the J curve effect had been operating, have led initially to an improvement in the current account position, before leading in the longer term to a deterioration. Looking at Figure 6 in the student's book, this is roughly what happened. In the first quarter of 1996, the current account balance was in deficit by nearly $3 billion. By the last quarter of 1998, this had improved to a surplus of £1 billion before plummeting by the second quarter of 1999 to a deficit of £7 billion.

However, the current account includes other items apart from traded goods and services. The other items such as investment income might have distorted the statistics. So in Figure 6, we can also see the trends in the balance in both traded goods and traded services. There seems no noticeable J curve effect on traded services. However, on trade goods, the balance improves between 1996 and 1997 as would be predicted by the J curve model, but then deteriorates again. Looking more closely at values, volumes and price, in Figure 8, there seems little impact on the trend in import volumes of the sharp rise in the value of the pound between 1996 and 1998, but perhaps this was because importers chose to reduce their UK prices when faced with a rising sterling exchange rate. In Figure 7, however, a J curve effect is possibly visible for exports of goods where values at first increase between 1996 and 1997 and then fall from 1998.

4. (a) One way the Bank of England could have intervened in the markets to correct a current account deficit would have been for it to reduce interest rates. A fall in UK interest rates, with foreign interest rates remaining the same, would have made the UK a less attractive place to save money for foreigners and would have increased the incentive for UK residents to place their money abroad. The demand for pounds would have fallen therefore and the supply risen, leading to a fall in the price of pounds.

A second way would have been for the government to introduce supply side policy measures aimed at increasing exports and reducing imports. For example, spending more government money on training in export industries might raise their competitiveness and lead to higher exports.

There are many other policies which the government or the Bank of England could pursue such as imposing tariff or quota barriers on imports, or using foreign exchange reserves to buy up pounds and reduce the value of the pound.

(b) The Bank of England reducing interest rates is likely to lead to a short term fall in the value of the pound but unless the interest rate change is large, it is unlikely to have much impact in the longer term. A large fall in interest rates would also have negative impacts on the current account balance. It would stimulate aggregate demand, leading to an increase in both consumption and investment spending. This would suck in imports and lead to domestic firms switching goods from the export market to the domestic market. The exchange rate impact on exports and imports of a large fall in interest rates could in theory be more than outweighed by the UK expenditure impact. Moreover, the fall in the exchange rate will lead to a rise in cost-push inflation because import prices will rise. The expenditure effect will lead to demand pull inflationary pressures. If inflation rises, this will offset the rise in international competitiveness gained by the fall in the exchange rate. This is unlikely therefore to be a very effective policy.

Using supply side policies is likely to be far more effective. However, supply side policies take a long term to work. Improvements, for example, in education and training might only impact on exports and imports in five, ten or fifteen years time. If the government is looking for a policy which will have an impact within 12 months, supply side policies are not the right policies to adopt. Supply side policies can also be ineffective. Spending an extra £2 billion a year on education might give no long run rate of return because the money was spent wastefully. Increasing the government budget for UK exporters to attend trade fairs abroad might have no impact because exporters are already attending all the trade fairs which are likely to generate sales.

The main problem with many of the other policy alternatives is that the UK is locked into treaty obligations which prevent these policies being used. Because of its EU and World Trade Organisation obligations, it cannot, for example, impose tariffs on a wide range of imports. Equally, the UK government cannot impose exchange controls because its membership of the EU which guarantees the free flow of capital across the EU.

86 Exchange rate determination

Question 1

(a) Table 1

Original value of the trade weighted index	Change in exchange rate %		New value of the trade weighted index
	Country X	Country Y	
100	+10	+20	114
100	+20	+10	116
100	-10	+10	98
100	+10	-10	102
100	-6	-6	94

(b) Table 2

Original value of the trade weighted index	Change in exchange rate %		New value of the trade weighted index
	Country X	Country Y	
100	+10	+20	111
100	+20	+10	119
100	-10	+10	92
100	+10	-10	108
100	-6	-6	94

(c) Table 3

Original value of the trade weighted index	Change in exchange rate %		New value of the trade weighted index
	Country X	Country Y	
80	+10	+20	94
80	+20	+10	96
80	-10	+10	78
80	+10	-10	82
80	-6	-6	74

Question 2

(a) J.
(b)(i) L - an increase in exports will increase the demand for pounds;
(ii) N - an increase in imports will increase the supply of pounds;
(iii) F, N or most likely E - a fall in interest rates will either increase the supply of pounds as money leaves the country, or reduce the demand for pounds as less is invested in the City, or some combination of both;
(iv) N - British companies will supply pounds onto the market to pay for the dollars needed in their acquisitions;
(v) F, N or most likely E - either speculators will sell pounds to buy euros or they will be deterred from buying pounds or some combination of the two;
(vi) H, L or most likely K - in the longer term, the discovery is likely to have a positive impact on the balance of payments and therefore the exchange rate is likely to rise; and so in the short term, speculators will buy pounds, or reduce their selling of pounds, or some combination of the two in anticipation of this;
(vii) N - UK tourists will supply pounds to buy their foreign currency to pay for holidays abroad;
(viii) F, N or most likely E - strikes will hit exports, reducing the demand for pounds, and could raise imports as domestic buyers switch to foreign goods, or some combination of the two.

Question 3

(a) According to the purchasing power theory of exchange rates, the rate of inflation has a significant effect on the long run value of a currency. To understand why, assume that two countries trade exclusively with each other. One has an inflation rate of 10 per cent whilst the other has an inflation rate of 0 per cent. There is therefore a 10 per cent inflation rate differential between the two countries. If exchange rates remain constant, then the country with the 10 per cent inflation rate will steadily become less and less competitive compared to the other country. Each year, its exports will be 10 per cent more expensive and imports will be 10 per cent cheaper assuming that firms do not adjust their domestic currency prices. The country with the 10 per cent inflation rate will then see its current balance steadily deteriorating. Eventually the situation will become unsustainable because it will no longer be able to borrow the money to finance this deficit. The only long term solution is for its currency to fall in value by 10 per cent per year to match the 10 per cent inflation differential. Then its exports will remain competitive over time.
(b) If the purchasing power parity theory were valid, then positive inflation differentials for the UK would lead to a falling exchange rate over time, whilst negative inflation rate differentials would lead to a rising exchange rate. There were positive inflation rate differentials occurred between 1996 and 1999. At this time, the sterling effective exchange rate was rising which would tend to disprove the theory. During the rest of the period 2000 to 2006, the inflation rate differential was mainly negative. For much of this period, the sterling effective exchange rate was broadly stable within a 5 per cent range again not providing much support to the theory.

However, it should be remembered though that there may have been other factors which affected the value of the pound in the short term over the period. Equally, the match in the data is not perfect. The trade weighted index is an average of exchange rates of our main trading partners weighted by their importance to our trade, whereas the inflation rate differential is only for the euro area, with the euro area accounting for around 60 per cent of UK trade. It should also be noted that for most of the period, there was a negative inflation differential and the value of the pound has increased comparing the start with the end of the period. Taking the period as a whole 12 year period, the broad trend has been as the theory would predict.

Question 4

(a) A deterioration in the current account on the balance of payments means that the demand for pounds from UK exports falls relative to its supply from UK imports. Hence, in theory, the value of the pound should fall, all other things being equal.

(b) There is some evidence that movements in the exchange rate have anticipated movements in the current account position. The appreciation in the value of the pound from 1978 onwards occurred before the improvement in the current balance from 1979. The fall in the value of the pound from 1981 to 1996 was accompanied by a deterioration in the current account position which did not return to near balance till 1997. However, between 1997 and 2006, the current account position broadly deteriorated and each year a substantial deficit was recorded. Yet the exchange rate was broadly stable. So the evidence is mixed.

Data question

1. (a) The period 1993 to 2000 can be split into two halves. In the first half between 1993 and 1995, the pound was weak against both the euro and in terms of the sterling effective exchange rate index. There was a substantial rise of the pound against the euro and against the basket of currencies of its main trading partners. The effective exchange rate for example increased by over 30 per cent between 1996 and 2000. Against the US dollar and the Japanese yen, the picture was much more confused. But taking the whole period 1993 to 2000, the pound was about the same value against both currencies in 2000 compared to 1993.

(b) The value of the sterling exchange rate index remained approximately the same between 2000 and 2006, before rising slightly in 2007. Against the euro, the value of the pound fell between 2000 and 2003 before stabilising during the rest of the period. Against both the US dollar and the Japanese yen, the pound appreciated in value significantly. Since the best overall measure of the value of sterling is the trade weighted index or sterling exchange rate index, it can be argued that in comparison with the 1993-1996, the pound was strong between 2000 and 2007. However, compared with 1997-2000, there was very little change.

2. A number of factors may have led to the changes in the value of the pound between 1993 and 2007 but the evidence from the data shows that no single factor has been dominant in causing changes.

The current account position should in theory have some influence. A deterioration in the current account position will lead to a greater demand for foreign currencies by UK residents in relation to supply. Through the period 1993 to 2007, the current account was in deficit. This in theory should have led to a deterioration in the value of the pound. As David Mann of Standard Chartered Bank said: 'With a growing trade deficit caused by a high value of the pound, there needs to be a market correction to raise exports and reduce imports.' However, the data shows little link if any between the UK's current account deficit and the exchange rate.

Perhaps this is because flows of capital have outweighed any current account effect on the exchange rate. One reason why monetary capital flows between countries is interest rate differentials. Figure 7 in the student's book shows interest rate differentials between the UK and three other countries, the USA, Germany and Japan. For almost all the period for all three countries, UK interest rates have been higher than those in other countries. In Japan, where interest rates were at or around zero for much of the period 1993 to 2004, there has been an interest rate differential of up to 7 per cent. This should have led to an inflow of capital into the UK to take advantage of relatively high interest rates in the UK. This will have put upward pressure on the pound, counteracting the downward pressure caused by the current account deficit. However, there is little correlation between individual years, interest rate differentials and exchange rates. On a short term basis, though, the value of the pound is affected by changes in interest rates. The Times article quoted in the data says that 'the pound tumbled yesterday after it emerged that the Bank of England examined the case for a cut in interest rates this month'.

It could be argued that, as The Times implies, it is not actual flows of money that are significant but speculation. At any point in time, it is speculation that drives currencies up and down in value. Some economists argue that over a long period of time, it is economic fundamentals that determine the value of an exchange rate. However, in the short term, speculation can drive a currency in any direction. Short term movements in the exchange rate are essentially chaotic and beyond analysis.

87 Exchange rate systems

Question 1

(a) $2=£1 (the intersection of the demand and supply curve).
(b) (i) Buy £3 billion per day (the difference between supply of £14 billion and demand of £11 billion);
(ii) none - the free market price lies between the two price limits;
(iii) sell £3 billion per day (the difference between demand of £7 billion and supply of £4 billion).
(c) (i) Buy £3 billion per day (the difference between supply of £5 billion and demand of £2 billion;
(ii) sell £3 billion (the difference between demand of £16 billion and supply of £13 billion).

Question 2

(a) Under the Bretton Woods system, the exchange rates of the world's major currencies were pegged against each other within a 1 per cent boundary. On a day to day basis, the price of a currency was fixed through free market trading. However, if the free market value of a currency threatened to break out of the boundary, then the central bank of the country would step in and either buy its own currency if supply was greater than demand, or sell its own currency if demand was greater than supply. It bought and sold currencies using its gold and foreign currency reserves.

In 1952, the ratio of world central banks' gold and foreign currency reserves to total world imports stood at 70 per cent. Given that world capital flows were controlled through measures such as exchange controls, it meant that central banks had considerable leverage over the foreign exchange markets. The markets knew that central banks, such as the Bank of England, had the resources to intervene heavily in the market for a period of several months. This discouraged speculative activity. Speculators in the foreign exchange market were most unlikely to make large gains from seeing the price of a currency rise or fall by 5 or 10 per cent in the space of a short period of time (although this could happen on the rare occasions when there was a devaluation of a currency under the system).

By 1966, world reserves had grown but world trade had grown even faster so that the ratio of reserves to imports stood at only 38 per cent. Central banks therefore had far less fire power in the market. The likelihood that speculators would carry on selling or buying a currency and forcing a devaluation or revaluation on a country was therefore now much higher. To a great extent, it was precisely these speculative pressures which eventually led to the abandonment of the Bretton Woods system in the early 1970s.

Question 3

(a) In a free float, the value of a currency is allowed to be determined by the forces of demand and supply. This means that the currency can go up or down in value on a minute by minute basis. Hence, the value of the dollar and the Swiss franc both fluctuate against other currencies according to the balance between demand and supply for each currency.
(b) The value of the US dollar went up because currency traders thought there was a greater likelihood that US interest rates would rise in the near future. If US interest rates rose, then monetary capital would flow into the USA to take advantage of higher US interest rates. Therefore, there would be an increase in demand for US dollars. Equally, US investors would be less likely to send their money abroad for investment purposes. So the supply of US dollars would fall. Higher demand and low supply would then increase the value of the US dollar. Currency traders were anticipating this rise by buying US dollars hoping to be able to buy them more cheaply today than they could sell them for tomorrow. Hence, the price of US dollars went up before any definite interest rise occurred. This can be shown in Figure 1. The increase in demand for dollars has shifted the demand curve from D_1 to D_2 resulting in a rise in the equilibrium value of the dollar from OA to OB.

The Swiss Franc went down in value because currency traders 'revised their estimates of lower Swiss interest rates compared to the euro'. A rise in Swiss interest rates against the euro would have led to a rise in the Swiss Franc. Hence, the currency traders' 'revisions' must have been that they thought there was a greater chance that Swiss interest rates would fall in the near future. For the same reasons explained above concerning the US dollar, a fall in Swiss interest rates would lead to a fall in the value of the Swiss Franc. However, there was a second reason for the fall of the Swiss Franc. This was news that Swiss investors have been moving funds out of the

Figure 1

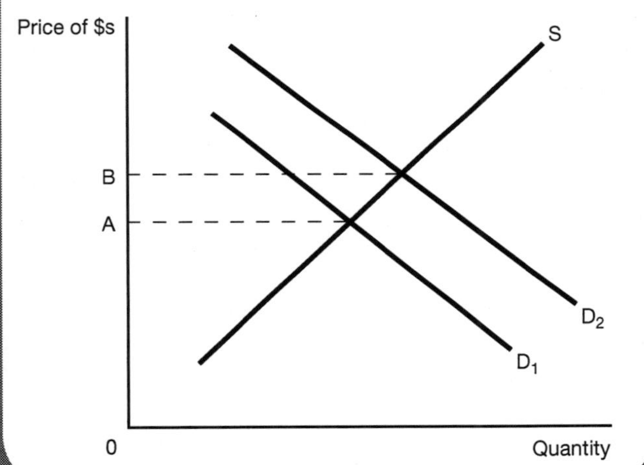

Figure 2

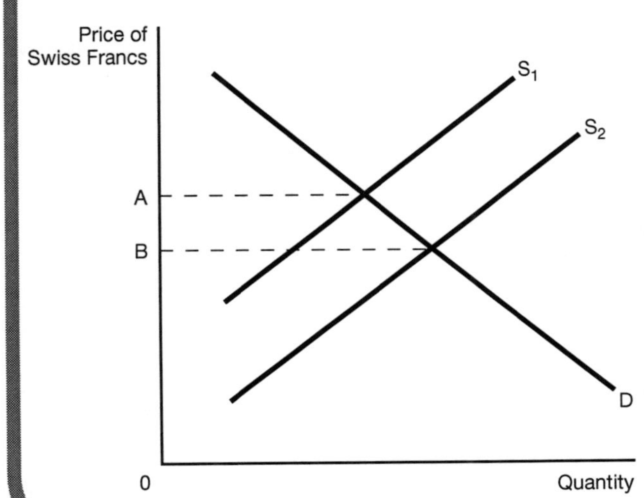

Swiss Franc to 'purchase foreign assets'. This would increase the supply of Swiss Francs onto the market and hence reduce the price of Swiss Francs.

Both pieces of news suggested to currency traders that the value of the Swiss Franc would fall in the future. Hence, currency traders on the 24 March 2006 sold Swiss Francs hoping that they could buy them back in the near future at a lower price. This will have increased the supply of Swiss Francs onto the foreign exchange markets reducing the exchange rate of the Swiss Franc. In Figure .2, the increase in supply of Swiss Francs is shown by the shift to the right of the supply curve for Swiss Francs from S_1 to S_2. As a consequence, the equilibrium price of Swiss Francs falls from OA to OB.

Question 4

(a) (i) A currency board is a fixed exchanged rate system where a country fixes the value of its currency to another currency. Notes and coins in the domestic currency can only be printed to the value of assets in the other currency held by the central bank. For example, between 1991 and 2002, the Argentinean peso was pegged to the US dollar at an exchange rate of 1 peso to $US1. Estonia's currency the Kroon was pegged against first the German currency, the deutschmark and then the euro between the early 1990s and 2007.

(ii) The main advantage of a currency board is that it links the inflation rate of the currency board country with the country whose currency is being used as the peg. For Argentina, it was a way of curing its inflationary problems by pegging its currency to a low inflation economy, the USA. For Estonia, it was a way of securing low inflation by pegging its currency against the deutschmark and then the euro. For Estonia, the currency board was a considerable success, partly because it effectively pegged its currency against its major trading partner, the EU.

For Argentina, the currency board proved a failure. By the time inflation had been reduced to US levels, the peso was overvalued against the US dollar. The result was that Argentina found it hard to export its products whilst imports were relatively cheap. The economy therefore ran a negative output gap for a number of years with high unemployment and deflation in the economy. Currency speculators predicted that the peso would fall in value against the US dollar and converted pesos into dollars prompting a succession of exchange rate crises. Eventually, the currency board collapsed in 2002. So the disadvantage of a currency board is that, unless the economic fundamentals are in place, the currency board is likely to collapse, leaving the economy in a crisis.

Data question

1. In an adjustable peg system, the value of a currency is fixed or pegged against other currencies in the short term, but may be changed in the longer term. The value of the currency is pegged through the central bank buying and selling its currency in order to fix its price.

For example, when the price of the renminbi threatens to rise, the People's Bank of China intervenes in the foreign exchange market to sell renminbis in exchange for foreign currencies such as the US dollar. When the price of the renminbi threatens to fall, it buys renminbis on the foreign exchange markets using foreign currencies in its reserves.

This can be shown in two diagrams. In Figure 3, the peg price of the renminbi against the US dollar is OA. Free market demand and supply curves for the currency are shown by D_1 and S_1. Demand for renminbis increases from D_1 to D_2, threatening to increase the equilibrium price of the renminbi to OB. The People's Bank of China prevents this by buying up FG of renminbis on the exchange markets for US dollars. Effectively, the People's Bank of China is prepared to supply any amount of renminbis at a price of OA. Hence the supply curve for renminbis becomes the kinked line S_2S_2.

In Figure 4, the peg price of the renminbi is still OA but an increase in supply of renminbis threatens to push the price down to OB. The People's Bank of China intervenes by buying up FG of the currency, using its foreign currency reserves which include US dollars. Effectively the People's Bank of China has kinked the demand curve for renminbis so that it becomes D_2D_2.

2. The Chinese government was under no short term pressure to revalue the renminbi because it could print as much of its own currency as it wanted to sell for foreign currencies. The pressure on the renminbi arose because the demand for renminbis was greater than the supply. Demand was greater because foreign customers wanted to buy more goods and services from China than the Chinese wanted to buy from abroad. With exports greater than imports, the only way the Chinese central bank could peg the value of the

Figure 3

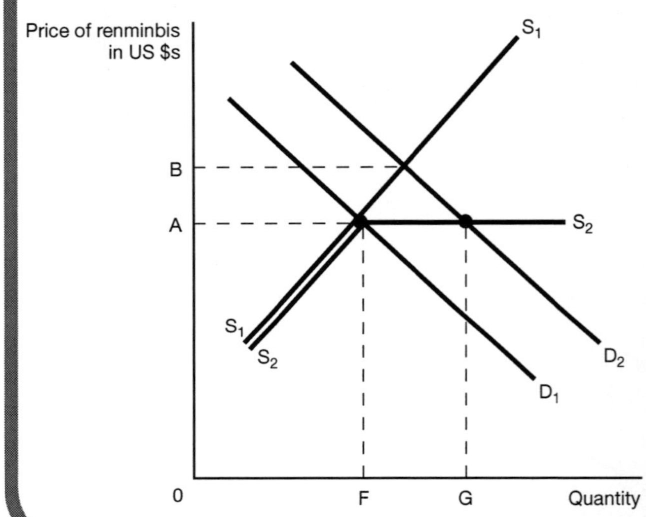

Figure 4

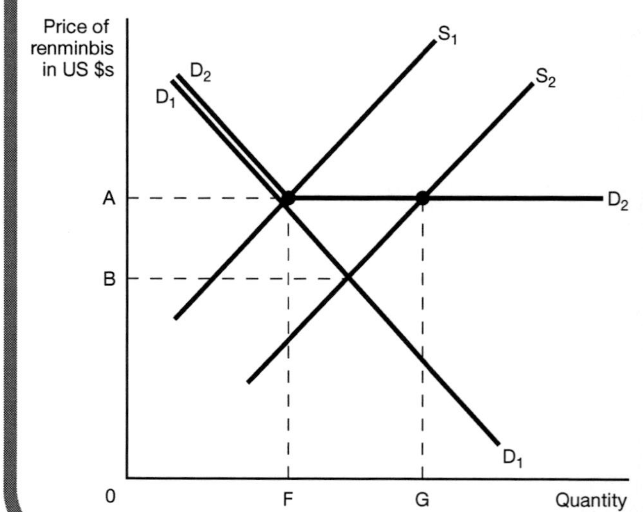

currency was by selling renminbis that it had effectively printed for foreign currencies. Because it could create as many renminbi as it wanted, the People's Bank of China was under no pressure to revalue the renminbi.

3. The renminbi is currently undervalued and is therefore likely to rise in price in the future. However, there are advantages to China of having an undervalued currency. It gives its exporting sector a competitive advantage and results in higher volumes of goods being sold for export. This sustains both jobs and incomes in China. The Chinese economy needs to grow fast if it is to absorb the large numbers of workers migrating from poor agricultural areas to richer industrialised areas. An undervalued renminbi is part of Chinese social policy and could be argued to be helping to prop up the Communist Party's grip on power.

On the other hand, an undervalued renminbi causes trade frictions, particularly with the USA which worries that its own jobs are being exported to China. It also lowers standards of living in China in the short term. If the renminbi were higher in value, the price in renminbis of imports would fall. The Chinese could buy more imports with the renminbis than before. An overvalued renminbi is effectively subsidising Chinese exports to the rich developed countries of the world.

Over time, the renminbi is likely to be revalued. When this occurs, the value of the $700 billion worth of foreign exchange that the People's Bank of China has accumulated will fall when valued in renminbis. The People's Bank of China will suffer a foreign exchange loss. This is a powerful reason why the central bank should not continue to buy US dollars are artificially high prices.

However, the Chinese government for the foreseeable future is likely to prefer the boost an undervalued renminbi gives to exports, economic growth and jobs rather than the boost to living standards that a revaluation would bring.

88 The advantages and disadvantages of exchange rate systems

Question 1

(a) Exchange rate instability imposes heavy costs on companies engaging in international trade. A company does not know at what price it can buy or sell its own currency. So if it signs a contract denominated in a foreign currency, it could gain money because of exchange rate movements or equally it could lose money. The loss arising from the fall in the value of the domestic currency could be quite considerable, and could more than wipe out any profit expected from the deal.

There are ways round the problem. For instance, as described in the article, smaller companies will often take 'evasive action' by charging higher prices for a contract than would otherwise be the case, insist on payment in their own currency, or delay making a monetary exchange until exchange rates are favourable. More sophisticated companies will hedge their currency transactions, taking out futures contracts to insure themselves against any loss they might make if the market moves against them. However, there is a cost in this in that the financial institutions involved in providing foreign exchange services will naturally want a fee. In the example given in the article, the cost of hedging to Van Halteren, a Dutch meat processor, was about £25 000 a year. Moreover, it is impossible to do this kind of deal to cover a long term contract of, say, 5 years.

Exchange rate stability would cut out these costs and therefore encourage world trade. Moreover, there would be a further substantial saving if some world currencies at least became one currency. The goal of European Monetary Union is to eliminate different European currencies and replace them with one common currency. This would not only provide perfect exchange rate stability with the consequent advantages to world trade, but it would also obviate the need to change currencies within Europe. At the time, the UK banks typically charged 1 per cent for small deals up to £10,000, and 0.1 per cent thereafter. Eliminating these charges would again encourage world trade by making European trade more profitable.

Question 2

(a) (i) The UK's inflation rate was above that of her main European trading partners. However, her growth rate was also greater.
(ii) The balance of payments on current account is likely to have deteriorated over time. Higher relative inflation rates will have led to UK exports becoming less competitive whilst imports will have become more competitive. Higher growth will have sucked in extra imports too.
(iii) Allowing the value of the pound to fall is likely to have been inflationary. If the pound falls, the price of imported goods increases. This feeds through directly to the Retail Price Index if the goods are final consumption goods and indirectly if they are supplies to UK industry.
(b) (i) The UK joined the ERM at a very high exchange rate which made it difficult for British exporters to compete internationally and conversely made imports price competitive. The UK then continued to have relatively high inflation rates resulting in the economy becoming even less competitive. Increasingly, the only way to prop up the value of the pound came to be the maintenance of high interest rates long after they were necessary to reduce the rate of inflation in the economy. High interest rates meant that consumer and investment spending remained very flat, prolonging the recession.
(ii) Britain's membership of the ERM is likely to have contributed to the fall in the inflation rate between 1990 and 1992. A high exchange rate kept import prices low. With consumption and investment spending depressed, there was little change in aggregate demand. Hence, there were few, if any, cost push or demand pull inflationary pressures.

Question 3

The break-up of the Bretton Woods system was caused by two main factors. First, it failed to be sufficiently flexible. It was envisaged, when the system was set up, that countries which moved into persistent surplus or deficit on their current account would revalue or devalue their currencies. In practice, devaluation and revaluation were rarely used as policy options and then only in an extreme crisis. Revaluations were rarer than devaluations. A country which ran a persistent surplus had no incentive to change. There was no pressure from within the system for it to revalue since it could carry on running a deficit on capital account (i.e. lending out more than it was borrowing) forever. A country which ran a persistent deficit would eventually be forced to devalue since it could not forever borrow money internationally to finance the deficit. Devaluation was seen (quite wrongly) as the ultimate economic failure of the country and its government both by domestic residents and by foreigners. So there was enormous pressure to put off any devaluation. But without the ability to revalue or devalue, in the changing economic conditions in the 1960s with the emergence of two large surplus economies, Germany and Japan, and a large deficit country, the USA, the system could no longer cope.

The second reason why it collapsed relates to the reserves of the world's central banks. The system could have coped if central banks had enough reserves to deal with speculative activity on the foreign exchange markets. But during the 1950s and the 1960s, the world's central bank reserves had fallen as a ratio of total world trade. Central banks were less able to dominate the foreign exchange markets with their buying and selling. Eventually, speculative activity became so large that central banks were unable to cope with fixing the exchange rate of their currencies. The system then collapsed.

Data question

1. There is a number of different arguments which could be used to support the entry of the UK into the single currency. One is that there will be lower transactions costs for those businesses and consumers. At the moment, consumers and firms have to pay banks commission and other exchange rate fees to convert pounds into euros or vice versa when they buy or sell goods and services from the eurozone. Joining the euro would eliminate these transaction costs. The government estimates this would be worth between 0.1 to 0.2 per cent of GDP, or £1 billion a year.

Another advantage is that it will reduce, although not eliminate, exchange rate fluctuations with our main trading partners. Approximately 50 per cent of UK trade is with other EU countries. Exchange rate fluctuations impose costs on businesses trading abroad. Either they have to accept that there may be exchange rate fluctuations which will adversely affect the value of an import or export contract or they have to adopt strategies to reduce the risk, such as hedging currency transactions. Such strategies almost inevitably impose costs on the firm and thus hit profitability.

Exchange rate fluctuations may also reduce trade between countries because some firms are unwilling to accept higher risk or pay higher costs for dealing with firms using a different currency. This reduces the benefits to be gained from international specialisation and leads to a country being able to consume fewer goods and services. The government estimates that 'British trade with the euro area could increase, perhaps by 50 per cent over 30 years' if Britain were in the euro area.

The government also argues that interest rates could be lower in the UK if were part of the euro zone. This would benefit both consumers and firms when borrowing money. British firms would also benefit from gaining access 'to a more integrated European capital market', making it easier to borrow money or raise equity funds.

Another argument in favour of the UK joining the single currency is that internationally mobile firms could decide to locate within the single currency zone rather than in the UK. They would do this in order to obtain the benefits of a single currency such as exchange rate stability within the zone.

The single currency could also benefit consumers by making pricing throughout the single currency zone transparent. Before the introduction of the single currency, European firms could hide behind different currencies to charge different prices in different countries. The car industry was the subject of frequent investigations in the UK in the 1990s for this type of price discrimination. With a single currency, it would become immediately obvious which are high price countries or regions and which are low price countries. Competition will then force prices down to the lowest possible level to the benefit of consumers.

However, there could be disadvantages. There will inevitably be transition costs. Retailers will have to replace many of their tills to work with the euro rather than the pound. Banks will have to work in both euros and pounds during the transition period. A construction firm might have to quote in both pounds and euros during the transition period. The Allied Irish Bank survey quoted in the data estimated these transition costs at £6.2 billion.

The UK could also suffer if its economy was out of phase with the rest of the euro-zone. The operation of interest rate policy will become the responsibility of the European Central Bank (ECB) and not the Bank of England. The ECB will set interest rates according to the average inflation rate throughout the euro-zone. If the UK is in recession but the rest of the euro-zone is in boom, then it will tend to increase interest rates to reduce inflationary pressures throughout the zone. But this will have the unfortunate effect of making the recession in the UK worse. This is the problem that Italy, cited in the data, faces.

Finally, many are concerned about the loss of sovereignty that a single currency will bring. Significant economic powers will pass to the ECB. Equally, though, there is considerable misunderstanding about the single currency. This is shown by the three quotes in the data under the title 'loss of sovereignty'. The medium sized manufacturer fails to realise that in ten years time it will be sterling which is likely to be the obscure currency whilst the euro will be the most significant world currency after the dollar. This is almost inevitable because the euro-zone is the world's second largest economy after the USA. The small construction company in the North confuses entry into the euro with the price of imports. The UK could continue to enjoy cheap import prices if it entered the euro at a high exchange rate. On the other hand, many manufacturing export companies would want the value of the pound to be low. The optimum value of the pound is an issue whether the UK is in the euro-zone or out of it. Finally, the big retailer from the Midlands seems very confused. Single currencies are not untenable. The pound sterling, for instance, is a single currency created from English and Scottish currencies. The US dollar is a single currency, used by all the states in the American union. As for a single currency leading to instability, this could be the case. But it is perhaps more likely to lead to greater stability as the economies of Europe become more closely linked.

2. Much of the debate about the single currency is centred on the political notion of loss of sovereignty. Words such as 'surrender' are used to imply that joining will not be in British interests. From an economic viewpoint, however, there are arguments both for and against joining at this point in time.

In the long term, as Gordon Brown recognised in his 2003 speech, there would be a positive impact on UK national income. This 'could rise over a 30 year period by between 5 and 9 per cent ... worth up to £3 billion a year, delivering higher living standards and lower prices for consumers and households'. However, the concern is that if the conditions are not right for joining now, the short term losses would outweigh the long term gains.

Economists disagree about whether the conditions are right today. Gordon Brown's five tests have been said to have been formulated in such a way that it will never be right to join the euro. As Figure 1 in the student' s book shows, there has been some degree of convergence between the UK and the eurozone countries in recent years, with GDP and interest rates tending to move in the same direction over time. What is true is that there will never be a perfect time to join. There will always be some costs in joining. Today is as likely to be a good time to join the euro as in ten years time.

89 Common markets

Question 1

(a)

• In a common market there should be no barriers to trade between member countries. For instance, there should be no tariffs or quotas on goods moving from one country to another. Freedom of movement of labour and capital should be permitted. In the data, a variety of examples of deeper integration are given.

One of the most visible signs of trade barriers is customs posts between countries. Just as there are none between countries in the UK, so in a common market there should be no customs posts between countries. The 1994 agreement, which brought about the abolition of customs posts in a number of EU countries, was a further sign of economic integration.

• Different monies can pose a significant barrier to trade. Firms in different countries have to purchase foreign currency to trade abroad. Banks impose charges for this and there is an exchange rate risk in any contract because the price of a currency may rise or fall in the short term. The creation of a single currency for the EU has eliminated these barriers to trade and thus helped create a single market.

• Different levels of tax in different countries distort markets. For instance, there is large-scale smuggling of tobacco into the UK because France and Belgium have low taxes on tobacco whereas the UK has high taxes. The UK loses tax revenues whilst there is an inefficient use of resources in distribution. Instead of tobacco being distributed in the lowest cost manner within the UK, much is now sent to France or Belgium only to be reimported illegally. Different levels of tax on labour further distort markets. Low tax countries are likely to experience a disproportionately large share of investment in labour intensive tradable goods or services industries to the disadvantage of high tax countries.

• In a common market, there should be identical labour standards throughout the market. Regulations which apply in one area should apply in another. So the 48 hour working directive was designed to create a level playing field across all member states in terms of hours of work per week.

• There are significant barriers to trade in services between member countries of the EU. For example, a bank in one country cannot necessarily open a branch in another country. The service sector is far more important in terms of output and jobs than either manufacturing or primary industry and yet there are considerable barriers to trade between member countries. Hence, bringing down these barriers is an important part of creating a common market.

Question 2

(a) Trade creation occurs when a country joins a customs union and as a result buys a product from a cheaper source than before. Trade diversion is the reverse; following membership of a customs union, the country is forced to buy a product from a more expensive source than before.

The accession of countries in Eastern Europe provided examples of trade creation in the agricultural sector. For example, Czech farmers could now sell milk and pork to German buyers for lower prices than Germans previously were able to get. Equally, Polish farmers could now sell agricultural produce into the Czech Republic because Poland had lower prices on some products than the Czechs. On a darker note, Germans living near the Czech border could now get a funeral at a cheaper price by getting cremated in the Czech Republic.

However, accession also brought with it trade diversion. Low cost Ukrainian, Rumanian and Russian agricultural produce was now denied access to former markets in Eastern Europe because of tariff barriers. This will have increased the cost of such produce to Eastern European consumers.

Question 3

(a) (i) Competition between EU service providers is likely to drive down prices. This is because firms in the EU with the lowest prices will be tempted to expand into countries and markets where prices are higher to gain market share and profits. In Figure 1, the demand and supply for a service product in the UK is shown. In this market, firms from other EU countries cannot compete because of restrictive legislation. Equilibrium price is OA. A new EU directive is now brought in which allows other EU firms to compete in the UK market. As a result, the supply curve shifts from S_1 to S_2. Equilibrium price now falls to OB.

(ii) The European Commission argues that a competition directive which covered all services would create 600 000 jobs. In Figure 1, competition in the UK expands output from OF to OG. Workers will be required to produce that increase in output. Hence, jobs will be created by increasing competition.

(b) Trade unions have been opposed to liberalisation of services within the EU. This is because it threatens both their wages and their jobs. What concerns trade unions is that services will be taken away from high cost locations to be performed in low cost locations. This is already happening in certain industries. Call centres today, for example, for UK clients can be located in Birmingham, London or India. Some IT software services can equally be located in London, St Petersburg or China. In the data, it says that low cost locations may exist because of 'lower wages ....environmental protection, ... and health and safety rules'.

In Figure 2, a demand and supply diagram for labour employed in service industries is shown In the UK. In a

Figure 1

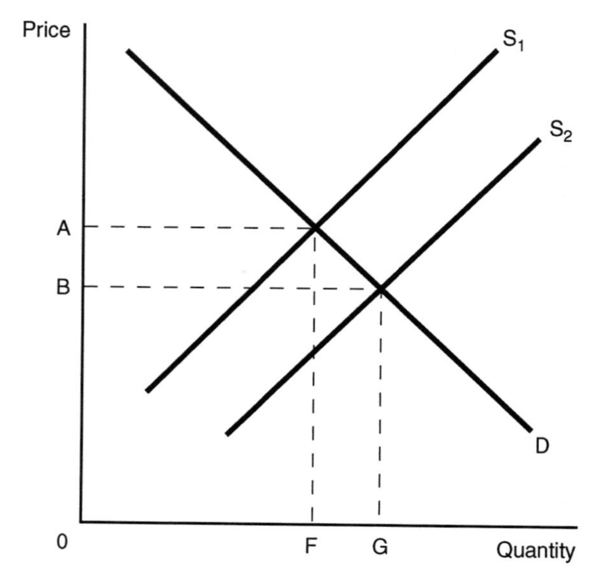

national market with no trade, the supply curve is S_1 and the equilibrium wage rate of labour is OA. Employment is OF. However, assume that if the market is opened up to competition, UK firms can employ any number of foreign workers at a wage rate of OB. So the supply curve of foreign labour is S_2. These foreign workers either work in their own countries, such as at call centres, or come to work in the UK, such as in the NHS. Then the new equilibrium quantity demanded and supplied of labour is higher at OH, but equilibrium wages have fallen to OB. UK workers prepared to work for a wage of OB will continue to have jobs. These are OH workers. HG foreign workers will be employed. FG will represent an increase in employment. HF foreign workers will replace HF UK workers who are not prepared to work at a wage rate of OB. Obviously, UK service sector unions will resist any directive which increases competition in the service sector of the economy because it will lower their members' wages and lose some their jobs.

Figure 2

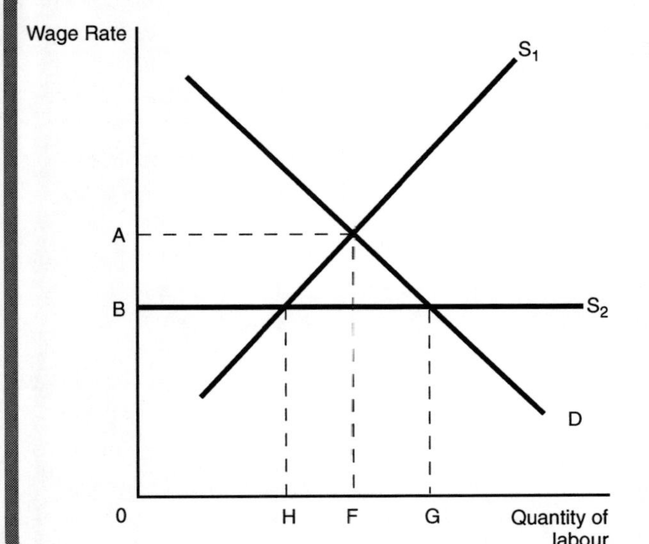

Question 4

(a) There is some correlation between net receipts from the European budget and income shown in Figure 1 in the student's book. To understand the correlation more clearly, it is important to remove both Luxembourg and Belgium from the statistics. Both countries receive large amounts of money from the EU because EU institutions are based in those countries. These payments are for salaries and facilities. So these countries are not typical EU countries.

If Belgium and Luxembourg are excluded, the poorer countries in the EU such as Latvia or Slovakia are the countries which receive the most per head from the EU. The correlation between forecast net receipts and GDP per head is high for countries which will be net recipients of EU funds.

It should be noted, however, that this is not true for countries which will be net payers into EU funds. For example, Germany, the second biggest net contributor to EU funds had only the 10th highest GNP per head in the EU in 2006.

As for Ireland, in 2006 it had the highest EU GNP per head at PPPs after Luxembourg but will still receive net an average 0.5 per cent of its GDP from EU funds between 2008 and 2013.

(b) The EU budget could be used to equalise living standards between different regions of the EU. For instance, the budget could be used to encourage job creation. Spending on infrastructure and training of the local workforce could provide the necessary backdrop to firms setting up in an area to reduce unemployment and raise wages. Equally, the EU may provide grants to firms investing in the creation of jobs. Alternatively, the EU could equalise incomes by giving income support to those on low incomes in a region. This is part of the function, for instance, of the Common Agricultural Policy which provides subsidies to low income farmers.

Data Question

1. Table 1 in the student's book highlights some of the key differences between Turkey and the EU 25. GDP per head at purchasing power parity rates in 2003 was 7.1 times higher in the EU than in Turkey (although note that this seems at variance with the data presented from a different source in Figure 4). In the labour market, only 45.5 per cent of the Turkish population of working age was in employment compared to 62.0 per cent in the EU. Partly this was due a higher unemployment rate of 10.7 per cent compared to an EU average of 9.0 per cent. But it is also due to very low employment rates amongst women. In Turkey, only 24.3 per cent of adult women are employed in the formal economy. The average wage in Turkey is only one tenth of that in the EU. Agriculture, which produces 11.5 per cent of Turkey's GDP is far more important relative to output than in the EU where it only accounts for 2.1 per cent of GDP on average. The share of GDP of industry and construction is roughly the same between Turkey and the EU, but service output is lower in Turkey.

Looking at Figure 3 in the student's book, it can be seen that Turkey has a worse governance record across all the indicators shown than either Germany or Poland. Twenty years ago, Poland was still a Communist regime and would itself have had relatively poor governance indicators. Partly because of the process of joining the EU, it has been forced to make considerable improvements to the quality of government and the rule of law. Turkey is still far behind this although it has made progress since 2000 when it became serious about wanting to join the EU.

2. (a) Existing EU members will make some gains from allowing Turkey to join. Enlargement will give EU firms greater access to the Turkish economy. There will therefore be gains from specialisation. EU consumers will benefit from being able to buy low cost Turkish goods. There would also be political advantages. Turkey has the potential to become a rogue state like Syria or Iran. To have such a state on the borders of the existing EU would be politically extremely damaging. It would therefore be far better, some argue, to admit Turkey to the EU.

(b) Turkey has a great deal to gain from EU membership. It knows that poor member countries over time have faster economic growth rates because of membership and can even overtake mature economies. Ireland, for example, has benefited enormously over the past thirty years from EU membership. Turkey also knows that it has performed economically in a very mediocre way over the past 50 years. Figure 4 in the student's book shows how China has been much more successful than Turkey in developing its economy.

The GDP gains for Turkey of membership would come from two sources. First, Turkish firms would have access to EU markets. Turkey's low wage costs would give Turkish firms a competitive advantage and attract existing EU firms to set up in Turkey. Second, Turkey would receive large amounts of EU aid both through the Common Agricultural Policy and through regional development funds.

However, Turkey would also benefit from a social and political perspective. Women would be major gainers because they would have much better access to education and would come to compete on equal terms with men in the job market. Turkey's citizens would gain from being better governed. Corruption would fall, the rule of law would improve and there would be greater political stability.

3. In the short term, there could be increased unemployment in EU countries as cheap imports from Turkey displace domestically produced goods. There might be large scale migration of Turkish workers to other EU countries which could disrupt their labour markets. EU countries may also have to increase their contributions to the EU budget to finance higher levels of spending associated with Turkish membership. Alternatively, if the budget contributions are kept at present levels, some countries will receive fewer benefits. On the political front, there is a concern that 'European civilisation' might be threatened by the accession of a large Moslem country.

However, there is considerable political will in Turkey to change in order to gain the benefits of membership. Enlargement in the past has mainly benefited existing members both economically and politically. Although doubts are expressed in Europe about possible Turkish membership, they tend to be expressed by right wing politicians worried about immigration and its effects on their country. Accepting any new member is a risk. However, just as offering membership to former Communist countries was a way of bringing countries which formerly had been a threat into the fold of the EU, so Europe has an opportunity here to turn what potentially could be a troublesome country both economically and politically into a partner with the same shared vision and goals.

90 Multinational companies

Data question

1. A multinational corporation is a company with significant production operations in at least two countries. For example, Shell is a multinational corporation because it operates oil fields and other oil installations across the world. Tesco has operations not just in the UK but also in Eastern Europe, the Far East and the USA.

2. (a) The multinational company will develop the field and seek to maximise its profit. In the process, all other things being equal, it will seek to minimise its costs. For example, it will pay as low wages to local workers as possible. It will seek to pay as little in tax as possible. It will spend as little on safety as the law demands but sufficient to protect its international reputation. It will also seek to maximise its revenues over time all other things being equal.

(b) It is likely to shift production to Slovakia over time. This is because it will attempt to profit maximise. Shifting production could save 15 per cent per year in production costs. However, the timing of the shift will depend on the fixed costs of moving. For example, if the company has recently invested heavily in its UK plant, then it is likely to have large sunk costs i.e costs which it will not be able to recoup if it closes down the plant. It is then likely that it will be more profitable to continue production in the UK for some time. If, on the other hand, the UK plant is due for considerable new investment, it is likely the multinational will close the UK plant and invest in Slovakia instead.

(c) It is likely to introduce the range because customers who buy 'value' products are unlikely to be very concerned about where the beef has come from or how the cattle have been reared and slaughtered. Customers who do value such information are more likely to buy more expensive ranges, such as organic product ranges. Introducing the value range will either give the supermarket chain a competitive advantage over other supermarkets or allow it to compete more effectively at the bottom end of the price range. Hence, the supermarket can sell more and be more profitable, its ultimate objective.

3. Friends of the Earth believe that multinational companies are 'out of control'. They have to 'by law ... maximise profits and keep investors happy'. As a result 'economic growth comes before people and the planet'. One possible solution to reduce the power of multinationals would be to break them up. They would then have less market power and would be less able to 'destroy environments', 'abuse human rights' and 'erode democracy'.

However, it is debatable whether multinational companies have these negative effects on society. Smaller companies are equally capable of destroying the environment for example. In Brazil, it is small farmers who are responsible for much of the destruction of the rain forest as they clear forest for their own use. If a multinational is not growing palm oil trees in Borneo, it will be smaller local companies doing so and selling the oil abroad. Small oil companies have no better a safety record in terms of accidents or 'leaking oil pipes' as large oil companies.

Moreover, there are economic advantages to multinational companies which explain why they exist. One is that their size allows them to exploit economies of scale in industries where economies of scale are particularly large. Breaking up multinational companies might lead to higher average costs of production and higher prices for customers. Another is that they have accumulated knowledge which smaller companies may not possess. They use this knowledge and the size of their research budgets to drive forward innovation. In agriculture, in contrast, farmers are too small to create ground breaking technological progress. In such industries, it is often governments or large multinational companies such as Monsanto, the seed manufacturer, or Caterpillar, the tractor manufacturer, which create innovation and technological progress.

All firms have some ability to act against the public interest. It is government's role to restrict firms in activities which create negative externalities. Breaking up very large multinational companies is one possible solution. But breaking up all large multinational companies is unlikely to be in the public interest. Equally, restricting firms to a particular size is unlikely to maximise economic welfare either. Instead, a more sophisticated approach needs to be taken and a wide range of measures implemented to ensure that firms operate at an optimal size and maximise their benefit to society.

Economics (Fifth Edition) AQA		AQA specification

AS Unit 1 Markets and market failure

Basic concepts and techniques

1	The basic economic problem	3.1.1
2	The function of an economy	3.1.1
3	Economic data	3.1.1
4	Positive and normative economics	3.1.1

Markets

5	The demand curve	3.1.2
6	The supply curve	3.1.2
7	Price determination	3.1.2
8	Interrelationships between markets	3.1.2
9	Price elasticity of demand	3.1.2
10	Elasticities	3.1.2
11	Normal, inferior and Giffen goods	3.1.2
12	Indirect taxes and subsidies	3.1.2

Efficiency and market failure

13	Markets and resource allocation	3.1.2
14	Production, specialisation and exchange	3.1.3.
15	Economic efficiency and market failure	3.1.3, 3.1.4
16	Public and merit goods	3.1.4, 3.1.5
17	Externalities	3.1.4, 3.1.5
18	Competition	3.1.4, 3.1.5
19	Monopoly and efficiency	3.1.4, 3.1.5
20	Market stabilisation	3.1.4, 3.1.5
21	Government failure	3.1.5

AS Unit 2 The national economy

22	National economic performance	3.2.1, 3.2.3
23	The economic cycle	3.2.1
24	The circular flow of income	3.2.2
25	Consumption and saving	3.2.2
26	Investment	3.2.2
27	Government spending, exports and imports	3.2.2
28	Aggregate demand	3.2.2
29	Aggregate demand	3.2.2
30	Equilibrium output	3.2.2
31	Economic growth	3.2.2
32	Unemployment	3.2.2
33	Inflation	3.2.2
34	The balance of payments	3.2.2
35	Fiscal policy	3.2.3
36	Supply side policy	3.2.3
37	Monetary policy	3.2.3
38	Exchange rate policy	3.2.3

A2 Unit 3 Business economics and the distribution of income

Business economics

39	Production	3.3.1
40	Costs	3.3.1
41	Revenues	3.3.1
42	Profit	3.3.1
43	The objectives of firms	3.3.1
44	Market structure	3.3.2

Economics (Fifth Edition) AQA		AQA specification
45	Perfect competition	3.3.2
46	Monopoly	3.3.3
47	Oligopoly	3.3.3
48	The kinked demand curve theory of oligopoly	3.3.3
49	Game theory	3.3.3
50	The theory of contestable markets	3.3.3
51	Other theories of the firm	3.3.3
Welfare economics		
52	Economic efficiency	3.3.3
53	Competition and efficiency	3.3.2, 3.3.5
54	Monopoly and efficiency	3.3.3, 3.3.5
55	Efficiency, the growth of firms and mergers	3.3.3, 3.3.5
56	Technological change	3.3.1
57	Public versus private sector provision	3.3.5
58	Environmental market failure	3.3.5
59	Cost-benefit analysis	3.3.5
Labour markets		
60	The demand for labour	3.3.4
61	The supply of labour	3.3.4
62	Wage determination	3.3.4
63	Trade unions	3.3.4
64	Labour market failure	3.3.4
65	Equality and equity	3.3.4, 3.3.5
66	The redistribution of income and wealth	3.3.4, 3.3.5
A2 Unit 4 The national and international economy		
Macroeconomics and government policy		
67	The business cycle	3.4.1
68	Economic growth and welfare	3.4.1
69	The new economics and happiness	3.4.1
70	Unemployment and the Phillips curve	3.4.1
71	Inflation and deflation	3.4.1
72	The quantity theory of money	3.4.1
73	Taxation	3.4.2
74	Government spending	3.4.2
75	Fiscal policy and demand management	3.4.2
76	Supply side policy issues	3.4.2
77	Money, its supply and demand	3.4.2
78	The rate of interest	3.4.2
79	The operation and limitations of monetary policy	3.4.2
80	The limits of government policy	3.4.2
The international economy		
81	Globalisation	3.4.3
82	World trade	3.4.3
83	Trade policy	3.4.3
84	Balance of payments issues	3.4.3
85	Government policy, the balance of payments and exchange rates	3.4.3
86	Exchange rate determination	3.4.3
87	Exchange rate systems	3.4.3
88	The advantages and disadvantages of exchange rate systems	3.4.3
89	Common markets	3.4.3
90	Multinational companies	3.4.3